SARISKA

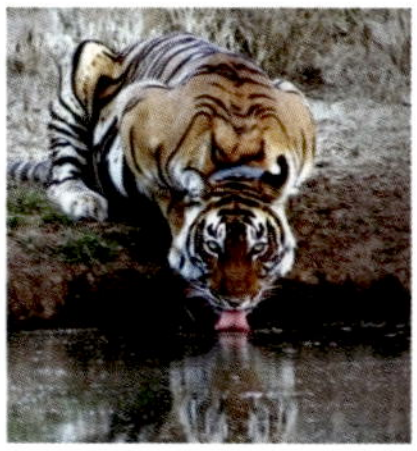

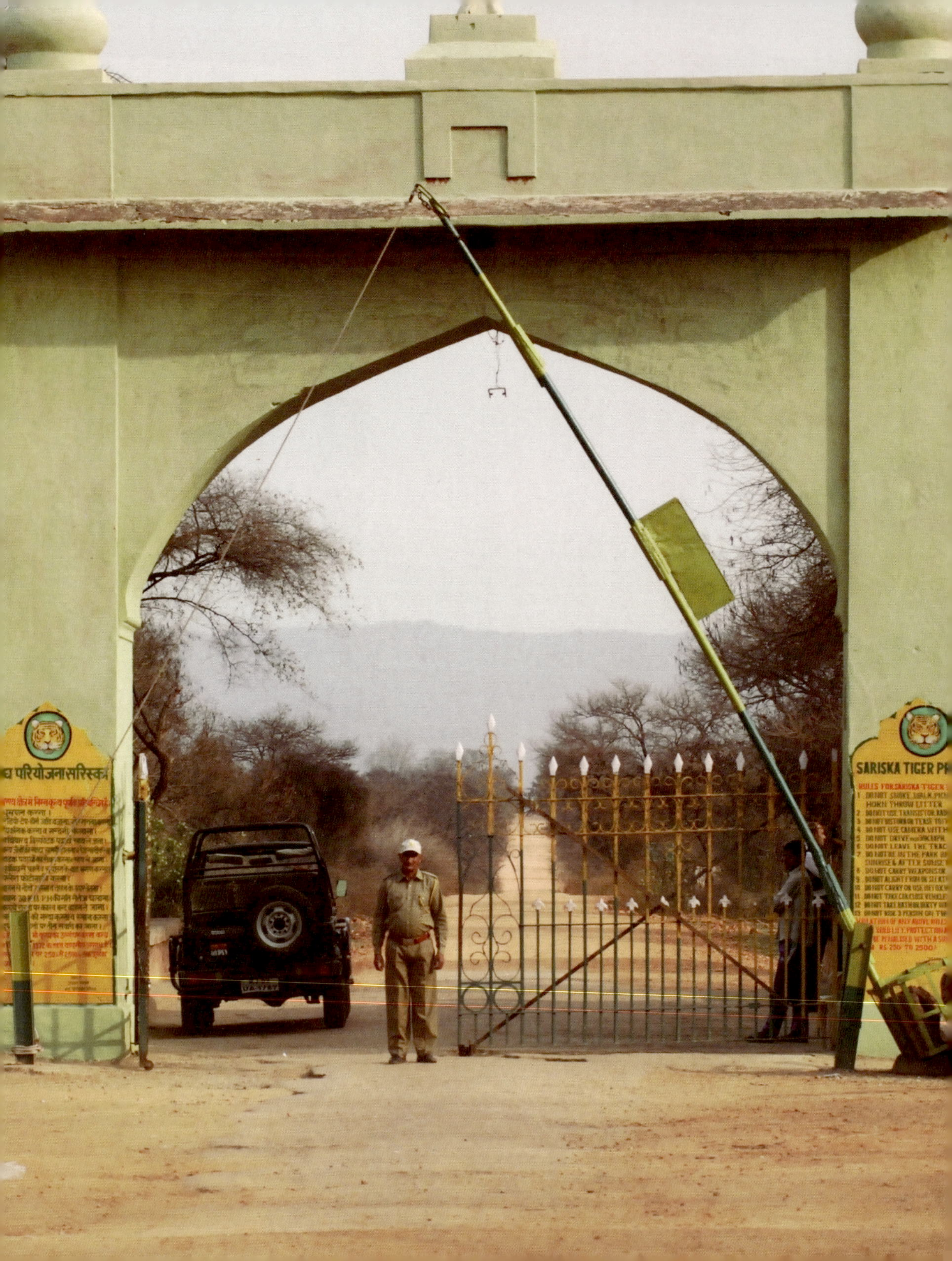
SARISKA TIGER

SARISKA

The Tiger Reserve Roars Again

Sunayan Sharma

NIYOGI BOOKS

Published by

NIYOGI BOOKS

D-78, Okhla Industrial Area, Phase-I
New Delhi-110 020, INDIA
Tel: 91-11-26816301, 49327000
Fax: 91-11-26810483, 26813830
email: niyogibooks@gmail.com
website: www.niyogibooksindia.com

Editor: P.K. Jayanthan
Design: Shashi Bhushan Prasad

ISBN: 978-93-83098-71-2
Year of Publication: 2015

Printed at: Niyogi Offset Pvt. Ltd., New Delhi, India

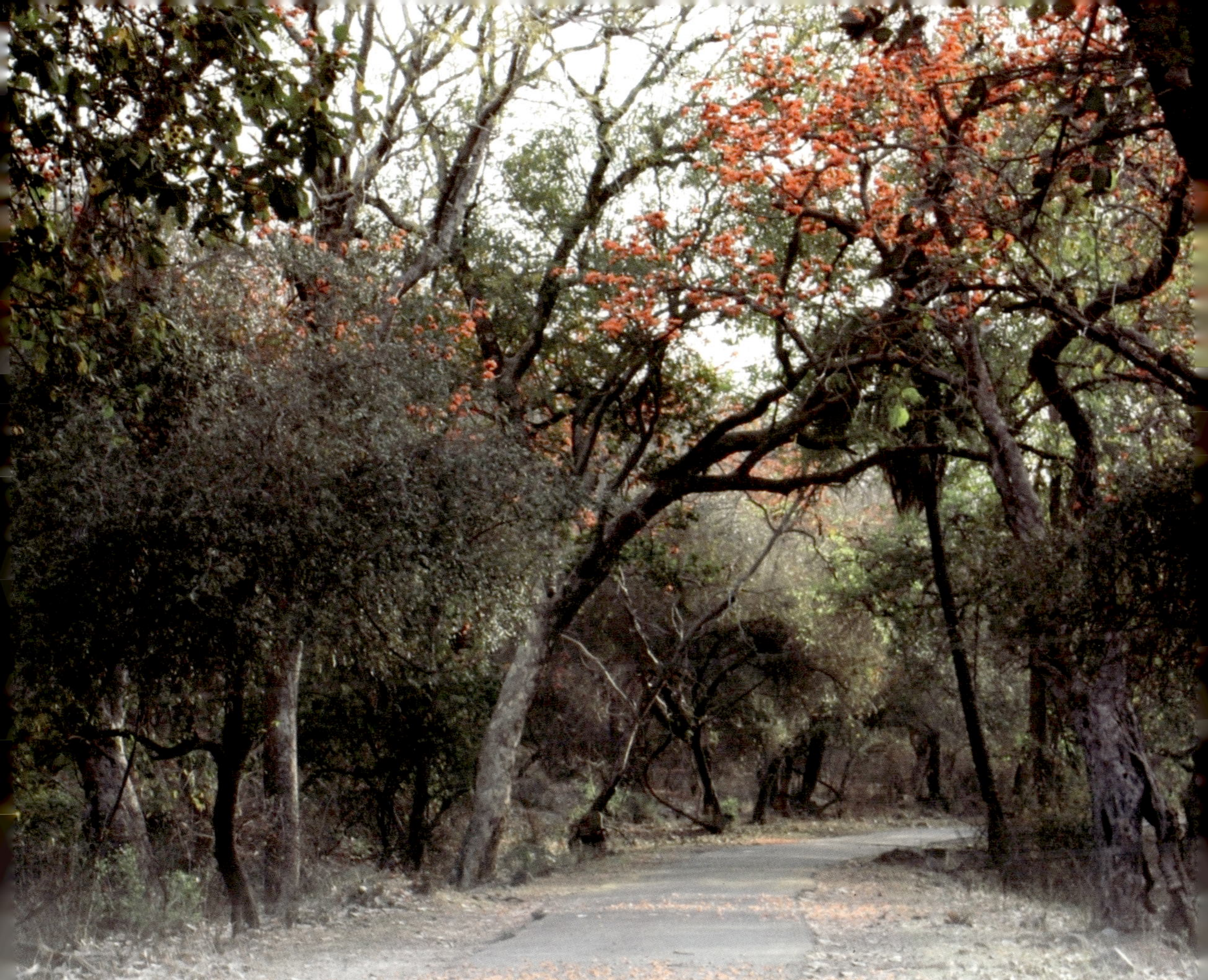

I dedicate this book
to my father
the late Pandit Vachaspati Shastri,
a great scholar of Sanskrit and vedic literature;
and mother
Smt. Vedwati Sharma,
an ideal mother with highly progressive thinking.

They preached, 'No worldly achievement can sustain
unless built upon the foundation of humanity.'

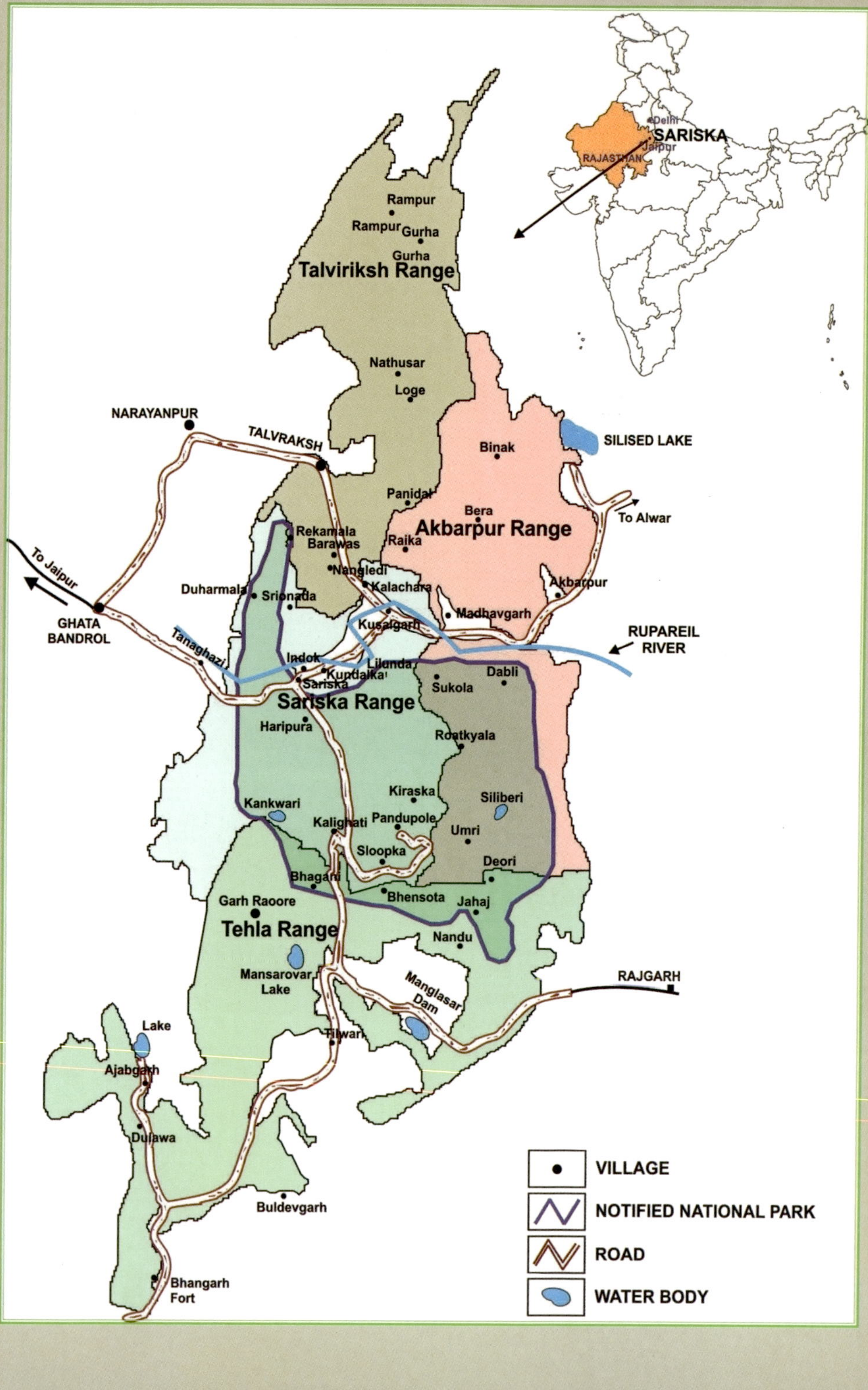
SARISKA
RAJASTHAN
Delhi
Jaipur
Talviriksh Range
Rampur
Rampur
Gurha
Gurha
Nathusar
Loge
NARAYANPUR
TALVRAKSH
SILISED LAKE
Binak
Panidal
Bera
Akbarpur Range
To Alwar
Raika
Rekamala
Barawas
Nangledi
To Jaipur
Duharmala
Srionada
Kalachara
Akbarpur
GHATA
BANDROL
Madhavgarh
Kusalgarh
RUPAREIL
RIVER
Tanaghazi
Indok
Lilunda
Kundalka
Sariska
Sukola
Dabli
Sariska Range
Haripura
Roatkyala
Kiraska
Siliberi
Kankwari
Kalighati
Pandupole
Umri
Sloopka
Deori
Bhagani
Bhensota
Jahaj
Garh Raoore
Tehla Range
Nandu
Mansarovar
Lake
Manglasar
Dam
RAJGARH
Lake
Tilwari
Ajabgarh
Dulawa
Buldevgarh
Bhangarh
Fort
VILLAGE
NOTIFIED NATIONAL PARK
ROAD
WATER BODY

CONTENTS

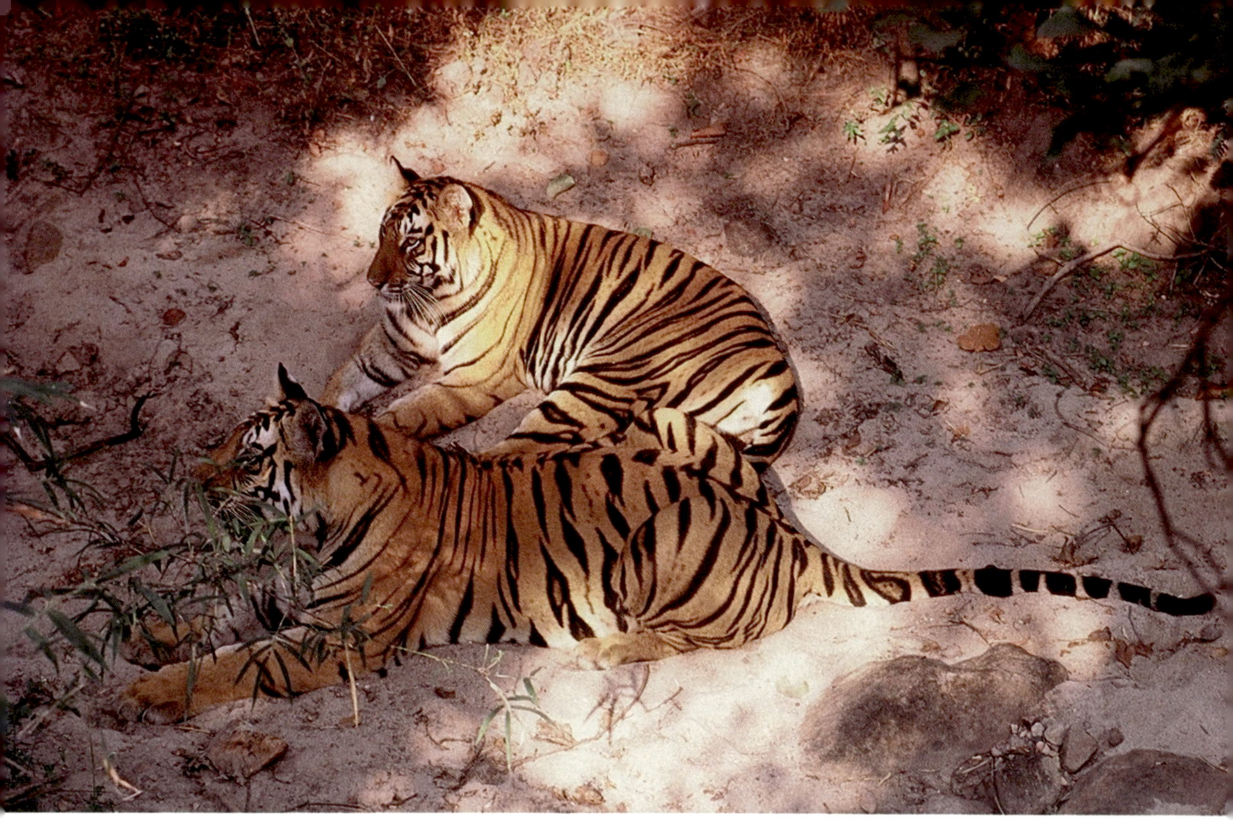

PREFACE

Sariska is one of the finest nature reserves in India. In 1973, I passed through Sariska on my way to Delhi. This brief encounter mesmerised me. I fell in love with its pristine wilderness.

Twelve years later, higher education at Wildlife Institute of India brought me back to Sariska again. I thought it was a God-sent opportunity to study the Reserve in all its dimensions. I set out to comb the most important parts of the Reserve.

I was spellbound when I came across the rich diversity of the flora and fauna of this Reserve. Tiger, of course, was the star attraction. But sambar, chital, blue bull, and wild boar were in abundance almost all over the Reserve. Large numbers of leopard and hyena also inhabited this Reserve.

In 1978 Sariska came under Project Tiger. Funds started pouring in. Habitat improvement efforts, especially water harvesting structures, were taken up. This helped herbivores as well as tigers to increase their population. Poachers, however, posed a great threat to their safety.

In the late 1980s, mining mafia became active and the habitat on the southern flank of the Reserve, falling under Tehla forest range, started depleting. In an effort to put an end to this illegal mining, Tarun Bharat Sangh, an NGO under the leadership of Rajendra Singh, filed a writ petition in the Supreme Court of India.

In 1991, I took over as Field Director of the Sariska Tiger Reserve. I realised that Sariska was faced with multifarious problems not restricted to mining. There was a heavy flow of vehicular traffic on the two state

FACING PAGE: Two majestic tigers in Sariska *(Photo by Dinesh Durrani)*

BELOW: A view of Sariska forest

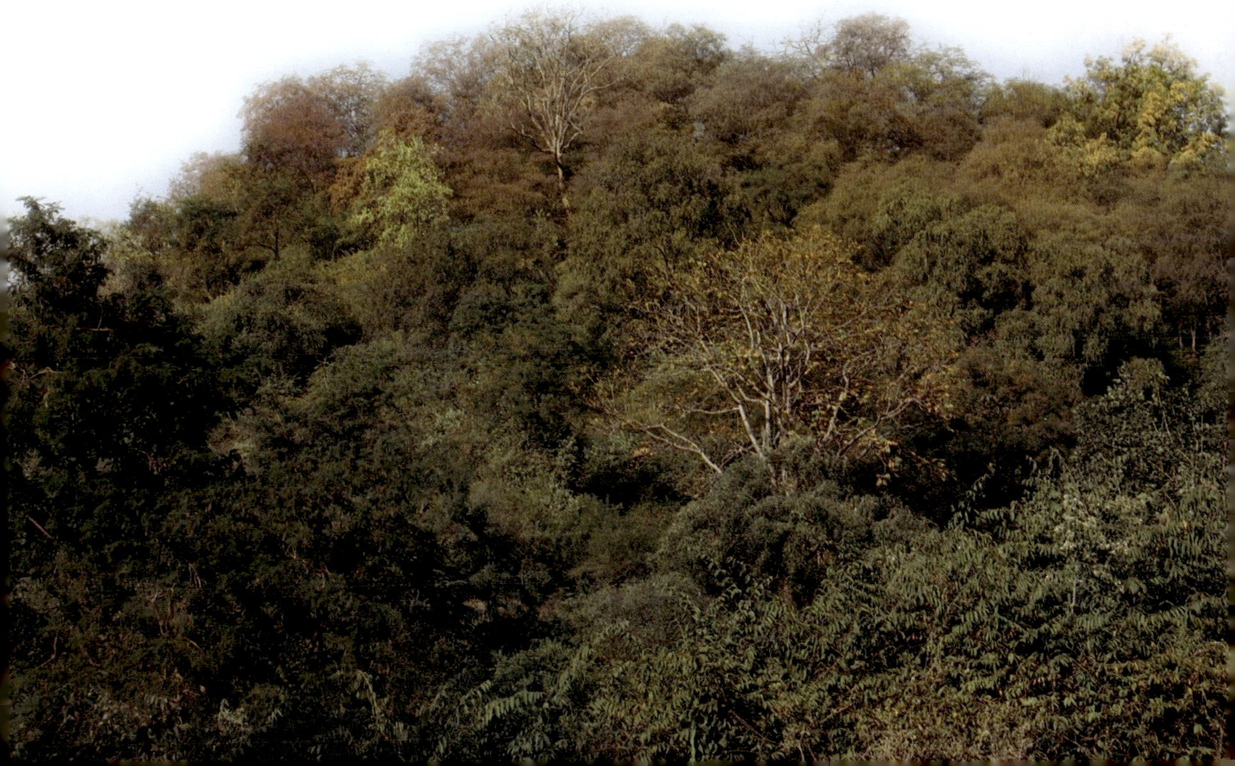

highways cutting through core area. No fewer than 28 villages/*guwadas* with about 10,000 cattle heads were located inside the Reserve. The entire Reserve was surrounded by about 300 villages. The burden of these villages for firewood and cattle-grazing was alarming and their rapid growth in numbers was posing a serious threat. The famous Pandupole temple located in the heart of the Reserve attracted a large number of devotees. Another famous temple of Bhrartrahari, located on the eastern side of the Reserve, also had regular pilgrimage traffic, causing serious disturbance to wildlife and its movement.

Bawaria community had been living on the periphery of the Reserve for ages. Traditionally, they are hunter-gatherers. The only other job they are skilled in is watching agricultural fields. Farmers engage them to guard crops against attack of wild animals in their agricultural fields located on the periphery of the Reserve. This gave them a free hand in killing wild animals like

BELOW: A tiger originally belonging to Sariska *(Photo by K.L. Saini)*

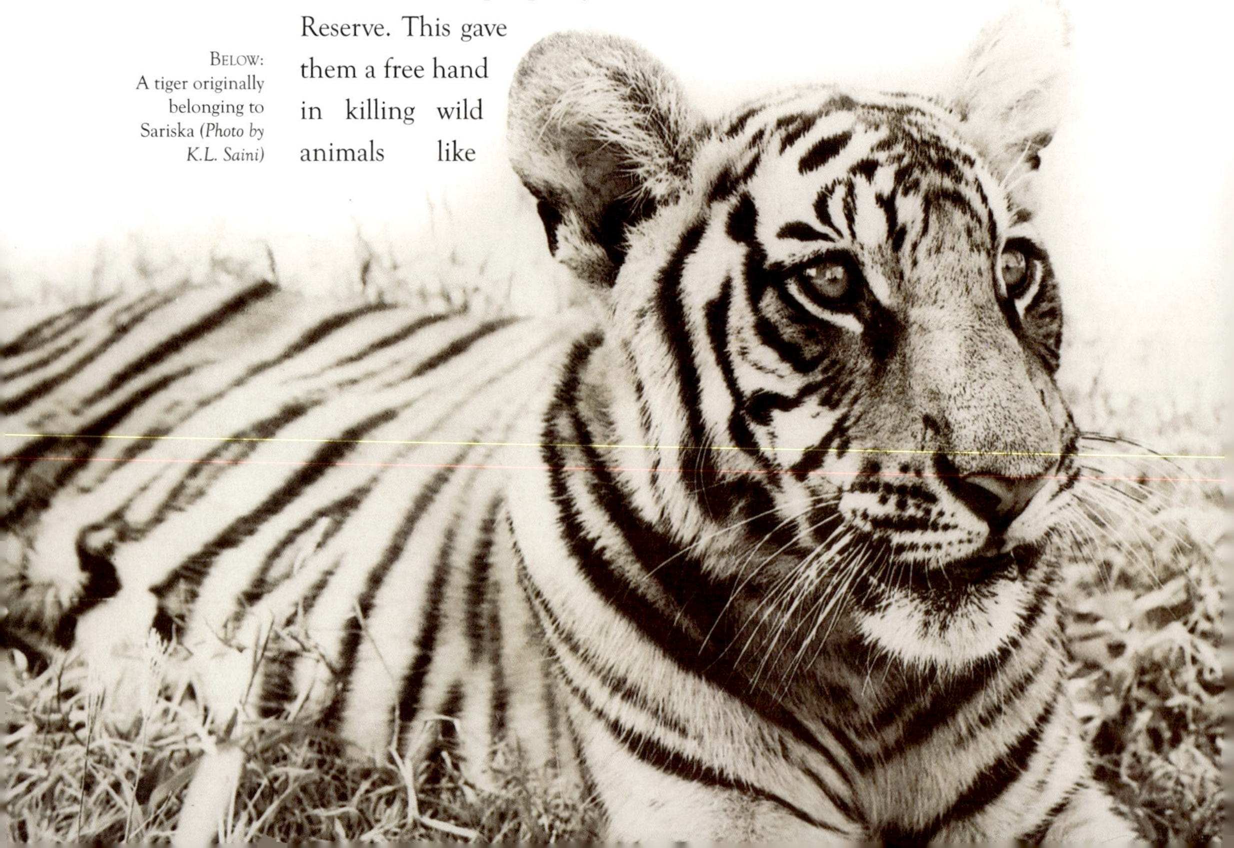

chital, sambar, blue bull, wild boar, and so on that strayed into the fields.

This also provided them with an opportunity to live close to the Reserve and hunt animals such as tiger, leopard, and so on when security of the Reserve was a little lax.

In spite of these problems, tiger still inhabited the whole place except Talvriksh range where its presence was remarkably low. In areas beyond Raika towards the northern boundary of the Reserve, it was even lower.

In the five years I was in office, several forest guard *chowkies* and patrolling tracks in deep interior areas were created or strengthened to tighten patrolling throughout the Reserve. Poachers were caught and seizures made even from Delhi. Several village forest protection committees were formed within the Reserve and on its periphery. This helped in restricting all kinds of offences, especially tree cutting. This also helped in building up trust between Reserve personnel and the villagers. This in turn led to the creation of an intelligence network among villagers against hardcore poachers. As a result there was marked improvement in the situation. Habitat development works began. Several *anicuts* and ponds were constructed, too. The number of tigers in the Reserve rose from 18 to 23.

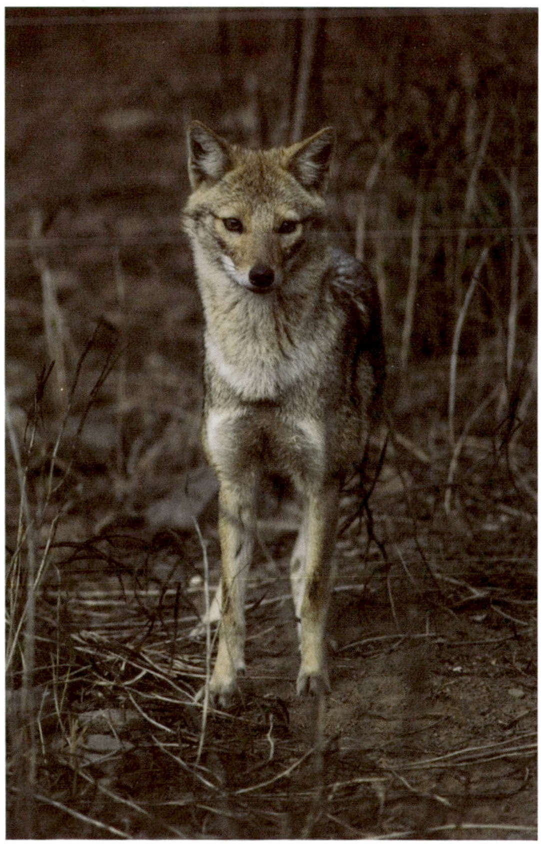

BELOW: A jackal in Sariska *(Photo by Daulat Singh)*

I spent a lot of time in the field as well as with the frontline staff. I checked on the forest guard *chowkies* regularly. I was acquainted with their problems, both personal and operational. Solving their problems was important. I tried to establish good rapport with them. They were motivated to work hard and be alert which put an end to poaching.

I was a satisfied man when I left Sariska in 1996. It was on the path to progress. Then in 2004 came the shocking news of annihilation of the entire tiger population of Sariska! It was unbelievable. Nothing could be more shocking than this! Sariska without its crowning glory, the tiger! What good is a tiger reserve without even a single tiger? Has the management of the tiger reserve collapsed completely?

The entire tiger population of Sariska was wiped out by poachers. This caused huge hue and cry within and outside the country among

BELOW: A tiger cooling off the summer season in Sariska

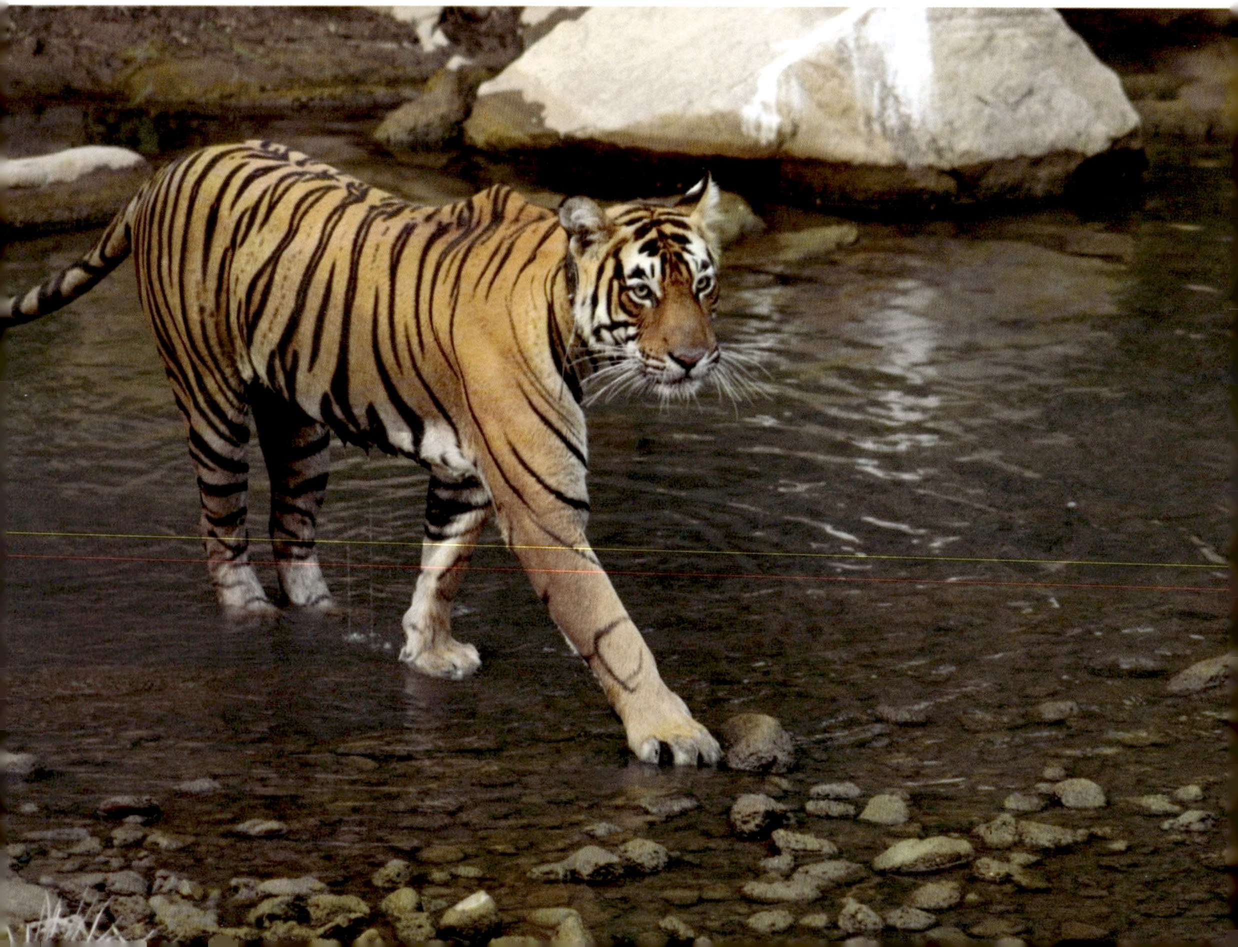

wildlife lovers. This could not have happened in a day. Obviously, poachers must have been able to operate unchallenged over a long period of time.

It is then that the state as well as central governments decided seriously to look into the matter. An empowered committee was formed by the state to look into the entire gamut of issues and suggest preventive measures for the future.

In the mean time, a committee headed by R.N. Mehrotra, Additional Principal Chief Conservator of Forests, was set up to enquire into the whole episode. The committee submitted its report within a week. Punitive actions were initiated against some reserve personnel on the basis of the findings of the committee.

The Government of India also formed a high level task force which came out with several recommendations for improvement in the management and development of Sariska as well as other tiger reserves in India.

The committees recommended translocation of tigers to Sariska. The proposal was approved by the Prime Minister of India. In the first phase, five tigers were to be brought from Ranthambhore. However, a lot of hue and cry was raised in Ranthambhore. The shifting of tigers was opposed tooth and nail by a lobby. Several controversies including problems of inbreeding were cited to stonewall the translocation. The government was pressurised to such an extent that the programme got deferred several times. Ultimately, the steering committee under the chairmanship of V.P. Singh succeeded in restocking tigers in Sariska by bringing in two tigers in June 2008. I was again called in to head Sariska at this crucial juncture. Later on, in February 2009, a female tiger was also brought in from the same source.

The first and the foremost task was to establish these tigers in their new home. It was a huge challenge. Shortage of field staff was the main handicap. Most of the staff members were aged 50 years or above.

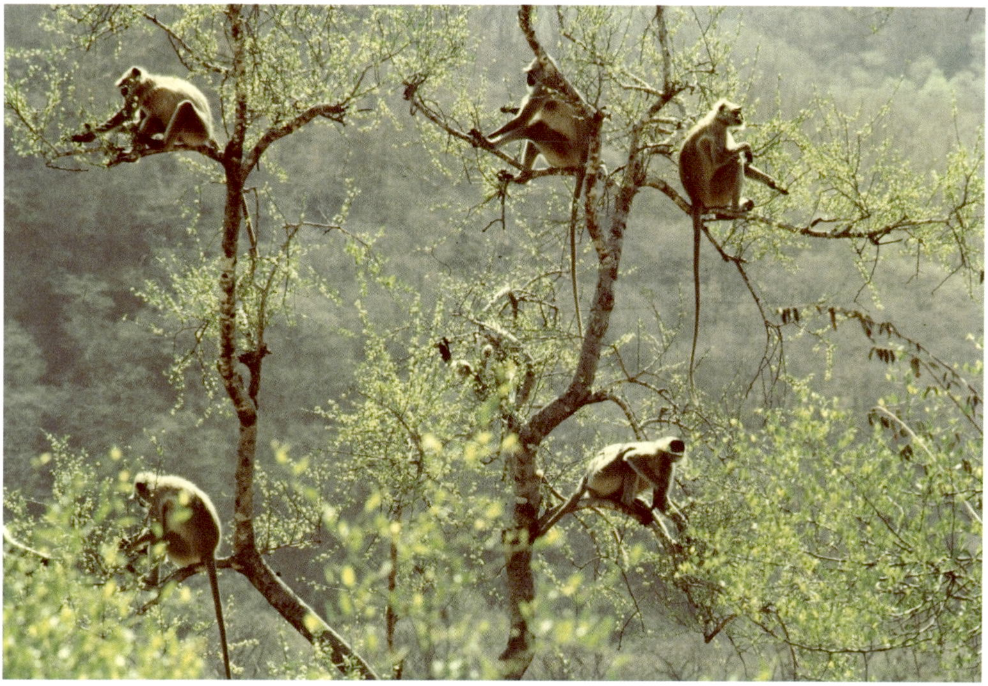

ABOVE: Sariska is blessed with huge langur population

Translocation of wild tigers into Sariska was the first such instance in the world. The scientists and critics both critically observed the results.

It was a good monsoon year.

Sariska has a series of hills and valleys. These hills pose a huge problem for the monitoring teams while following a tiger. At the same time, these tall hills did not offer any resistance to these tigers. They were agitated due to the displacement from their home. The tigers remained highly disturbed for the first two months. They tried to run away from the Reserve several times in the hope of returning to their home.

It was very tough to follow the tigers day and night. Dense shrubs and grasses due to heavy rains during the monsoon made our task tougher. It was even more difficult preventing them from running away from the Reserve. This called for putting in untiring labour. This also placed our lives at stake.

Since poaching was responsible for the debacle in Sariska, we tried to locate, arrest, and punish the poachers.

The protection network was strengthened; new guard posts were created in the main poaching prone areas; and fair weather tracks were created in these remote areas. It was extremely difficult due to the inaccessibility of the terrain. However, regular patrolling on these tracks helped halt all kinds of animal poaching.

Central Government offered funds liberally for shifting villages from the core areas of the Reserve. Before I was reposted to the tiger reserve, one *guada* (permanent cattle camp) of Bhagani had already been shifted, thanks to Mr Somshekhar, the then Field Director of Sariska. I could shift several families from *guada*s of Umri and Kankwadi.

The shifting of villages is a highly sensitive issue. Therefore, it takes time. The Reserve management has to have patience and commitment. I am hopeful that at least the core forest will be free of these settlements soon.

BELOW: A view of the rich flora of Sariska forest

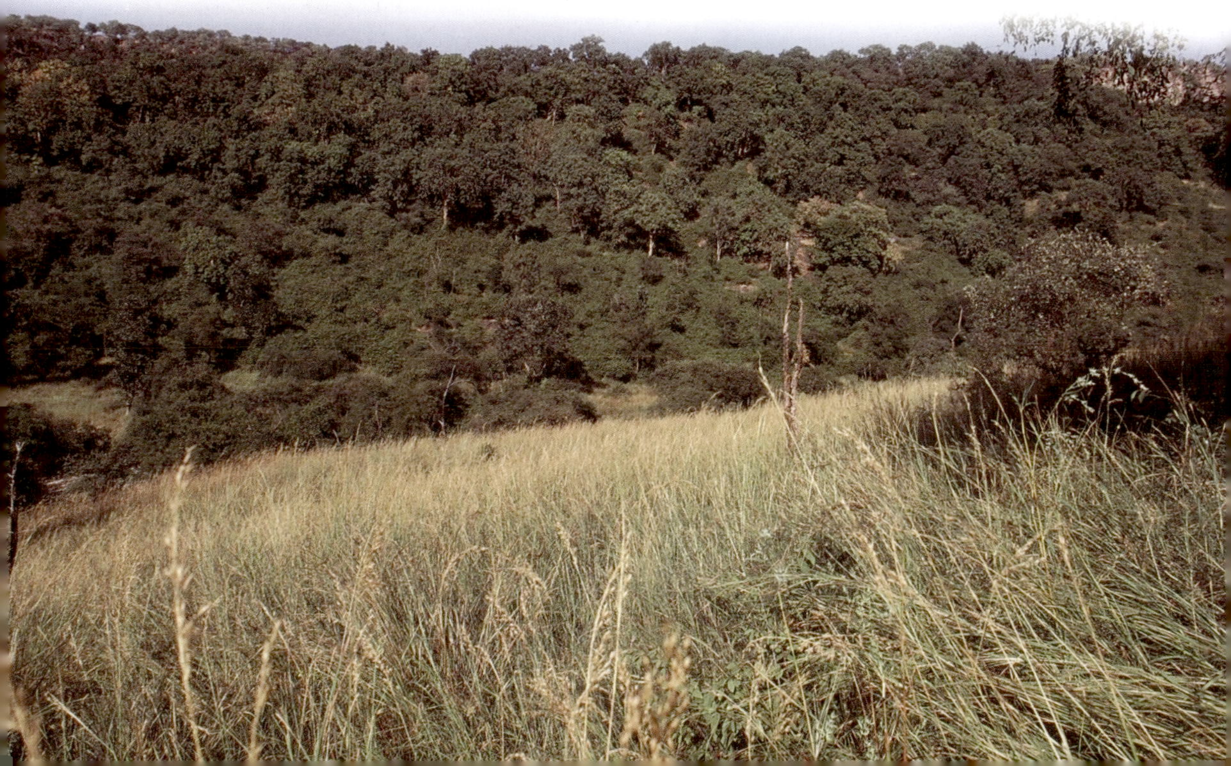

With the reintroduction of the tiger, the roar of the tiger began to be heard in Sariska again. Tourists and wildlife lovers returned to enjoy the wild beauty of Sariska.

There are, however, more problems to grapple with. The Reserve management is on its toes all the time. Above all, positive political will is very important. No conservation effort can succeed without a strong political will.

I saw the golden era of Sariska as well as the days after the tragedy. I was fortunate to be part of its revival. I felt it was my bounden duty to place the facts relating to the ups and downs of Sariska before the wildlife, especially Sariska, lovers. Hence this book.

This book is divided into three parts: (I) The Past Glory; (II) The Debacle; and (III) The Rebuilding.

BELOW: Once diminished Valture population is slowly returning to Sariska

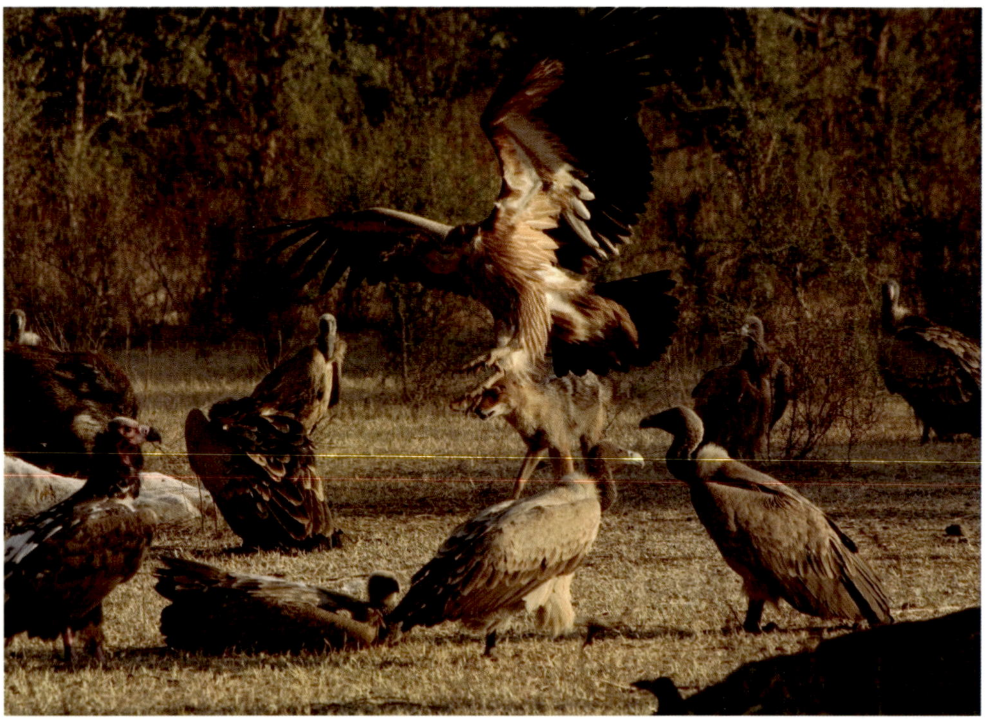

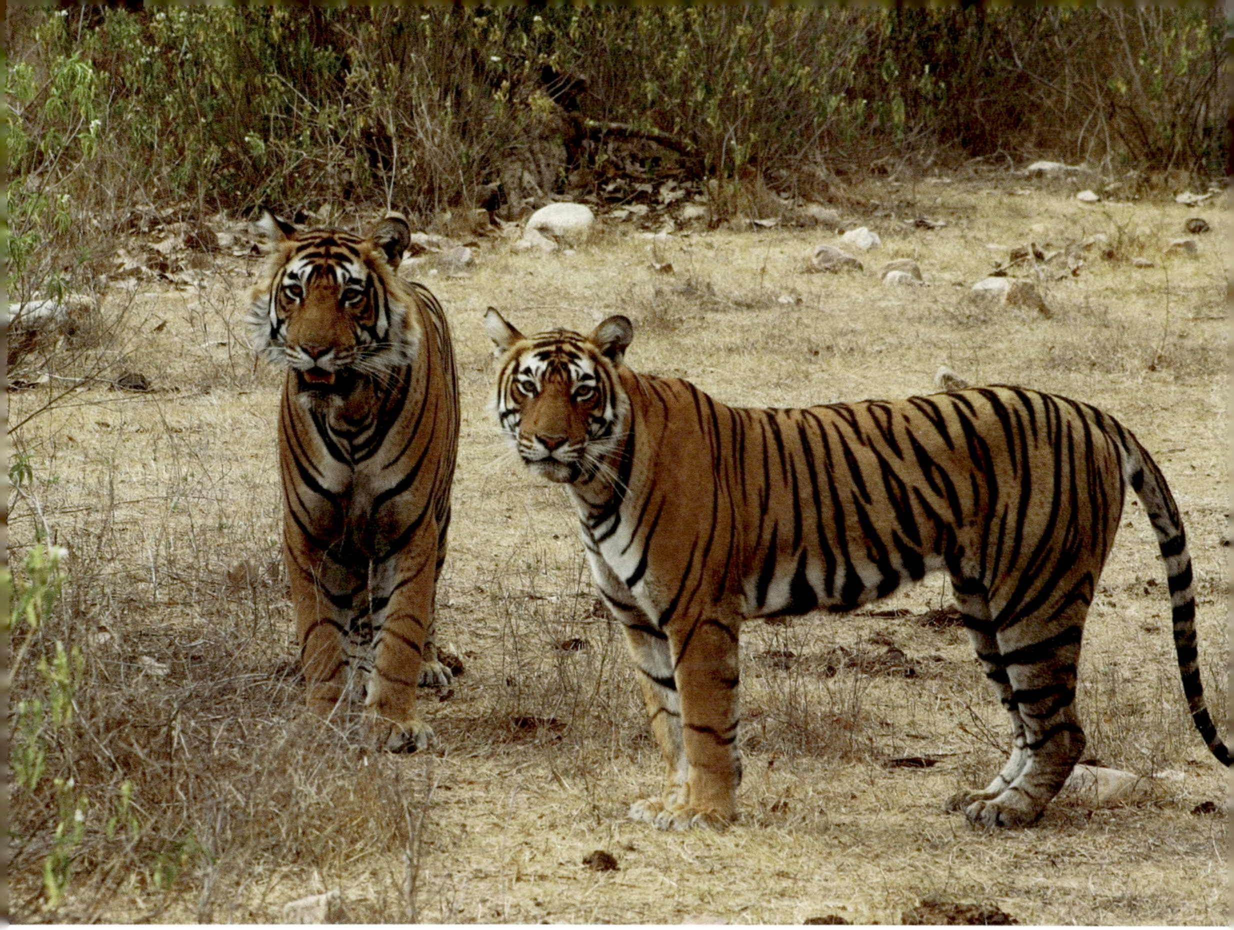

Part I describes the rich flora and fauna of Sariska as well as its cultural, historical, and archeological significance. It also dwells on the human and other biotic pressures. A serious effort has been made to describe the pre- and post-independence managerial practices to meet drinking water requirements of the wildlife inhabiting the Reserve.

ABOVE:
Posing for photos majestically!

Part II describes the problems arising out of decimation of the entire tiger population of Sariska by poachers in 2004. Report of the Mehrotra committee, set up by the state government to gather first-hand information on the genocide of the tiger population in Sariska Reserve, is the highlight of this part.

Part III deals with the main recommendations of the State Empowered Committee (SEC) and Tiger Task Force (TTF) set up by the central government as well as their implementation by the steering committee set up by the state government. This part also deals in great detail with the historical translocation of wild tigers in Sariska and the resulting controversies.

I have tried to share my experience in settling the translocated tigers in Sariska and the various steps taken to strengthen wildlife protection measures.

After my retirement in 2010 I joined Sariska Tiger Foundation, an NGO, as its senior vice president. This organisation works for the improvement of Sariska's forest cover and wildlife to its optimum potential. It also emphasises the need for the people living in the periphery of Sariska to live in perfect harmony with its wildlife.

Unfortunately, however, very little attempt has been made to present the rich wildlife and cultural heritage of this jewel of the Aravallis in all its grandeur. Hence my humble attempt. Interactions with wildlife

BELOW: Sambar stag in velvet

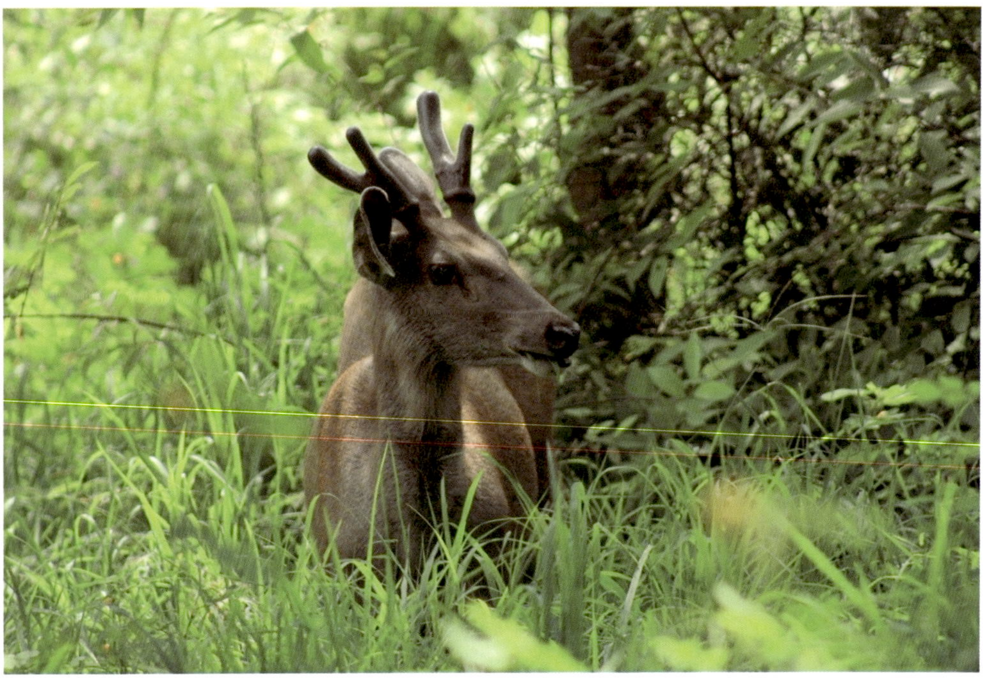

enthusiasts at Sariska made me aware of the immense interest that the total loss of tigers in Sariska as well as their re-introduction has generated.

In India, particularly in Rajasthan, our precious forests and wildlife reserves are passing through critical times for want of political will on conservation. On the one hand, recruitment of frontline personnel stopped 25 years ago. On the other, biotic pressures have increased manifold with the exploding human population. As per the latest survey, trade in wildlife products is now the third largest illegal activity globally after drugs and human trafficking.

While the challenges to conservation measures are increasing at a fast pace, government apathy is increasing, too. Consequently, the forest cover as well as wildlife are vanishing very fast. How long can our mother nature endure this? We must put an end to this senseless plunder immediately.

The responsibility has to be shared by nature lovers also. It is a war-like situation for the conservationists.

As a dedicated soldier in this endless war, I feel proud to sing praises of the heroes who have contributed to this great cause. I urge other responsible citizens, especially politicians, to come forward and take up cudgels and keep the flag of conservation flying high by helping to put an end to the plunder of nature and preserve this precious heritage for future generations.

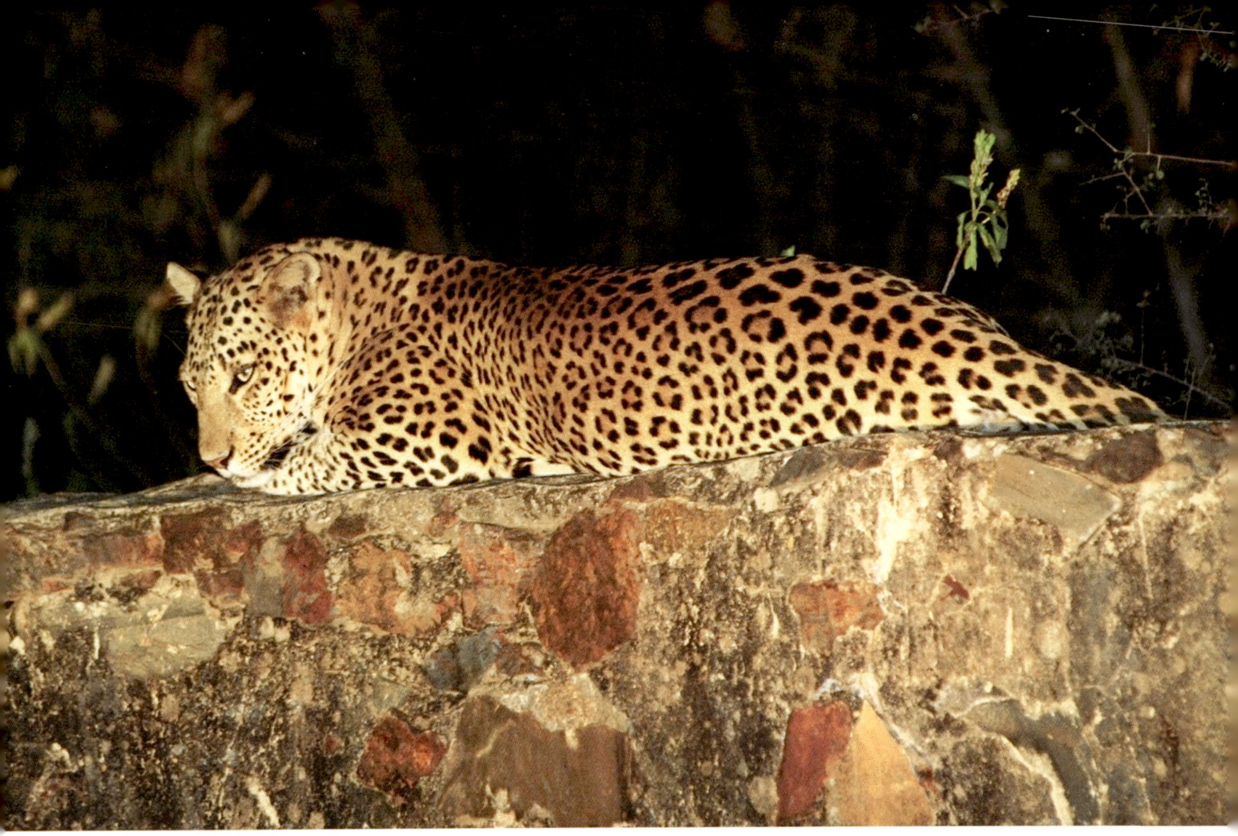

FOREWORD

I have known Sunayan Sharma for over 20 years, first as an inquisitive and quick learner under training at the Wildlife Institute of India (WII), and then as a committed field officer in Sariska. Post-retirement he remains active in the tiger rehabilitation programmes in Sariska Tiger Reserve.

Sariska is a difficult park to manage. Not because of any natural deficiency but because of weaker governance. Sariska too faces several constraints that plague many protected areas in our country. The problem of highways, relocation of villagers, ineffective participatory management of religious tourism, and lack of adequate frontline staff in fieldworthy age are the most critical constraints that stall efficacious management of the Park, as Sunayan convincingly brings out.

The true value of Sariska as a vital aquifer for this semi-arid region of Rajasthan, and tiger conservation for achieving it, is apparently lost on the political powers that be. Sariska, easily is the best specimen of Aravali forests, and is a treasure trove of biodiversity with tiger at the crest, as Sunayan strives to bring out in this book. The freakish history of the treatment of the park during the past few decades points to the lack of concern and indecision that resulted in the Sariska debacle of 2004, when the Park was bereft of all its tigers. Sunayan's book deals with this crisis of governance with lessons for those responsible for the Park administration and those in political and administrative top hierarchy.

This first-person account of Sariska's natural history in the backdrop of rich local political history and archaeology is absorbing and greatly informative. The thrilling notes on a close encounter with a courting pair of tigers and the much-belated but fiercely-welcome arrival of two cubs would rivet any reader's attention. Graphic details such as mitigation of constraints of water shortage and establishment of an effective network of anti-poaching patrol camps and an encounter with poachers would certainly engage any reader. A serious scholar of natural history and a keen visitor to the Park would find the book a potent means of information on Sariska. The author's keen eye and deep understanding with authentic citing of geographic locales around which he weaves the true story of Sariska is remarkable.

FACING PAGE: A leopard taking rest after a good meal *(Photo by Dinesh Durrani)*

H.S. Panwar
Founder Director
Wildlife Institute of India

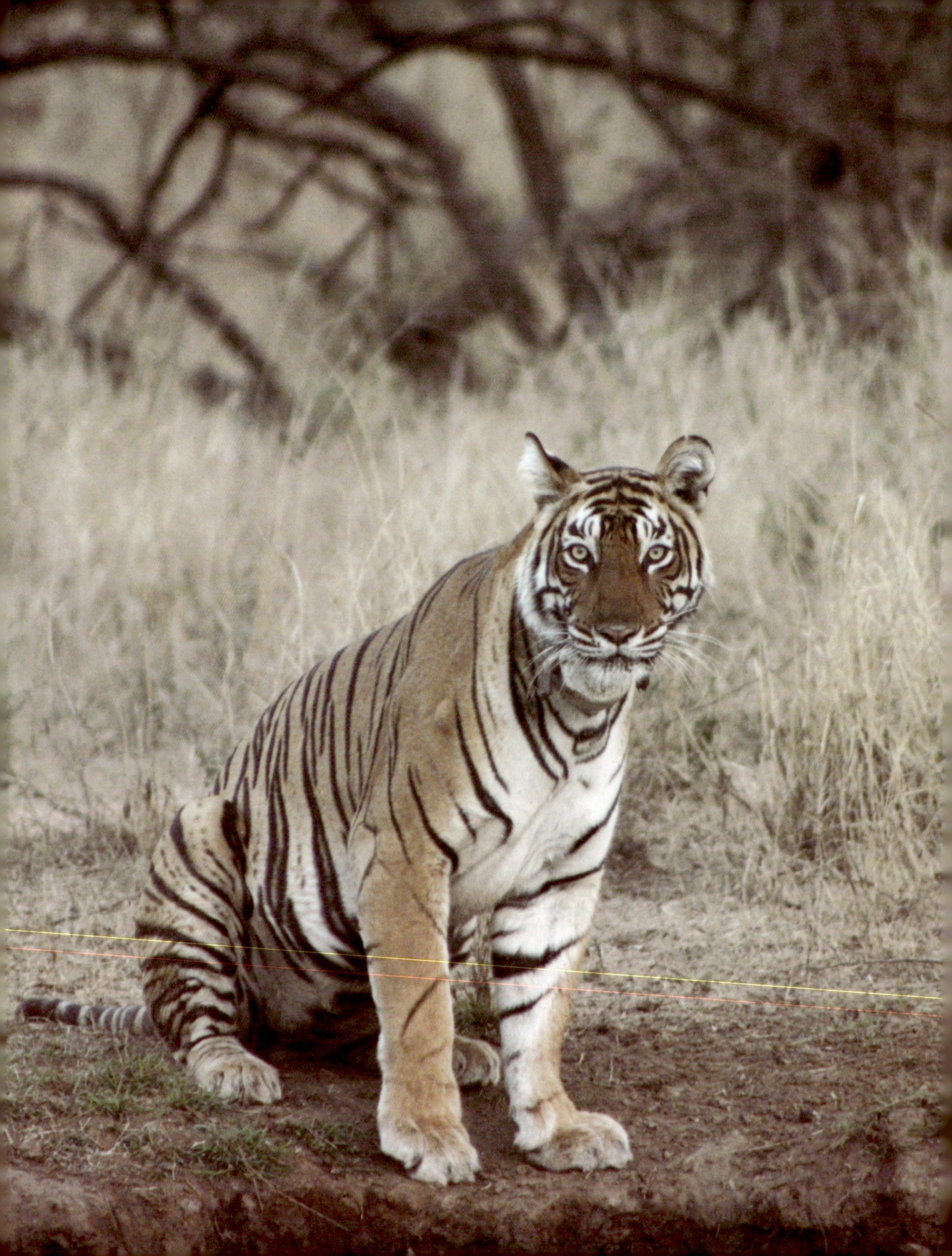

1

PAST GLORY

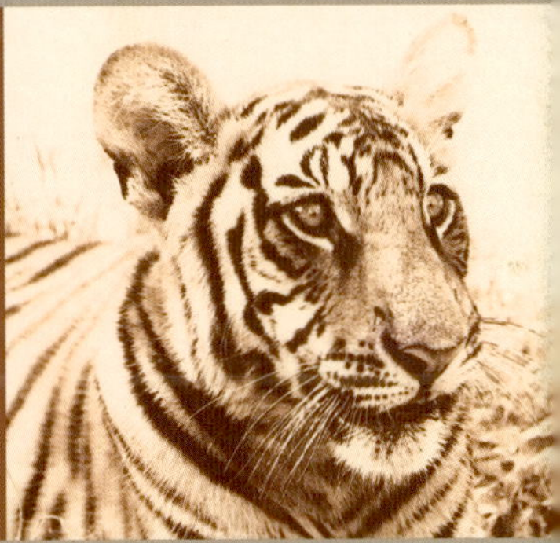

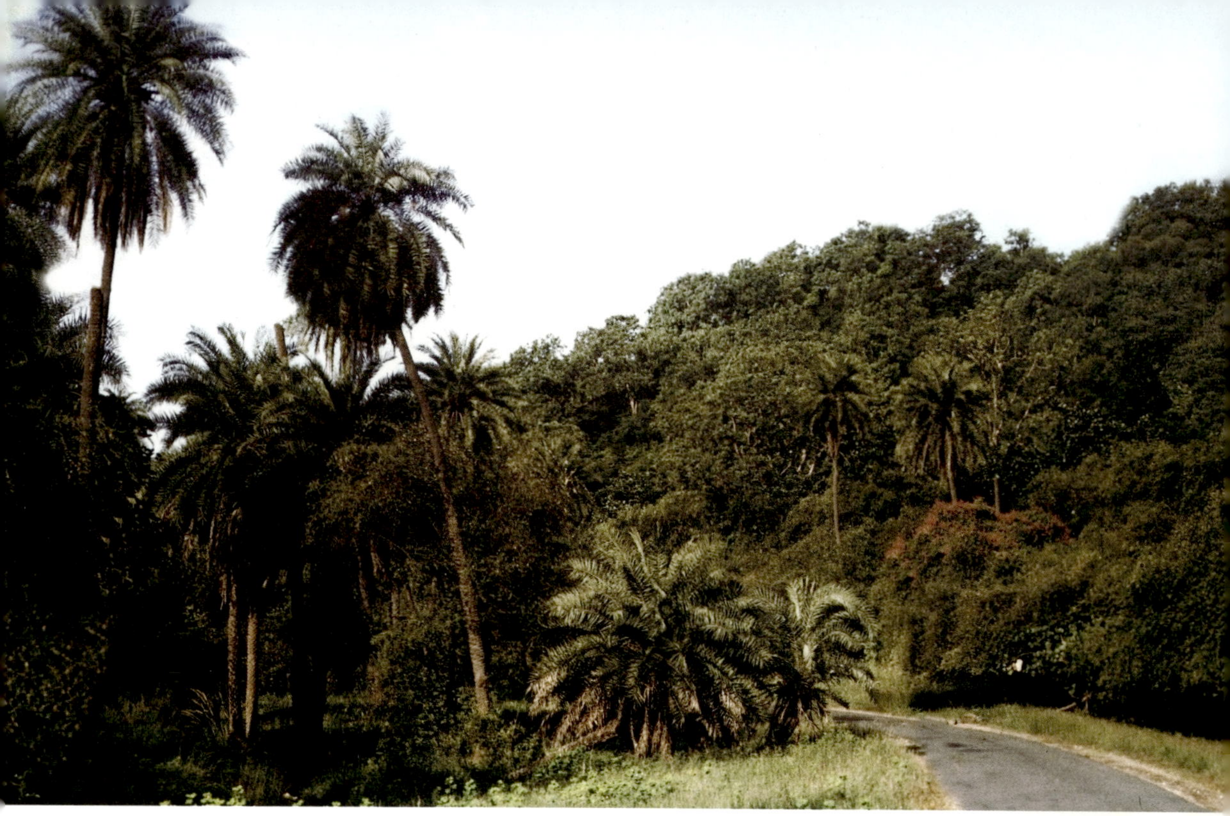

SARISKA, MY VALENTINE

LOVE AT FIRST SIGHT

Sariska has always been romantic which perpetually fascinated me. My first visit to Sariska was merely by chance. I had completed a two-year forestry training course at Dehradun and was posted at a government saw mill in Banswara.

In an early morning in October 1973, I was travelling to Delhi through Sariska-Alwar. In those days, the national highway between Jaipur and Delhi used to pass through Sariska-Alwar.

As I crossed Thanagazi, the heavenly fragrance of Sariska made the place self-evident. The jungle was quiet and the fragrance in the air was overpowering. A cautious herd of Sambar crossed the road. Soon after, the entire jungle suddenly echoed to the whooping call of langurs. It was playtime for them. We stopped the vehicle and stepped out. The breath of fresh and pure air was indeed refreshing. The impact of this atmosphere was so electrifying that it left me spellbound for a while.

I would have loved to enjoy the beauty of this jungle a little longer but the call of duty and lack of time did not permit me to do so. I continued my journey after a cup of tea.

This brief experience had hypnotised me and I immediately fell in love with Sariska. The sweet memory of this experience is still fresh in my mind.

Facing page: Highway passing through the core of Sariska

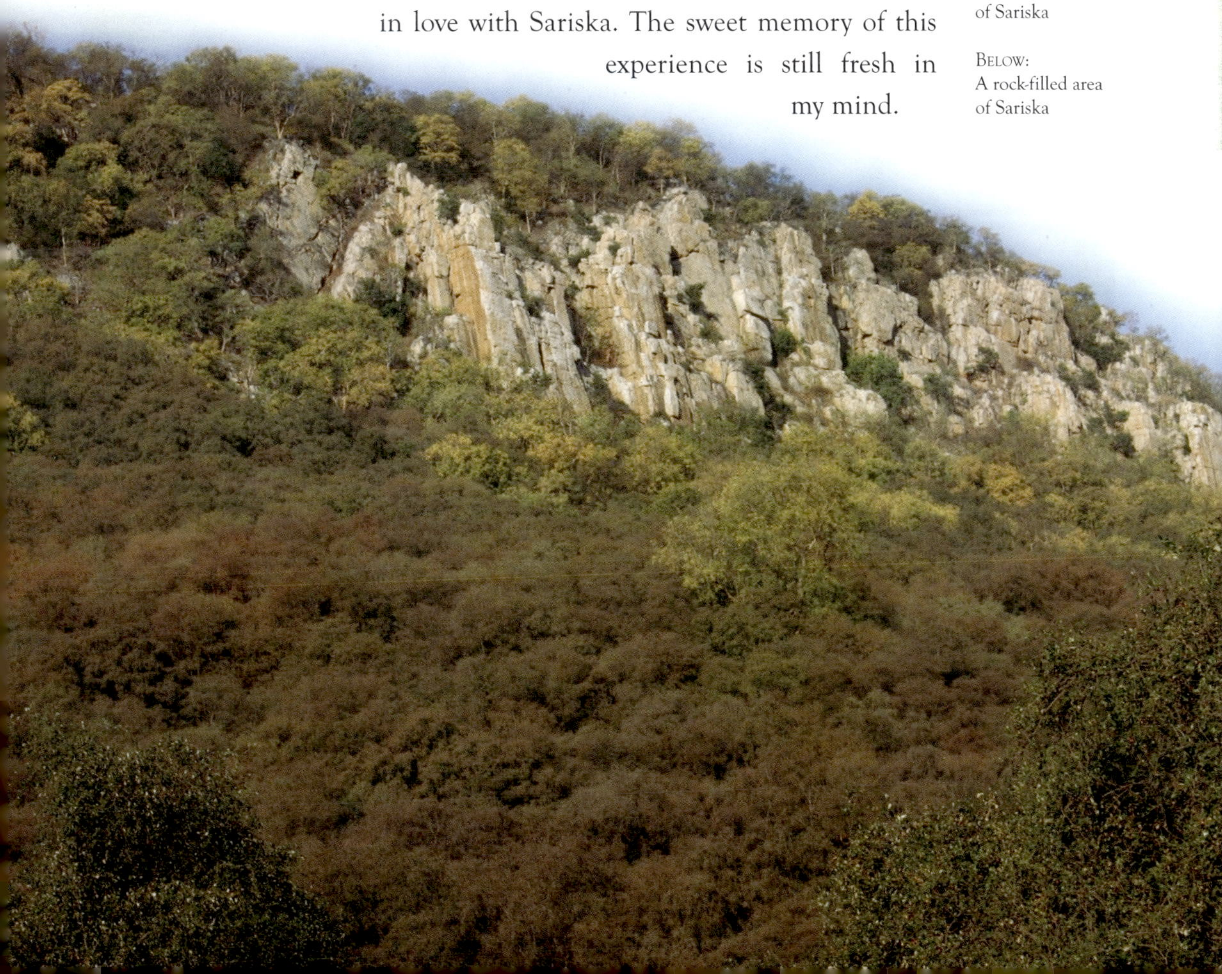

Below: A rock-filled area of Sariska

MY SUBSEQUENT TRYSTS WITH SARISKA

I had been working with the forest department and had served in several parts of Rajasthan. I, however, did not get an opportunity to visit Sariska again. Such an opportunity was presented to me in October 1985. I camped at Sariska for a week with fellow trainees of a course in wildlife management. We learned various census methods as well as techniques of tranquilising wild animals. The camp, thus, provided ample opportunity to wander through the core area of Sariska Tiger Reserve.

One night I was seated at the legendry watch tower of Kalighati along with two colleagues, Tejvir Singh and Uday Vohra. In those days, the Kalighati waterhole used to be a small cemented trough. This is the richest patch of Sariska as far as the forest and wildlife are concerned. Till late night we kept a watch on the animals visiting the waterhole.

BELOW: Deers using an earthen waterhole in Sariska

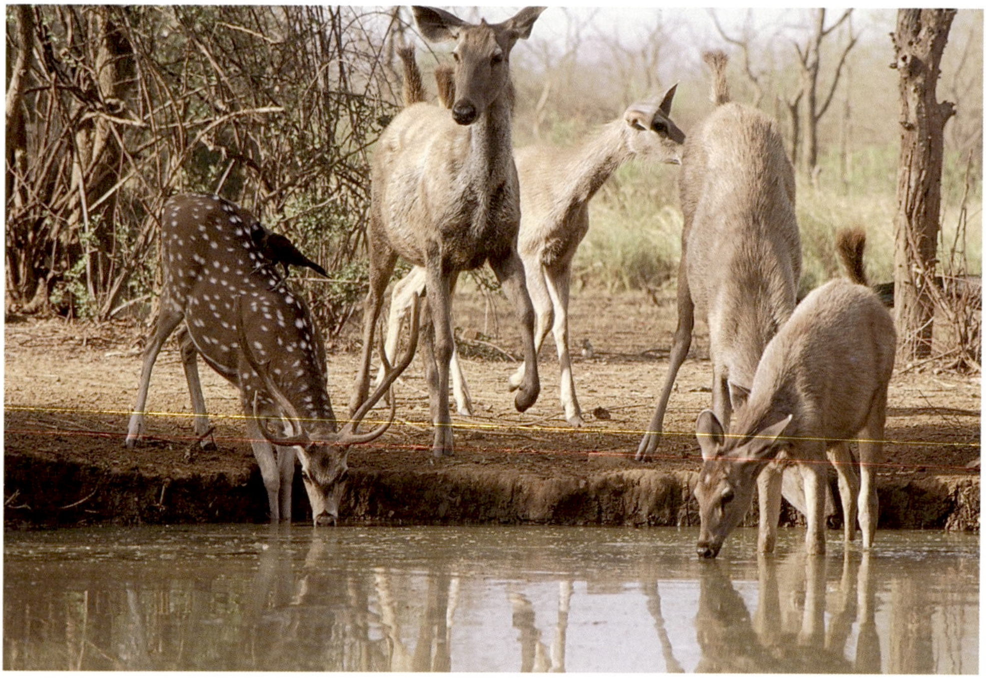

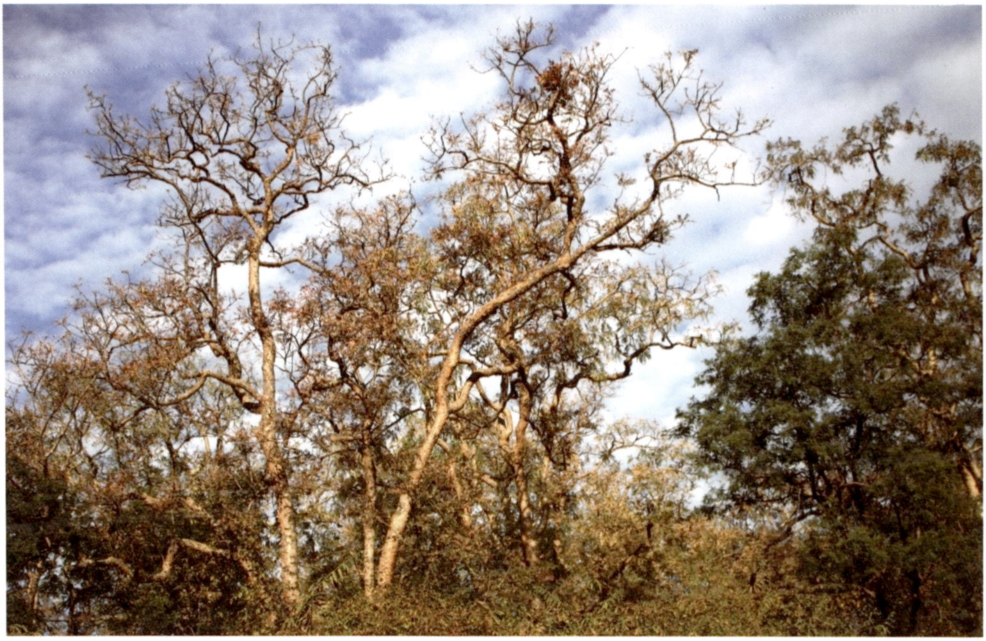

Above:
A colourful view of Sariska

A few chital, sambar, and wild boar visited the waterhole. Since it was a dark night, it was not possible to see the small animals clearly. The forest guard accompanying us had, however, told us that Indian palm civets lived close by and visited this waterhole frequently. We desperately waited for the tiger. There were strong alarm calls three times from chital and sambar but there was no sign of the tiger.

Early next morning, I checked the waterhole for pug marks of tiger or leopard just in case one had visited the waterhole without our noticing it. While I was absorbed in this exercise, I heard a typical 'soo-soo' sound. I turned around and found a wild boar, a huge tusker, heading towards me. Though the animal was not exactly charging, it looked visibly annoyed. I climbed the parapet of the well used for filling the waterhole. The animal, however, continued the chase. I panicked and shouted for help. My colleagues rushed to my aid. That deterred the boar from chasing me. It backed out and headed towards the waterhole.

It drank some water and then silently vanished into the bushes, and I heaved a sigh of relief.

Later, while we were busy examining the waterhole and surrounding areas for pug marks, one huge sambar stag appeared at a distance. It was a beautiful animal. I was carrying an ordinary camera not very suitable for wildlife photography. But I was tempted to photograph the stag. I approached the animal cautiously. It started moving away. I kept following it hoping for a better photographic opportunity. This led the stag to the road between Kalighati and Tehla. I was behind the animal. While moving away from me it was continuously munching on Grewia flavescens shrubs, which were in abundance there. We were very close to Kalighati chowki when the stag crossed the road and moved towards another Grewia bush. It was so absorbed in its feeding and also probably distracted by my pursuit that it did not notice a tiger resting under the shrub. The tiger was as surprised as

BELOW: A view of the thick forest of Sariska

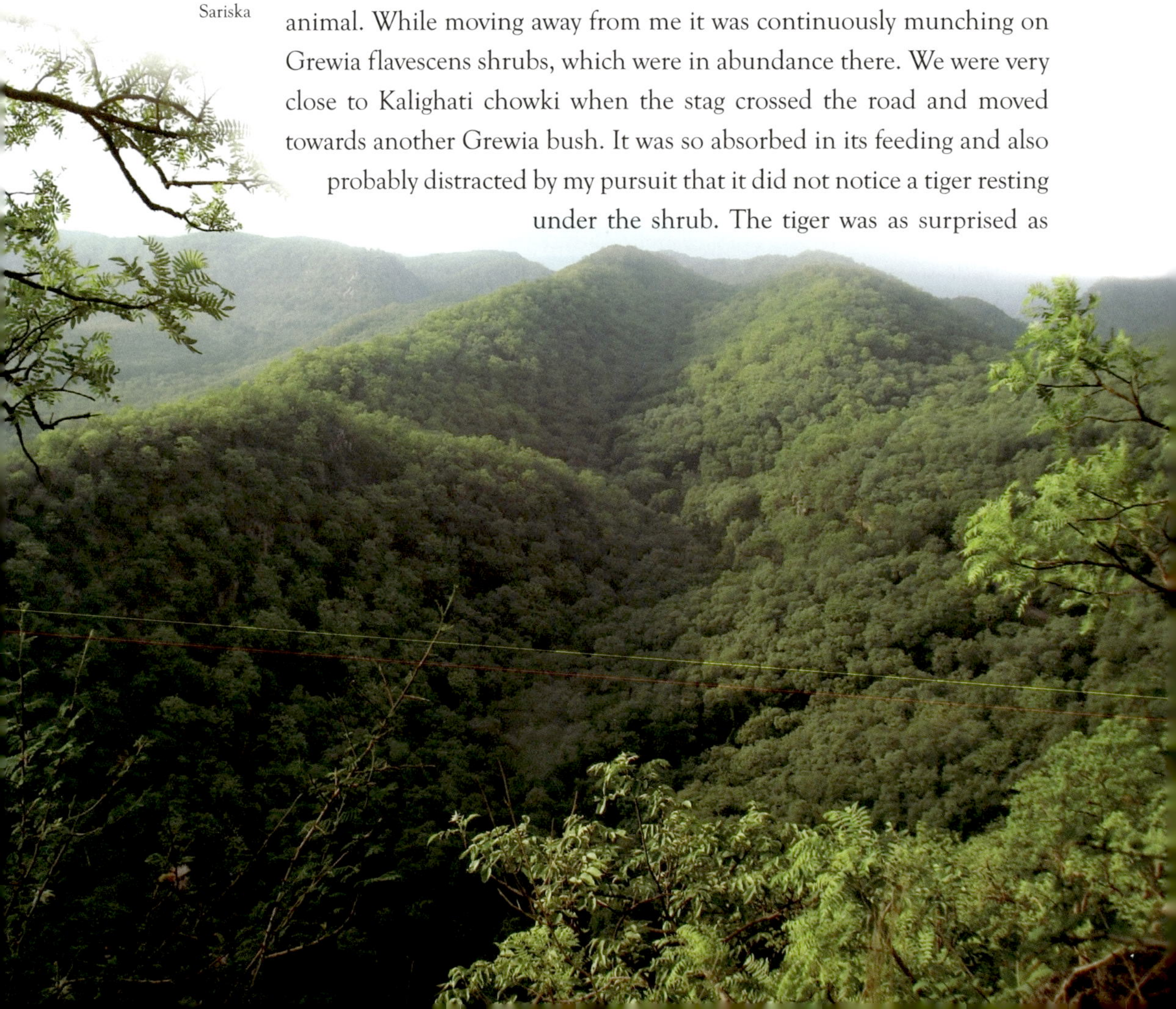

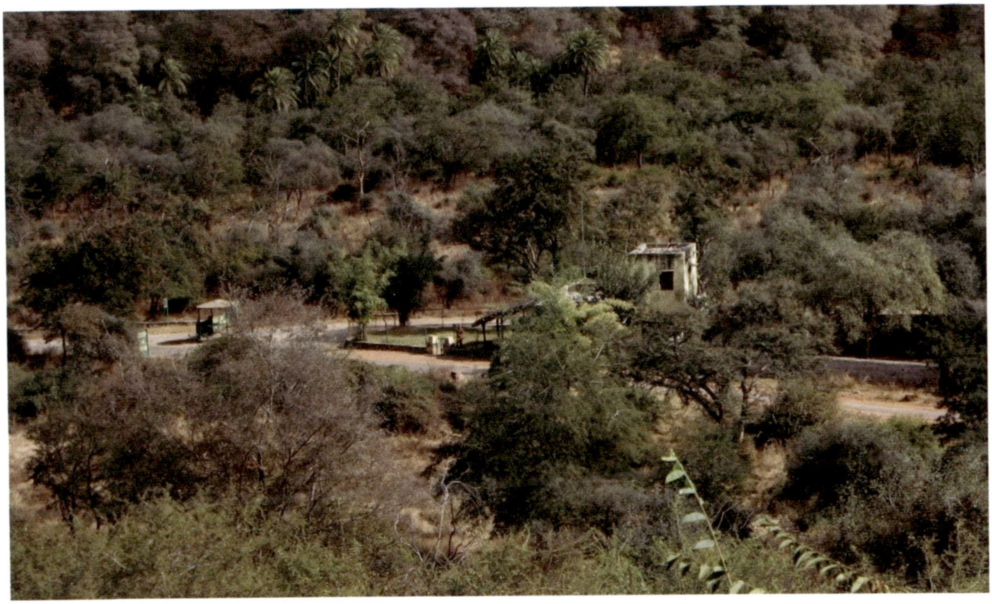

the sambar stag when they came face to face with each other. Even as I watched, the sambar suddenly leapt emitting a high pitched metallic dhank. I was completely taken aback. The tiger, also shaken from its siesta, slowly slipped into the tall grass of the valley. I could get only a glimpse of the back of the tiger. By the time my colleagues joined me, the tiger had already vanished.

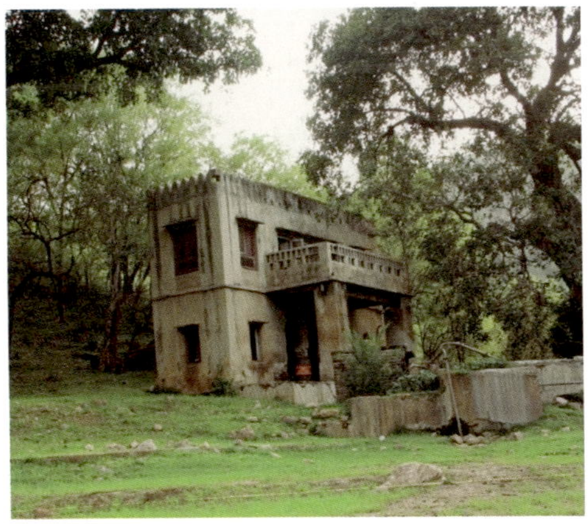

This was my first tiger sighting at Sariska. So exciting! This educational tour provided us with an excellent opportunity to get familiarised with the rich flora, fauna, and topography of Sariska.

In August 1991 I joined Sariska as field director.

TOP:
Kalighati forest chowki

ABOVE:
Kalighati watch tower

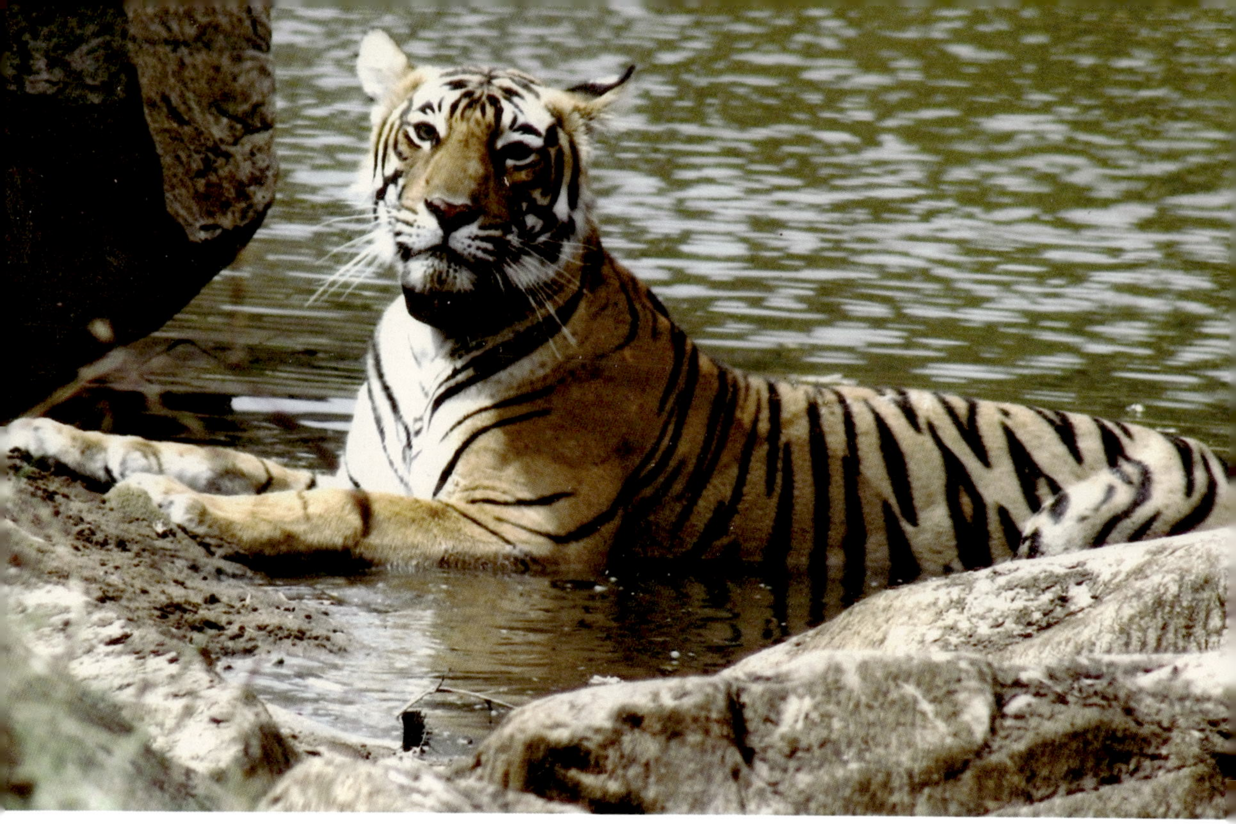

SARISKA TIGER RESERVE

LOCATION, TOPOGRAPHY, AND FLORA AND FAUNA

Sariska Tiger Reserve (76° 17' to 76° 34' E and 27° 5' to 27° 33' N) is located in Alwar district of Rajasthan, India. The Reserve is spread over an area of 882 sq. km of the ancient Aravalli hill range.

The Reserve is a beautiful blend of tropical dry deciduous and tropical thorn forest. It is dotted with numerous narrow and broad valleys such as Sariska-Bara, Sariska-Kalighati-Slopka, Kankwadi-Ghar-Rajore, Sariska-Udainath, Umri-Siliberi, Raika-Pani Dhal-Loj, Deora-Lilka-

Binak, Kalikhol-Vera-Binak, Nathusar-Rampur, and so on. These valleys provide excellent habitat to the faunal diversity of the Reserve.

The classification of Sariska indicates that it is dry forest notwithstanding the change that takes place during the monsoons. With the onset of monsoon, heavy undergrowth comes to life. The transformation in that season is complete with a lush green cover all over. Even the tracks have tall grass growing all over them. During summer (March to June) the temperature soars to 45 °C and the entire jungle turns ash brown except for some patches in the valleys.

Sariska is probably one of the most visited wildlife parks in India. The main reason for this could be its proximity to important cities like Delhi and Jaipur, as well as its beauty and wildlife.

The first reference to Sariska forests goes back to the time of *Mahabharata*, the great epic. The Pandavas lived in Virat Nagar and

FACING PAGE: Cooling off after a good meal

BELOW: Wild pigs suckling piglets

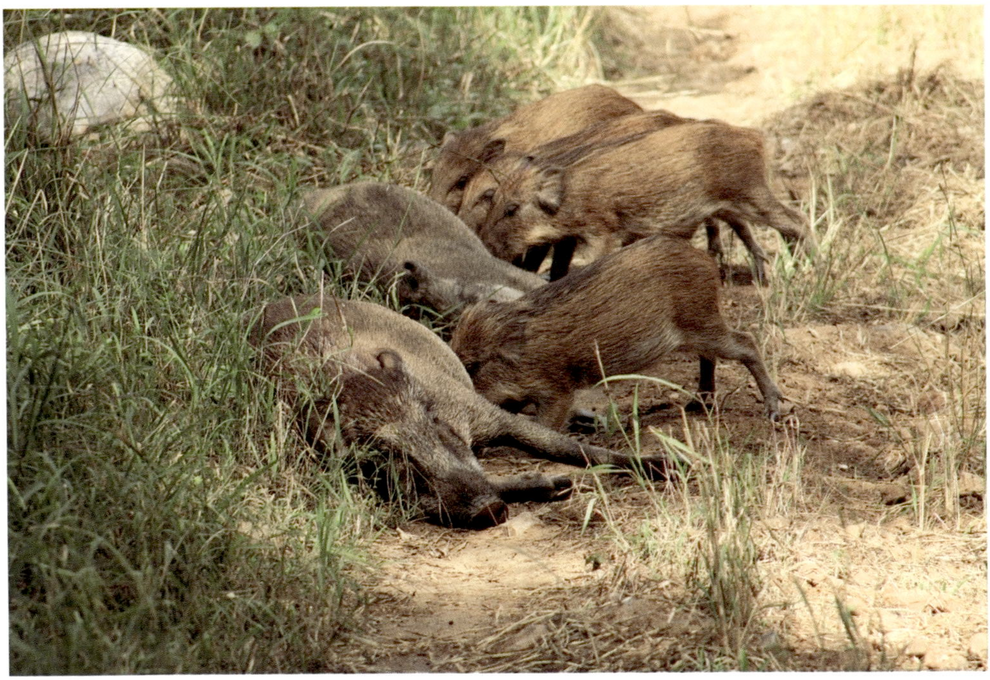

Sariska forests for one year in hidden exile. Pandupole, named after them, is still a much visited place in Sariska.

During the 9th to 10th centuries AD, the area gained prominence under the rule of Gurjar-Pratihar dynasty, who established a powerful empire over a vast portion of Northern India.

In the olden times the entire area of Alwar and Bharatpur was known as Matsya (fish) Pradesh.

The princely state of Alwar was founded by Pratap Singh, of the Kachhwaha lineage, in the second half of the 18th century. Alwar's earlier name was Ulwar. The first letter 'U' was replaced by 'A' by the then ruler of the state so that its name comes at the top in alphabetical listing introduced by the British! Sariska was established as a hunting reserve by the erstwhile rulers of Alwar.

BELOW: Deers enjoying an earthen waterhole

Sariska was notified as a wildlife reserve in 1955, which made it unlawful to hunt or capture wild animals from there. It was declared a

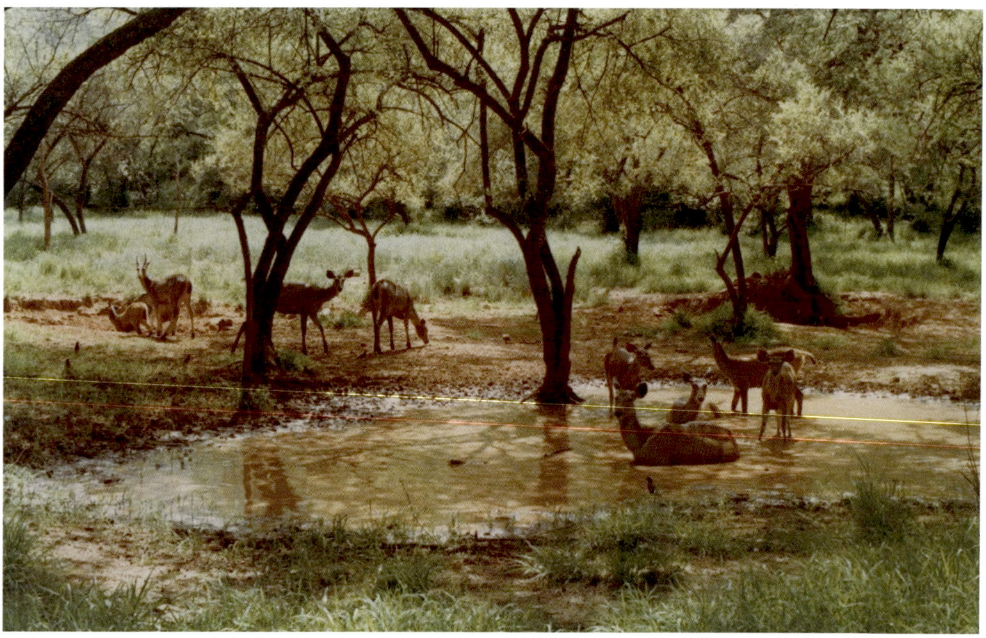

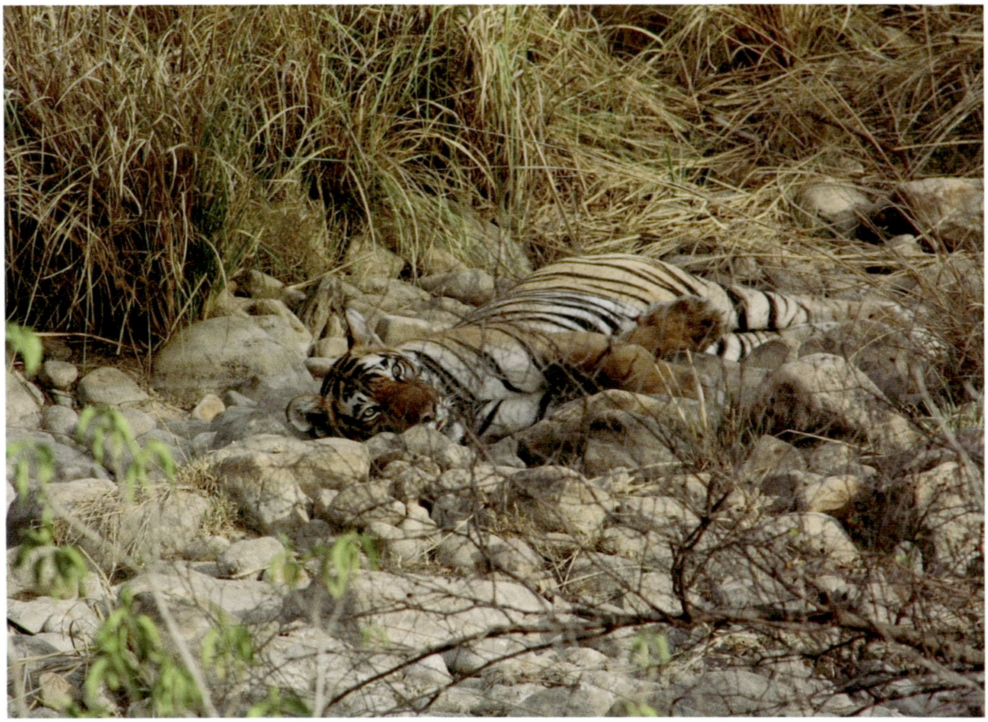

ABOVE:
A tiger taking rest after a meal

wildlife sanctuary in 1958. Sariska's potential for tiger conservation was acknowledged when Sariska was declared as a Project Tiger Reserve in 1978. To further strengthen protection measures, the core I area of the Reserve, spread over 274 sq. km, was notified as a National Park in 1982. Later, some adjacent forest areas of Alwar Forest Division were added to it.The Tiger Reserve thus spread out to occupy 882 sq. km.

Aravalli is one of the oldest hill ranges of the world. Sariska is the only Tiger Reserve which falls wholly in this range. Sariska and Ranthambhore, another Tiger Reserve in Rajasthan, form the western border of tigers' distribution in the world.

Sariska and Ranthambhore have different topography. In Ranthambhore merely the fort and adjacent areas covering about 60 per cent of the National Park, fall in the Aravallis. The rest of the park,

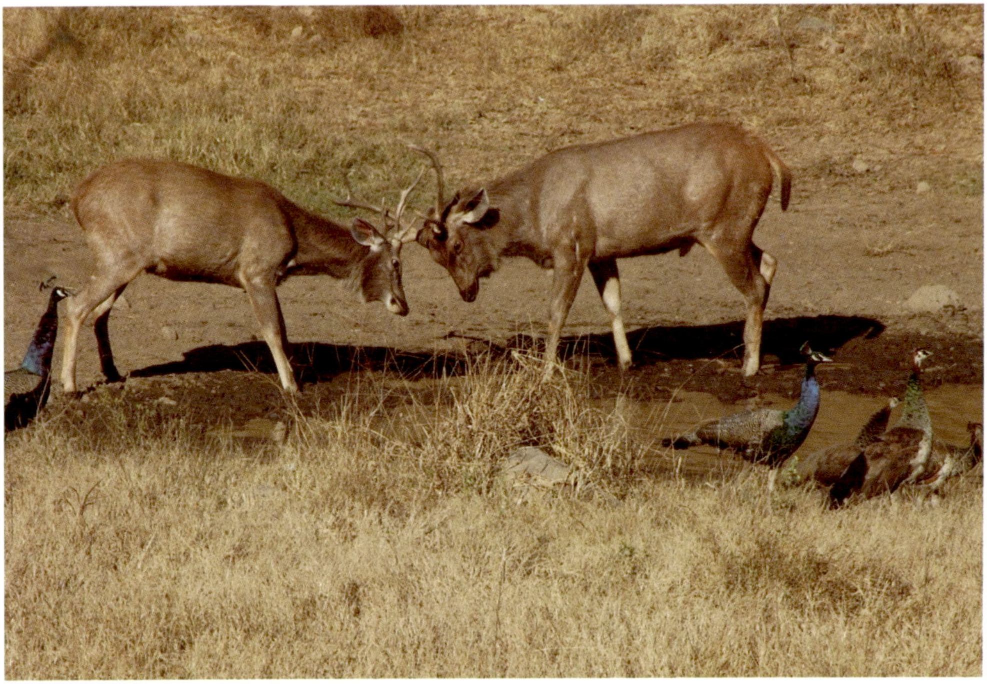

ABOVE: Some exercise, playfully though

which supports huge tiger population, falls in Vindhyan formation with flat surface. Sariska lies in Aravallis with hills, valleys, and gorges.

Sariska has scrub-thorn arid forests, dry deciduous forests, rocks, and grasses. The wide range of wildlife found here is a wonderful example of ecological adoption and tolerance, for the climate here is variable as well as acute.

Anogeissus pendula (Dhok) is the dominant tree species covering over 90 per cent of Sariska forest. *Boswellia serreta* (Salar) and *Lannea coromandelica* (Gurjan) grow at rocky patches. *Acacia catechu* (Kattha), though rare in pure patches, is generally found in valleys. Bamboo, though spread all over the Reserve, can mostly be seen along springs and moist hills. Some valleys support Zizyphus (Ber) species. *Butea monosperma* (Dhak) popularly known as 'flame of the forest', is gregarious in almost all the flat and wide valleys. The site becomes most picturesque

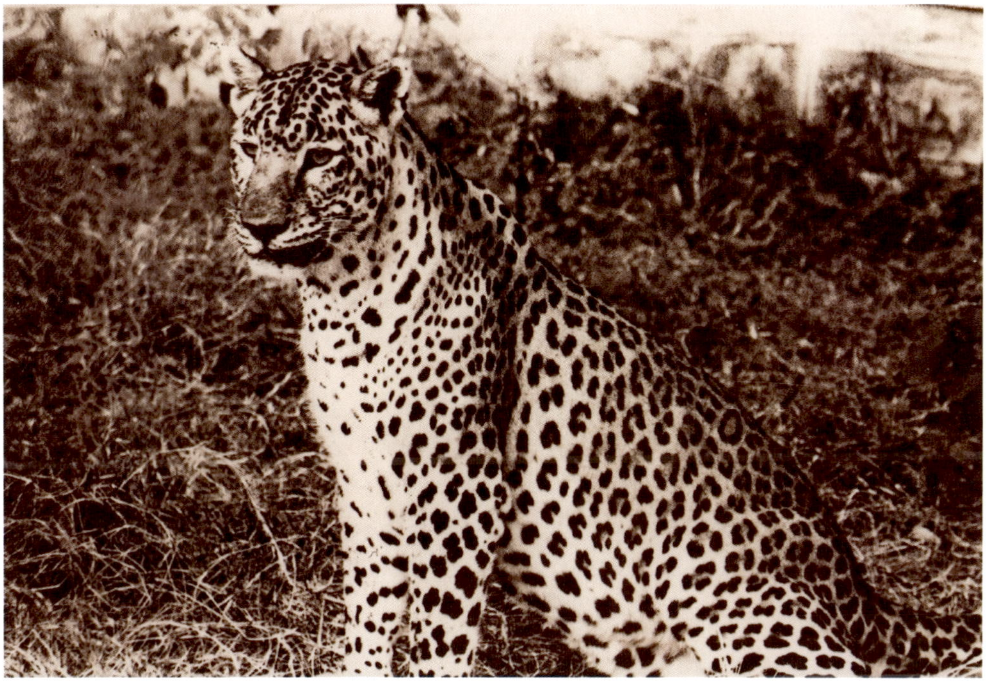

Above:
A leopard in deep thought *(Photo by K.L. Saini)*

during summer when the entire forest blooms with the flame of the *Butea* flowers.

During summer when the grass becomes dry and non-palatable, the highly nutritious dry leaves of *Anogeissus pendula* (Kardhai or Dhok) fall on the forest floor and provide the best possible nutritious food to sambar, spotted deer, and blue bull. *Capparis* spp. also plays an important role in providing green fodder to animals during peak summer when most other plants dry up.

Fifty five species of grass enrich the important ground flora of Sariska. These are scattered all over the Reserve and play an important role in the distribution of wildlife. Grass is the main source of food for the herbivores and omnivores. The main Sariska-Kalighati-Slopka-Umri valley supports a large number of faunal species. This is the richest part of the Reserve for edible grasses, apart from various other shrubs and fruit-bearing trees which provide food to various faunal species round the year.

Ber (*Ziziphus numuleria*) was planted in the past in groves at several places in the Reserve, especially in the main valley between Sariska headquarters and Umri crossing. They have proved to be a boon for the herbivores, particularly langurs, who eat less and drop more on the forest floor where spotted deer, sambar, blue bull, and wild boar congregate in large numbers to feed on the dropped fruits.

Several *Phoenix sylvestris* groves can be seen along the 3 km stretch between Umri crossing and Pandupole. Like Umri–Pandupole valley, the Kankwadi Lake–Tuda valley as well as Pila Pani have got rich crop of *Phoenix sylvestris*. Kankwadi fort and the lake at its feet surrounded by Phoenix groves is a picturesque site in Sariska.

BELOW: Slopka forest during monsoon

Sariska is home to numerous carnivores such as tiger, leopard, jungle cat, caracal, civet, hyena, jackal, etc. Tiger and leopard feed on spotted

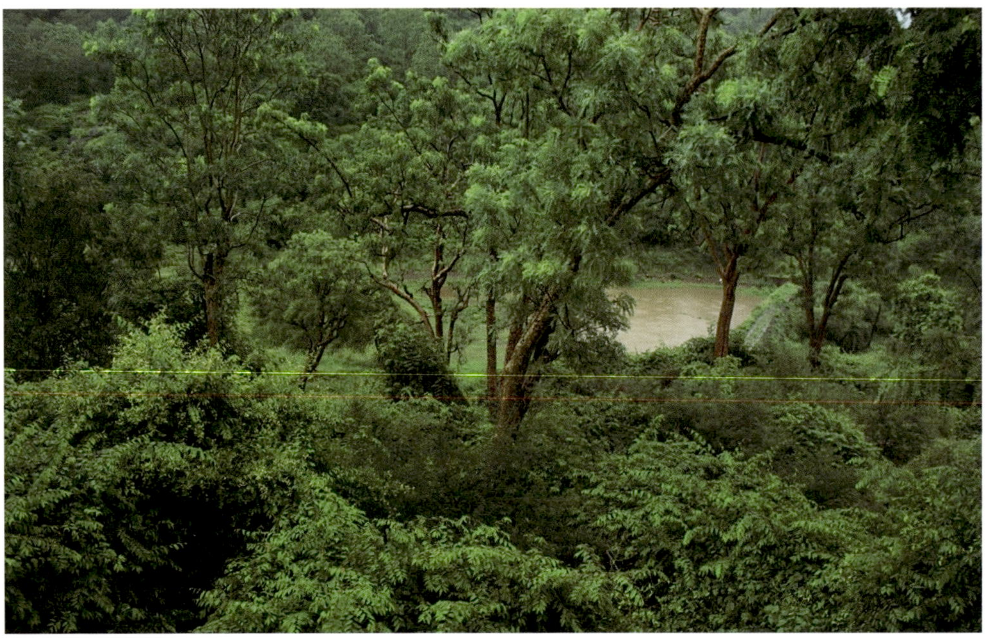

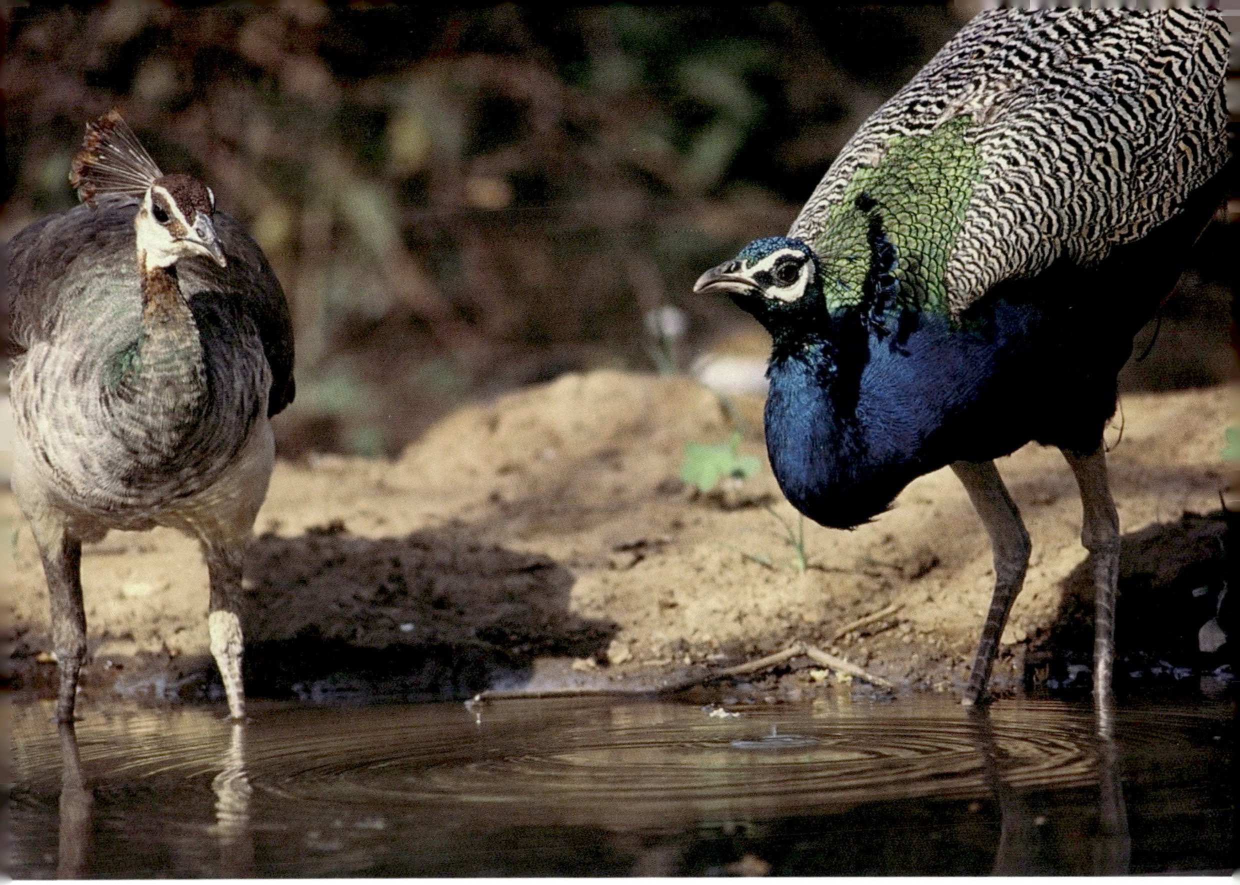

ABOVE:
Peacock and Peahen enjoying water from an earthen waterhole

deer, sambar, blue bull, wild boar, and langur. Sariska in general, and Talvriksh in particular, supports a huge population of rhesus monkeys.

Sariska also has a rich and varied bird population. The largest population of peafowls in India is found here. Grey partridge, bush quail, sand grouse, painted spur fowl, tree pie, golden backed wood pecker, golden oriole, crested serpent eagle, and black winged kite are other common birds found here. Several resident and migratory waterfowls inhabit various water bodies, especially those located in the central and southern areas of the Reserve. The Silised lake on the edge of the Reserve is home to a large number of crocodiles.

The Sariska forest had several forts and temples. Most of these are now in ruins except for Sariska Palace and Kankwadi Fort. Sariska is a classic example of a rare amalgamation of natural history and archaeology.

ADMINISTERING SARISKA

The mere size of Sariska makes the management of the Reserve very difficult.

Human population in and around the Reserve has continuously been increasing. Their demands include unrestricted grazing and browsing as well as for passage of motor vehicles through the core even after sunset. Mining leases had been issued even in the Reserve.

After joining in 1991, I toured the Reserve extensively to understand the field problems at ground level. My long experience as a forester had taught me that the solution to wildlife and forest management problems lie in human management, including the Reserve personnel. My tours were to study the field as well the living conditions of the staff. Wildlife sanctuaries and forests are open assets which make the job of a forester more difficult.

BELOW:
Blue bulls mating

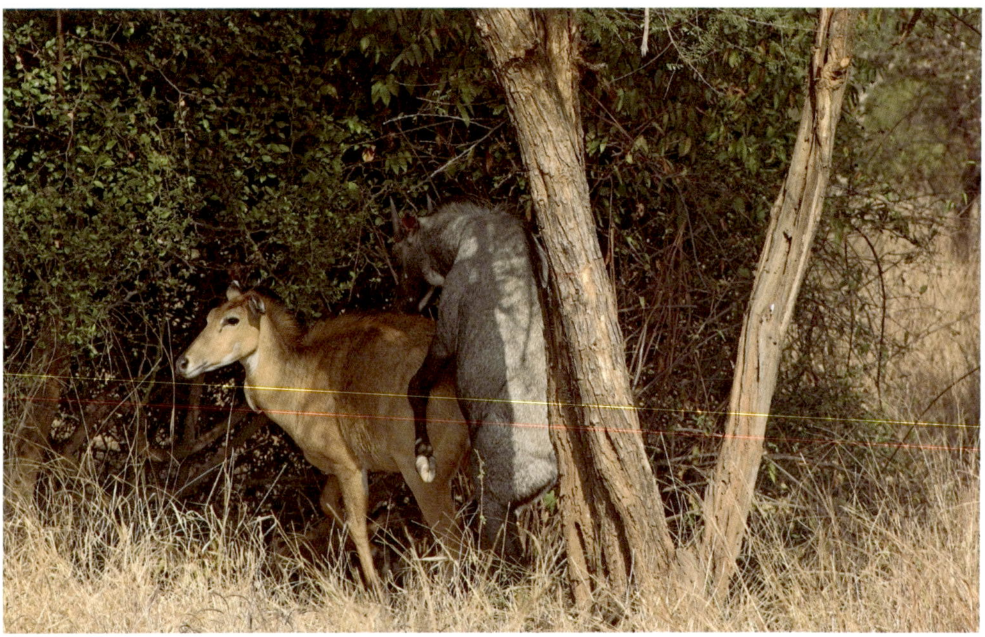

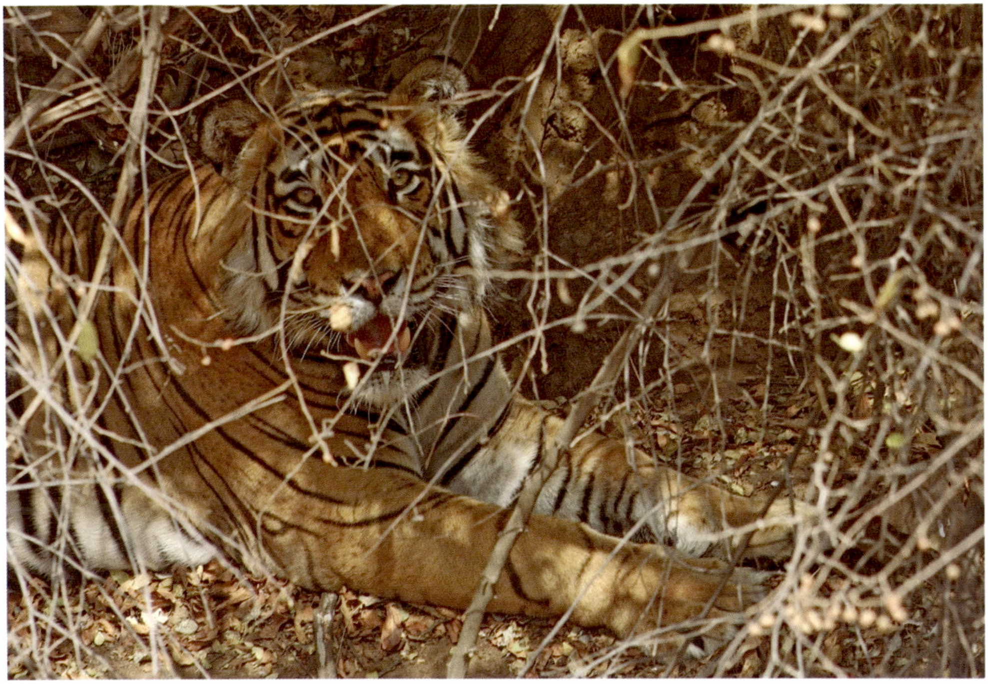

ABOVE: Occasionally sun gets too hot for tigers

During these visits I listened to their problems. This helped me understand the ground realities. These early lessons helped me a great deal in successfully tackling even the most difficult problems that I encountered in future. These interactions also enriched my knowledge of the flora and fauna as well as the archaeological assets of the Reserve.

For administrative purposes, Sariska has been divided into four ranges, namely Sariska, Tehla, Akbarpur, and Talvriksh, each headed by a range officer. These ranges are further divided into circles (*nakas*), each headed by a forester or assistant forester called Nakedar. Each *naka* is further divided into several beats, each headed by a forest guard or game watcher.

Every beat or *naka* is important from the protection point of view. But Kalighati naka falling under Sariska range is very special as it controls the most luxuriant forest with the highest density of wildlife in this Reserve. Kankwadi Fort also falls under the Kankwadi beat.

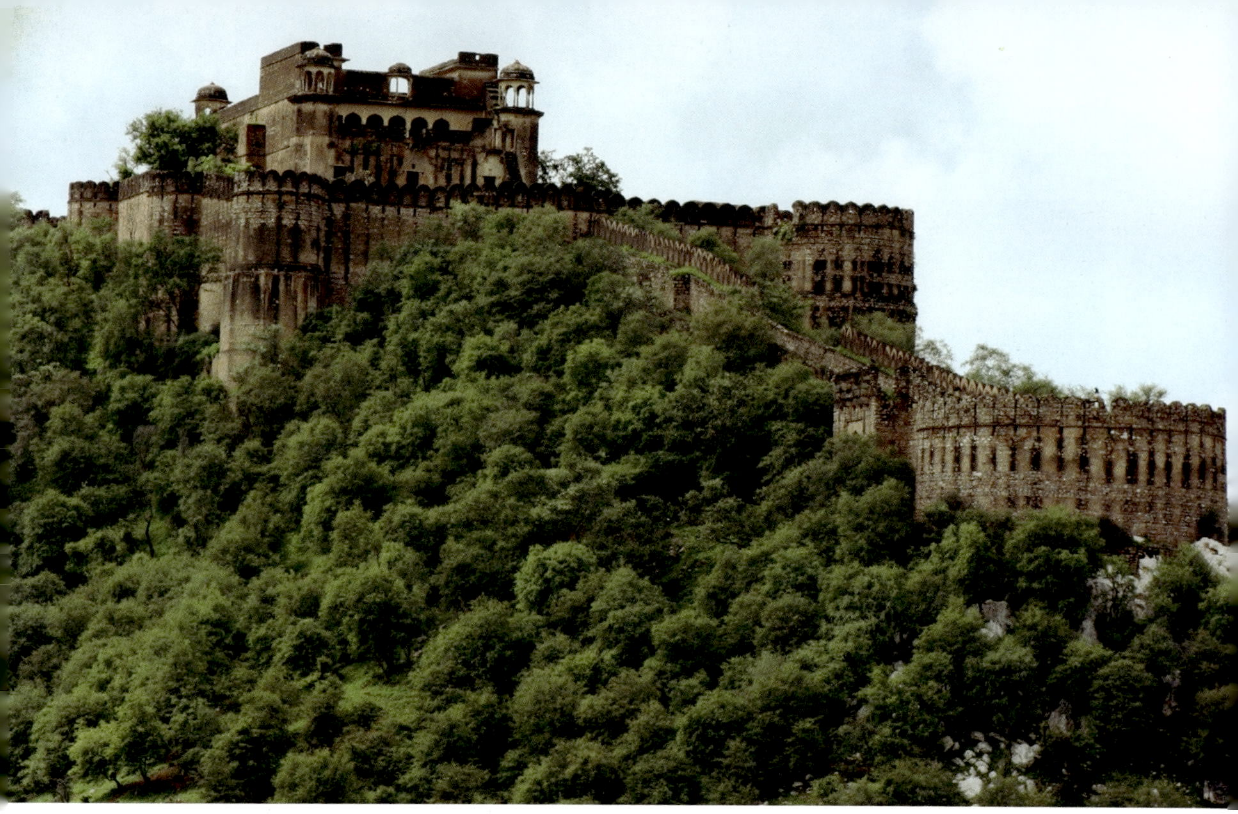

SOUTHERN FORESTS AND ITS ARCHEOLOGICAL AND CULTURAL HERITAGE

BHENSOTA PLATEAU

In late October, the days are warm but mornings and evenings are cold. The weather being ideal, we generally used to undertake long walks. During one such walk, while inspecting the grasslands of Doraka valley and sloping hills full of *Anogeissus pendula*, I decided to check further upwards crossing the boundary of Kalighati *naka*. After crossing the middle slope along the *nallah*, the dense growth of bamboo made our walk rather tough. We crossed the hill and reached the plateau of Bhensota. This 6-km-long narrow plateau had rich grass, bamboo, and several patches of Dhak (*Butea monosperma*) trees. Water from this beautiful plateau drained towards its southern slope beyond which are located Ghevar and Nadu villages. These villages have a sizeable human and livestock population. I then realised the importance of this area for wildlife and the potential threat it faced. Thereafter, patrolling along this area was intensified.

KANKWADI VALLEY AND FORT

Kankwadi fort is an important archeological landmark in Sariska. My first visit to Kankwadi was replete with bone-chilling experience. During

FACING PAGE: Kankwadi Fort

BELOW: The majestic Cabri gate, 7 km ahead of the Kankwadi Fort

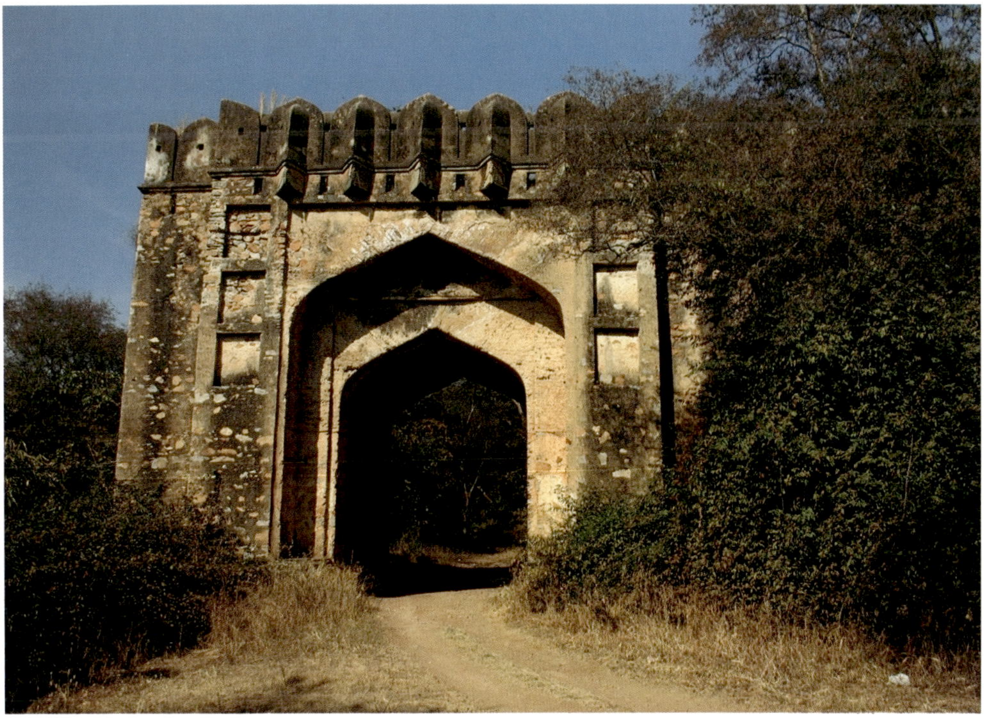

my early days in Sariska, when I studied the ways of the tiger, it was usual for me to keep track of tiger movement in Kalighati as well as surrounding areas. Kabul Singh, one of the most experienced forest guards, who had spent his entire service in Sariska, informed us that a tigress frequently took rest in Kankwadi fort during the day time. This piece of information got me excited. I travelled to Kankwadi the next morning along with Kabul Singh and Ram Prasad, Nakedar of Kalighati.

On Kalighati–Tehla road, after about 3.5 km, an earthen hilly track of about 8 km took us to the fort. This earthen track gets extensively damaged during monsoons because people from about a hundred Gujjar households use it round the year for travel and transport. These cattle owners were settled in four hamlets, close to each other, at the foot of the fort.

A forest guard outpost was established here to contain the damage done by the villagers. This track passes through a narrow valley rich in soil. Bamboo grows on the lower hill slopes on either side of this valley. Sambar and chital are always present here in good numbers. The upper areas of these hills are used by leopards cautiously for fear of confrontation with the larger carnivore, tiger.

The abandoned medieval fort is situated in the heart of the Reserve. It tells a grim story of the Mughal Empire. It is believed to have been built by the Mughal Emperor, Aurangazeb, in the 17th century where his brother, Dara Shikoh was imprisoned for several years.

Thousands of date palms grow around the fort. This is said to have grown from seeds thrown by the Mughal soldiers guarding the fort after eating the fruits. It is a small but beautiful fort. Beautiful paintings can still be seen on the walls.

In the main building I took a closer look at the space under the platform of the elevated ground floor. The place is quite spacious with an earthen floor. I saw there several pug marks, body marks, and other evidence to prove that a tigress used to rest there frequently.

Suddenly I realised that there was a peculiar body odour. Probably the tigress must have been there till a little while ago. Or maybe she could be around even at that point of time! I had a gut feeling that the tigress left the place only when she saw us approaching. That sent a chill down my spine. The staff too was frightened. I realised my mistake due to lack of experience. I apologised to my team. I vowed to be more careful in the future. I found the tiger's pug marks in the fort later on several occasions. The fort itself was in ruins. Ceilings and walls had collapsed. The Rajasthan government carried out extensive restoration and renovation work at the fort in 2009–10, turning it into a tourist attraction once again.

GARH-RAJORE VALLEY

Several villages such as Kaniawas, Muthrawat, Rajore, and Garh lie in the valley at the south of Kankwadi Fort. Kaniawas is largely inhabited by members

BELOW: Ruins of a temple in Garh–Rajore complex

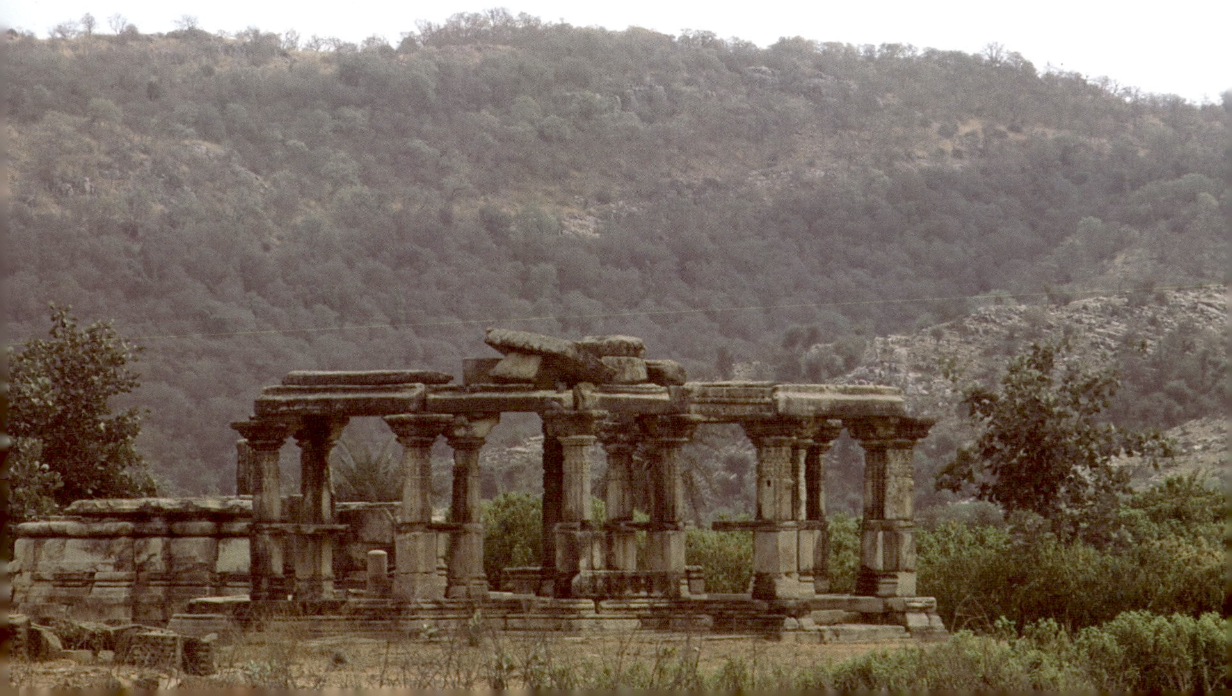

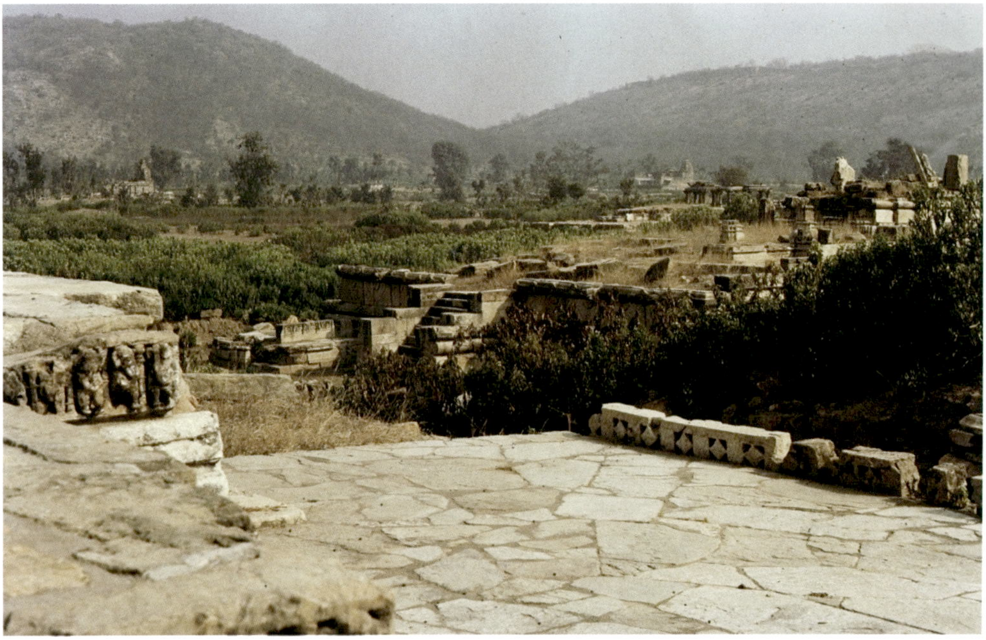

ABOVE: Ruins of temples in Garh-Rajore complex

of the Gujjar community while the other three villages are dominated by those from Meena community, generally farmers. The tobacco of this area is of high quality. Therefore, apart from cattle rearing, tobacco farming is also one of the main sources of livelihood for these villagers. Members of the Meena community are generally meat eaters. Therefore, herbivores and prey species are always under threat in this area. Therefore, if the management of the Reserve is not alert, they would dare to poach even the big cat!

This valley has a special status from the archeological point of view as well.

There are ruins of thousand-year old Shaivite and Jain temples in the archeological Garh-Rajore complex. Barely 9 km from Kankwadi, Neelkanth temple, belonging to the 9-10th centuries, still remains intact. The Jain temple with an 18 ft defaced statue of Lord Mahavira must have been a mute witness to the political turmoil in the past. This complex was probably a deserted township. The complex houses several dilapidated temples within an area of about 1 sq. km. It is believed that the complex used to be a university where students from all over the country studied different subjects, particularly philosophy. These temples doubled up as residential schools for these scholars. Several invaluable statues of Hindu gods and goddesses had been smuggled out of here in the past. Currently Archeological Survey of India (ASI) protects the remaining material, collected from the ruins of these temples. Some *bawadis* (stepped wells) have been revived by ASI.

During one of my rounds, I saw some labourers repairing an old *bawadi* close to the Neelkanth temple. I was initially happy to see restoration work on the well but was aghast to find that old and invaluable statues were being used as stones for the work! I reprimanded the contractor for this irresponsible act. He promised not to use any such statue in future in the work. He was, however, not ready to take out the ones already buried deep in the masonry. I threatened him with stoppage of payment. Only then did I succeed in rescuing these precious statues

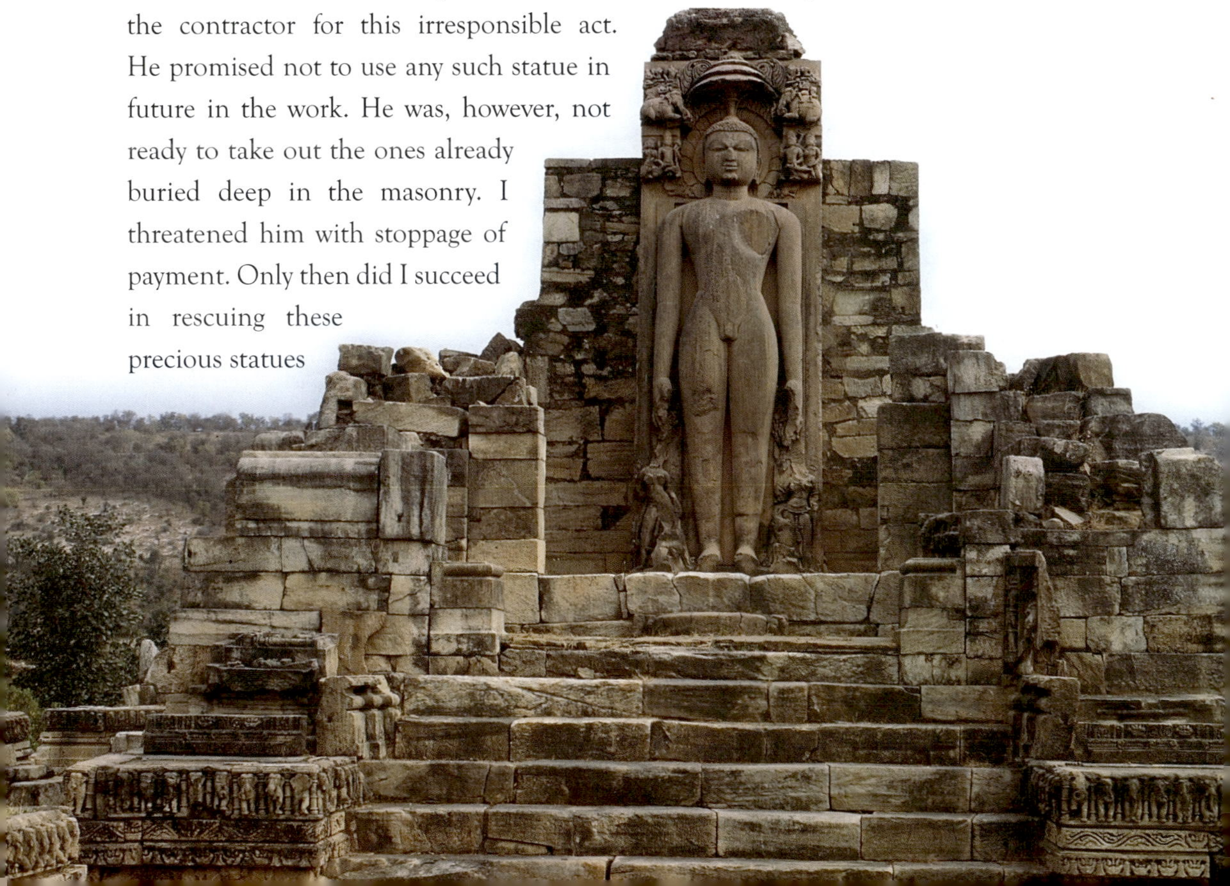

BELOW: Statue of Bhagwan Mahavir in Garh-Rajore complex

This part of the Reserve falls under the administrative control of the Tehla range. Another approach road to Garh-Rajore complex exists through Dabkan. Even today an old fort wall made of red stone and a huge gate stands on this approach road at the entrance to the complex. This area is also called Para Nagar and was under the rule of the mighty Gurjar-Pratihar dynasty. Later, it changed hands to powerful Bad Gujjar kings. During the reign of Mughal emperor Akbar, in AD 17th century it was merged with Jaipur state. Then the entire Garh-Rajore complex was fortified with a massive wall and several small structures for the security personnel at the top of the hill. These structures overlook Dabkan village and Mansarovar lake.

In the latter half of the 18th century the complex finally came under Rao Raja Pratap Singh who founded Alwar state. It seems that during the rule of Alwar, no temple or structure was maintained except for Lord Shiva's temple. That is probably how this rich cultural heritage got ruined.

DABKAN VALLEY AND TEHLA FORT

Dabkan village is populated by Gujjars who generally do not hunt wild animals. Being cattle rearers they had encroached upon most of the grazing lands of Dabkan forest block. They even took their cattle to Richhunda-Bhagani valley seriously threatening herbivores, especially chital, sambar, and blue bull inhabiting the valley. This also increased the chance of cattle lifting by tiger or leopard leading to conflict and consequent threat to the big cats.

The Tehla range headquarters is about 4 km from Dabkan marked by an old red fort standing on a 100 m high hillock surrounded by thick Dhok trees. Presently, this belongs to the forest department. Tehla township is located at the foot of this fort with the beautiful huge Mansarovar lake. Thousands of resident birds feed on the fishes of the lake. During winter, a large number of migratory birds enjoy the submerged and floating vegetation in this lake. Barheaded Geese have a special preference for this lake. With each passing day, the lake water shrinks and new vegetation gets exposed in the process. The geese feed freely on this green vegetation.

The forest surrounding the lake supports a large population of sambar, chital, blue bull, wild boar, and many other wild animals. This lake provides drinking water to the entire wildlife of this region throughout the year.

The road connecting Tehla and Pratap Garh forms the lifeline of the people of this area. On the one hand, the hills here are predominantly decked with dense growth of Dhok, and on the other, they are full of rich dolomite minerals. This has attracted miners, who started mining in revenue areas. Later they managed to obtain mining licenses in the forest areas of this Reserve. This, however, came to an end with the intervention of the Supreme Court.

Parashar ji, named after the ancient saint, is a beautiful perennial spring situated on the way from Tehla to Pratap Garh on the south of

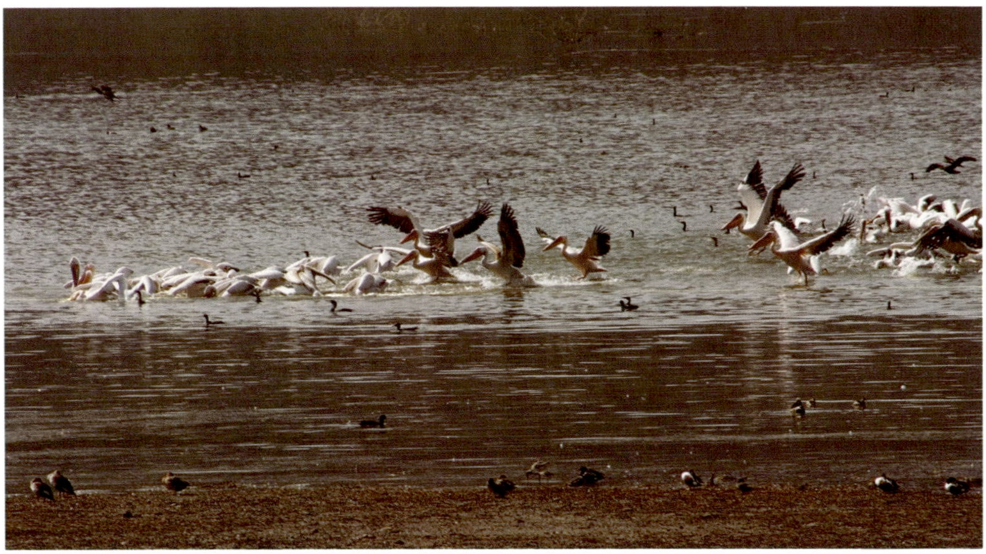

BELOW: Winter visitors to Mangalasar dam of Sariska

Dabkan and Garh-Rajore. Naraini ji temple is situated further south of Parashar ji. Several villages are located along this road with huge human and livestock populations. Pressure on the adjacent forests is, therefore, immense. A forest outpost has been created at Naraini ji to protect the forest but it is not very effective. This part of the forest is very crucial as it acts as a corridor, especially for big cats, and should be zealously guarded.

The area located further south to south-west of Naraini ji, that is between Gola ka Bas and Ajab Garh, is a beautiful and highly fertile valley with perennial water springs flowing from Ajab Garh to Gola ka Bas. The ruins of the old forts here establish the existence of old civilisation. Stories of magic and ghosts abound in this area.

BHAN GARH FORT

The historic fort of Bhan Garh is located in the Reserve at about 8 km to the south-west of Narainiji, 45 km from Sariska, and about 20 km from Dausa town on Jaipur-Agra National Highway. The hills of this fort also mark the boundary

BELOW: Haunted fort of Bhan Garh (partially repaired)

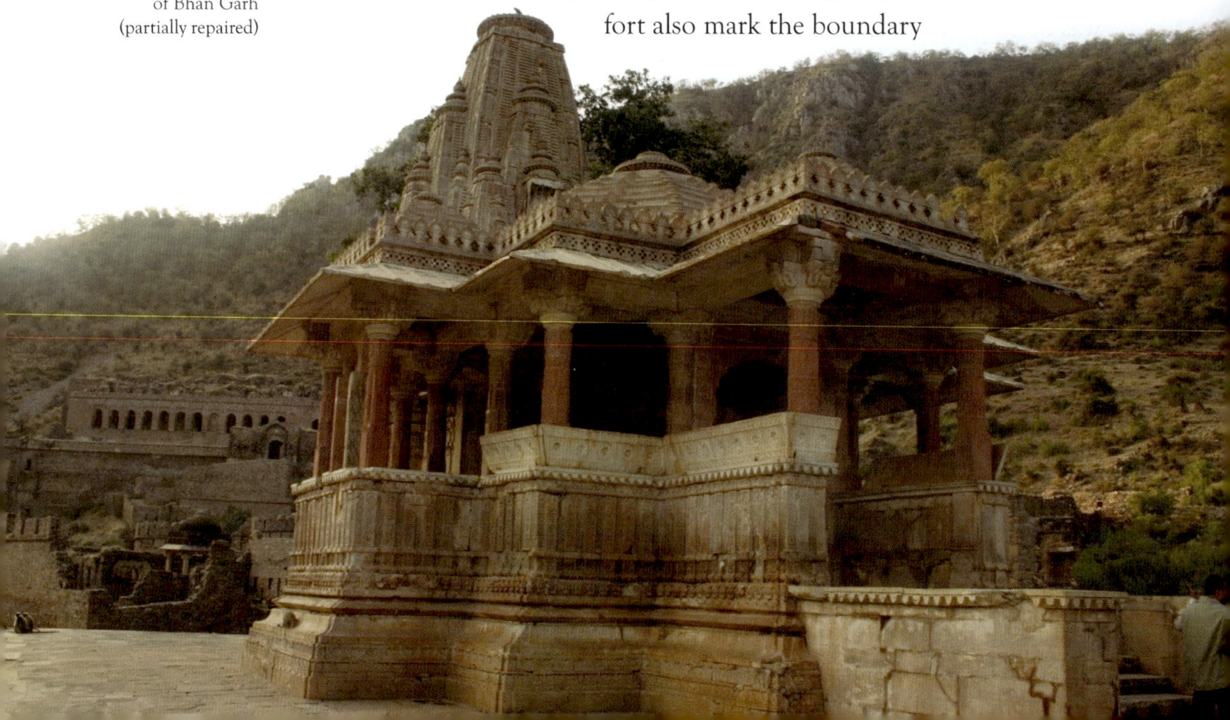

of the Reserve. The south-western slope of the hill falls under Jamwa Ram Garh sanctuary. There is a popular story about the city.

> Long ago queen Bhanumati, known for her magical powers, engaged an eminent magician to further enhance her magical powers. This magician fell in love with her but felt his love would not be accepted because of the difference in status between them. So he played a trick. He charmed the oil brought for the personal use of the queen. The oil would hypnotise the queen and he could then control her. The queen, being a magician herself, realised the trick and became furious. She decided to punish the magician. She showered her magical powers over the oil and poured it on the magician. The magician suddenly turned into a rock. During the process, however, he cursed the queen that the country would soon be destroyed.

This myth has been depicted in the form of a small stone tomb (*chhatari*) outside the fort. Shortly afterwards, Bhan Garh city along with the fort was destroyed due to the curse. From then on, no human being dares to stay overnight inside the ruined city.

Known as the city of ghosts, Bhan Garh is a treasure trove of great archeological value, especially the ruined fort and the market buried under the soil. Old temples situated here are also of great architectural value. ASI has taken up its revival. Some remarkable work has already been done. It has renovated the first storey of the fort. It is now in the process of unearthing the main market. The market had residences on the first floor and shops on the ground floor.

AJAB GARH

Ajab Garh is situated about 15 km from Bhan Garh. It has a beautiful lake and a small fort on a hill. This is also believed to be a ghost town haunted by evil spirits. The Raj Garh–Tehla–Pratap Garh road passes through this township. The shops and houses in the town have either been reduced to ruins or are decaying. Even today, many locks can be seen on dilapidated gates of shops. It looks as if these shops have never been opened. Not surprisingly, no human being lives in this old township.

> A popular story is that long ago this township was inhabited by members of the Meena community who had magical powers. Once they had a conflict with a powerful magician of another community. As a result, Meenas killed the magician, who cursed them as death descended on him. The Meenas got scared of the curse and they immediately vacated this beautiful township and settled at Sattais ka Bas (settlements of twenty seven), not very far from Ajab Garh. These have now been developed into major settlements.

BELOW: Residential colony of Ajab Garh deserted by natives

Ajab Garh valley supports a dense growth of Dhak trees. Unfortunately, it has been encroached upon by local people. Most of this valley used to be part of Bandipul–Dulaba forest (under Narainiji reserve

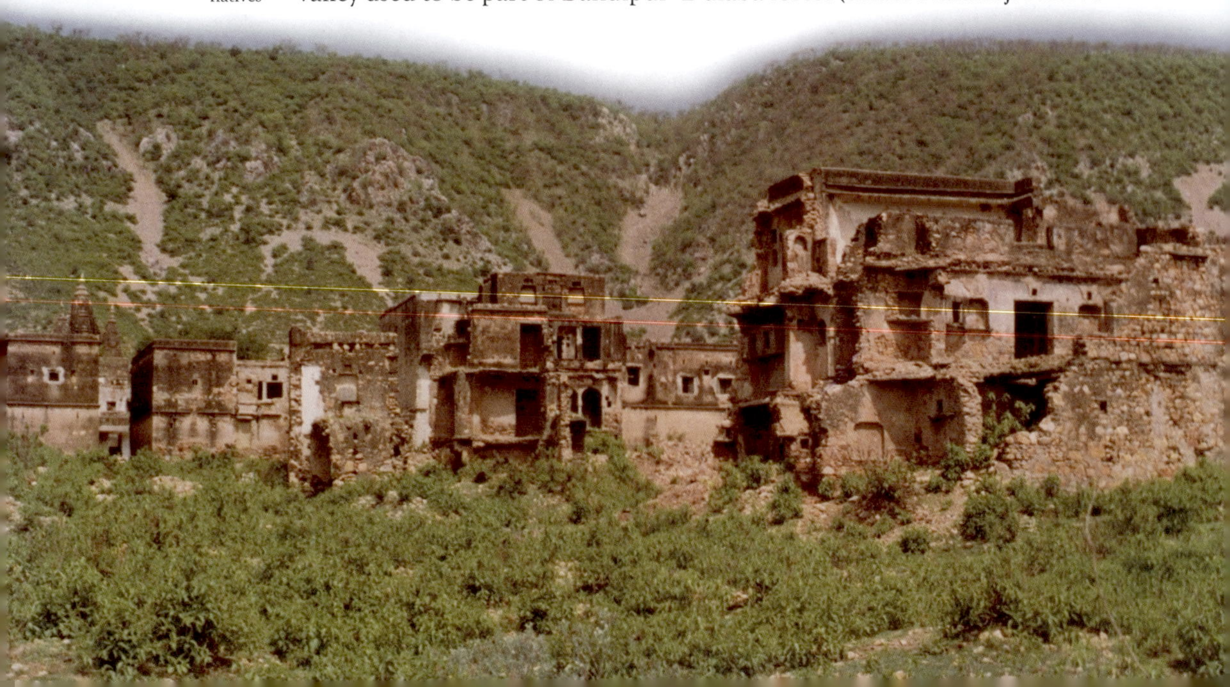

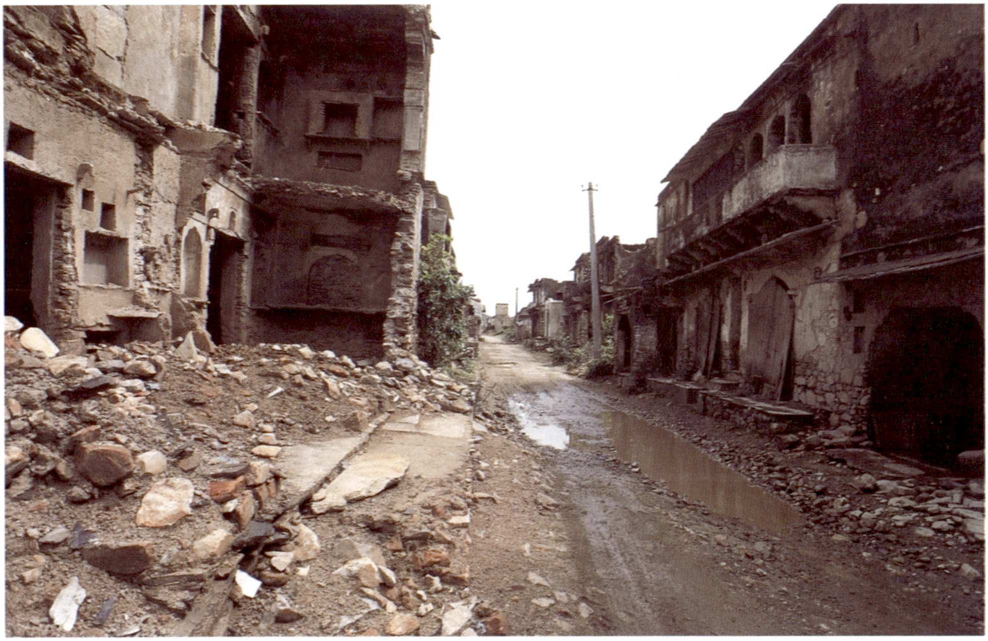

ABOVE: Residential colony of Ajab Garh deserted by natives

forest). In order to rehabilitate people of Kraska and Kundalka villages located in the core area of Sariska, about 472 bigha (120 ha) of land from this block was transferred to revenue department in 1975. The shifting was, however, abandoned due to political pressure. Subsequently, even those who had shifted returned. Many of them sold the land received as compensation at Bandipul–Dulaba to non-beneficiaries. Thus, this crucial portion of the reserve forest, which used to support a number of tigers before de-reservation, was allowed to be encroached upon. Several of them have got huge chunks of land allotted in their names from the revenue department.

Rich in water and vegetation, this valley used to serve as an excellent corridor for tigers between Sariska and Jamwa Ram Garh sanctuaries. Before Independence, this area used to be popular for tigers. A number of tiger hunting expeditions were organised here for the royal families. Serious effort by the government is needed to bring back its past glory.

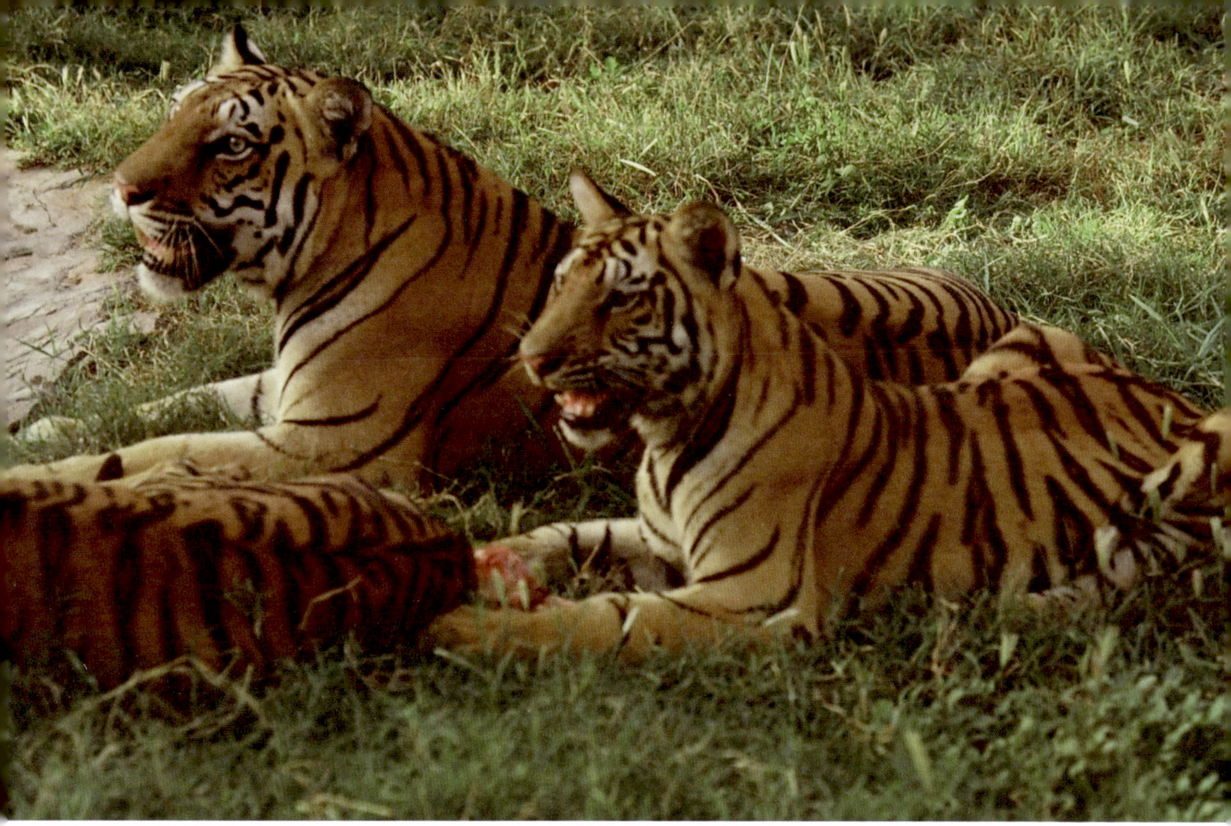

TIGER HUNTING - A ROYAL PASSION

In India, tiger hunting was regarded as a great sport by kings in the olden times. Earlier bow and arrows and spears were used in this sport. The *shikaris* (hunters) used horses, chariots, or elephants to chase the *shikar* (hunted).

Shikar was definitely a sport which needed not only immense power and courage, but also proper skills and intelligence. In the absence of these the hunter could become the hunted. This adventure sport continued till shooting guns were available. The British resorted to hunting by guns for security. The sport loving hunters continued to use horses while kings used elephants.

As the British rule in India gathered strength, many Indian kings used all kinds of tricks to appease the British officers to gain favours from them. An invitation to a *shikar* camp was always tempting to senior British officers and seldom got turned down. Thus, by the turn of the 20th century, the adventurous and thrilling sport of *shikar* became a political game.

Fixed shooting boxes (*haudis*) were set up to facilitate shooting in comfort under secure conditions. For fast hunting, goats and buffalo claves were used as baits. Baits were tied on a platform close to the shooting box. This arrangement not only quickened the process but also economised it substantially. This resulted in indiscriminate killing of tigers and leopards.

SHIKAR IN SARISKA IN EARLIER DAYS

Sariska was an excellent hunting location in the princely state of Alwar. In order to appease the British, the then ruler of Alwar built a beautiful palace at Sariska.

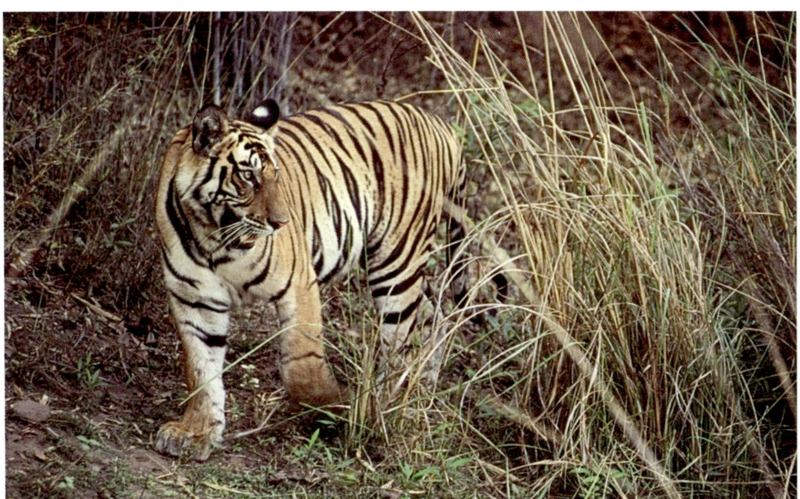

FACING PAGE:
The original royal tigers of Sariska

LEFT:
Searching for food? A view from Sariska *(Photo by Dinesh Durrani)*

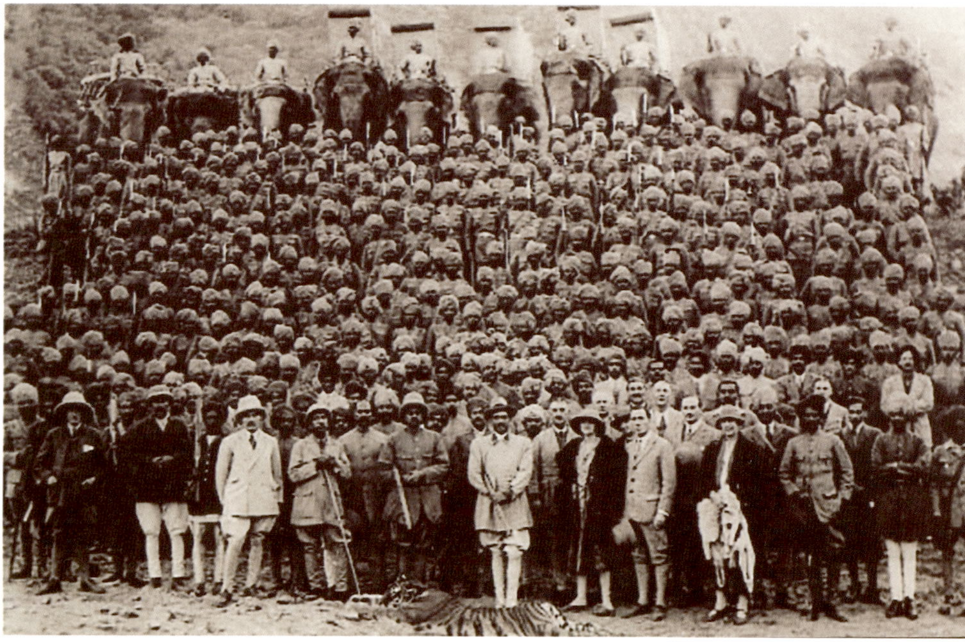

Above: H.H. Jai Singh, Maharaja of Alwar (in centre) with British overlords

Maharaja Jai Singh, who ruled over Alwar from 1892 to 1937, was a sportsman in the true spirit. He was a sharp shooter and a great horseman. He won several polo competitions in India and England. He framed several stringent rules for *shikar*. No one, including members of the royal family, was allowed to violate them. The Maharaja himself observed these rules very religiously. He set a target of not killing more than eight tigers a year. Nobody was allowed to kill a female of any species in order to ensure regular replenishment of the population.

The pressure to please the British was so immense that several shooting boxes were constructed in Sariska, such as in Bandipul, Tarunda, Kalighati, Ghamodi, Silibery, Tuda, and so on. At Tarunda one massive wall was also constructed for *shikar*. This was called *hathi* (elephant) wall. Hidden behind the wall, *shikaris* mounted on elephants used to shoot the tiger or leopard approaching the bait tied close to the wall or at the nearby water hole.

On a sunny winter day in 1921, a *shikar* was organised by Maharaja Jai Singh for his British guests. The Maharaja and his guests were on elephants hidden behind the *hathi* wall. A team of drummers led the tiger towards the Maharaja and his guests waiting at Tarunda. The drummers were cautiously chasing a tiger from Kala Kua area. It is believed that Kala Kua tigers were more aggressive and ferocious compared to others. By the time the tiger reached Tarunda, it became very furious and violent due to the torturous and continuous drum beat and the chase by a battery of people. It suddenly turned back and attacked one of the drummers. The Maharaja shot the animal using his gun. The tiger was wounded and gave up the poor drummer. It, however, jumped at the Maharaja furiously. Everyone got scared at this sudden turn of events. The Maharaja, however, taking advantage of the *hathi* wall, shot the animal straight on its head. This shot proved fatal to the daring tiger. The 11-feet long tiger's trophy is still preserved in the Sariska Palace Hotel.

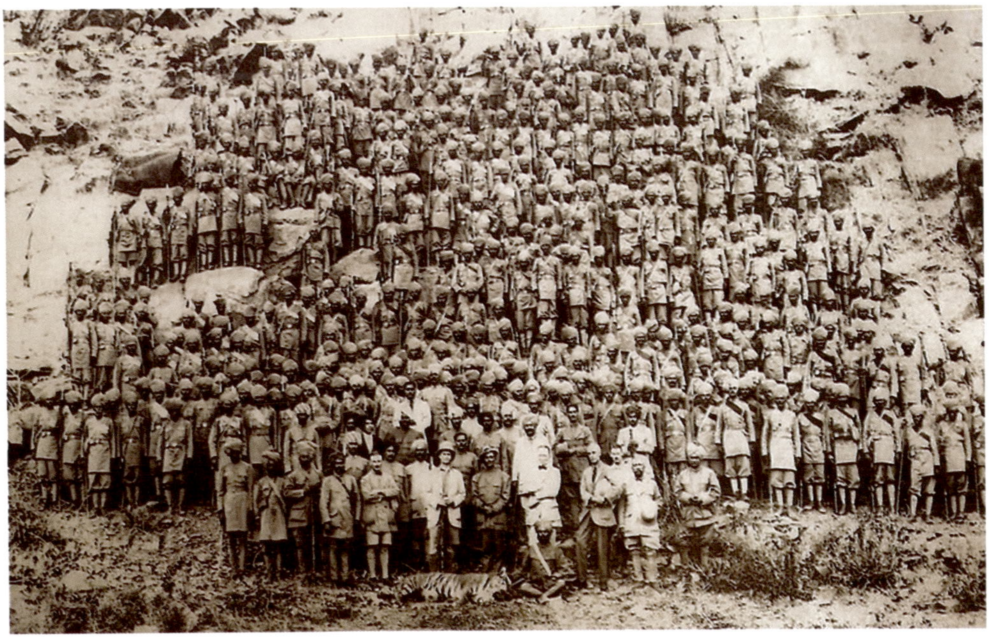

BELOW: Tiger hunt organised by the Maharaja of Alwar in 1926 for his British guests in which a dozen elephants and about 300 people were involved

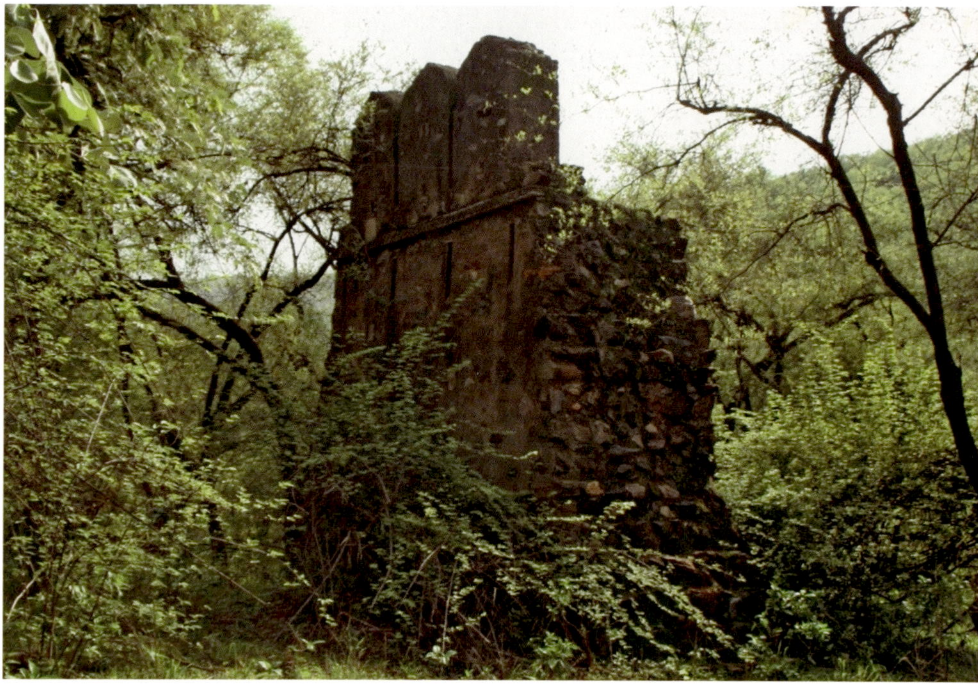

ABOVE: Hathi wall at Tarunda

After Maharaja Jai Singh passed away, officials started flouting the *shikar* rules. Shockingly, around this time some people mixed opium in water at certain points like Tarunda, Sarunda, Kundli, and so on. The big cats became intoxicated upon drinking the water and could not escape the greedy hunters who killed them for the skin or a head trophy.

Even after Independence, a lot of *shikar* outings used to be conducted at the Reserve. By 1970 hunting of tigers was banned. In 1972, hunting of any animal in Sariska was completely prohibited. Several legal and administrative rules were enacted to ensure protection of wildlife. However, poaching could be checked only partially because of several factors such as increase in human and livestock population and shortage of efficient and dedicated staff. The total wiping out of the tiger population in Sariska in 2004 had resulted from this situation.

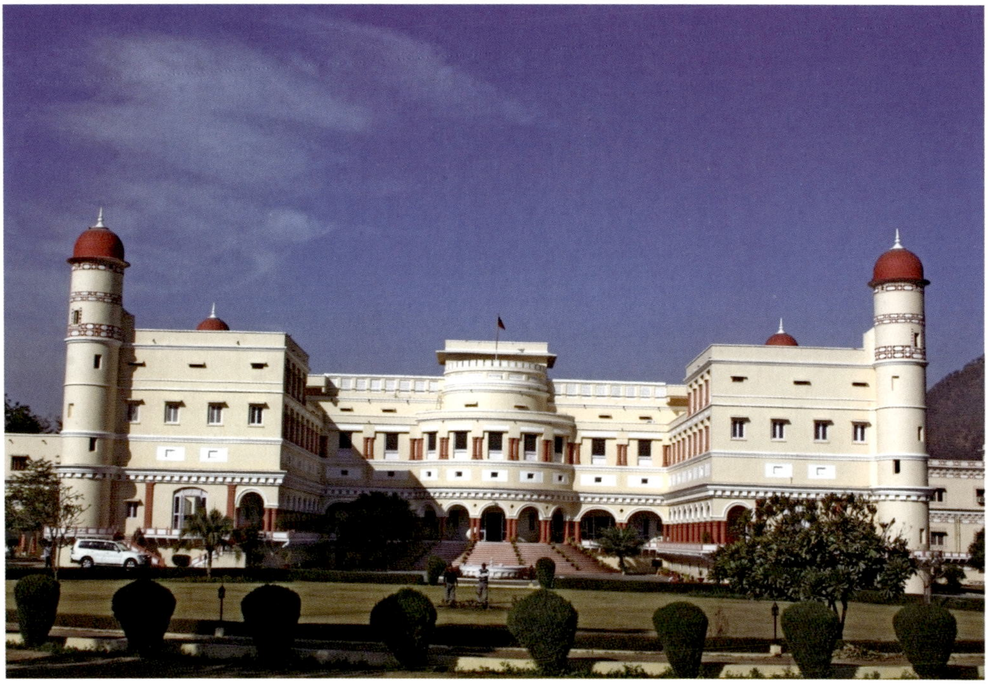

SARISKA PALACE

ABOVE:
Sariska Palace

The century-old Sariska Palace breaks the monotony of the forest that surrounds it. Situated on the Delhi–Alwar–Jaipur highway, near the gate of the Tiger Reserve, the foundation of the palace was laid in 1890 by the visiting son of Queen Victoria, the Duke of Connaught. This majestic palace stands on the bank of Rupareil, the only river flowing from the west to the east of this Reserve.Currently it belongs to Ranjeet Singh of Bikaner who has converted it into a heritage resort.

TIGER, THE BIG BROTHER

Several species of carnivores have enriched the wildlife of Sariska. However, the tiger has been unanimously accepted as the big brother.

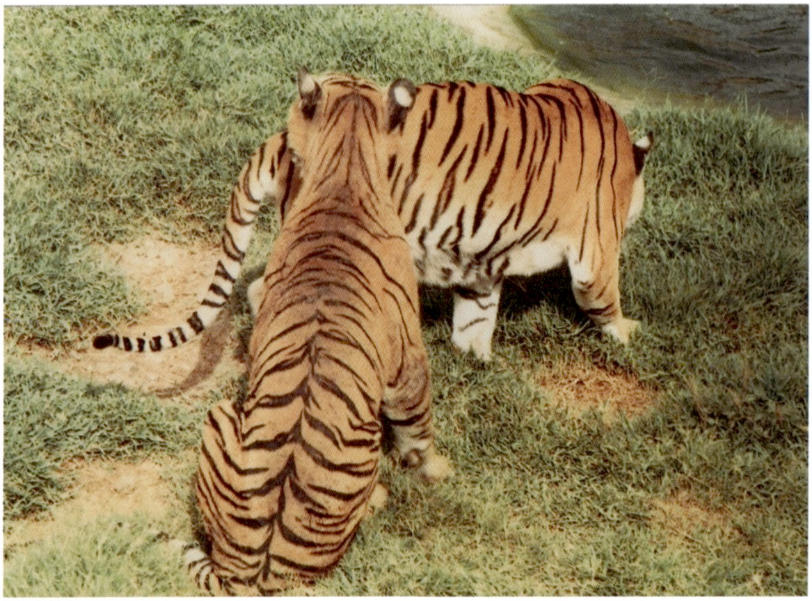

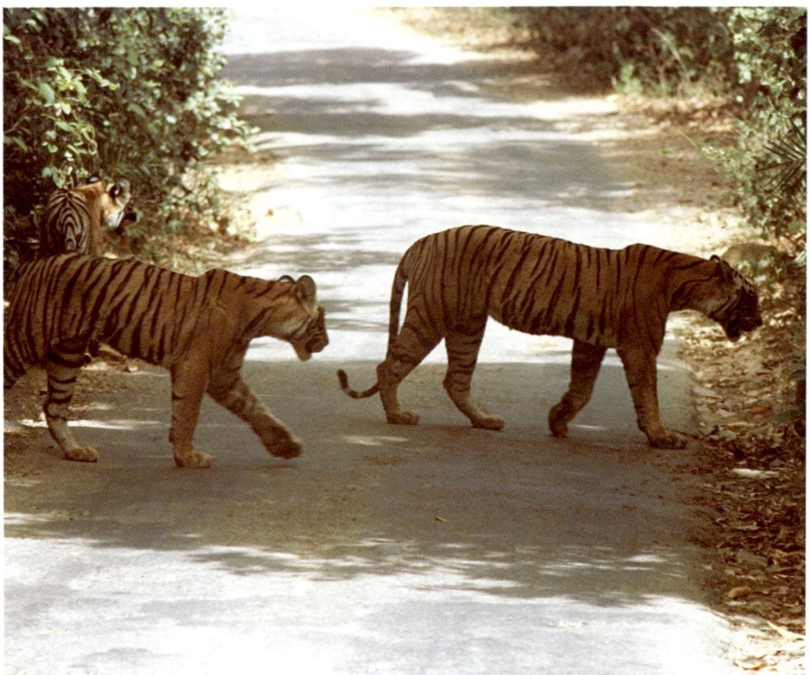

ABOVE: Tigers originally belonging to Sariska *(Photo by K.L. Saini)*

RIGHT: Tigress and cubs close to Karna ka Bas (1994)

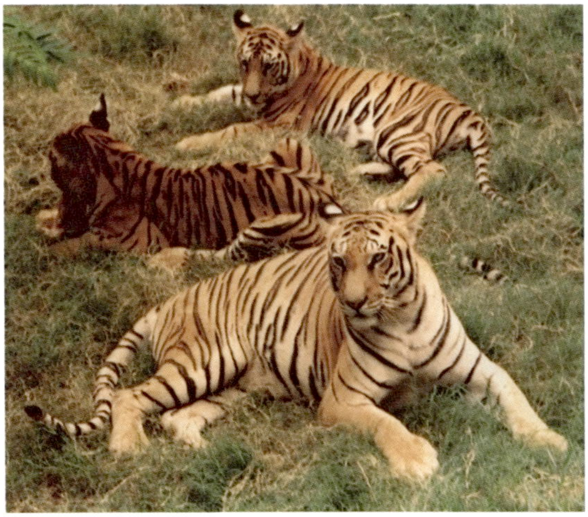

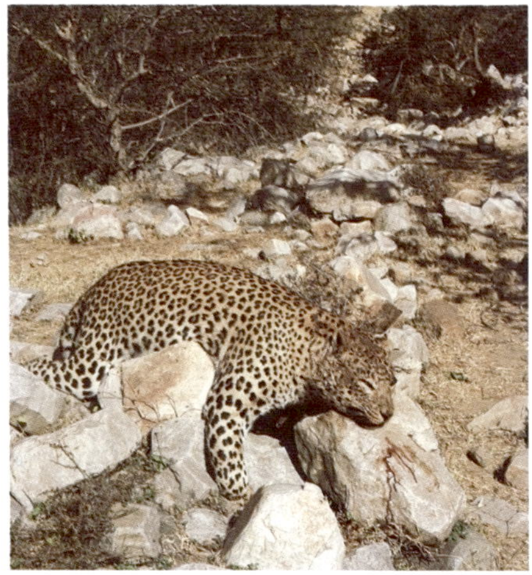

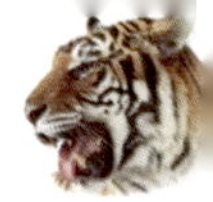

ABOVE LEFT: Tiger cubs originally belonging to Sariska *(Photo by K.L. Saini)*

ABOVE: A leopard killed by a tigress in Siliberi (1993)

No animal, young or old, ever comes in conflict with the tiger. This is the unwritten law of the jungle respected by every animal inhabiting the Reserve. There have been, however, rare occasions when two or more wild boars (tuskers) may be seen driving away a tiger.

Once during the monsoons a fully grown young tiger was caught by a python. Though the tiger ultimately succeeded in rescuing itself from the deadly grip of the python, the duel was breathtaking. In this area tigers need to be on the alert especially while passing through the open grass lands during monsoon.

Packs of wild dogs are known to hunt tiger. Sariska did not have any wild dogs. But in early 1986 a pack of three dogs was spotted. From then on its sighting became fairly regular. The park authorities were worried that they might start threatening the tiger population. Tigers, however, did not seem to have suffered at all. The wild dogs disappeared one by one within a span of a few years. I had seen only one lonely dog wandering in important tiger areas such as Umri, Slopka, Kalighati, Brahmnath, and Tarunda during 1991–93. The last sighting was in 1993. Surprisingly, a pair reappeared in 1999 and roamed freely in Sariska–Kalighati valley.

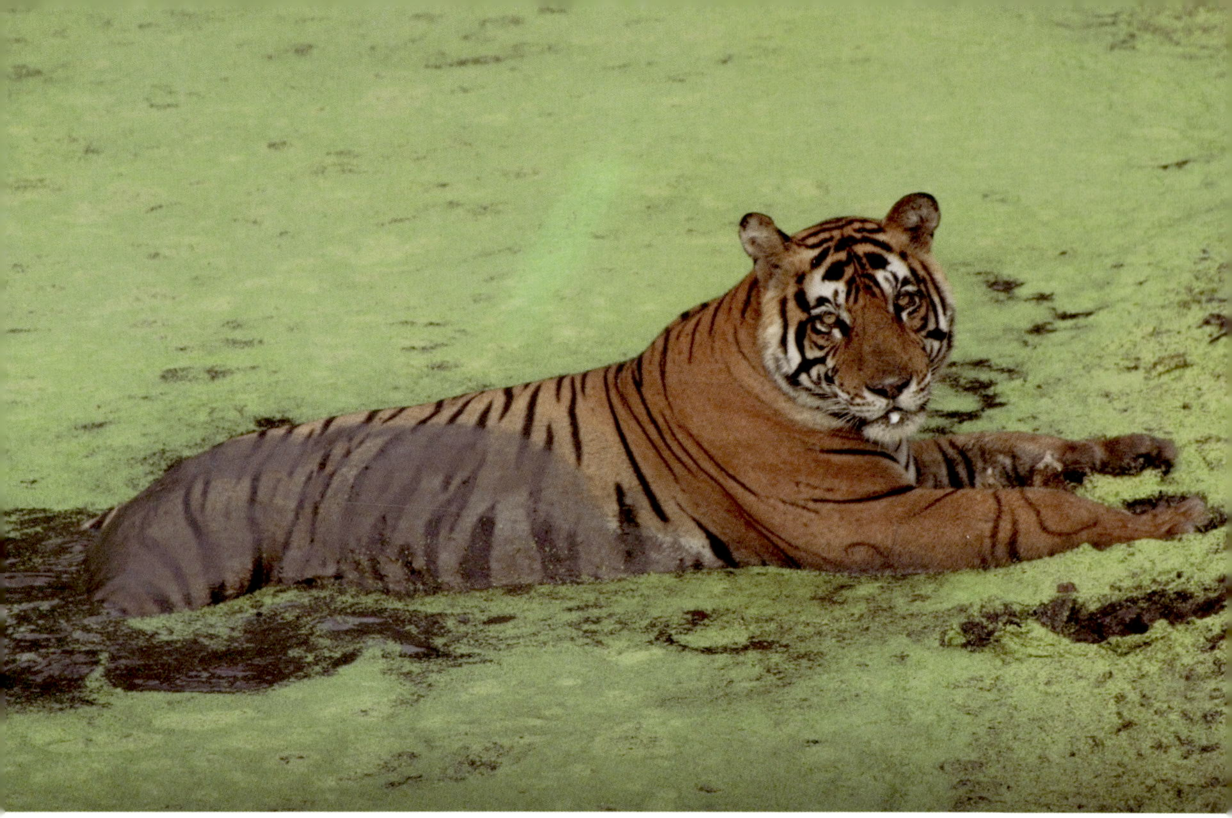

WATER MANAGEMENT IN SARISKA

Wildlife depends, to a large extent, on the natural sources of surface water. It is no different in Sariska. The diversity of wildlife species and their numbers in an area is determined chiefly by the availability of surface water round the year. In wildlife terminology it is called carrying capacity of a particular area.

Herbivorous animals of Sariska also migrate to adjacent areas in search of food and water when these dry up in the Reserve. Over a period of time, the human greed for land has resulted in the encroachment of fallow and pasture lands surrounding reserves. Several townships have also come up around them. The southern boundary of Sariska has been packed with dolomite (marble) mining.

The devout farmers of yore have given way to materialistic young men intolerant towards wild animals that venture into their fields to quench their thirst. They either drive these animals away or even kill them. This has resulted in growing conflicts between the local farmers and the Reserve management. The frequent failure of monsoon creates water scarcity in the Reserve that has added to the woes of the management.

Sariska is a dry deciduous forest with typical Aravali Hill formation. These hills are generally very steep. As a result, rain water rushes down the hills to the valleys as seasonal streams and flows out of the Reserve. This typical phenomenon is responsible for dry conditions in the Reserve. A few dams were constructed by erstwhile rulers on the periphery of the Reserve, namely Manglasar, Somasagar, Silised, and one inside the core area, Kankwadi, which support the wildlife inhabiting the surrounding forests. But again water from these dams (except Kankwadi) was largely used for irrigation. Apart from these there is the seasonal river Rupareil passing through the Reserve from

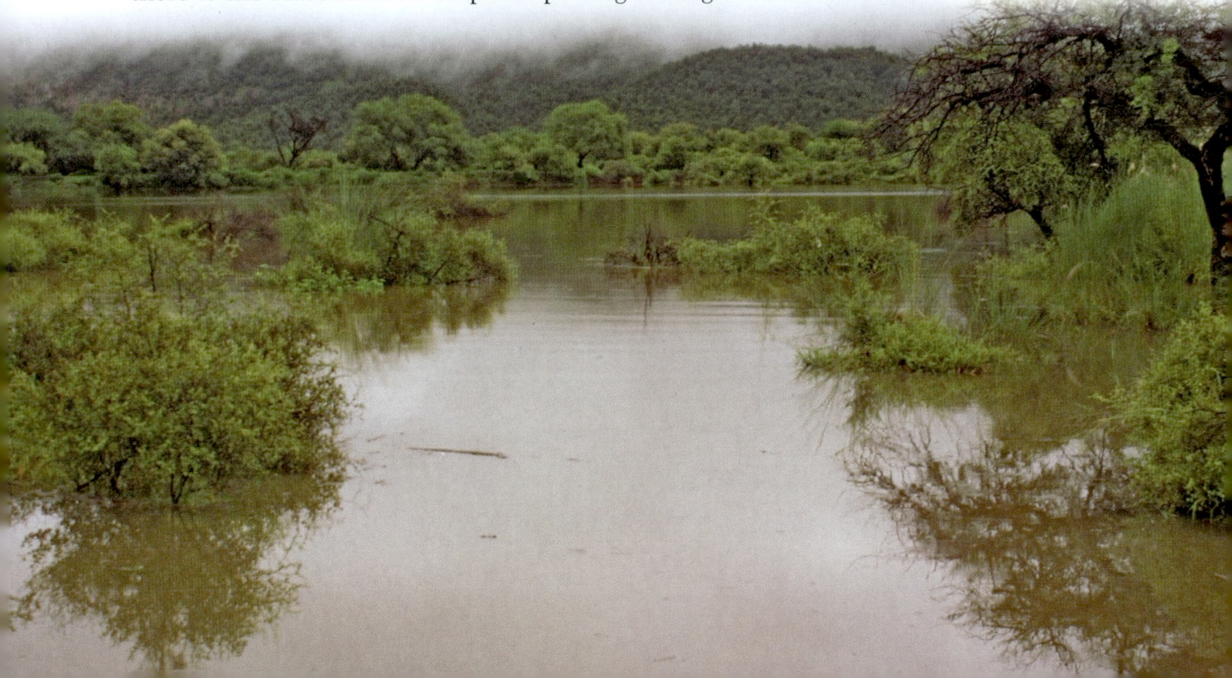

FACING PAGE: Tiger cooling off in Brahmnath anicut

BELOW: Karna ka Bas lake in monsoon

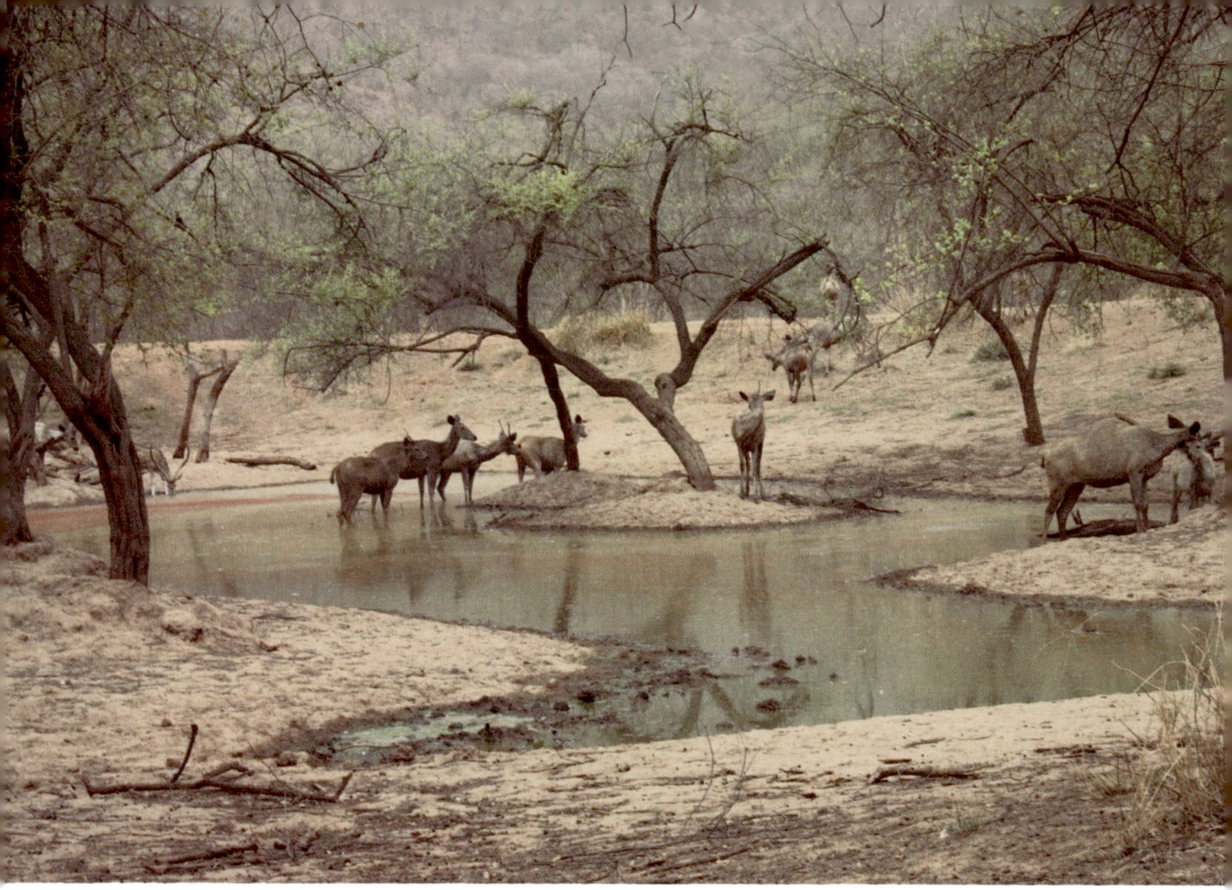

ABOVE: Earthen water hole (Baheda Johadi)

Thanagazi side to Alwar city, that is, from west to east. This river traverses through the Reserve for about 20 km.

Till the 1990s, the Pandupole *nallah* used to hold water for about 2 km for most part of the year. Due to decrease in rainfall, the periodicity of its flow has shrunk to four to five months. Water, however, remains in a few pools throughout the year. The Maujnath spring is perennial but in summer it shrinks considerably. The Udainath spring is also perennial but is largely used by domestic animals from the neighbouring Gujjar dominated villages.

The pool of water at Bandipul, just behind the Sariska Palace, used to support a large number of animals till recently. After construction of dams upstream of Rupareil, it has considerably dried up. Also, constant disturbance from traffic on the highway prevents wild animals from using this waterhole.

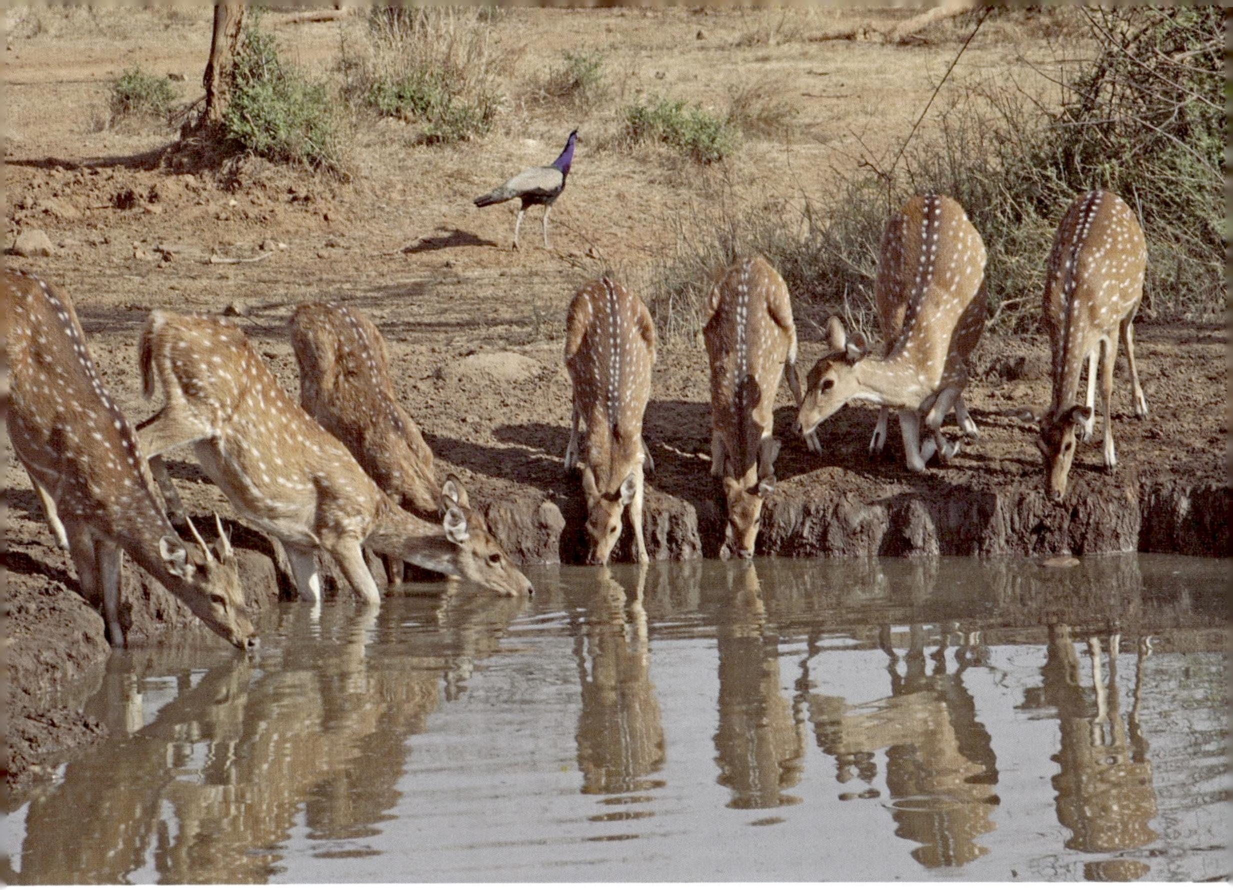

ABOVE:
An earthen water hole at Brahmnath

There are some perennial springs like Paras Nath (Tehla range), Talvriksh, Chotta Bhrartrahari (Talvriksh range), Bhrartrahari (Sariska range) and Naladeshwar, located in the periphery of the Reserve. The wildlife has to share them with a large domestic population from neighbouring areas. During summer, especially in May–June, drinking water becomes scarce. In fact, water emerges as a critical limiting factor for the wild population of herbivores and omnivores of the Reserve.

Before Independence, the *shikar* department of the princely state of Alwar created several water tanks, mostly in the Sariska valley. These used to be filled with drinking water transported from outside on bullock carts.

After Independence too, barring the initial years, this practice continued. During 1980–87 many more cemented waterholes were constructed at Naya Pani, Kund, Kundali Road, Brahmnath, Kalighati (near watch tower), Slopka, Siliberi, Raika, Pani Dhal, and so on.

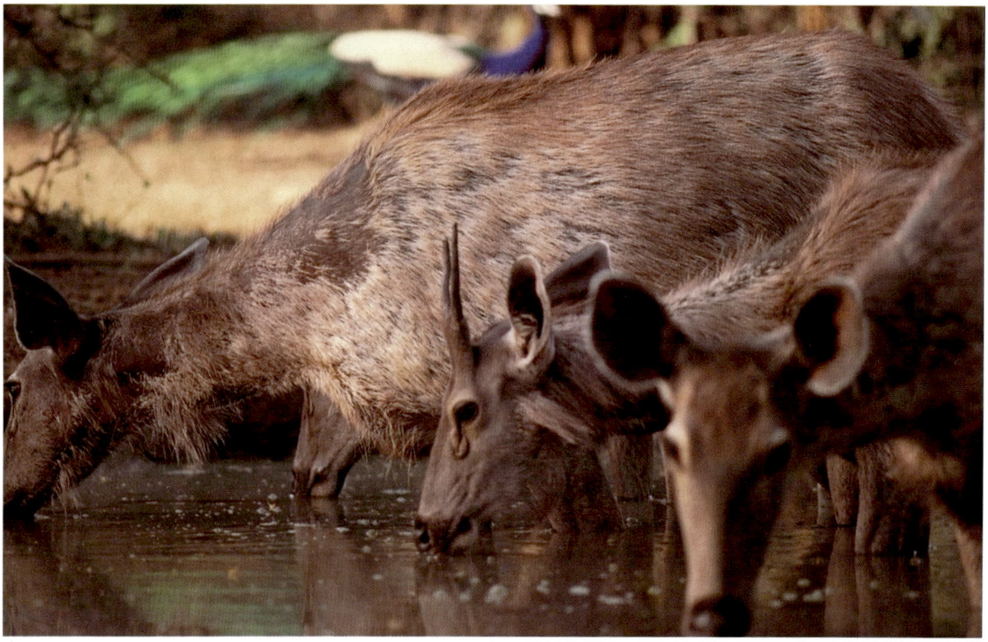

ABOVE: An earthen water hole at Naya Pani

Cemented waterholes are not animal friendly. Sambar has the habit of entering into the water. Cemented tanks are slippery and thus hamper this natural activity. They often urinate in the water. The pollutants so emitted will be absorbed by soil but not by cemented surface. The water, thus, gets polluted. Besides, the water level goes down in a few days of consumption by animals. It then becomes inaccessible to most animals even in crouching posture due to the slippery, slanting surface of the tanks. The animals do not enter such waterholes lest they slip. Thus, precious water brought from outside cannot be properly used to quench the thirst of the animals.

The cemented water holes, except at Tarunda, were replaced by large earthen waterholes in 1988. A realistic shape was given to these waterholes so that they merged naturally with the surrounding area. Transportation of water from far was also abandoned. These earthen water tanks were connected to wells with the help of underground pipelines. Diesel engines were fitted to these wells to lift water. This improved system proved to be excellent. The basic need, however, was to store as much rain water as possible in order to reduce dependence on artificial water supply. To address this problem, the first anicut was built at Karna ka Bas in 1985–86 which was extended and improved during 1989–91. At present, it is the most important water body of the Reserve, hardly 3 km from Sariska headquarters.

In 1985–86, another anicut was constructed at Phenta ki Pal. Looking at the huge quantum of water collected in this *nallah*, the anicut's design was inadequate. The anicut could not stand the pressure and gave way to water through its main structure. Located on the main Kalighati–Slopka road, it stuck out as an eyesore. Nothing could be done about it as it was beyond repair.

Several districts of Rajasthan, including Alwar, came under the grip of a famine in 1986–87. One anicut, named Bhrartrahari Sagar, was constructed near Kundalka. The famine continued in the following

Below: Maujnath Anicut overflowing in Monsoon

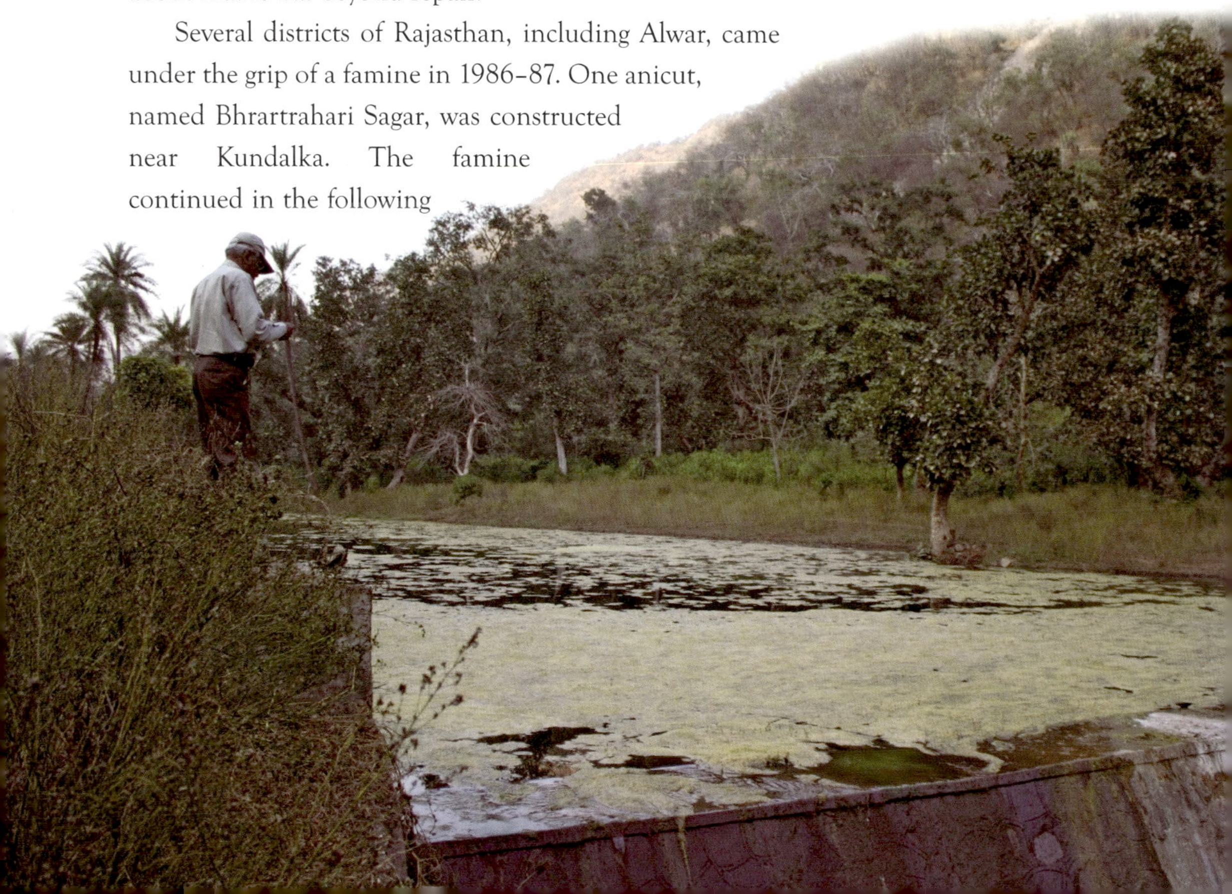

year. As part of relief work, another anicut, named Gopi Chand Sagar, was constructed close to Kundalka, adjoining Bhrartrahari Sagar.

Yet another anicut, Hira Man Sagar, was constructed on Haripura *nallah*. Bhrartrahari Sagar and Gopi Chand Sagar also helped in controlling the entry of cattle inside the core area from Kundalka village. In the same year, one anicut was constructed at Tarunda and another at Kankwadi. The Tarunda anicut, connected to a beautiful masonry waterhole, however, could not hold water and failed. In fact, most of the *nallahs* in Sariska are full of boulders and sand. This helps water to drain bypassing the foundation. Though such anicuts fail to work as waterholes for wildlife, they improve the moisture level downstream. The improved moisture level supports the vegetation during summer and drought years.

In 1989–90, one huge anicut was built in Umri valley. This, too, suffered the same fate as that of Tarunda. A team of senior engineers from Rajasthan irrigation department visited Sariska in 1991. They inspected the anicut site. They observed that it failed because of the

BELOW: A cemented water hole

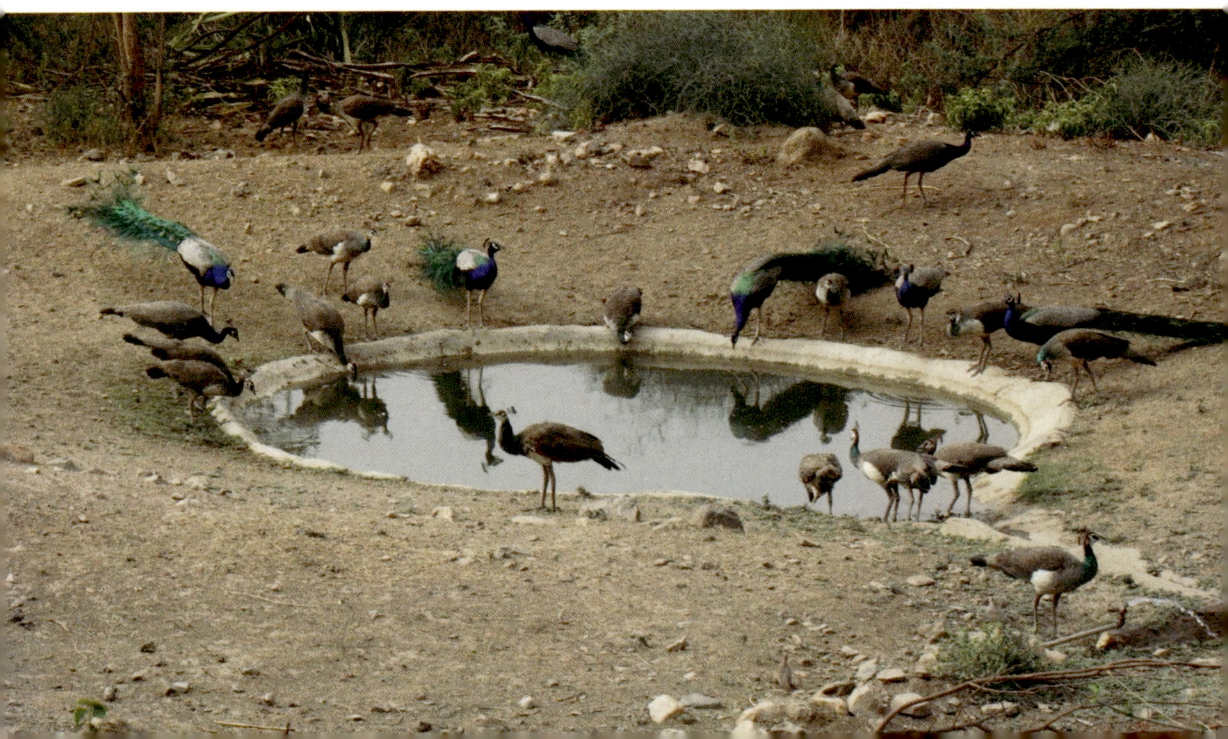

boulders and sand on the *nallah* bed. Removal of earth from upstream to increase the water holding capacity of the anicut also contributed to the water percolation. I, therefore, cautioned my staff not to disturb the upstream soil while constructing any anicut or earthen pond.

I came to know that a boy feeding cows had been attacked by a tiger close to Madho Garh some time ago during summer. Earlier a holy man passing through the Alwar–Sariska highway had been attacked and killed by a tiger under a culvert close to Madho Garh. Shortage of drinking water had compelled the tigers to enter human settlements in Madho Garh. Such incidents sometimes generate conflicts between villagers and the Reserve management leading to damage of forest and wildlife.

I then decided to construct an anicut near Madho Garh. However, to ensure safety of wild animals against poachers, the waterbody needs to be away from human settlements. Considering all aspects and after discussing with field staff, I selected a site in Ghamodi *nallah*. The first rains filled this anicut and no water percolation occurred. Being close

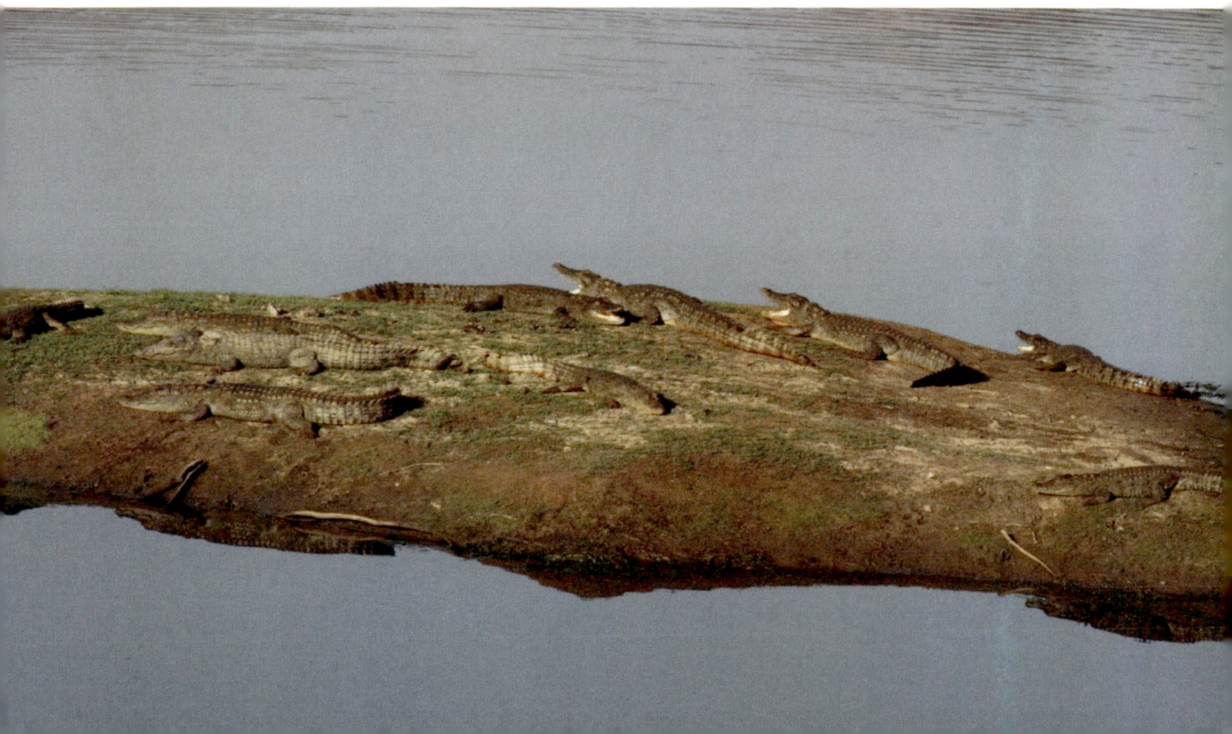

BELOW: Crocodiles basking in Karna ka Bas lake

RIGHT: Pandupole nallah, the lifeline of Sariska

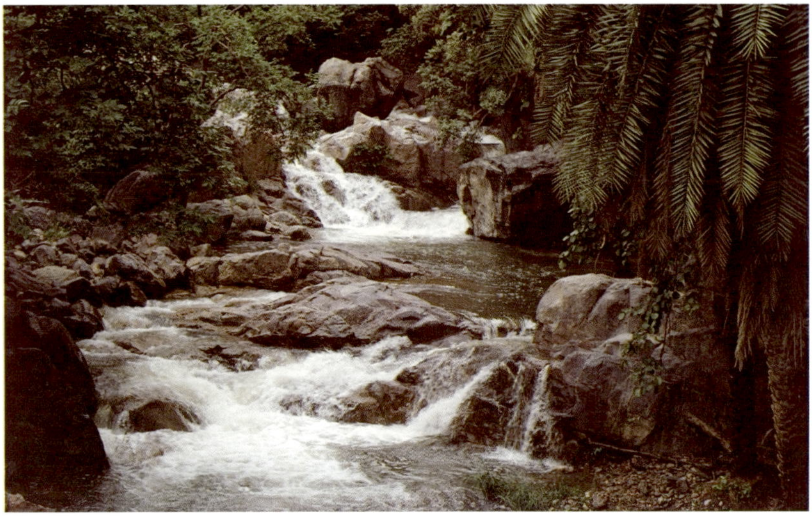

to Bhrartrahari and Kushal Garh chowkies, safety of wild animals could also be ensured by regular patrolling. After this no man-animal conflict took place in Madho Garh.

Thirsty animals, both wild and domestic, shared waterholes at Haripura village. This was not a good idea. Chances of cattle lifting might increase in such circumstances. This could also lead to conflicts between villagers and the Reserve. Construction of an anicut was the solution. Therefore, I selected a site close to the forest guard chowki at Ghanka. The anicut could store water up to its full capacity and no percolation was noticed. This waterhole proved to be a boon for wildlife inhabiting this part of the Reserve. Wild animals, especially tigers, which earlier crossed the busy Alwar-Jaipur highway in search of water at Bandipul, were now happily fulfilling their requirements here. It also helped reducing accidents on the highway.

Encouraged by these successes, I got five more anicuts built at Algual, Bandipul, and Kankwadi (all in Sariska range), Narandi (in Akbarpur range), and Pani Dhal (in Talvriksh range) the following year. All of them proved successful.

Algual is a perennial spring located in the foot hill of Kraska plateau in the centre of the core area, hardly 4 km from Sariska headquarters as the crow flies. Using this water source, my predecessor Fateh Singh had built an earthen waterhole at Naya Pani. He laid a 3-km-long underground pipeline connecting this spring to the Naya Pani waterhole and placed a diesel water pump at Algual. Water was transported through pipeline to Naya Pani water hole. Naya Pani water hole started attracting a large number of herbivores and carnivores round the year except during monsoon when water is available in puddles throughout the Reserve.

This method of water transportation was quite effective. But the diesel engine created a lot of noise. Also, it was very expensive considering the costs of pump maintenance, diesel, and salary of the pump operator.

One day, while on an inspection of Algual area, suddenly it occurred to me that if a larger and deeper pool of water could be created there, the pressure of the water itself may push it up to Naya Pani through the pipeline without having to use a diesel pump. Though its viability was not guaranteed, I wanted to give the idea a try. In order to create

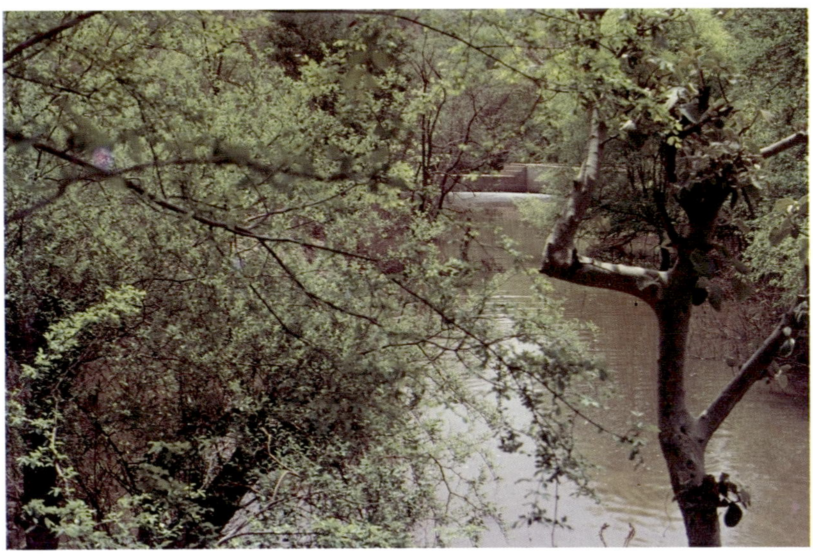

LEFT:
Bandipul Anicut

a deeper water pool, an anicut was constructed at Algual about 100 m upstream of the existing water point. Fortunately, impervious rocks were found which did not allow water percolation. A lot of water was collected here in the beginning of the monsoon. By October, Naya Pani water hole had dried up and the overflow from the new anicut began to fill it up. The pump was disconnected. We were elated to find that the water flow continued unabated without using the pump! It was a moment of great joy for us. This system works very efficiently even now.

Narandi anicut was named after the 8-km-long Narandi valley, stretching between Nahar Sati and Rotkyala. Grass cover was sparse; the area was full of Dhak and Semal (*Bombaxciba*) trees. During summer these trees bloom with their gregarious red inflorescence to make it extremely attractive.

Dearth of grazing ground brought down the number of grazing animals like nilgai and spotted deer. The hills decked with Dhok on either side of the valley, however, supported a large sambar population. Several other species of herbivores and carnivores also inhabit this area. In this valley, after Nahar Sati or Siliberi, the closest water point was at Aman, about 7 km away. During summer when the temperature rises to 45 °C finding drinking water is tough and proves fatal at times for wild animals, especially sambar. The worst situation could be during drought when Aman gets dried or shrunk and sambar has to compete with domestic animals of Gujjars of Rotkyala village. Construction of an anicut was the only solution to this problem.

Site selection for the anicut was difficult because the embankments did not give us any idea about the property of the rocks. We depended on the knowledge and experience of neighbouring villagers. The work of the anicut was completed in March. To our surprise, water started collecting immediately. Even during peak summer, the anicut had enough water to quench the thirst of every animal that visited this spot. Nothing can be more satisfying than seeing the fruits of one's work. In 2009 the height of this anicut was increased to enhance its water-holding capacity.

In 1993-94, four more anicuts were constructed at Harsawal in Akbarpur range, Talvriksh in Talvriksh range, Kala Kua in Sariska range, and Bhagani in Tehla range. These anicuts were also successful, except Harsawal, where, in spite of our best efforts, water somehow found a way out through the earthen embankments. Here an underground pipeline was also laid to carry water up to Umri outpost to fill an earthen saucer for wild animals and birds as well as to help the staff manning this outpost.

There is an interesting incident behind the construction of the anicut at Harsawal. One day in July 1992, I was studying tracking reports of tiger or leopard movements pouring in from various beats. Intercepting these reports, a message was received that some poachers were sitting close to a waterhole at Harsawal. There was only one forest guard at Umri who had gone to Siliberi to seek assistance. Siliberi, equipped with a wireless set, was about 3 km from Umri.

BELOW: An earthen water hole *(Photo by Daulat Singh)*

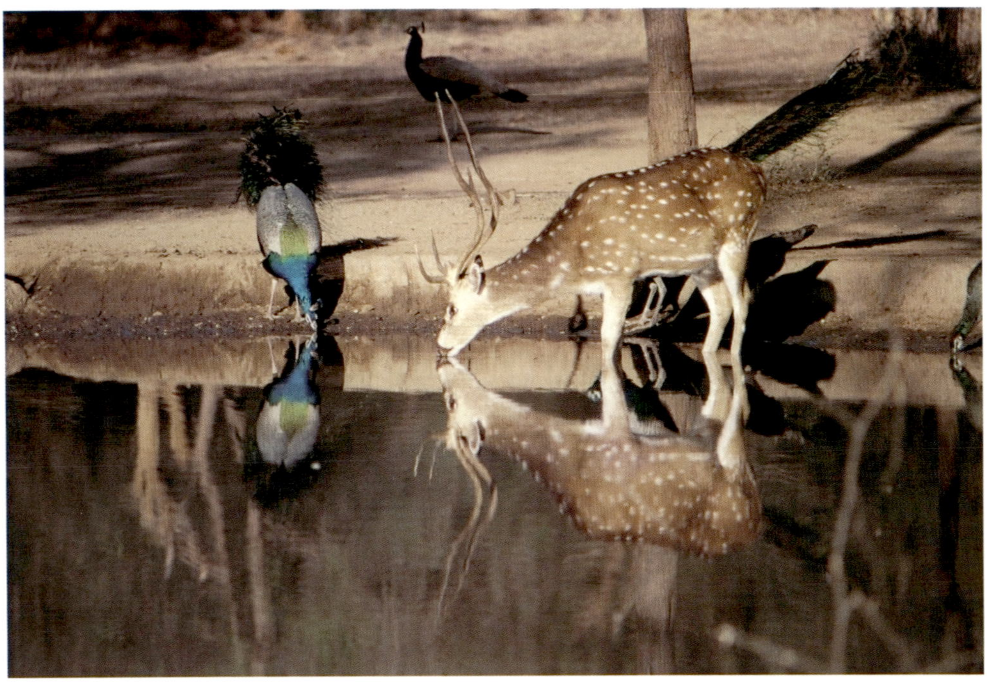

It was dinner time for the staff. However, this was not an occasion for a leisurely dinner. I instructed the Assistant Field Director and the Range Officer of Sariska to move to the site with staff immediately as it was an emergency. It took them sometime to reach the spot. It was about 1 km up the hill on foot from Umri. Umri is about 21 km from Sariska. We all met at Umri and moved to the site. When the poachers saw us approaching, they fled under the cover of darkness.

A thorough inspection the next morning revealed that the poachers had built a hide on a tree overlooking a water hole which had little rain water but could attract wild animals. We were worried that a tiger which had been sighted in that area could fall victim to these poachers. Apparently after the poachers had fled, the tiger came to drink water from Harsawal's perennial waterhole about 100 m away from this site.

Investigations revealed that the poachers were a mixed group of Bawarias and locals who had entered the area on foot through the high hills. On the way up they had also killed and cooked a peacock. A case of trespassing and poaching was registered. Raids were conducted in houses of suspected Bawaria poachers. Ultimately we succeeded in arresting one Surjan Bawaria, who confessed to killing a leopard in Nadu village the previous summer. We also managed

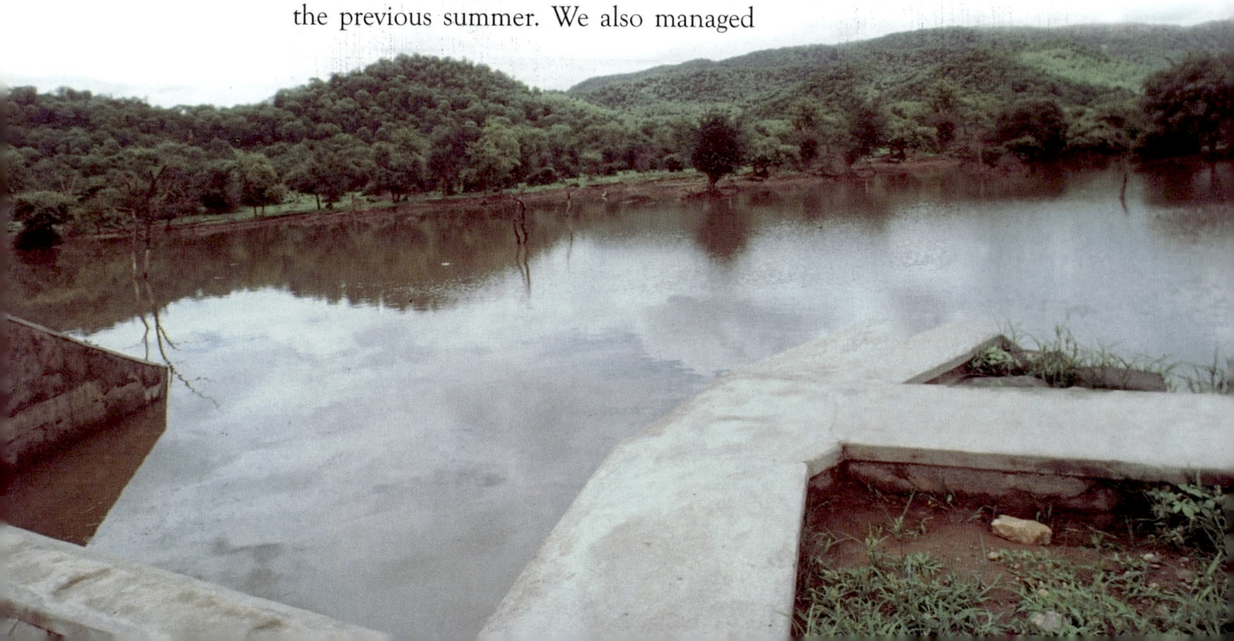

BELOW: Kala Kua anicut

to catch the middleman, Hira Lal Khatik, from Thanagazi village and recovered a leopard skin from Mangolpuri in Delhi. The trial court at Raj Garh awarded three years' rigorous imprisonment each to both of them. This was the first case from this Reserve of poachers being given such exemplary punishments.

Our work pressure was immense due to shortage of field staff. I had raised this issue several times with my seniors but they too were helpless because there was a shortage of frontline staff throughout the state.

After the Harsawal incident, one day the Rajasthan Forest Minister visited Sariska along with the Principal Chief Conservator of Forests (PCCF) and the Chief Wildlife Warden (CWLW) of the State for a meeting on this Reserve. During the meeting, I brought up my demand for increase in frontline staff before the Minister. To reiterate my stand, I cited the Harsawal poaching incident. The CWLW had told me not to bring up the incident before the Minister. But considering the gravity of the matter, I opted to disregard his advice.

The Minister could not understand how I dared to bring up the story before him. He was furious and opined that the Reserve was not in safe hands. The PCCF and the CWLW were impressed with my record. But the Minister knew nothing about it. I pleaded with the Minister to visit the Harsawal site in order to understand and appreciate the problem. He, fortunately, agreed.

It was a hot sunny day. We reached Umri outpost where a lone forest guard was on duty. The Minister was shocked to learn that there was just one forest guard manning the outpost. I told him that the guard looks after his entire beat of around 15 sq. km.

The minister, who had served in the military, immediately realised that the life of the guard was very unsafe at the outpost. He felt there should be no fewer than three persons posted there. I apprised him that more or less the same situation persists in all the 72 beats of the Reserve.

We climbed up the hill to have a clearer look at the spot of the incident. On seeing from the top the folds of high hills through which the poachers had come, the minister could appreciate the problem and thanked me for bringing him to the site as well as for apprising him of the actual problem. He promised to arrange for more staff. He fulfilled his promise and soon enough Sariska got additional staff which helped us immensely in strengthening the wildlife protection measures.

It was also decided to tap water from Harsawal spring close to Umri outpost. This would avoid poaching risk at Harsawal located in the interior. It was thus that the Harsawal anicut was constructed.

Encouraged by the positive results, several more sites were identified for constructing anicuts. Three anicuts were built in Talvriksh range at Loj-Renu, Berawas, and Nagal Hedi during 1993–94. The anicut built at Binak in Akbarpur range in the north of the Reserve was a great success.

During my second posting, I wanted to raise its head wall by 2 ft to increase its water holding capacity. When I inspected the site, however, I was shocked to notice unrestricted cattle

BELOW: Richhunda Anicut

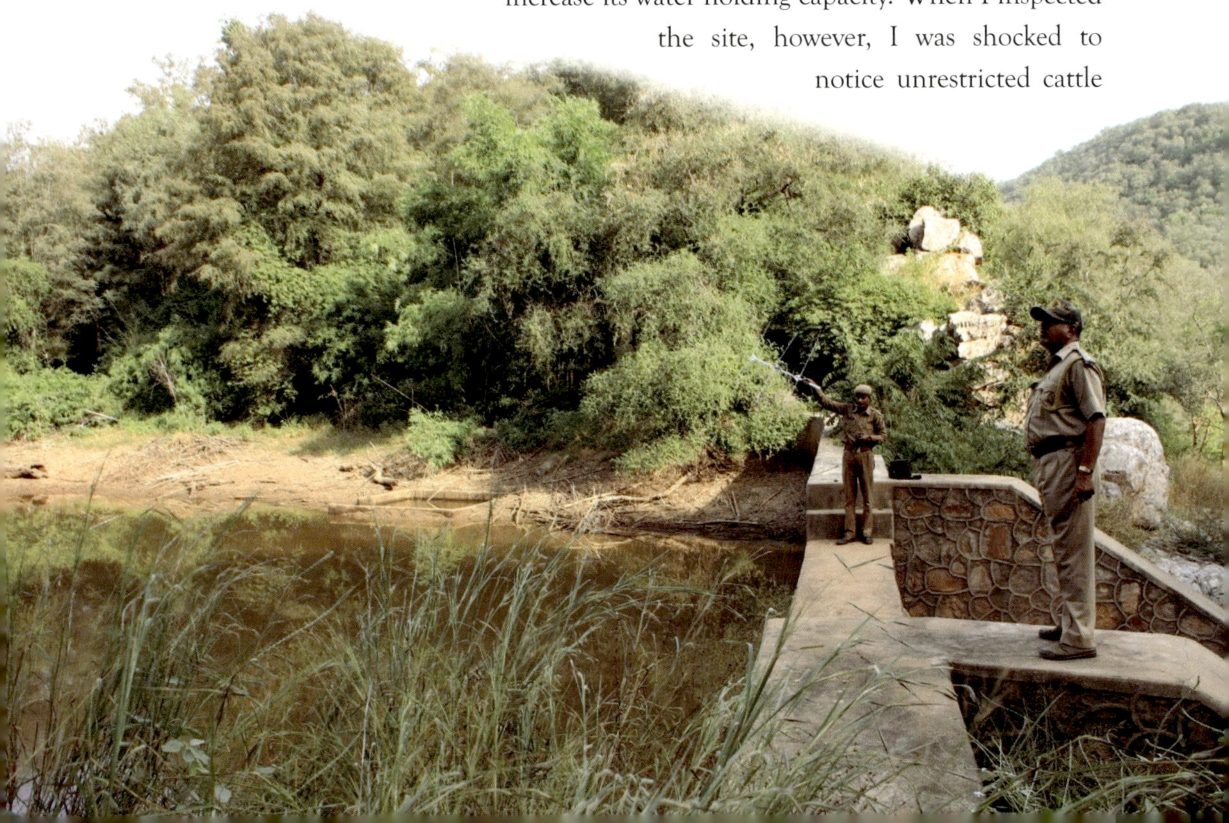

grazing. My first task was, therefore, to put an end to this menace in this part of the Binak beat.

In Sariska range, one anicut was constructed close to Kundalka village and adjacent to Gopi Chand Sagar constructed earlier. These two anicuts along with Bhrartrahari Sagar not only helped in forming a small lake but also put a halt to unauthorised entry of cattle in this area from Kundalka.

One anicut was constructed in Kundali in Sariska range. I had great hopes from this but all were in vain. It did not hold water for long. On my second posting, I succeeded in renovating the anicut using a lining of thick poly sheet on its bed so as to hold water.

In 1995–96, two anicuts each were constructed in Talvriksh (at Berawas and Nathusar), Tehla (Boretha Naka), Sariska (Sarunda and Slopka), and one in Akabarpur range. All of them provided excellent results.

Slopka, being at the heart of the Reserve, had always been a favourite spot of all kinds of animals, particularly tiger and sambar. Slopka *nallah* used to be perennial but decrease in rainfall had resulted in reduced water flow currently.

One afternoon while returning from Siliberi I noticed hundreds of spotted deer waiting to cross the road in order to reach the artificial waterhole at Slopka. The waterhole was being fed by a pump fitted on an open well. The vehicular traffic on the road was almost continuous. The animals were getting impatient. Suddenly a fawn jumped on to the road and just escaped being killed in an accident. At the other side of the road I saw the mother waiting for the fawn. It was certainly very risky for the animals.

My driver Badri had more than 40 years of experience in this Reserve. He knew the ins and outs of the forest area. He told me that an anicut built on Slopka *nallah*, which receives water from the huge catchment area stretched up to Kraska, could hold water throughout the year. He also showed me a spot where water remains throughout the year albeit in small quantity. This meant that water from the upstream hills keeps trickling down round the year and impervious rocks exist in the *nallah* bed, close to this water pit.

That very day I conducted a detailed survey of the *nallah* and discussed the matter in detail with my colleagues. We then finalised the site for an anicut about 50 m upstream from this water point. The decision proved correct. Even as construction progressed, a lot of water got accumulated and a water pump had to be used to remove the water during construction. The anicut had enough water to support the wildlife of the entire area throughout the summer.

BELOW: Brahmnath anicut in Monsoon

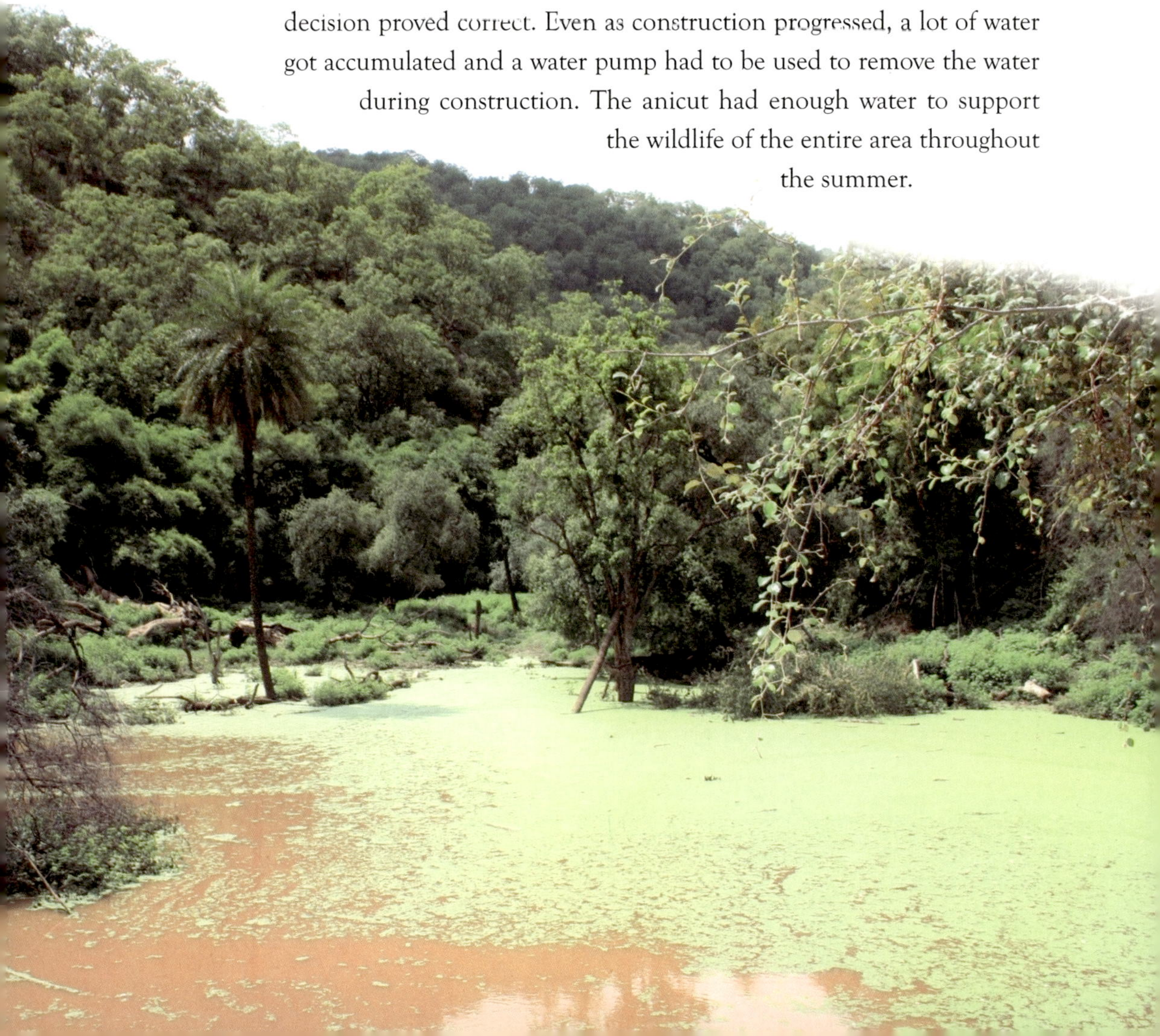

> Hardly had the construction finished when, taking advantage of this water, a sub-adult tiger made this its prime hunting spot. A dominant male often passed through this track. The sub-adult was clever. On spotting the adult it disappeared into the bushes. It would reappear only after the adult had gone.

Unfortunately, several years later, villagers were allowed to develop a huge water pond in the catchment of the Slopka anicut at the Kraska plateau. This encouraged them to increase the number of livestock. In addition, a number of check dams too, were constructed. This reduced water level considerably in the Slopka anicut. In Reserves such as Sariska, where water is very critical, water harvesting should be undertaken very diligently and after considering all facts. During my second posting at the Reserve in 2009, I got these undesirable checkdams removed and restored the anicut.

During 1996–98, 13 anicuts were constructed in various ranges. Each one had its own utility but the ones at Maujnath, Brahmnath, and Richhunda proved to be most successful of all.

Apart from anicuts, several earthen ponds were constructed in order to tap rain water. About 30 such ponds were created between 1990–91 and 1997–98.

This water management strategy was a boon to the entire Reserve. It helped in storing rain water much beyond the rainy season. This in turn helped in the dispersal of wildlife especially the population of ungulates and wild boar throughout the Reserve. Dependence and burden upon artificial waterholes also reduced noticeably and the wells got recharged. The Raika–Loj–Nathusar seasonal river started flowing up to November–December. The water situation got tremendously improved in the entire Reserve. This helped in successfully fighting the harshness of the dry years in the recent past. No casualty of wild animals was reported from any part of the Reserve for want of drinking water.

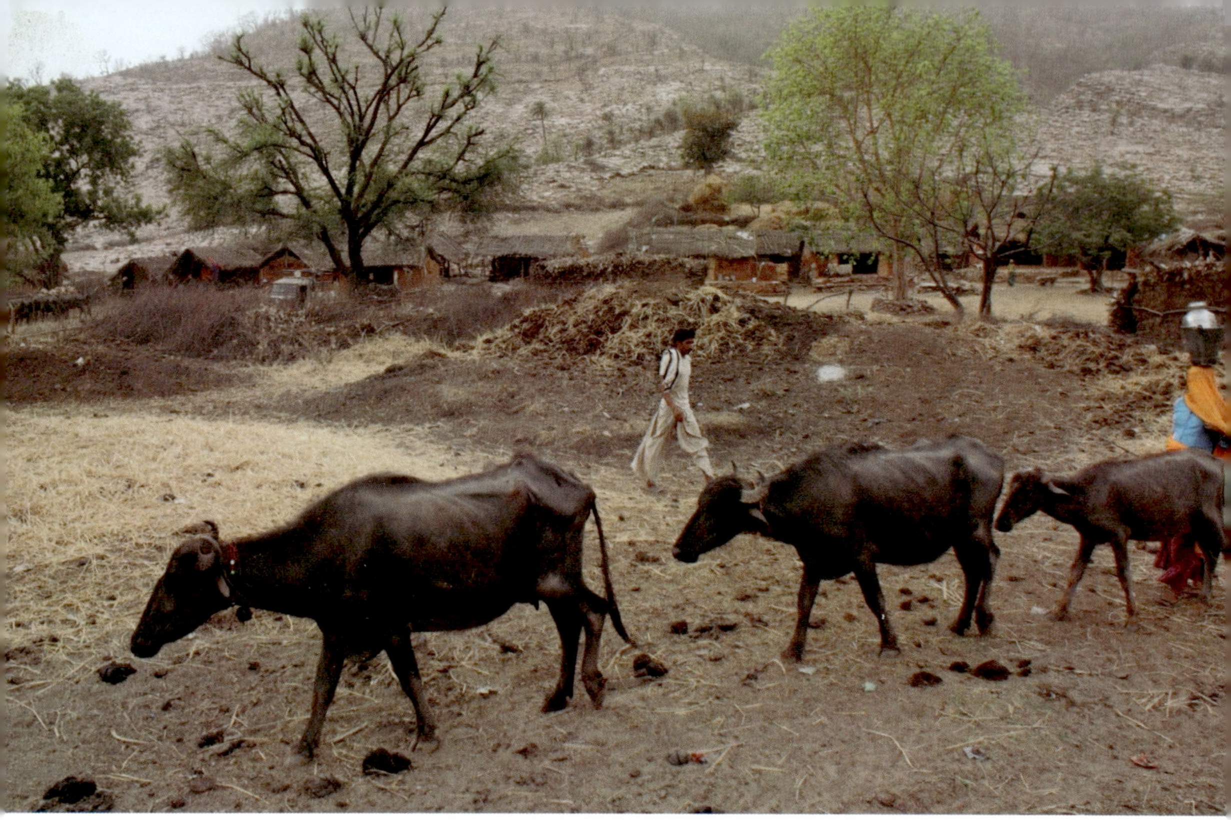

SARISKA - ITS PRESSURES AND CHALLENGES

Sariska was known all over the world for its tigers. In 2004, however, it was revealed that it had lost its entire tiger population due to poaching. An excellent tiger reserve, which used to be frequented by several wildlife lovers, had thus been laid completely waste. There are also several other factors threatening the existence of this important tiger reserve.

BIOTIC PRESSURES

The rich forest areas attract cattle rearing communities and they settle in and around them. Sariska is no exception. The cattle rearers are called

Gujjars here. Like everywhere else, the human population is on the increase here also.

Before Independence, Gujjars used to live in complete harmony with wildlife. They used to obey the orders of the rulers strictly and never harmed animals. They were pure vegetarians. Further, they were of immense help to forest guards whom they used to treat with great respect.

When there was sufficient rainfall, there was no dearth of fodder or water. In fact, their cattle posed no competition to the wildlife. Since the cattle were not moving out of the forest, chances of their contracting diseases from outside were also ruled out. Thus there was hardly any danger of wild animals contracting diseases. In those days, people were not allowed to keep sheep, goats, camels, and so on, as they cause serious damage to forests. The Gujjars and their cattle were part of the ecosystem.

The problem started after Independence when politicians started interfering in the affairs of the sanctuary. People became bolder and grazing became rampant. Highways were constructed through Sariska. Motor vehicles started plying through these. Villagers began keeping more cattle to increase business and profit. They

FACING PAGE: Umri village (evicted in 2011–12)

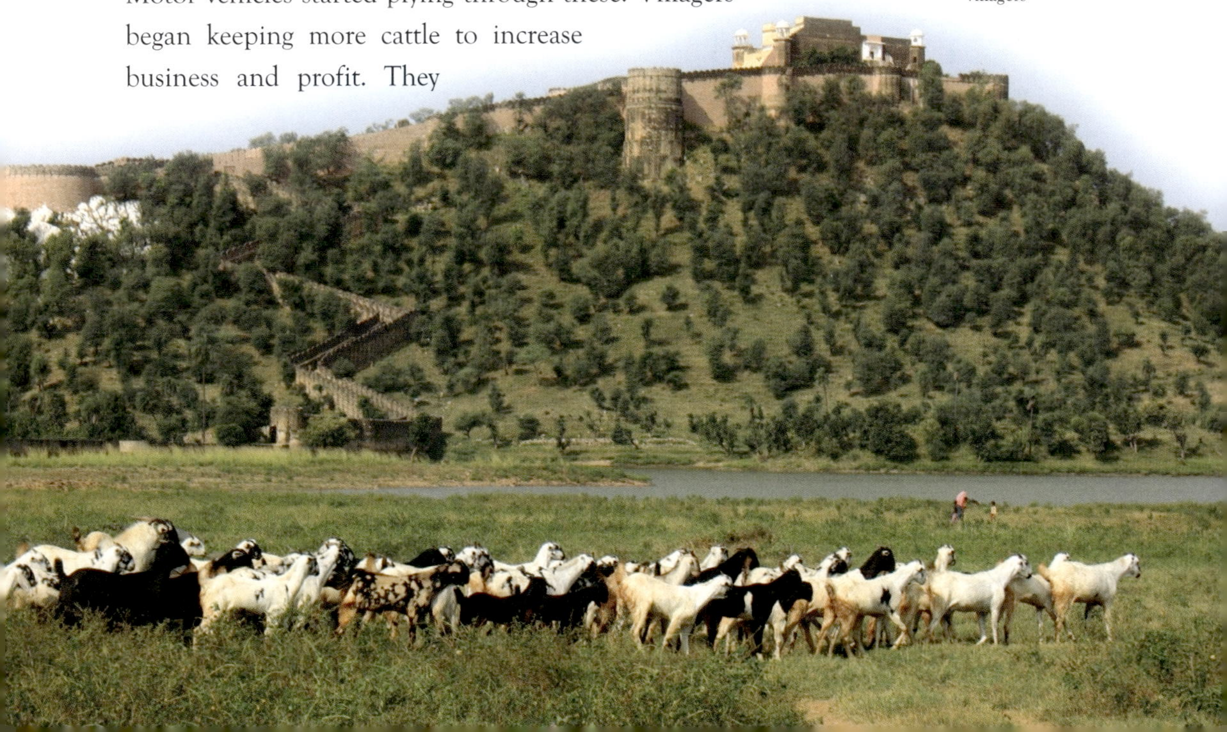

BELOW: Goats reared by Kankwadi villagers

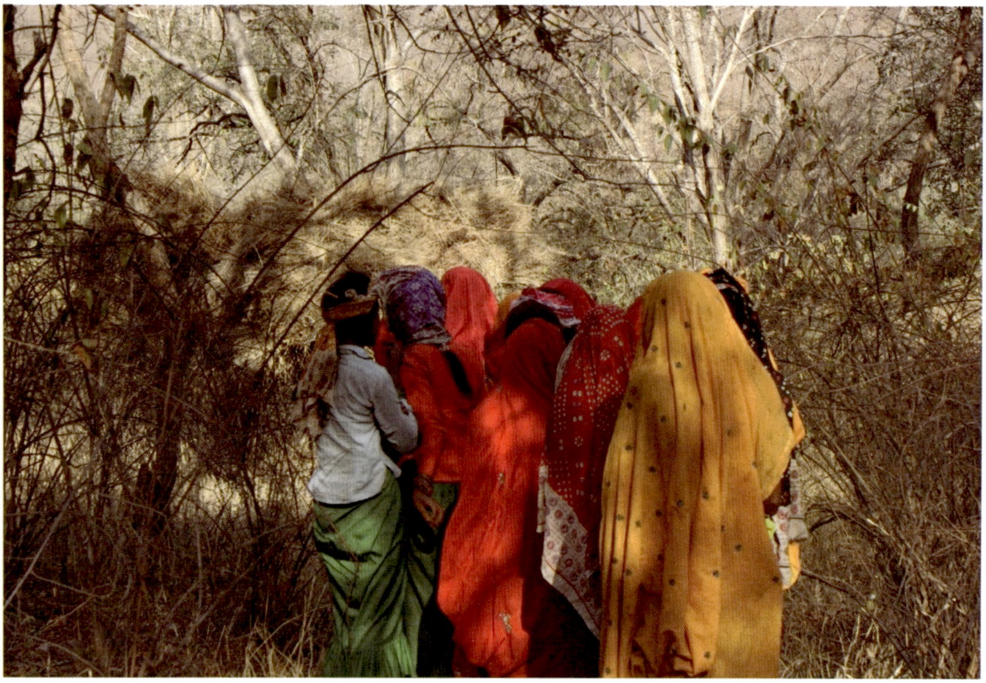

Above: Ladies illegally collect grass (Plateau of Bhensota)

also started preparing milk cake to earn even more profits, which adversely affected firewood in the forest.

Roads and highways, no doubt, made life easy for humans. This encouraged more Gujjar families to settle in the prime forest areas of Sariska. The forest administration went haywire due to pressure from people on the one side and politicians on the other. This paved the way for people to rear goats and sheep as well. These people opposed Reserve management tooth and nail as it hampered their unrestricted use of the area.

The increased human and animal presence in Sariska created immense potential for conflicts between humans and wild animals. Twenty-eight villages with nearly 12,000 human and 33,000 livestock population (as per the 2008-09 census by the Reserve management) existed in the Reserve. The inhabitants of these villages are fully dependent on the forests for their genuine and not-so-genuine requirements of fuelwood, fodder, thatch grass, timber, bamboo, and so on.

In addition to this, about 300 villages are located within a 5-km radius of the Reserve (with over 1.5 lakh people and 2.75 lakh livestock as per the 2002–03 census). They also depend largely upon the Reserve to meet their daily forest-based needs. This led to large-scale deterioration in and degradation of the peripheral as well as core areas of Sariska.

The temple at Pandupole, in the heart of Sariska, attracts about a lakh of devotees and tourists every year. About 50,000 people visit the temple during the three days of Pandupole mela in July–August.

State highways number 13 and 29A pass through the Reserve. The latter passes through the heart of the Reserve. It links Sariska to Tehla. On an average, 2000 vehicles, including government buses, ply on state highway number 13 every day. This seriously affects the peace of the core area. It is a constant threat to wildlife and its habitat. There have been several cases of tigers, leopards, and other wild animals being run over by speeding vehicles. As the number of vehicles increases, so does the number of hit-and-run cases.

Poachers always take advantage of this free accessibility. An alternate route for this highway has been developed but has not been used. Traffic on Sariska–Tehla road through Kalighati needs to be stopped immediately in the interest of this invaluable wildlife and Reserve, and the people at large.

The famous milk cake industry of Alwar, too, is largely responsible for the immense biotic pressure on the Reserve.

Villagers living in the Reserve make a living by selling milk. Villagers of Umri had a jeep for transporting milk to Tehla market daily. Milk venders from other villagers have also started pressurising the Reserve management to allow dairy vehicles for transportation of milk to the markets of Tehla and Bhrartrahari.

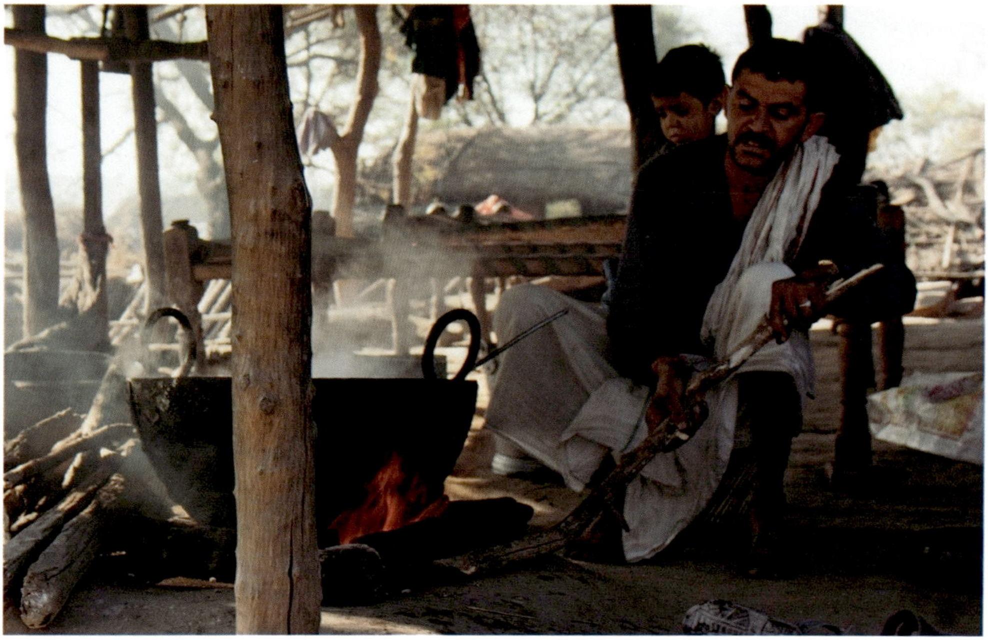

ABOVE: A villager preparing milk cake at his home in the core area of the Reserve

Entry of commercial vehicles inside the Reserve, especially the core area, is bound to create several problems. The demand of the villagers to allow dairy vehicles might be considered reasonable on humanitarian grounds. However, from the point of view of wildlife protection it is disastrous.

The villagers living in the Reserve are deprived of all kinds of civic amenities such as medical aid, electricity, and education. They are, however, not willing to move out of the Reserve. Even lucrative offers of a million rupees per adult male have not succeeded in motivating them to move out of the Reserve. They are interested in living inside the Reserve and adding more cattle heads to have added quantities of milk with practically no additional maintenance expenditure. They also prepare milk cake at their houses using firewood collected from the forest. This milk cake fetches them high returns. Thus the famous Alwar milk cake market flourishes at the cost of Sariska Tiger Reserve. Villagers living in the Reserve collectively oppose restrictions on such activities. On several occasions, the villagers have leveled false allegations against the field staff of entering their houses and misbehaving with their ladies. Media, politicians, and human rights activists take advantage of such stories. These handicaps coupled with shortage of staff forms a big challenge for the Reserve management.

HUMAN RESOURCES

The number of frontline staff entrusted with the duty of protection falls far short of the requirement. Also, no recruitment of foresters and rangers has taken place for nearly three decades. As a result, the Reserve has an ageing frontline staff. There is a serious shortage of young and enthusiastic rangers. This is a matter of serious concern as there would be no one with experience to take over from those retiring from service.

The average age of the guards, foresters, and rangers working in the Reserve is above 50 years. They are physically weak and cannot cope with the increasing demands of the job. In such a situation the protection of the area is bound to suffer. More personnel should be urgently recruited to protect the Reserve and to deal with poachers and other forest offenders effectively.

When I joined the services of the forest department of Rajasthan in 1973, there were several excellent forests in the state. Protection of these precious natural resources was a great challenge. Since access to these areas was very difficult, the staff posted there were deprived of the facilities of a civic society. The wildlife reserves posed similar problems to the staff. Therefore, transfer from territorial forest postings to a wildlife reserve was hardly a pinch to the frontline staff. However, the situation has changed drastically. In the entire state, only Sariska has very dense forest currently.

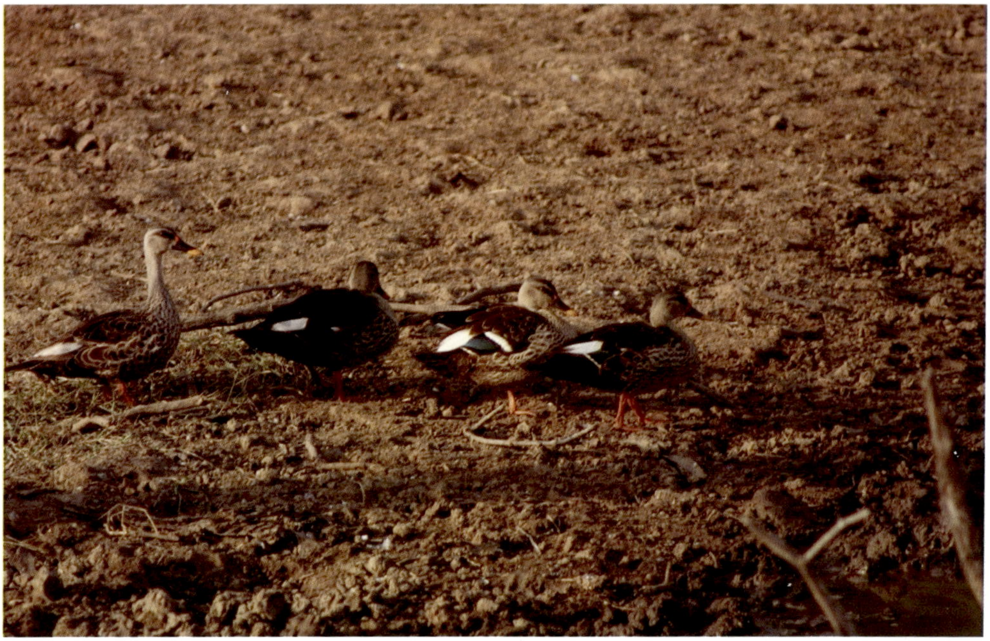

ABOVE: Spot Bills at Kalighati water hole

With the growing demand for tiger skins, bones, and other parts in some Asian countries, protection of the animal has become an uphill task. Constant monitoring is required. Even daily tracking of tigers is not sufficient. Beat guards need to cultivate their own information systems in the villages to get timely information on tiger or leopard movement as well as incidences of cattle lifting immediately. This needs a very strict round-the-clock vigil. On top of that, if a tiger or leopard gets poached, the guard is likely to be punished.

In territorial forests life has become very easy for the frontline staff. Roads have come up in forest areas which used to be non-penetrable two decades ago. Buses and taxis ply along them. Things have changed drastically in recent years. Compared to a few decades ago, hardly 10 per cent of frontline staff, including Range Officers, now stay at the protection outposts, nakas, or ranges in non-wildlife forest divisions. Nobody is, therefore, interested in being posted to wildlife reserves like Sariska.

Therefore, in order to attract efficient and sincere personnel to wildlife reserves, it is necessary that the power to post and transfer field staff and officers must vest with CWLW of the state and should not be influenced by external pressures. It is also essential to provide adequate incentives like compensation for excess work, allowances for double establishments and mess facilities at wildlife area postings, especially in tiger reserves, where working conditions are very tough.

RELIGIOUS TOURISM

Several popular temples are located in the Reserve. The wild beauty of Sariska attracts a huge number of nature and wildlife lovers from all over the country and abroad. Sariska also attracts more than 1.5 lakh pilgrims every year, especially from Alwar, Jaipur, Dausa, and neighbouring districts of Haryana. Such a large number of pilgrims are beyond the carrying capacity of the Reserve and is actually hazardous. This needs to be regulated. Criticisms are bound to occur in case of such regulations. However, in the larger interests of the people and society, suitable steps must be taken at the earliest.

Pandupole Temple

Pandupole is made of two words, pandu and pole. Pandu stands for 'Pandavas', the five heroes of *Mahabharat*, and 'pole' means gate.

According to *Mahabharata*, the Pandava brothers, in a gamble with their cousins, the Kauravas, lost their right to the throne and accepted an exile of 13 years with the last year in disguise. If they were found out during this period then they would have to undergo exile once again.

It is believed that the thick forests of Sariska provided a safe hideout for the Pandavas during the last year of the exile. However, enemy spies started searching the forest.

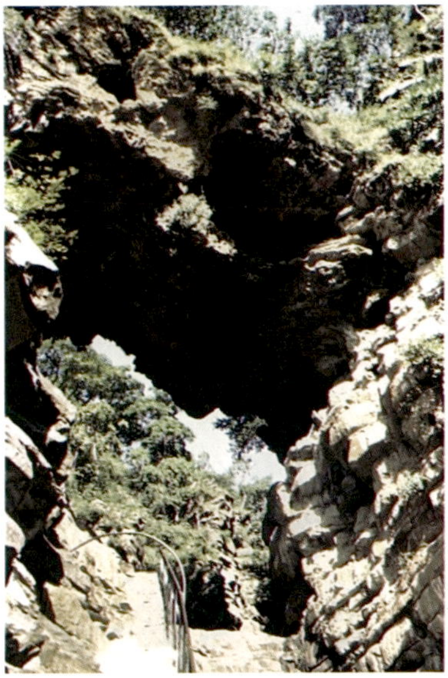

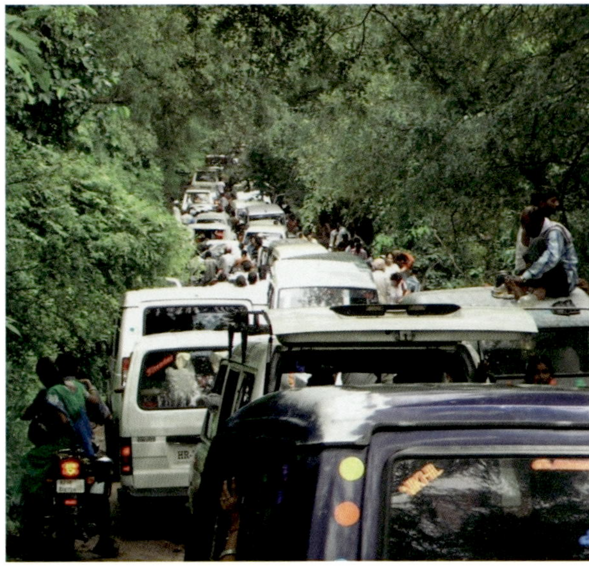

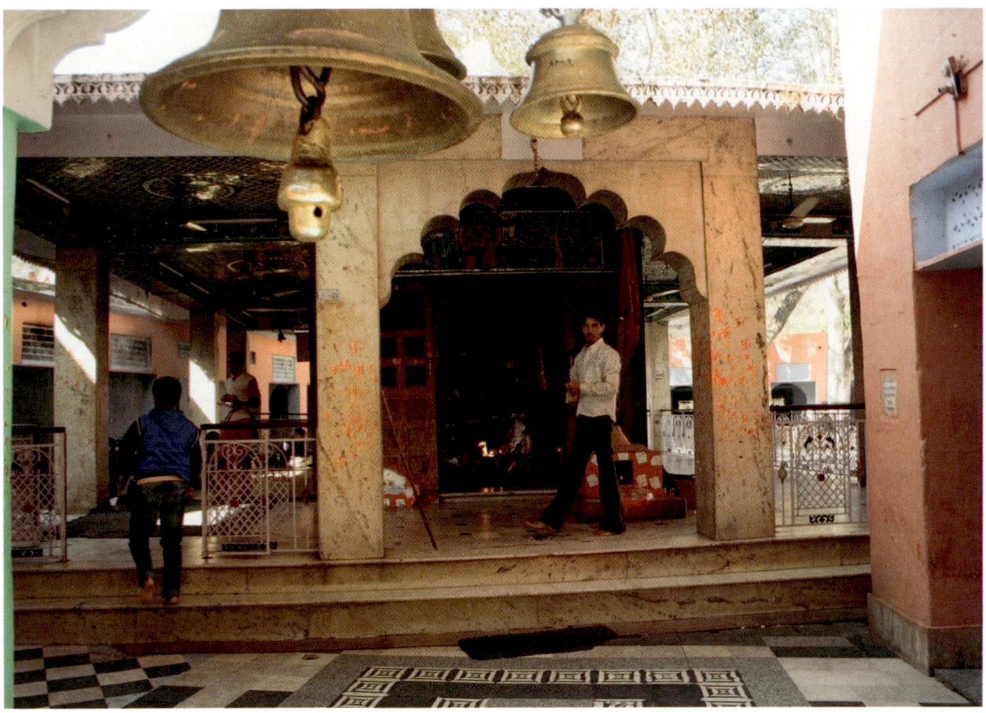

The Pandavas rushed towards Pandupole where they got trapped by hillocks on all the other three sides. They could not go back for fear of running into the enemy. Bhim, the mighty one, created a gateway through the hillock using his mace. Pandavas thus succeeded in hoodwinking the enemy. This gateway thus got its name Pandupole. Pandupole is situated at about 21 km from the main entrance of Sariska Tiger Reserve.This is a 20 ft × 15 ft wide hole at a height of 300 ft from the ground.

During monsoons a spring flows through this gateway and is the source of great attraction to tourists visiting Sariska. Pilgrims also visit this legendary gateway because of its mythological importance.

The entire valley spread between Umri and this gateway, about 3 km long and 200 m wide, is popularly known as Pandupole. This is one of the most picturesque sites with perennial water source flowing between the steep hills standing on both sides. The micro climate with dense green forest in this valley supports a large web of wildlife. The rare dusky horned owl can easily be spotted on the tall trees in the middle of the stream here. The steep hills offer ideal habitat to leopards and their sighting is common in this part of the Reserve.

A temple of Lord Hanuman, one of the heroes of the great Hindu epic *Ramayan*, is also situated in this valley at about half a kilometre from Pandupole. It is believed that Lord Hanuman spent his old age at this place, and blessed Bhim with immense power and strength during their exile in this valley.

A temple of a reclining Hanuman exists here. The temple draws a number of visitors every day, especially on Tuesdays and Saturdays, considered special days of Lord Hanuman. An annual fair is held at this shrine in Bhadva (August–September) which attracts several thousands of devotees. This causes immense disturbance to the wildlife of the Reserve.

FACING PAGE ABOVE LEFT: The historic Pandupole gate

FACING PAGE ABOVE RIGHT: Pilgrims going to Pandupole temple on a 'free entry' day

FACING PAGE BELOW: Pandupole temple

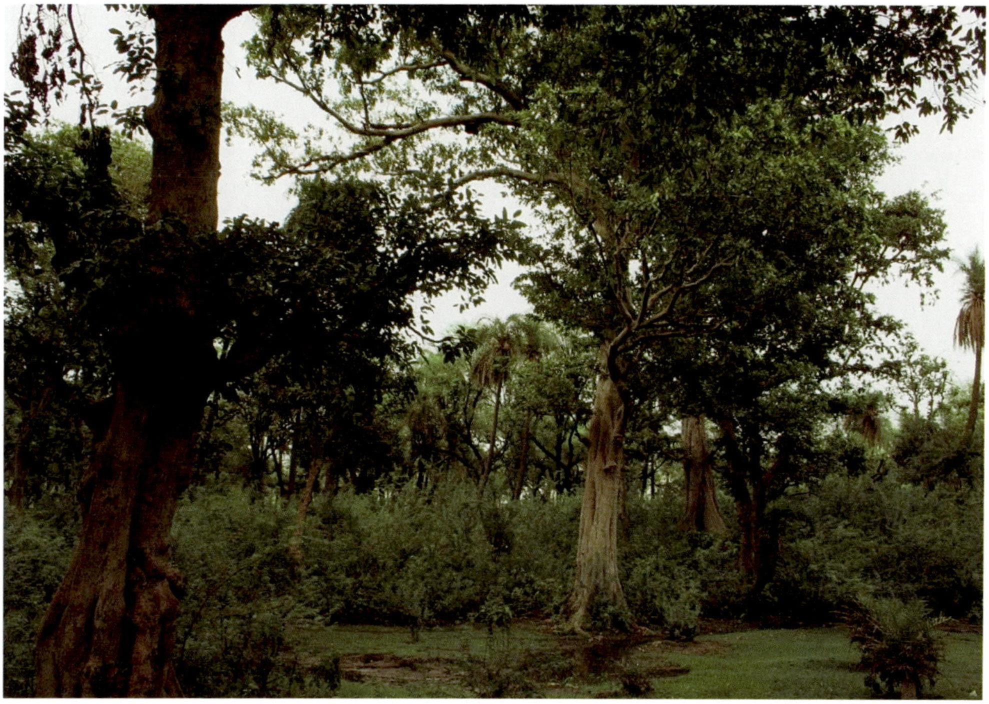

ABOVE: Tall Tal trees *(Terminalia arjuna)* in Talvriksh

Ganga Mandir with Tiger Head

The Ganga mandir at Talvriksh is religiously, historically, and mythologically important. Located at a distance of 18 km from Sariska and 10 km from Kushal Garh, this beautiful valley with tall Tal (*Terminalia arjuna*) trees is spread over a large area and a stream flows through it. A large number of vibrant monkeys occupy the place, which sometimes fall prey to leopards inhabiting the hills. Initiatives by the Reserve authorities to improve the conditions further have attracted the wildlife.

According to mythology, during the Vedic period, Mandav Rishi, who created the Upanishads, meditated at Talvriksh. Ganga appeared here in the form of hot and cold springs in order to facilitate the rishi to attain *moksha* (end of the cycle of births and deaths).

Talvriksh, located at the western boundary of the Reserve, is also the headquarters of one of its administrative ranges. Among the several temples here, Ganga mandir is the most popular. It is believed that this temple has been in existence from pre-historic times. A tiger head is displayed at the entrance to the temple.

According to the legend, a long time ago, the king of Alwar hunted a tiger at Talvriksh and took away the trophy. That night a saint appeared in his dream and accused him of killing him while meditating in the form of a tiger and roaming in the jungle of Talvriksh. The king woke up and immediately summoned his ministers. They told him that he had unknowingly committed a serious sin. Killing of a meditating saint will not be pardoned by God. The king will have to atone for his sin. He was advised immediately to hold a

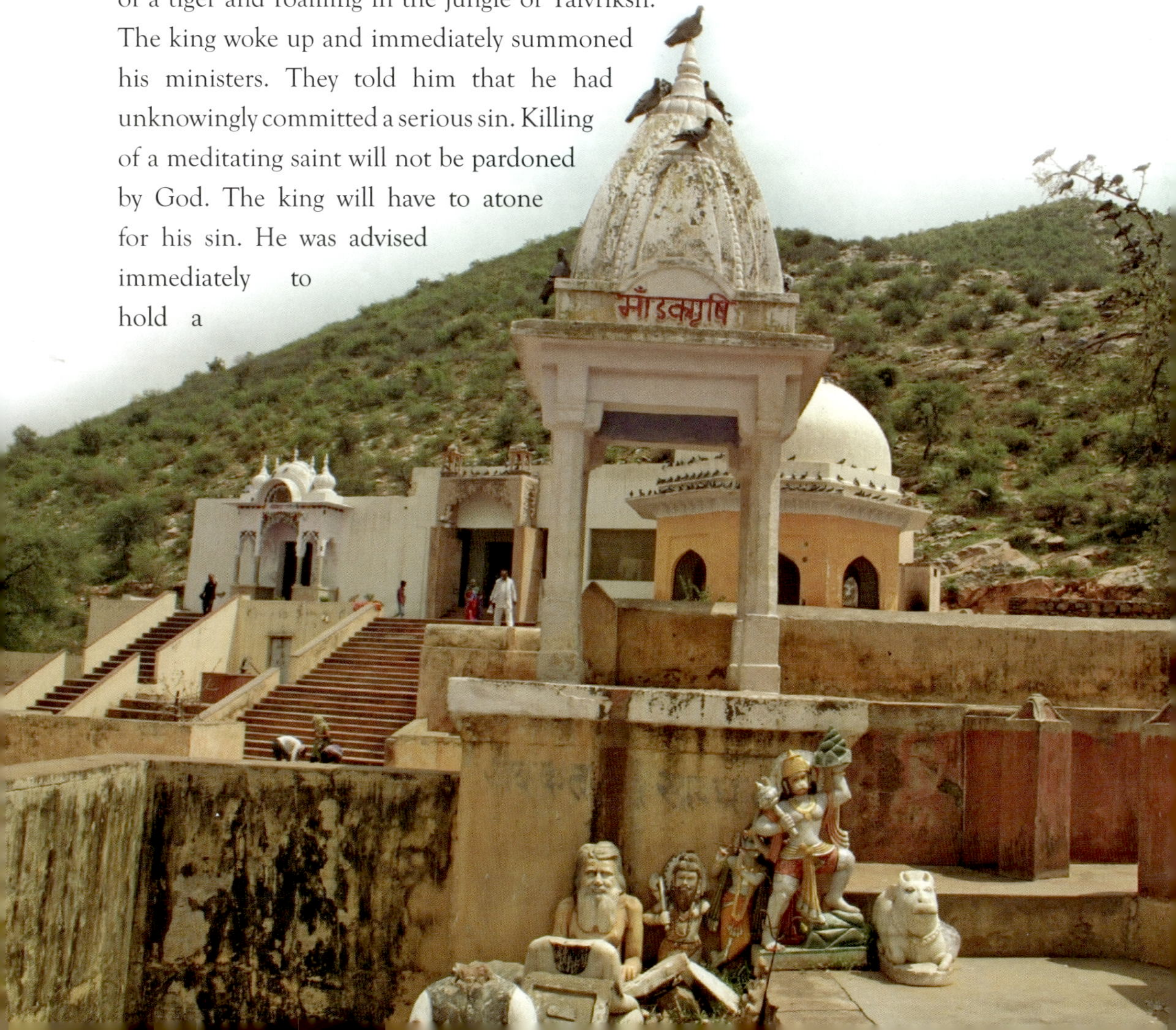

BELOW: Temple of Mandav Rishi

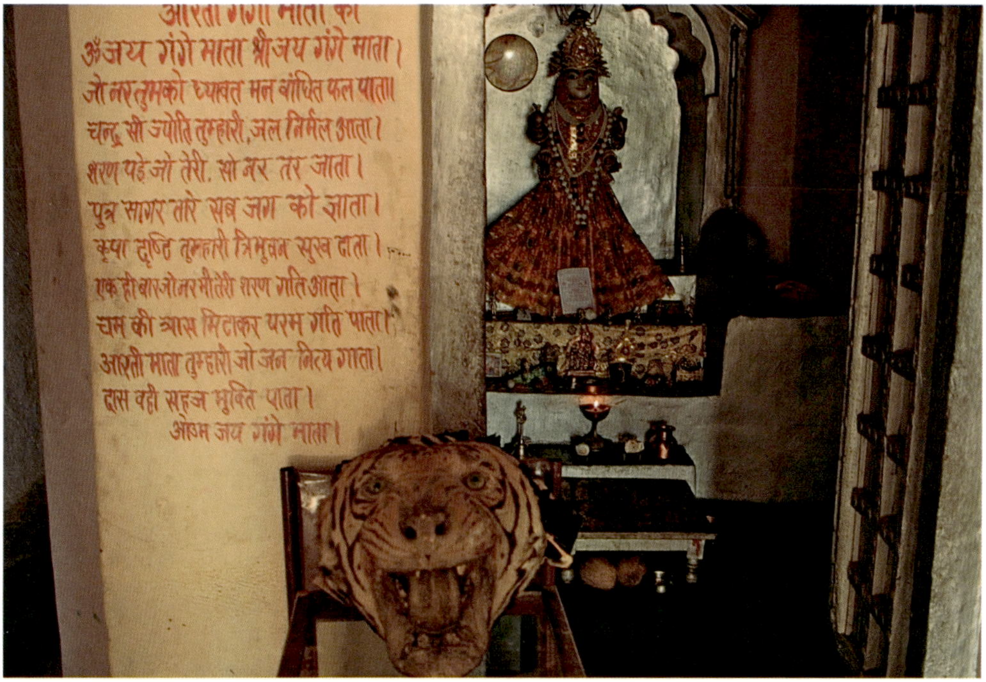

ABOVE: Ganga mandir with tiger head

yagya and observe fast for 10 days. The king followed the advice with great diligence and returned the tiger head to this temple. Since then, it has become a part of the temple.

It is also believed that during the time of Mandav rishi, a prosperous city called Champawati Nagar used to exist towards the north of Talvriksh, ruled by mighty king Loam.

Some thieves planned to rob the palace. Before embarking on the heinous act, they visited saint Mandav to obtain his blessings. The saint was, however, meditating. So they left without his blessings. They managed to steal several valuables from the palace. While returning they again visited saint Mandav. But he was still in deep meditation. The thieves believed that they had the saint's blessings. They did not think it proper to disturb him. They, however, wanted to show their gratitude to him. They, therefore, placed a beautiful necklace around the neck of the saint before taking leave of him. The saint was not aware of anything.

The following morning the king came to know of the theft. He also learned that the thieves had come from Talvriksh side. In Talvriksh, his soldiers found saint Mandav wearing the precious necklace of the queen. The saint was still under meditation. They carried him to the king in the same posture. The courtiers managed to awaken the saint from his deep meditation. The saint was surprised to find himself in this situation. The furious king charged him with theft. The saint denied the allegation. He explained that he was in deep meditation and was not aware of anything. The king was not convinced. He awarded death punishment to the saint. The saint got very annoyed. He cursed that the country would soon lose its prosperity. The king did not relent.

The saint was soon brought for execution. The loop was fitted around his neck. It suddenly transformed itself into a garland. The king realised his mistake. He repented and pleaded that the curse be taken back. The curse, however, had started taking effect and the country's ruin had begun.

When his anger subsided, the saint regretted inflicting the curse that would devastate the people and the country. He, however, could not take back the curse. He meditated for several years to please Lord Shiva who ultimately appeared before him and advised him to entreat mother Ganga to save the people from the curse. Accordingly the saint went into meditation for several years. Ultimately mother Ganga was pleased. She appeared at Talvriksh in the form of hot and cold springs. Thereafter the impact of the curse slowly declined. Champawati was devastated. A new civilisation under the Gurjar–Pratihar dynasty flourished in this area in the 9th century AD.

Bhrartrahari Temple

Bhrartrahari was the powerful king of Ujjain (Central India) during the 2nd century BC. He was the elder brother of the legendary king Vikramaditya, who founded the Indian calendar known as Vikram Samwat in 57 BC.

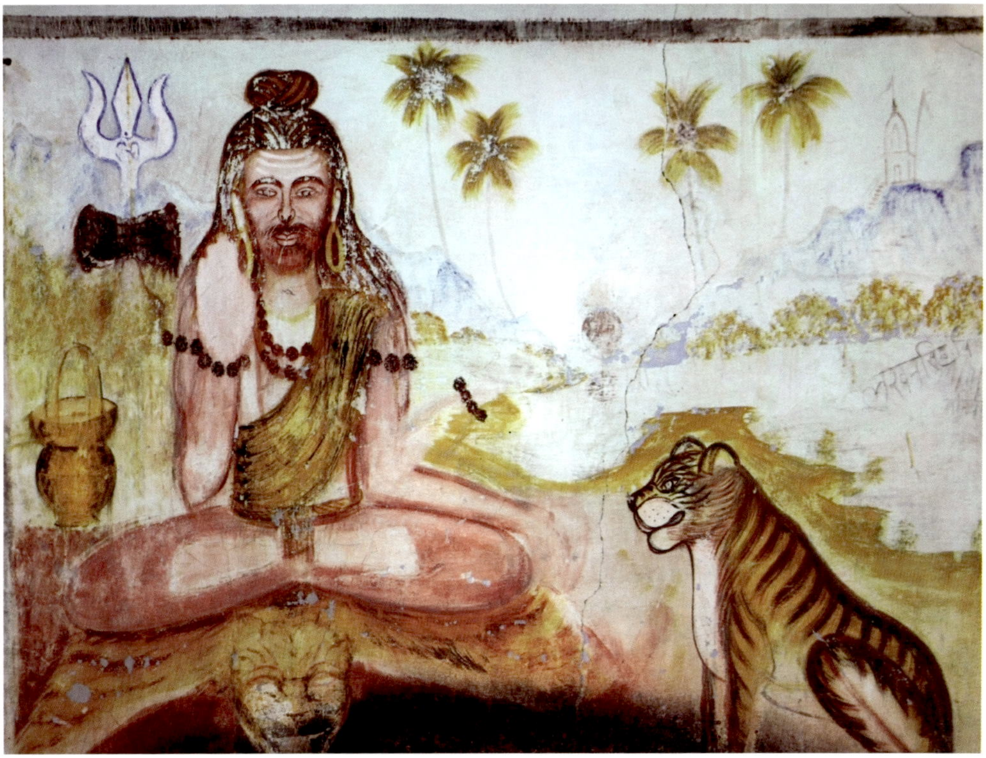

ABOVE:
Painting of Saint Gorakh Nath at Tarunda in the National Park

Once a saint visited Bhrartrahari in his court. He gifted the king a special fruit. Whoever eats it would become immortal. The saint thought that Bhrartrahari, being such a benevolent and caring ruler, should serve his people forever. The king gifted the fruit to Pingla, his favourite queen so that she becomes immortal. The queen gifted it to her coachman with whom she had an affair. The coachman in turn gifted it to his beloved prostitute. The prostitute, however, was not happy with her life and did not want to prolong it. She thought that the kind-hearted Bhrartrahari is the only person who deserves immortality. So she presented the magic fruit to the king. The king soon learned how the fruit had travelled back to him. He also learnt about the infidelity of his beloved queen. This was highly shocking for him. He thereafter lost interest in worldly affairs.

He handed over the kingdom to his younger brother, Vikramaditya, and became a sanyasi. He left the palace and wandered far and wide and produced three master pieces in Sanskrit, *Shrangar Shatak, Vairagya Shatak,* and *Neeti Shatak.*

When he reached Sariska, he settled there. He observed deep meditation for several years. He finally attained *samadhi* (death) on the 8th of Shukl Paksh (moon light fortnight) of Bhadava (August–September). A shrine-cum-temple was built on this spot by his followers.

Bhrartrahari temple is located 5 km from Sariska. The temple attracts thousands of pilgrims every year. On the anniversary of his *samadhi*, a festival is held here which draws thousands of devotees from all over India, especially from Alwar and Dausa districts.

Nahar Sati Temple

Nahar Sati temple is located east of Pandupole in the Reserve. It is a small temple with small tiger statues on either side of the entrance.

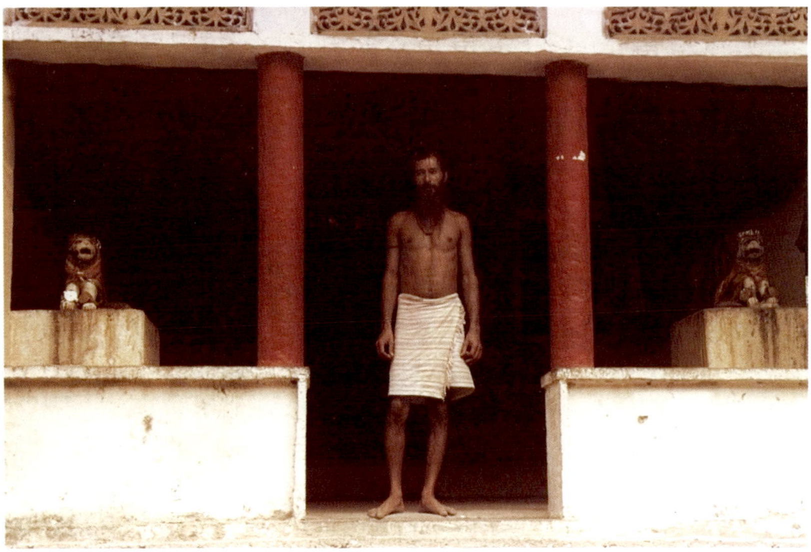

LEFT:
The Nahar Sati Temple in 1996

Legend has it that about a thousand years ago, a tiger took a woman's child from her lap. She was wearing a veil and did not look at the tiger. She thought it was her father-in-law who took the child. Later on, however, she learned that her father-in-law did not do it. She was worried and started searching for the child. The child was finally found in the den of a tiger. The child was safe. She picked up the child and the tiger did not obstruct. Nor did the tiger hurt her or the child. She believed that it was her husband who came in the form of a tiger. He had been away for long at some far away place for work. The villagers, however, did not think so and killed the tiger in anger.

The custom during those days was that women immolated themselves on the funeral pyre of their husbands. Such women were called Sati. This woman, too, immolated herself on the funeral pyre of the tiger for she believed that the tiger was her husband. A temple was later built on this site. Nahar is the local word for tiger. The temple thus came to be known as Nahar Sati temple.

In 1967 the old temple was renovated by devotees. The temple is very close to one of the most important protection outposts of the Reserve at Siliberi.

Basically, the concept of this temple glorifies the dignity of the tiger. This fact could have been encashed for protecting the tiger. But unfortunately over a period of time devotees got deviated from this noble objective. They expanded the temple structure considerably and converted it into a commercial venture attracting a large number of picnickers from the nearby Baleta township. This endangered the safety of the wildlife in the area. During my second posting I was aghast to notice the unauthorised expansion. Strict legal action was initiated against the temple authorities. Since then no further construction work has taken place. But the Reserve management needs to keep strict vigil lest it resumes.

Bagheshwari Mata Temple

Bagheshwari Mata temple is situated on the south of Sariska. This is the entrance to an important tiger habitat, the famous Bhagani valley. Many tigresses have produced litters in this forest. The deity of this temple, like Goddess Durga, has a tiger for her vehicle. Worshippers believe that with the blessings of the Goddess, they can live peacefully along with their livestock, in the tigerland. During the reign of the royals before Independence, the villagers living on the periphery or inside the Reserve lived in perfect harmony with the wildlife, especially carnivores like the tiger and the leopard. During those days the temple played an important role in maintaining harmony. The tiger then was not an enemy. The villagers worshipped the animal as a deity and did not harm it. Greed of the people has, however, changed this concept over time. As a result, the temple no longer acts as protector of the Reserve.

> Due to the presence of these temples, there is heavy traffic of pilgrims through the Reserve throughout the year, especially during rainy season. Unlike other protected areas in the country, which generally remain closed during the monsoon for forest regeneration, protection, and maintenance, Sariska Tiger Reserve remains open on Tuesdays and Saturdays during this period as well. The problem gets aggravated during the annual fairs of Pandupole and Bhrartrahari temples, when the number of pilgrims go up to more than a lakh. This damages the sanctity of the Reserve, as well as the ecosystem. Therefore, the decisions taken with regard to controlling the vehicular trafic inside the Reserve need to be implemented at the earliest.

MINING

Mining is another major problem that this Reserve has been facing since many years. Commercial mining was closed in Sariska by the Supreme Court in 1993. The powerful mining lobby, however, has been continuously demanding the reopening of these marble mines. Their threat persists and the smallest laxity on the part of the management can open the doors of the Reserve to miners leading to its complete ruin.

With every change in government the lobby becomes active. On quite a few occasions, they did succeed in getting the government to check the Reserve's boundary demarcation repeatedly. So far, fortunately, they have not succeeded in getting the boundary changed. But they are still waiting for a favourable opportunity. The Reserve management needs to be constantly vigilant lest they succeed in their motive.

Sariska was severely damaged due to about 240 mines in the Tehla range, on the southern side of the Reserve, during the 1980s. Tarun Bharat Sangh, an NGO, filed a Public Interest Litigation (PIL) in the Supreme Court in 1990 against these mines. Field Director of Sariska was also made a respondent along with the mining department of the state. The mining department had granted mining leases in the Reserve. Being the then Field Director of Sariska I was made officer-in-charge (OIC) of this case by the state government. The powerful mining lobby, backed by mighty politicians, was fighting tooth and nail. The state government, through the mining department, straight away denied forest status to this mining land. As officer-in-charge, I had, however, filed an affidavit in the apex court that all the mines in question were sanctioned on the notified forest land of the Reserve. I was under tremendous pressure from very powerful agencies including the state government. The then Secretary (Forests) instructed me to file an additional affidavit requesting the court to allow mining under the existing leases. I refused as his instruction was against the interests of wildlife. The Secretary was furious. I knew he could spoil my career. But this did not deter my commitment towards the tigerland of Sariska.

At one time, it was felt that the petitioner would lose the case. But my affidavit came to his rescue. Citing my affidavit the petitioner demanded that if its contents are true then the government cannot deny 'forest status' to the areas under dispute. If, however, they are false then contempt of court proceedings should be initiated against me.

It was a hard time for me. The powerful mining lobby and the state government were very unhappy with me for filing this affidavit in the apex court. The advocate also threatened to initiate criminal proceedings for breach of trust against me. He alleged that I had been helping the petitioner by briefing him on my affidavit. He claimed that otherwise the state government and the mine owners would have won the case.

My affidavit, no doubt, had altered the entire complexion of the case. The apex court's verdict on 8 April 1993 was that mining activity in Sariska Tiger Reserve should be completely closed down.

BELOW:
The 'golden' Sariska

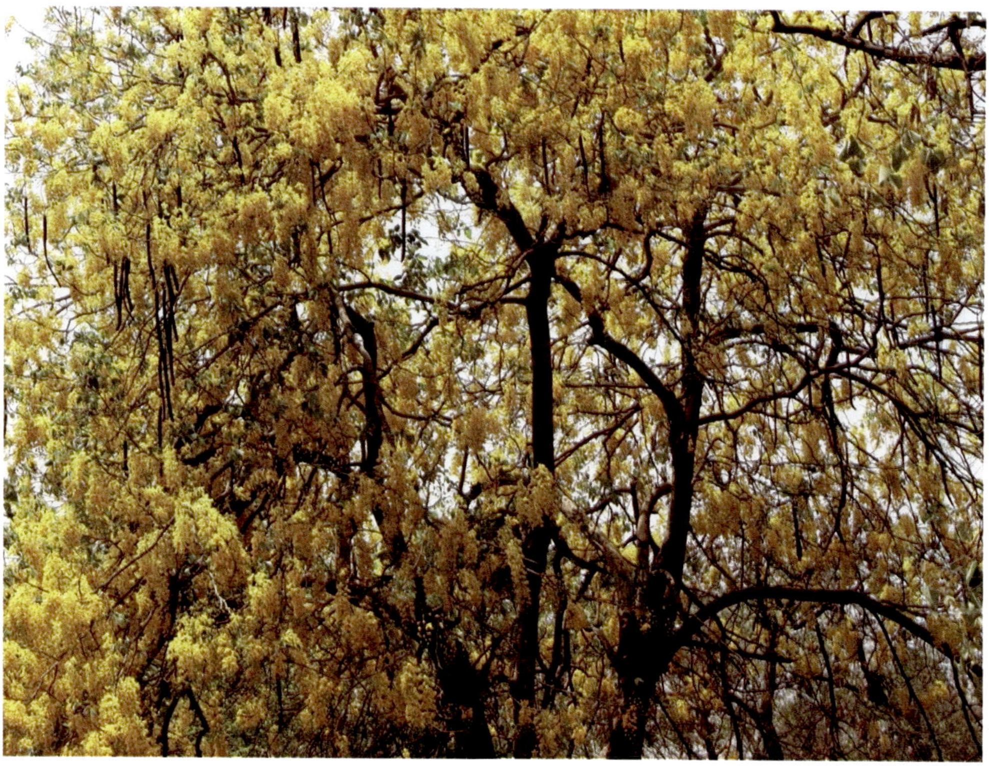

As the officer-in-charge of the case on behalf of the government, I lost the case. But as the in-charge of the Reserve I won the case in the interest of the Reserve in general and the tiger in particular. It was a day of celebration for wildlife lovers across the country. I paid a heavy price for this fight in the interest of wildlife. But, God helped me and truth and sanity prevailed. Government of India wanted to reward me for my valuable services in closing down the mines in the Reserve. I, however, requested them not to do so lest the state government feel further offended.

POLITICAL INFLUENCE, A STUMBLING BLOCK

Forest officials are discouraged, demoralised, intimidated, and even manhandled while carrying out their duties. As a forest officer, I have witnessed this throughout my career.

Conflicts between villagers and wildlife reserve personnel are a countrywide phenomenon. After the complete annihilation of tigers in Sariska in 2004, the problem increased manifold. The management was compelled to improve protection measures to ensure safety of the remaining wildlife wealth of the Reserve. The villagers instigated by local leaders started flouting rules with impunity. They wanted to put further pressure on the already demoralised staff.

On 24 August 2006, the entrance gate of the Reserve at Tehla was burnt down by miscreants. They also set ablaze records maintained at the entrance office. The miscreants forced entry into the Reserve using trucks and tractor trolleys. They indulged in large scale arson and looting in front of a handful of forest staff. A large number of cattle were also pushed deep into the forest. All this was done with the backing of local political leaders.

A criminal case was registered against certain bad elements. However, lack of immediate and strong police action encouraged the villagers to exploit the Reserve resources to the maximum. Local leaders, during

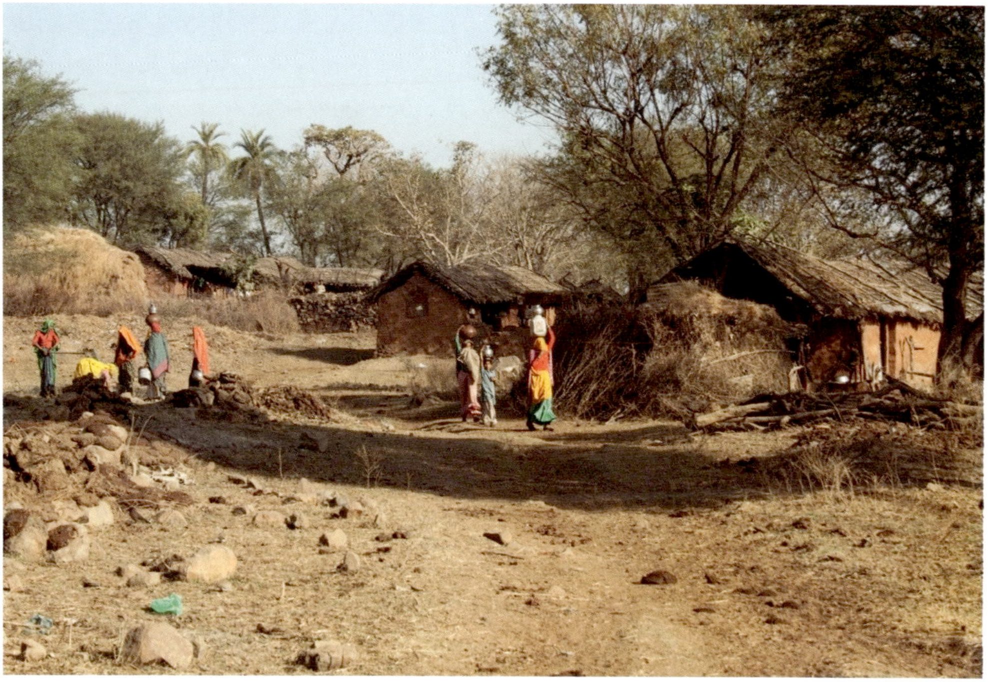

Above:
A village in the core of Sariska

their election campaign assured villagers of free cattle grazing facility in the Reserve as well as unrestricted entry for vehicles through the core area. Such promises naturally arouse the aspirations of villagers and they considered the local leaders their benefactors.

When I joined Sariska again in July 2008, I held several meetings with the villagers to build harmony with them. This helped in controlling this rampant grazing to some extent.

There was tremendous pressure on the Reserve management to go slow on the offenders. Such a reaction from us was bound to encourage other offenders as well as repeat offences. Therefore, we could not, and did not, compromise on this issue at all.

On 25 January 2009, I was on a routine inspection of the Reserve. When I returned to my residence at Sariska headquarters at around 8 in the evening, I found that my house was surrounded by the local MLA and over 200 people. As soon as I reached, I was immediately surrounded. They misbehaved with me in all possible ways. I was kept hostage in my own house for over two hours. The crowd demanded unrestricted grazing and mining rights as well as entry of vehicles to villages located inside the core area of the Reserve. They also demanded schooling, health, and other modern facilities for villagers residing in the core area.

The MLA in his aggressive speech portrayed the forest personnel as villains who were against the welfare of the people. The atmosphere was charged. The aggressive crowd wanted to extract a commitment from me on their demands which I could not accede to immediately.

By then, however, the Reserve staff had also gathered in large numbers and was ready to confront the crowd. I knew fully well that a confrontation would result in serious injuries on both sides. More importantly, it might create permanent hostility between the staff and locals. That, in turn, might result in frequent scuffles between villagers

BELOW: Village buffaloes at a water hole for wild life at Tarunda

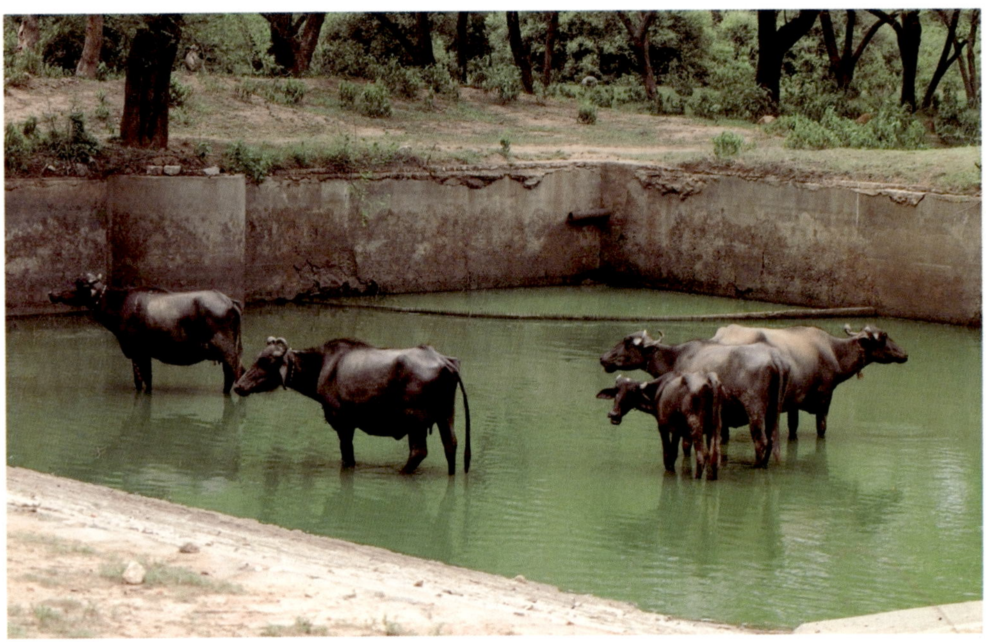

and the Reserve staff. Protection measures already in place would suffer greatly in such a situation. I could not let this happen at any rate. I, therefore, kept my cool and asked the staff to stay calm despite the humiliation I was undergoing at the hands of the crowd. The situation was tense till the Deputy Superintend of Police (DSP) from Alwar reached the spot.

This was taken as a terrible setback to our round-the-clock hard work in the face of high risks. The reserve staff got truly agitated and decided to go on strike the same night demanding the arrest of the MLA. I held several meetings with them and at last succeeded in convincing them that by not reporting to duty they are only assisting the miscreants.

The Superintendent of Police (SP), Alwar, played a crucial role in settling the dispute to some extent. He managed to convince the MLA not to intervene in the Reserve administration in future. This could be considered as a success for me. But the friction generated with the villagers could not be assuaged immediately.

BELOW: Siliberi stream, the life line for wild life of this area

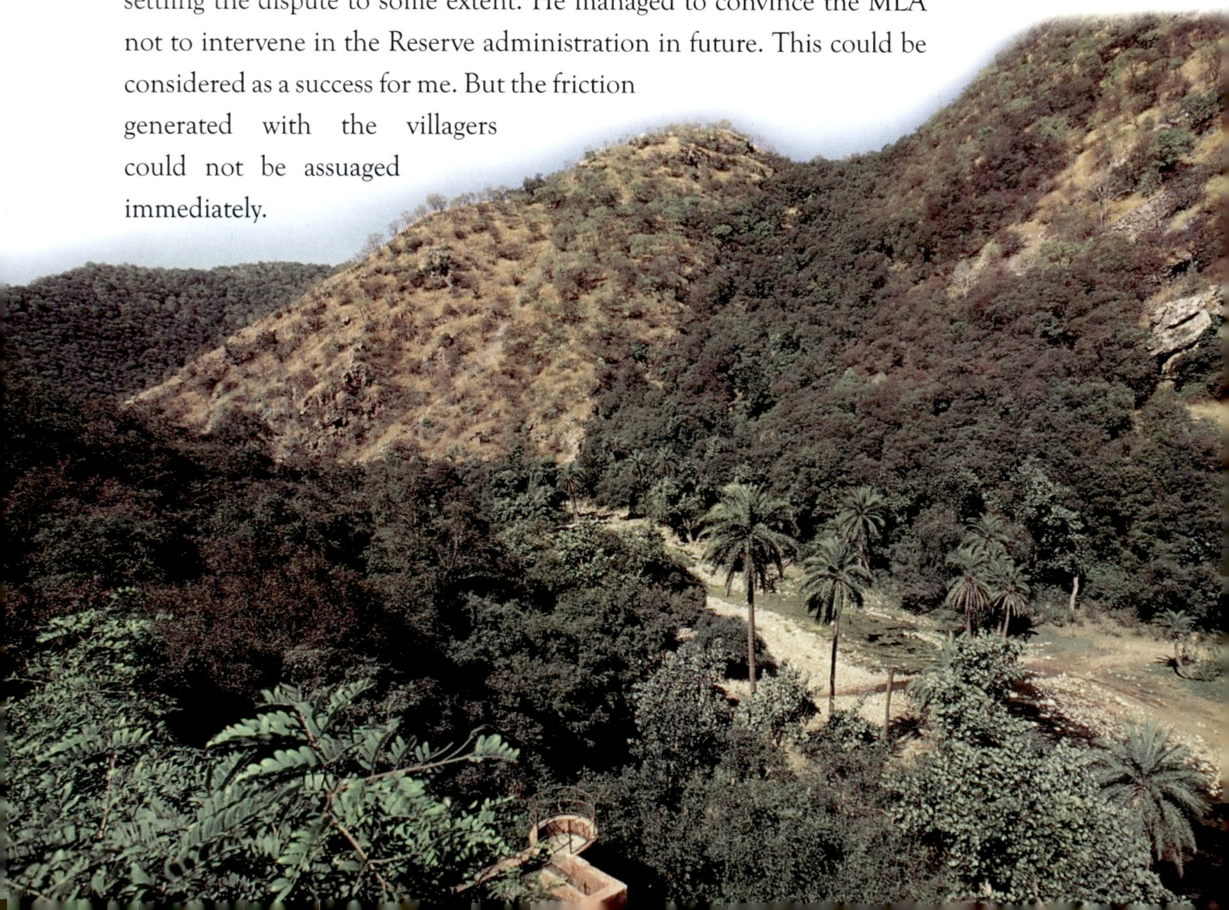

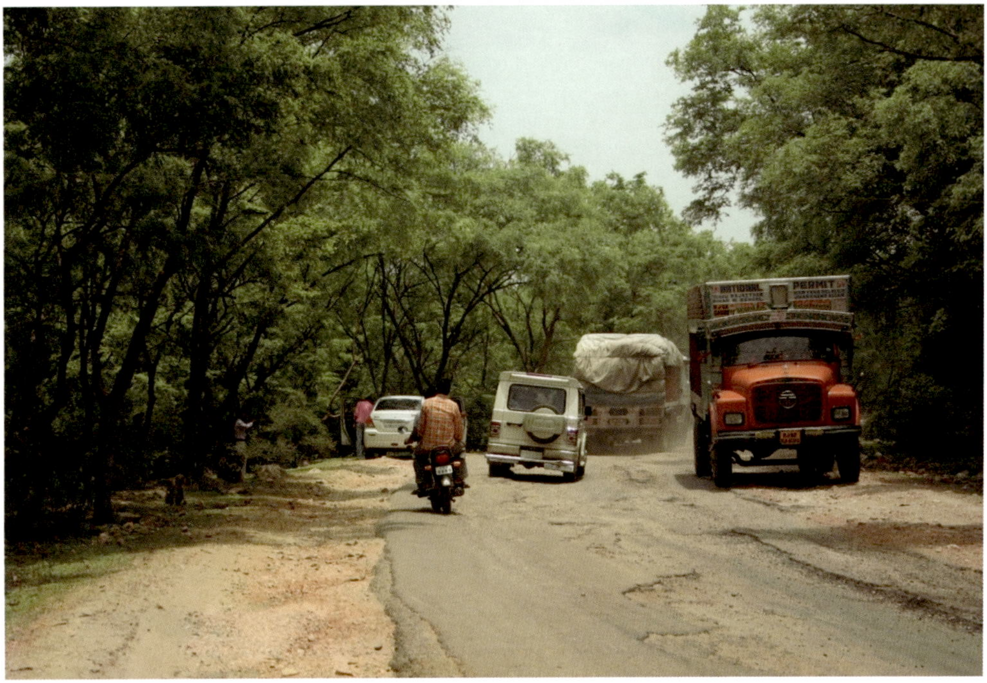

Above: State Highway number 13, passing through the core of Sariska

There was yet another incident of political interference in August 2009.

In pursuance of the Supreme Court's Order issued a few days earlier, it was decided to divert heavy traffic along Kushal Garh-Sariska-Thanagazi stretch on state highway number 13 to Kushal Garh-Talvriksh-Narayanpur-Ghata Bandrol route. With the help of police, barricades were erected at Kushal Garh and Ghata Bandrol crossings and the traffic was diverted smoothly.

The local MP (Member of Parliament) then led an agitation against the diversion of heavy traffic from the National Park. Some agitators pelted stones at some government vehicles at Kushal Garh barrier. Police acted swiftly and arrested the hooligans and registered a case against them. The situation was peaceful thereafter and traffic diversion was effected smoothly for a week. As a result, the 14-km stretch of core area of the Reserve was silent without heavy traffic disturbing the tranquility of the forest. But, alas, this silence was short lived!

On 6 September, the MP addressed public meetings at Tehla and Thanagazi barely a few kilometres from the headquarters of Project Tiger at Sariska. More than ten thousand people attended the meeting at Thanagazi.

In his power packed speech, the MP promised the people not only to reverse the traffic diversion, but also to get them right of free grazing within the Reserve area. This was shocking as the MP had been made aware of the provisions of the law on various issues earlier in the day in a meeting with the CWLW and the management of the Reserve.

Under the leadership of the MP, a crowd broke the barricades in a sudden move. Thus, our entire effort and that of the law enforcing agencies became a waste and the traffic started flowing as before. The MP did not stop here. Intoxicated by his success he went on to pressurise the state government to accept several of his other demands harmful to the Reserve. These demands were fortunately not granted by the government. But the resumption of heavy traffic, especially trucks, through the heart of the core, had demoralised not only the Reserve personnel but also the top level management of forest department.

It was also sad and painful that the internationally acclaimed wildlife activists who opposed the translocation of tigers from Ranthambhore to Sariska chose not to support the Reserve management on important issues such as this.

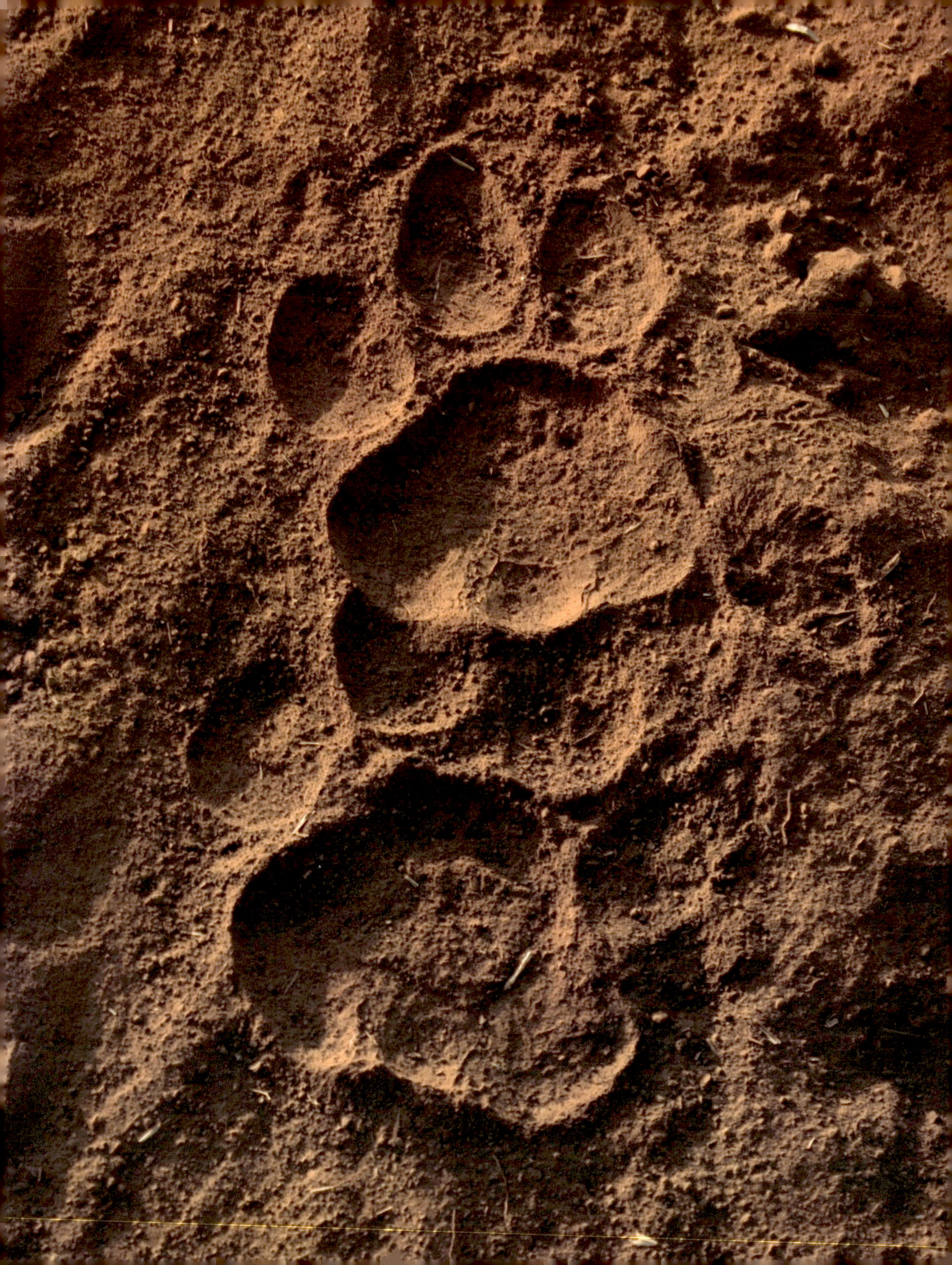

2

DEBACLE IN SARISKA

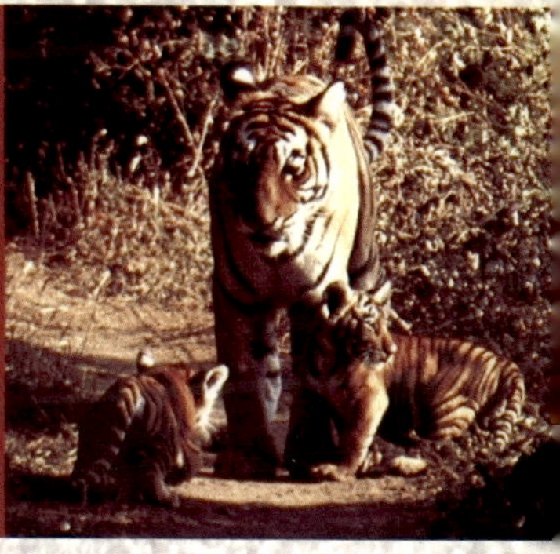

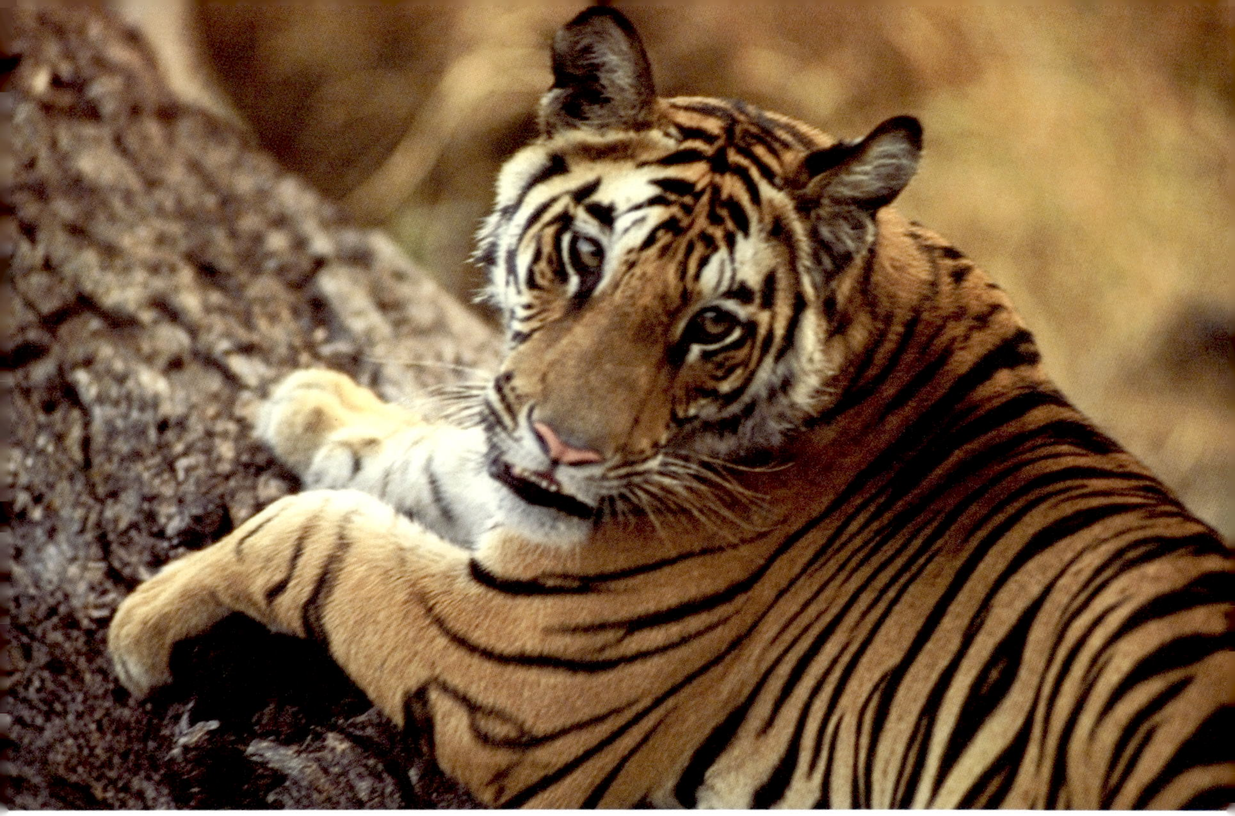

TRAGEDY IN SARISKA

One could never imagine such a black period when Sariska, the land of saints like Raja Bhrartrahari, and jewel of the Aravallis, would lose its treasure, the tiger. The complete wipe out of the majestic animal from Sariska in 2004 sent shock waves throughout the nation.

While serving as Field Director at Sariska during 1991–96 and later, too, I felt and enjoyed the presence of tigers all over Sariska. So it was almost impossible for me to imagine the place without its pride! Total criminal negligence by the Reserve management could only have been responsible for this disaster which was indeed a national shame.

Investigation into the disaster revealed that tiger poaching had been going on for quite some time. Instead of taking steps to prevent poaching the Reserve management was busy hushing up the incident! This in turn encouraged the poachers and resulted in total wipeout of the tiger population in Sariska.

It was Sanjay Kashyap from Delhi who bought the matter in the open. In December 2004 after a Sariska visit he informed World Wide Fund for India and the Indian Express about zero presence of tigers in Sariska Reserve. It was then that the governments started acting on the information.

It was further revealed that tiger sighting in Sariska had reduced considerably by 2003. By 2004–05 there was hardly any tiger sighting in the park. In February 2005, the Rajasthan Government accepted that there were very few tigers left in Sariska Tiger Reserve.

FACING PAGE: Posing for a photo! *(Photo by Dinesh Durrani)*

In a swift response to the crisis, especially in the three most prominent conservation areas of Sariska, Ranthambhore, and Keoladeo National Park, Bharatpur, the Chief Minister constituted a State Empowered Committee (SEC) on forest and wild life management in February 2005 under the chairmanship of V.P. Singh, Member of Parliament and noted conservationist.

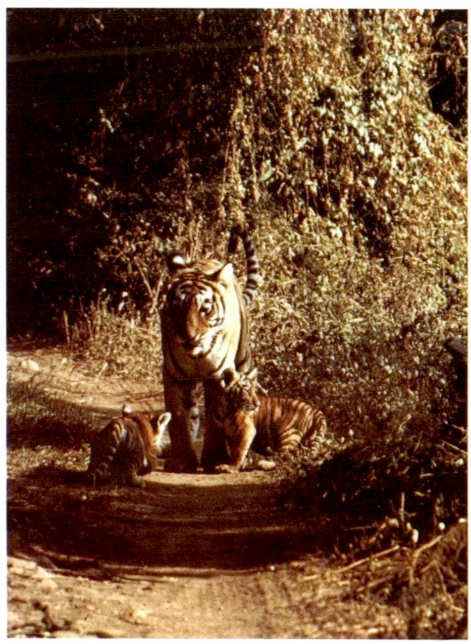

BELOW: Tigress with cubs in Kala Kua area in 1992

In March, the Wildlife Institute of India surveyed the entire stretch of 882 sq. km and confirmed that there was no evidence of the presence of tiger in Sariska Tiger Reserve.

In May the same year, the Minister for Environment and Forests, Namo Narain Meena, informed the Parliament that Sariska does not have even a single tiger due to extensive poaching. This official confirmation generated a major uproar in the

RIGHT: Tigers mating (*Photo by K.L. Saini*)

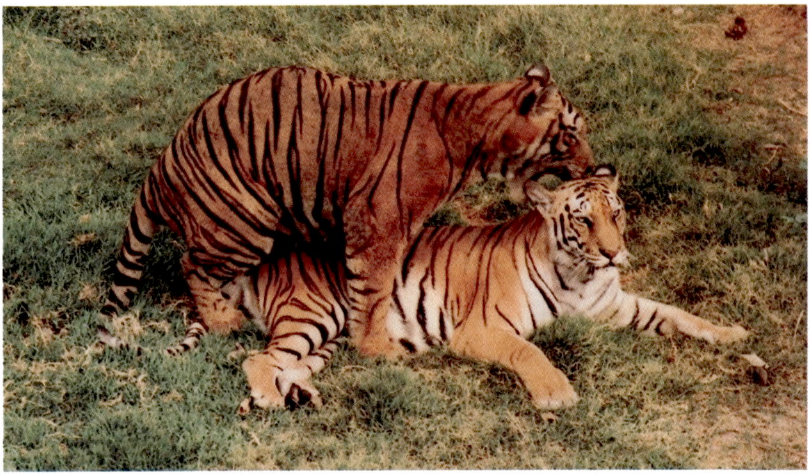

wildlife conservation community around the world. The reverberations of this shock were experienced even in the Prime Minister's Office. The Prime Minister asked the Rajasthan Chief Minister to look into the matter immediately.

The SEC focused on the failure of the management at Sariska and tried to fix accountability. More importantly, it decided to develop a shared vision and an action plan for the future. The aim was to secure continued presence of the tiger and its healthy habitat at Sariska.

The Chief Minister also initiated action for an enquiry into the disappearance of tigers from Sariska Tiger Reserve by a committee headed by Mr R.N. Mehrotra, a senior forest officer. The Mehrotra Committee submitted its findings to the government in March 2005. The report stated thus:

> There was a regular decline in the tiger evidences since June 2004 which ultimately reduced to nil in November / December 2004. This establishes the fact that the decline in the number of tigers started in 2003 which correlates with the timings of the poaching as revealed by poachers caught in 2005.
>
> On the basis of the action taken by officers of the Reserve in March

2005, statements of the accused after their arrest, inspections made by this author and the complaints received in the office of the Field Director, it can be concluded that though tiger poaching had been going on for past many years, its intensity increased sharply after May 2004.

No evidence is found to indicate that any effort was done to find out the reasons for the decline in the tiger population between May 2003 and May 2004. This establishes the failure of the management in performing its duties.

On 27 August 2004, Mr Mohar Singh, resident of Pratap Garh, district Alwar, wrote a letter to the Field Director which was received on 2 September 2004. In this letter were given the names and other details of the poachers. The top management of the park was supposed to take immediate action on the letter but after a lapse of more than a month on 15 October 2004 the Field Director sent this complaint to Range Forest Officer Tehla for necessary action and feedback on the same. The Officer reported after four months, on 27 February 2005, indicating no serious investigation or action was taken by him.

It is worth mentioning that many persons whose names appear in this complaint were later arrested by the Reserve management in tiger poaching cases in March 2005. The decline in tiger number could have been checked had immediate action been taken on this complaint. This case clearly indicates the shortcomings of the management in the discharge of its duties.

An accused, Balya Bawaria alias Ram Chandar, son of Nadia, has confessed in his statement on 8 March 2005 that he along with his brother Kalya, Hanuman Bawaria and Phulya entered the Reserve from Narayani Mata side. They reached Parashar ji, Aunkari earthen pond via plateau at 2.30 in the afternoon that day. Around 4.00 pm, above the Kala Kund *nalah* (on earthen road of Ghanka plateau), they put up one trap after digging a pit and a second trap was fitted at about 1.5 km distance on the earthen road to Kalighati. Around 4.00 am, a tiger trapped in the second trap was killed by them with a gun and the dead body dragged into the bushes some 20 steps away, where it was skinned. Ghanka chowki is located only 1.5 km from this place of incidence!

Four poachers could enter the Reserve in broad daylight with guns passing through various beats / *nakas* and reach Ghanka beat where they stayed for more than 12 hours on the plateau and water point of Kala Kund. Again passing through above beats / nakas in broad daylight, along with the tiger skin, they return back! After 15–20 days, two poachers come back and take away the carcass of the tiger as well! The fact that the staff posted on the concerned beats / *nakas* does not take notice of anything during this entire period shows the neglect of duties at their end.

It is evident from Haripura and Ghanka tiger poaching cases of 2004 that right from the beat in-charge to the Field Director, no officer / employee showed any interest in performing their duties with regard to protection of tigers. They showed carelessness and tigers were killed in broad daylight in the core area while they were posted there. They did not conduct proper patrolling and local investigations which is why poachers openly placed traps for tigers and shot and skinned them and even took away the carcass later.

REVIEW BY THE PRIME MINISTER

Central Bureau of Investigation (CBI) also got into the act and, along with experts from WII, started its enquiry into the tiger crisis in Sariska. Simultaneously the prime minister convened a meeting of the National Board for Wildlife in India to review the conservation efforts in the country. The prime minister also constituted a high level Tiger Task Force (TTF) to review the tiger conservation programme in the country with Ms Sunita Narain, a noted environmentalist, as its chairperson.

The prime minister convened a meeting of the chief wildlife wardens of the states and the field directors of the tiger reserves at Ranthambhore in May 2005 and discussed the problems faced by them in the field. He promised several things including funds for resettling the villagers from

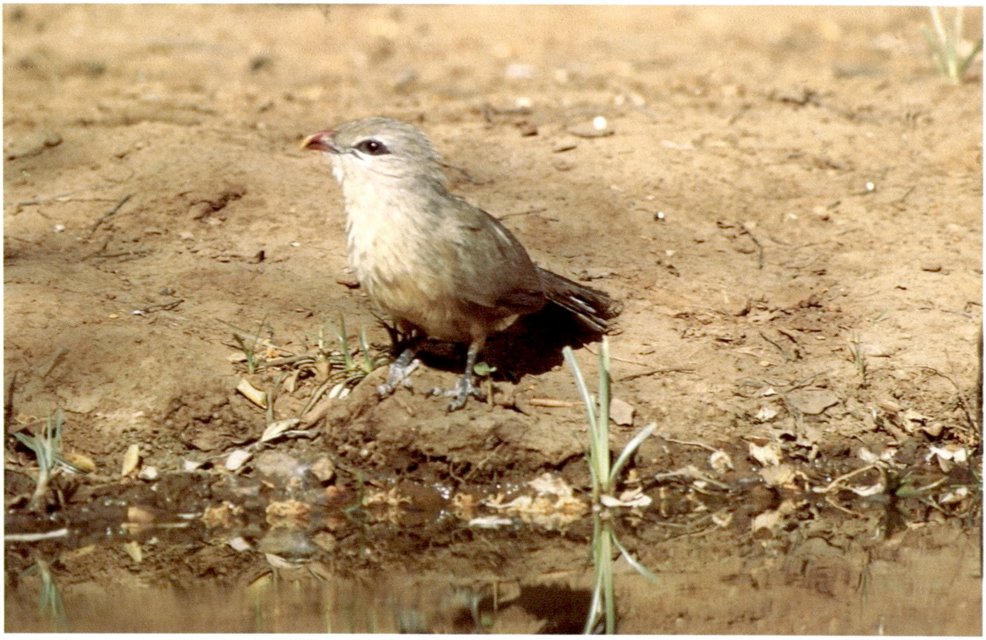

ABOVE:
Sirkeer Cookoo in Naya Pani area of Sariska

protected areas. The main focus of this meeting, however, was on making tiger reserves inaccessible to poachers.

RECOMMENDATIONS OF THE TIGER TASK FORCE

The TTF made observations and recommendations in respect of all the tiger reserves in the country in order to ensure that no repetition of the Sariska episode takes place anywhere.

For Sariska, it recommended improvements in the internal management of the Reserve and fixing of accountability for the debacle. It emphasised on the shifting of some villages from the core area but with utmost care. It showed its deep concern about the heavy vehicular traffic passing through the heart of the Reserve, especially the pilgrimage traffic between Sariska-Tehla and Sariska-Pandupole.

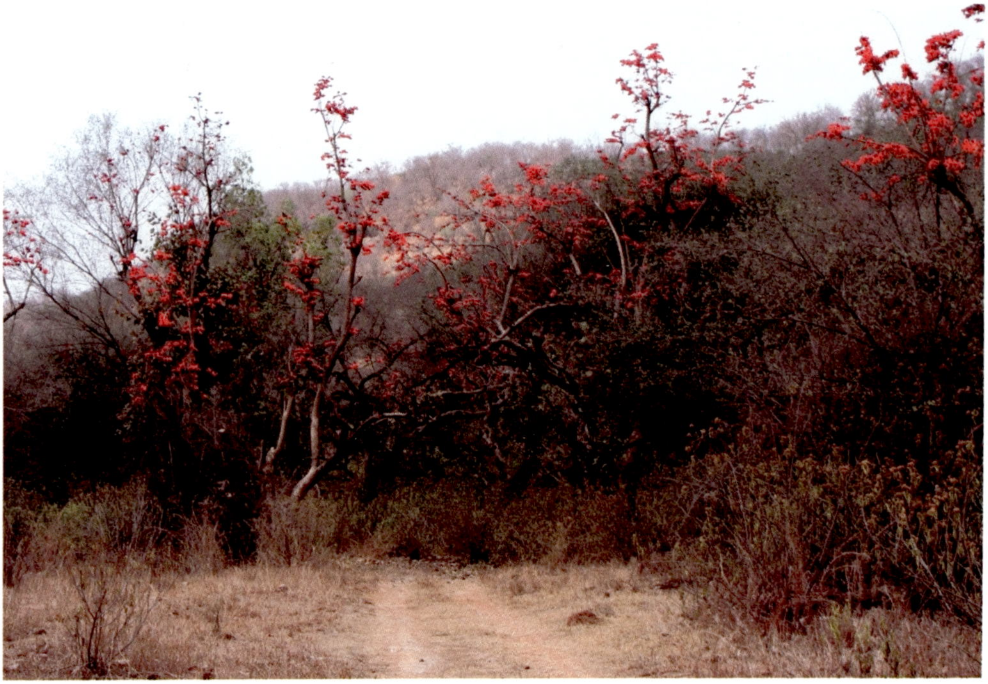

ABOVE: Colourful Sariska

On re-introduction of tiger into Sariska, the Task Force observed,

> ...Sariska is an important reserve supporting the largest intact habitat of the tiger in the Aravalli ecosystem. The condition of the habitat is good and, therefore, needs to be protected. The Reserve is also the catchment for innumerable streams in this otherwise dry region. ... urgent steps need to be taken to restore the park and to rehabilitate tigers in the reserve....

Excerpts from SEC Report:

> The sanctum-sanctorum of the reserve needs to be kept free from all kinds of disturbances. For this purpose, it is necessary to rehabilitate villages located inside Core I of Sariska Tiger Reserve with immediate effect.

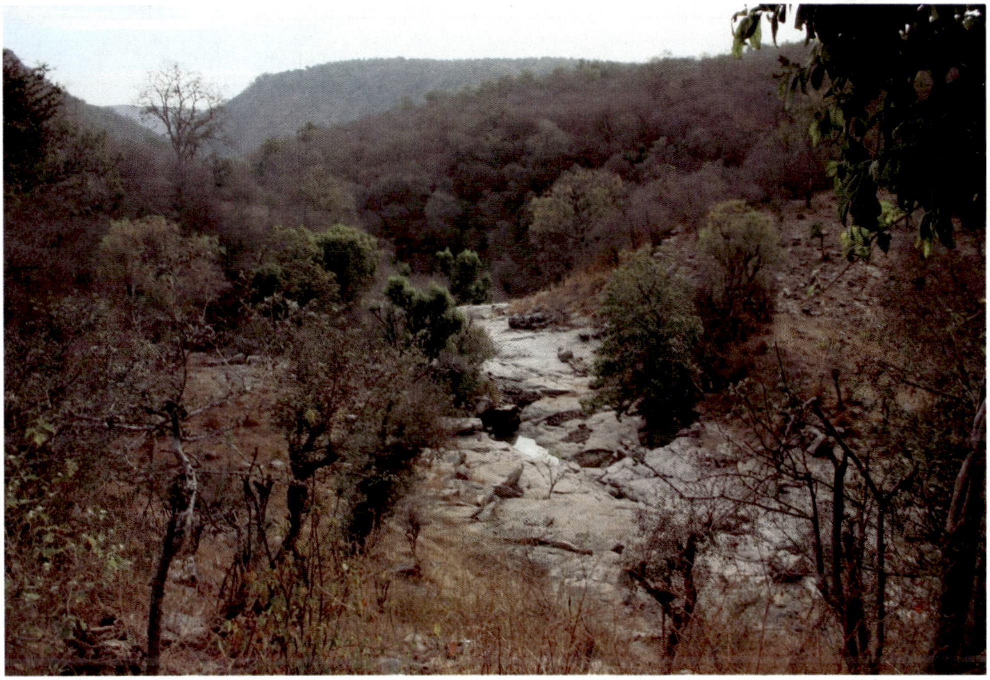

ABOVE:
Rotkyala area of Sariska

> The tiger population to be re-introduced needs to be identified from the identical/similar habitats. The most suitable tiger reserves are Ranthambhore and Kanha (MP) and it would be advisable to have a mix of population from these reserves. Considering the stress conditions and threats to the tiger habitats it is necessary to regularly exchange animals among these reserves in future.

The Committee also recommended the diversion of traffic on state highway number 13 between Khushalgarh and Thana Ghazi to Kushal Garh-Talvriksh-Narainpur-Ghata Bandrol route. The committee expressed its serious concern about the ever-growing vehicular traffic of pilgrims to Pandupole temple located at the heart of the core area.

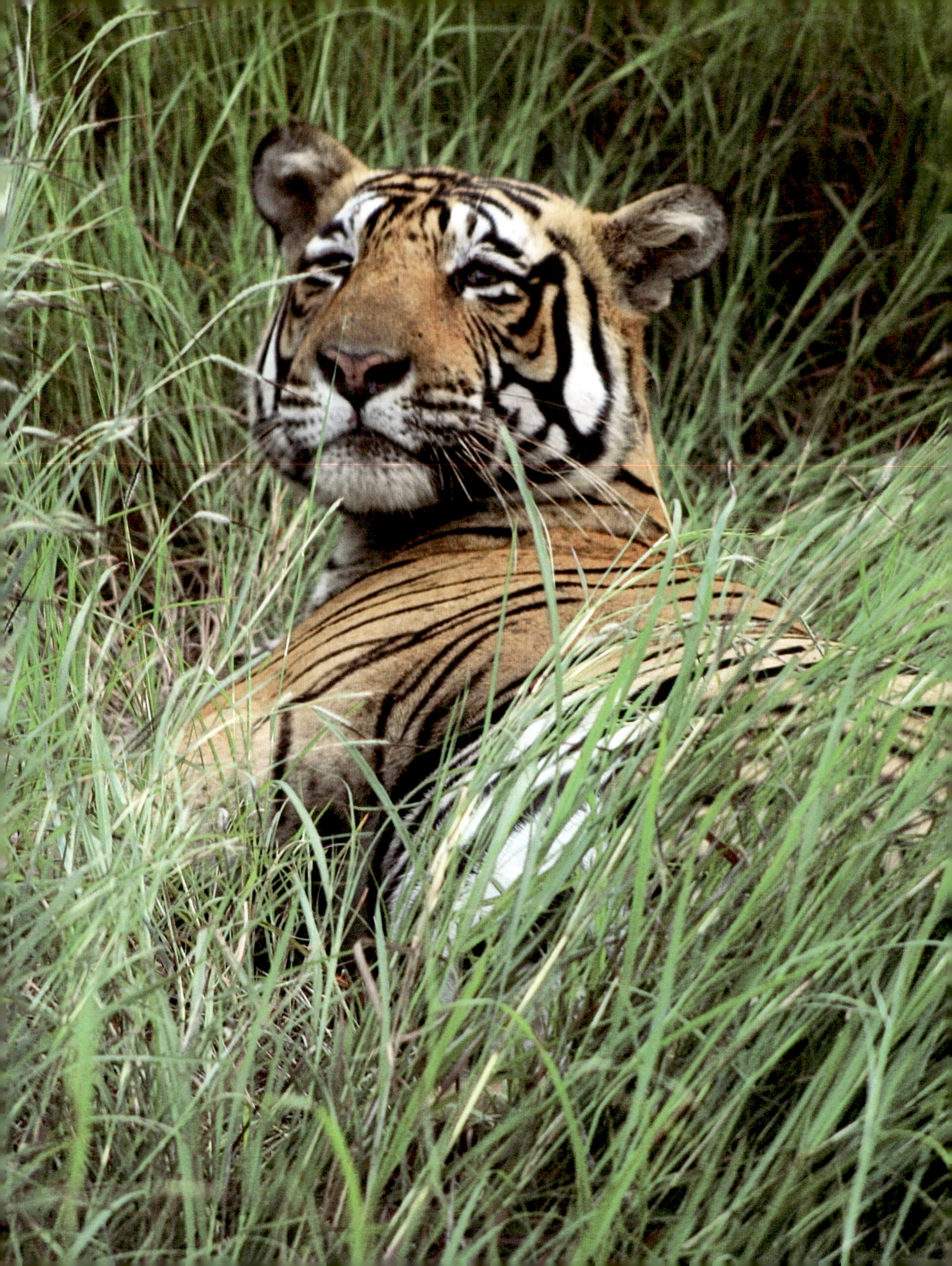

3

REBUILDING SARISKA

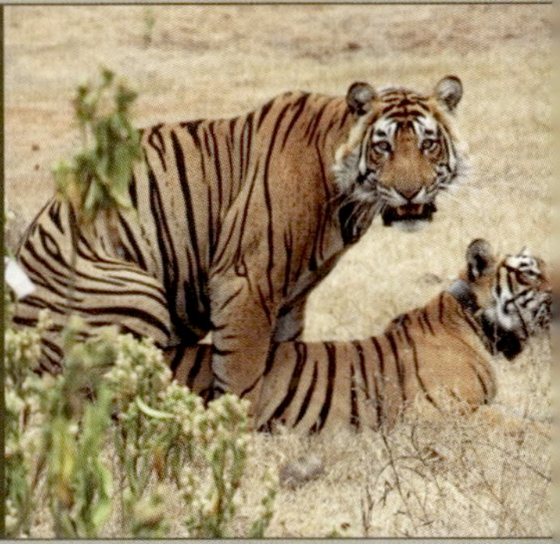

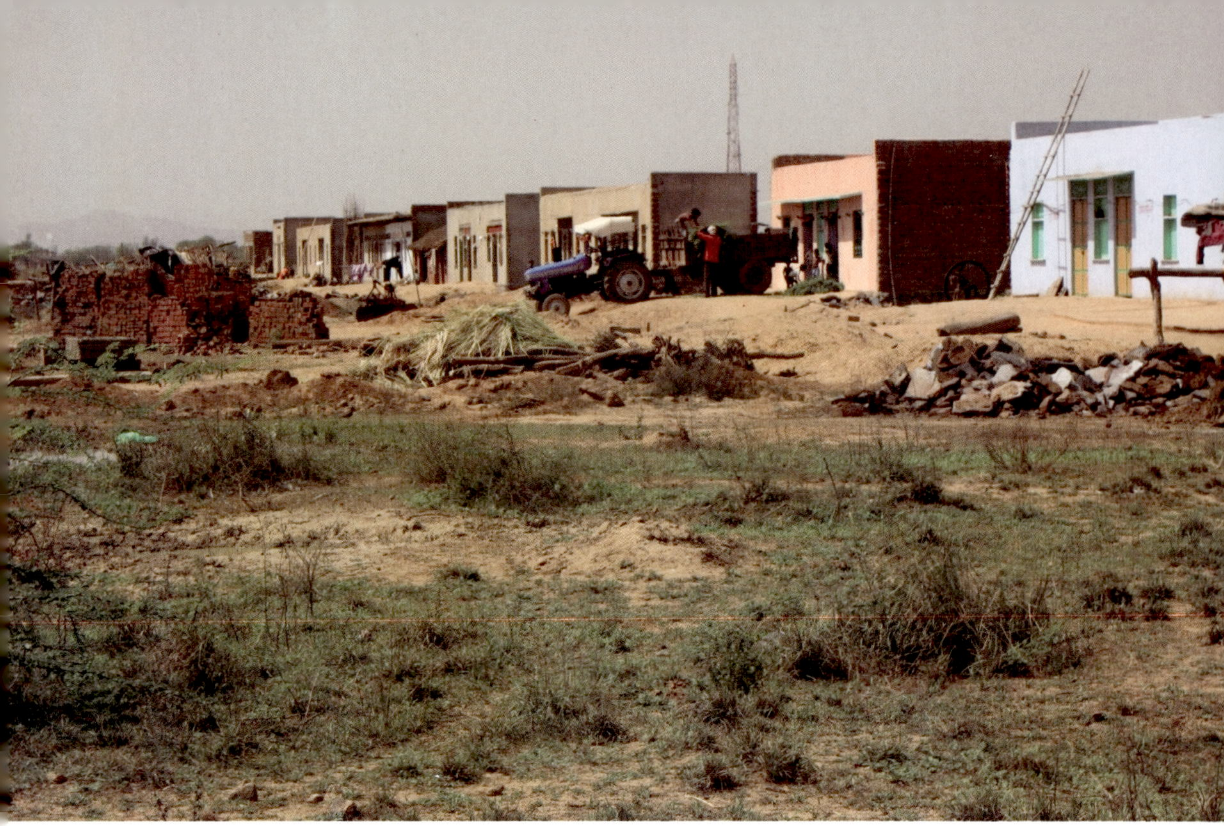

REBUILDING SARISKA

PROTECTION AND HABITAT

The revival of Sariska started with the formation of the SEC headed by V.P. Singh at the state level and TTF headed by Ms Sunita Narain at the Central level. Reports of both these committees discussed at length the problems persisting in the Reserve and stressed upon initiation of immediate steps to address those. As a follow up, the posts of field staff lying vacant for many years were promptly filled.

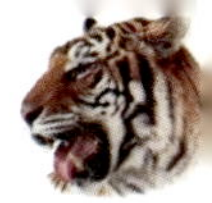

The office of the Sariska field director was shifted to Alwar in order to give a free hand to the deputy director, who was responsible for protection of the Reserve. The field director was specifically entrusted with the work of shifting the villages from the core area of Sariska. Protection measures were strengthened. Night patrolling was introduced in the entire Reserve, particularly on poaching-prone jungle tracks. Village Bhagani located on the southern side of the core of the Reserve with 21 families was successfully rehabilitated outside the Reserve, at Bardod Rundh, close to the township of Bahrod on Delhi–Jaipur Highway (NH 8).

The successful rehabilitation of village Bhagani convinced people in other villages inside the Reserve to agree to move out of the Reserve. Village Kankawadi with about 170 families and village Umri with about 80 families were the next in the plan to be rehabilitated.

The other villages to be shifted from the core area on a priority basis were Rotkyala, Sukola, Kraska, Lilunda, Haripura, Dabli, and Reka Mala.

The State Empowered Committee succeeded in getting a landmark decision from the Supreme Court to reduce vehicular traffic through the National Park area.

My efforts to regulate traffic as per the Supreme Court order were sabotaged by local politicians. However, sooner rather than later, the Supreme Court order is bound to be implemented.

FACING PAGE: Bhagani and Kankawadi villages relocated at Bardod Rundh

BELOW LEFT: Villagers' meet at Bardod Rundh

BELOW: Kankawadi villagers felicitating the author at the time of eviction

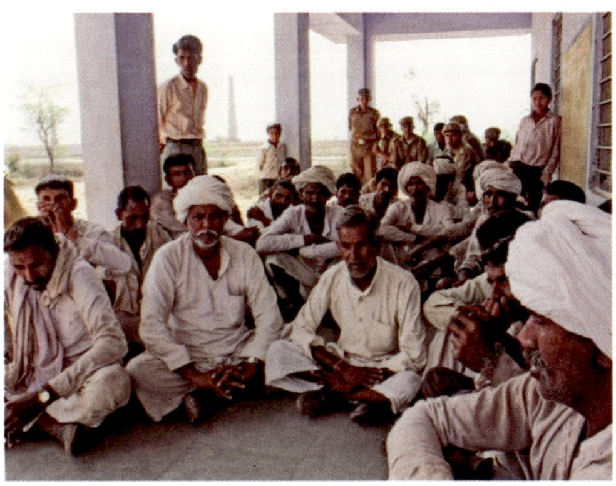

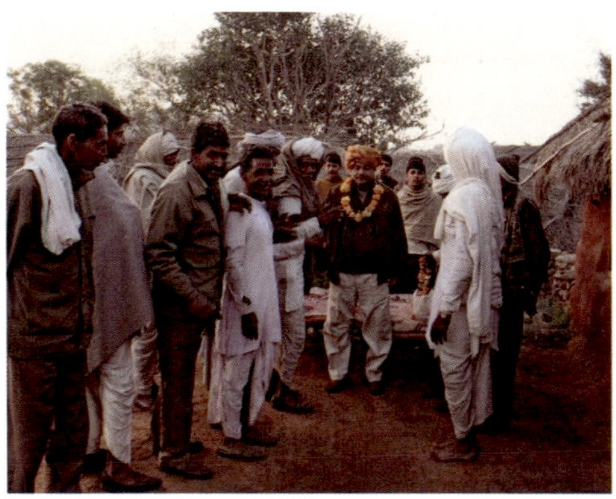

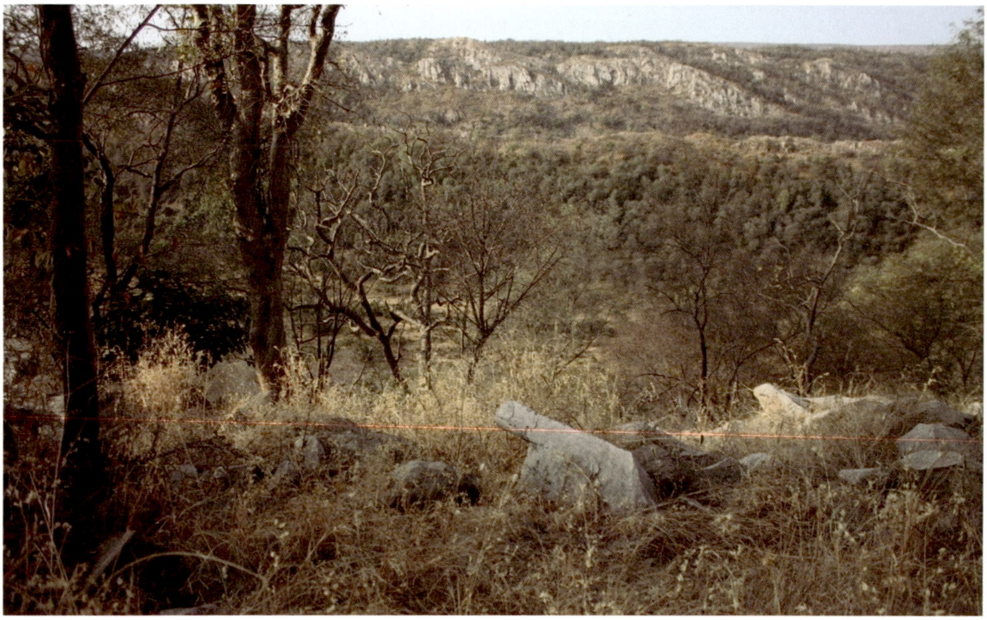

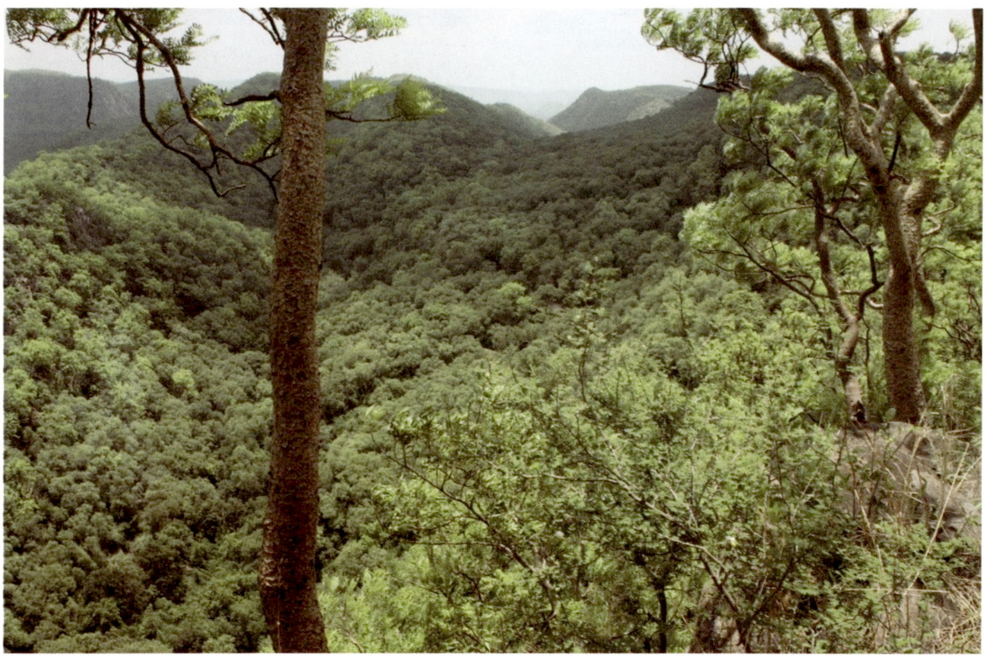

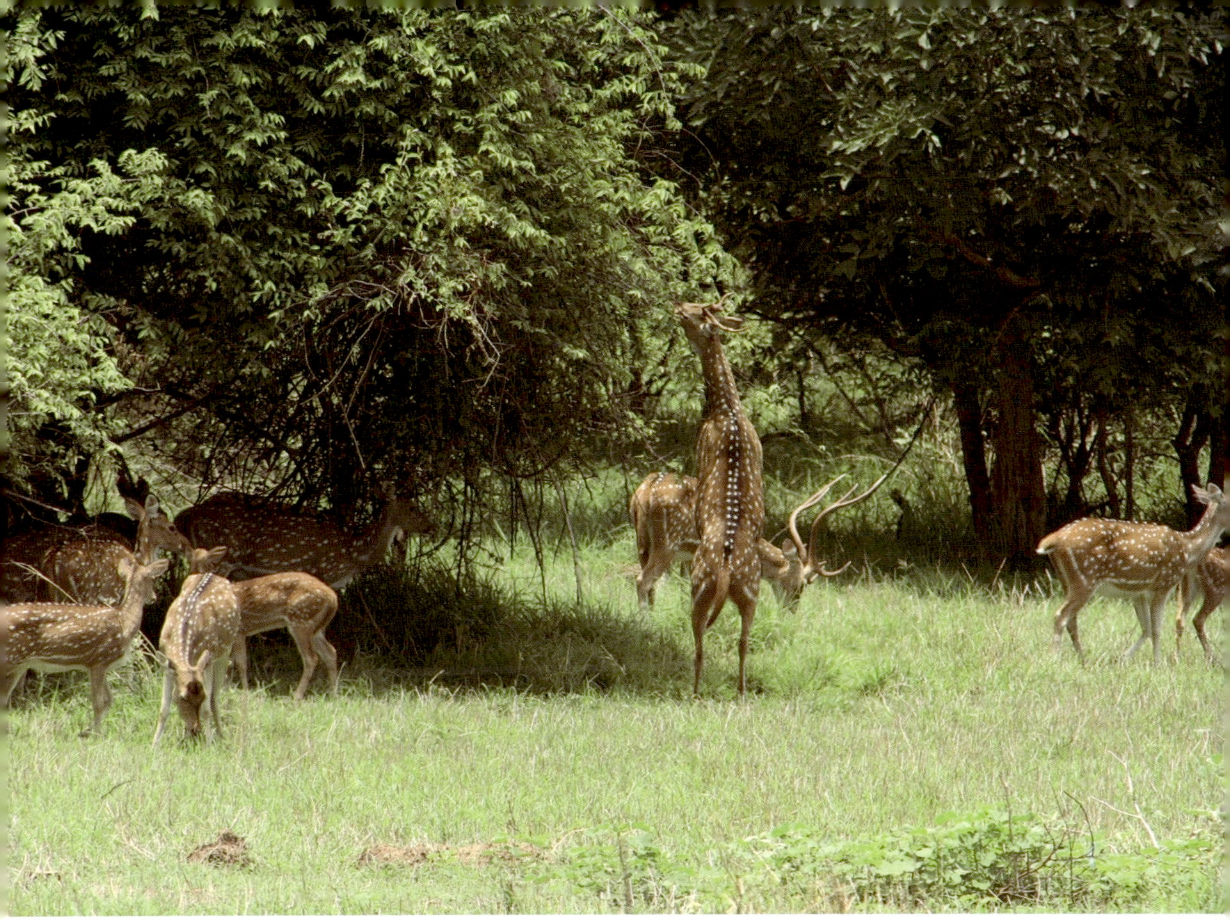

The concerned roads have since been handed over by the Public Works Department to the Reserve authorities. This has put a halt on maintenance of these roads before full compliance of the court orders. As a result, by 2012 these roads had totally worn out causing great difficulty to local transport as well. Wildlife tourism too suffered a lot. Local people led by politicians organised agitations which once again adversely affected their relations with the Reserve management. Such hostility is very unhealthy for the protection measures in the Reserve. One hopes that the government will take up this issue seriously and find a permanent solution in the interest of the people and the Reserve.

In order to regulate the pilgrim traffic on state highway number 29A passing through the core area of the Reserve, it is proposed to start a

FACING PAGE ABOVE: View of Kankwadi valley from Sunny Point

FACING PAGE BELOW: View from Mehrotra Point

ABOVE: Bana Plateau in 2009

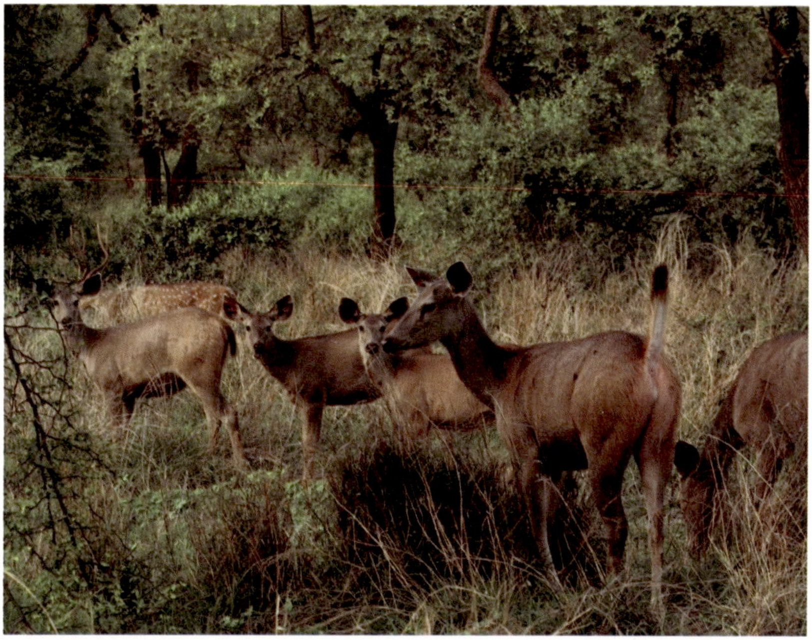

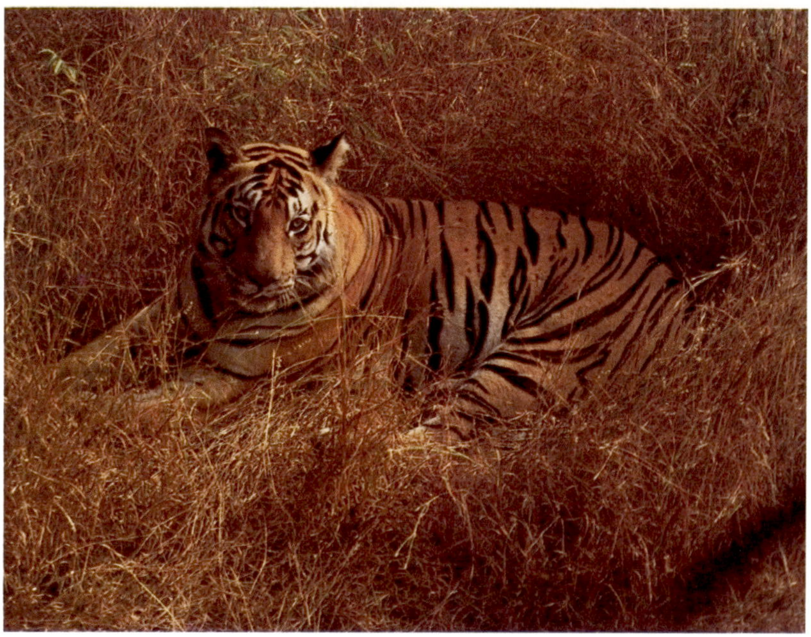

ABOVE:
Bana Plateau
in 2009

RIGHT:
Sunbathing
after a feast!

government-operated conducted bus service shortly as per the decision taken in a meeting under the chairmanship of the Additional Chief Secretary of Rajasthan.

In order to strengthen the human resource capacity of the Reserve, 150 posts were created for ex-army personnel on annual contract basis. Unfortunately, ex-army personnel do not find enough charm in this job owing to the tough working conditions. It may be worth mentioning that many of these recruits did not join and many others ran away after a few days' service. As a result, in spite of the best possible efforts, only about 50 posts could be filled. Recruitment of adequate number of field staff and officers for the Reserve, therefore, should be undertaken immediately.

When I rejoined Sariska in July 2008, I discovered that though some new protection posts (*chowkies*) had been created, many remote and poaching-prone areas remained unattended. The high hill plateau about 20 km long and 1 to 2 km wide stretching between Kalighati and Ghar–Rajore was one of the most vulnerable areas for poaching. As per the report of the Mehrotra Committee three tigers were poached on this plateau. According to the management, the fair weather road running from one end to the other through the centre of this plateau is the major cause for this.

BELOW: Patrolling tracks, vantage points and chowkies between Kalighati and Rajore

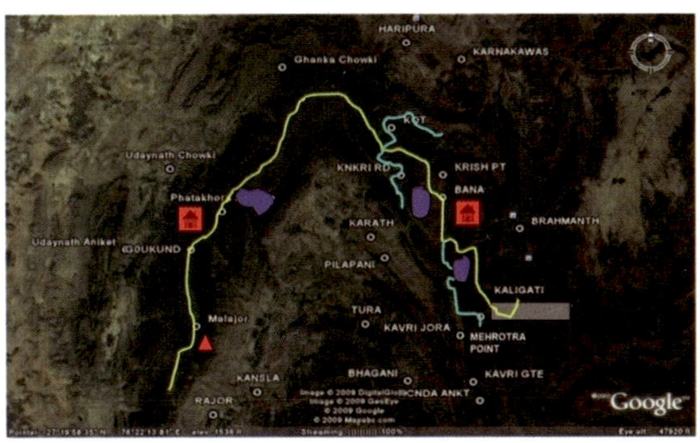

I accorded the highest priority to protection and habitat development of this important but secluded part of the Reserve. The bumpy track was repaired in order to make travel easier and faster. This helped in frequent patrolling of the plateau in a vehicle. In order to enable regular patrolling in larger areas I created an additional track for jeep on top of the plateau and parallel to the Kabri

Gate–Kankwadi road. One section of it terminates over Kabri Gate while the other at a vantage point over Kalighati–Tehla road overlooking a vast expanse of the best core area of this Reserve. The inspiration of Mr R.N. Mehrotra, Chief Wildlife Warden played a key role in the creation of this point. Therefore this spot was dedicated to him by naming it as 'Mehrotra Point'.

Four more vantage points were created on this track for patrol guards to keep a strict vigil over any illicit activity or fire over a vast area. These vantage points, located at high points, also helped in excellent wireless and mobile phone connectivity. One vantage point overlooking Maujnath (northern side) and another overlooking Tarunda were also created in order to keep a strict vigil on the northern side of the plateau.

Keeping in mind the tough working conditions of Sariska, I

BELOW: View of Maujnath Kutia from Nemi Point

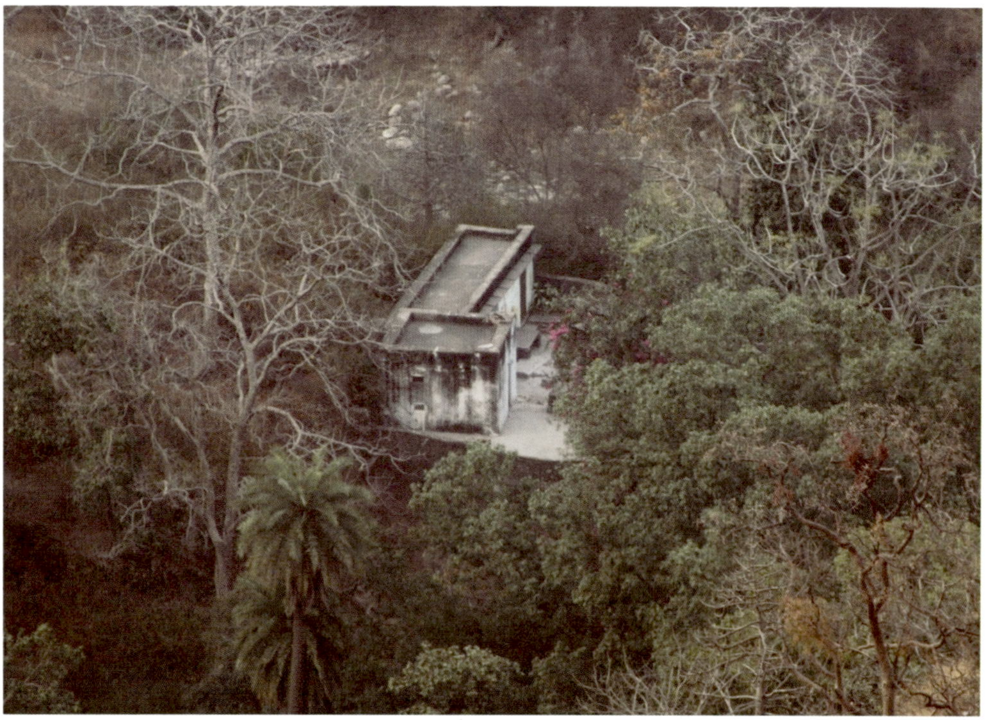

rewarded some outstanding staff personnel by naming some places after them. One vantage point was named R.P. Point, after Ram Prasad who served for a long time with high dedication as a Forester at Kalighati check post. The point overlooking Maujnath was named Nemi Point after Nemi Chand Meena, the first Forest Guard of the newly created Bana Chowki. He worked in a temporary Chowki in a very isolated place. The vantage point overlooking Tarunda gives a clear view of the entire forest valley up to Sariska Palace, residence of the director of the Reserve and Karna ka Bas Lake, etc. It was named Vidhyadhar Point after a very hard working and sincere Range Officer, Vidhyadhar, without whose active participation these points could not have been created and water brought to this plateau for staff and wildlife. I could not resist the temptation of naming a point overlooking Kankwadi Fort from this new track which terminates at Kabri Gate as Sunny Point, after my nick name used by my beloved wife. (Sadly, these names were later removed from these vantage points.)

Another jeep-worthy approach road was constructed to connect this central spine road to Kankwadi area.

Protection posts were to be constructed at the earliest at Bana, Phatyakhora, and Mala Johadka, three strategic locations on the plateau. Due to paucity of funds masonry work could not be taken up immediately. Initially, therefore, these chowkies were made of mud, bamboo, grasses, and brushwood. They were gradually converted to masonry structures as and when funds became available.

It was very difficult to get the budget for masonry chowkies sanctioned from National Tiger Conservation Authority (NTCA). They were scared of possible criticism by powerful conservationists. This is a very unfortunate situation. Conservationists must be practical as far as field matters are concerned. Field situation is not at all rosy as it may seem to a tourist who stays in five star hotels and visits the Reserve for a few hours in the safety and comfort of a jeep. In tiger country or in any wilderness, if we wish to ensure the presence of field staff, we must provide them with at least minimum facilities like water for basic needs including drinking, and shelter in which one can sleep without fear of being attacked by wild animals. Tents or grass-thatched shelters do not serve this purpose. Thefts are common in such hutments in fields when the staff is out on patrol duty.

These newly created protection posts were located in fairly tough areas; so no one was willing to work there. A unique formula was, therefore, devised of posting four personnel at each of these posts, in place of just one, comprising a Forest Guard, a Work-charge Employee, a Home Guard, and an ex-Army personnel. One person from the neighbouring villages was also posted here for local help. Later, the facility of the masonry chowkies also motivated the staff to work here.

This plateau was completely devoid of water. The closest source of water was located down the hill far from the spot. It was a challenge to supply safe drinking water to men posted at these remote areas. Initially, water used to be transported on donkeys. It was, however, an arduous task. Due to acute financial constraints only a very limited quantity of water could be provided regularly which was hardly sufficient for the staff living at these chowkies. Due to this problem it was not possible to depute extra force to these posts even during emergencies.

It was clear that this arrangement could not last long and adequate facility for water needs to be created. To begin with, plastic drums were installed and water was transported on a regular basis to Bana chowki in a multi-utility van. Meantime, a detailed plan was prepared for a permanent solution to the problem. It was proposed to install pipelines to transport water to Bana from Kalighati. It was an ambitious plan. Bana is situated on the plateau at a height of about 600 ft from the ground. It is about 5 km by road from Kalighati. The plan was to lift water from the Kalighati well using a submersible pump run with the help of a heavy duty generator set. Serious doubts were raised from many quarters on the

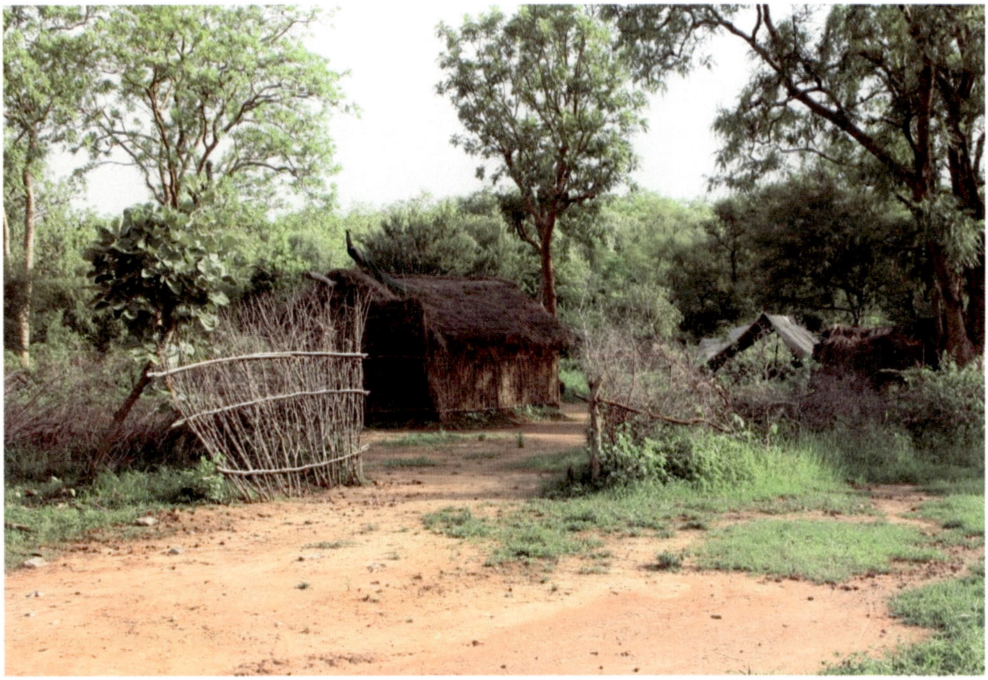

ABOVE: Phatyakhora chowki thatched with grass

success of the plan. I, however, could not abandon the ambitious plan.

A suitable generator set was bought. A steel pipeline was also laid between the Kalighati well and the highest point on the hill near Bana. The submersible pump was hung in the well and the motor switched on. Initially it seemed to be doing well, but soon it succumbed to the heavy work load. Experts were consulted again. Motors of different capacities were tried but all in vain. Many trials were conducted. The Range Officer of the area and the Forester of Kalighati started losing heart. But I was determined to try everything possible to make it a success because the future strategy of protection and development of this important plateau depended on the availability of water in this area.

Ultimately, after consultation with some irrigation experts, a motor with a special design was ordered to be manufactured. But the delivery took a long time. Mr Jairam Ramesh, central Minister for Environment

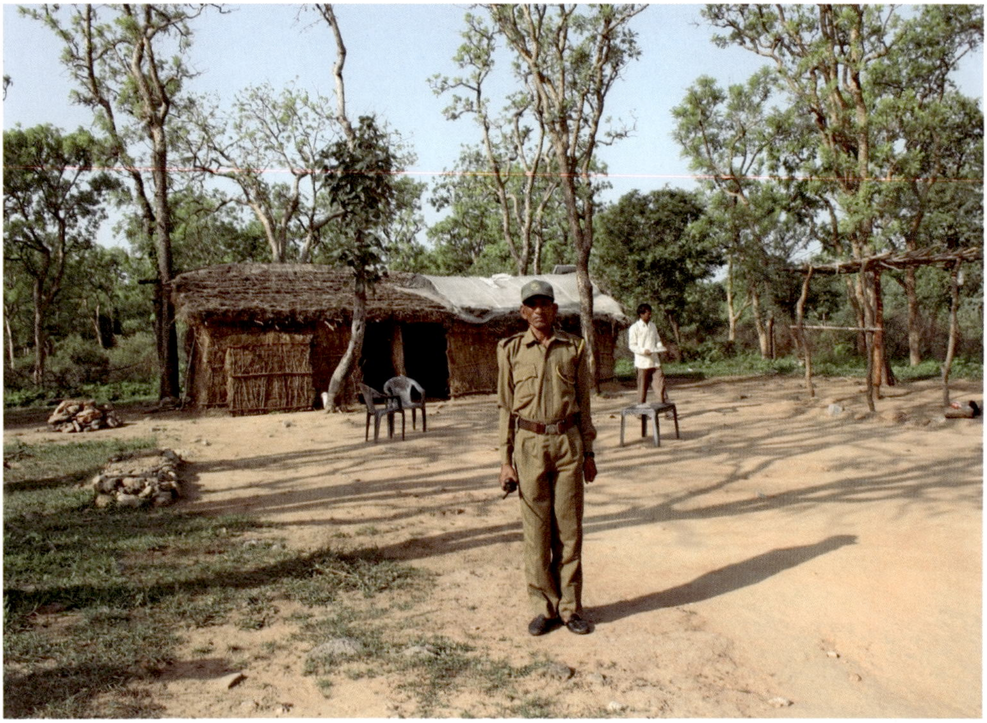

Above: Mala Johadka chowki thatched with grass

and Forests was to visit Sariska to attend a national level Field Directors' Conference in mid-July 2009. I was desperate to show this facility to the minister. Despite regular reminders and constant follow-up, we did not receive the motor in time.

Finally, the machine was delivered in August 2009. This attempt turned out to be a success. We were all jubilant. The day water reached the plateau was one of the most joyous days of my life. I organised a small party for the staff, who had left no stone unturned in helping to fulfil this dream. As anticipated, this 5-km-long pipeline between Kalighati and Bana, was indeed a boon for wild animals and their protectors.

Similar water problem at two other chowkies had to be solved, too. Phatyakhora is situated at about 10 km from Bana, and Mala Johadka, 3 km from Phatyakhora. This problem was solved in March 2010 with the availability of funds. A deep bore well was dug at Ghanaka in the valley. A submersible pump was used to draw water from the well and push it to the top of the Phatyakhora hill. A heavy duty silent generator was purchased and steel pipelines were laid up to Phatyakhora. The experience of Bana water supply helped us here. Buddha, the efficient technician of the Reserve, took little time in bringing water to Phatyakhora.

On 29 March 2010 I reached Phatyakhora. I saw water gushing out of the steel pipe to the recently dug water hole. I could not hold back my tears. How could one believe seeing water supply in such quantity at a remote place like Phatyakhora? The effect was so mesmerising that, forgetting all tenets of discipline, one of the home guards posted there started bathing semi-nude in the tank. What a sight it was to see hundreds of Red Vented Bulbuls bathing in the water pool! This was, of course, a great moment for everybody. I realised history had been created in the management of this Reserve.

Taking advantage of the gravitational force, it was possible to draw

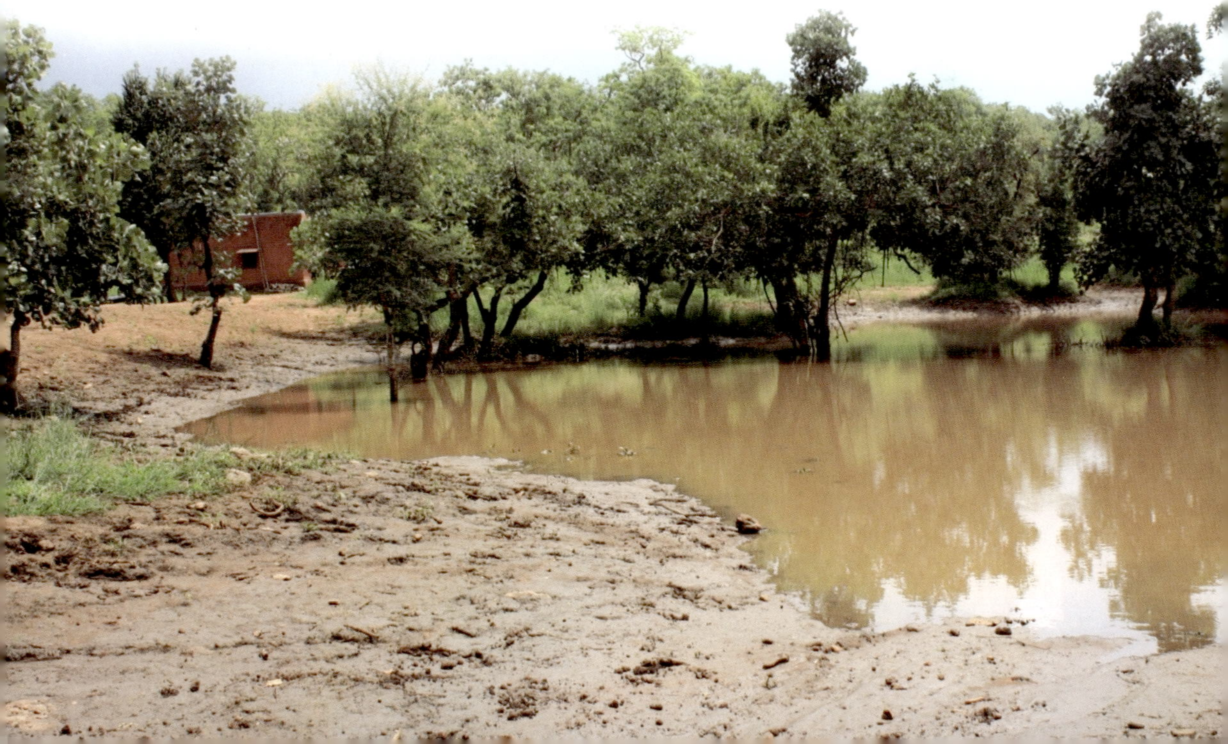

BELOW: Masonry chowki and the earthen water hole at Bana

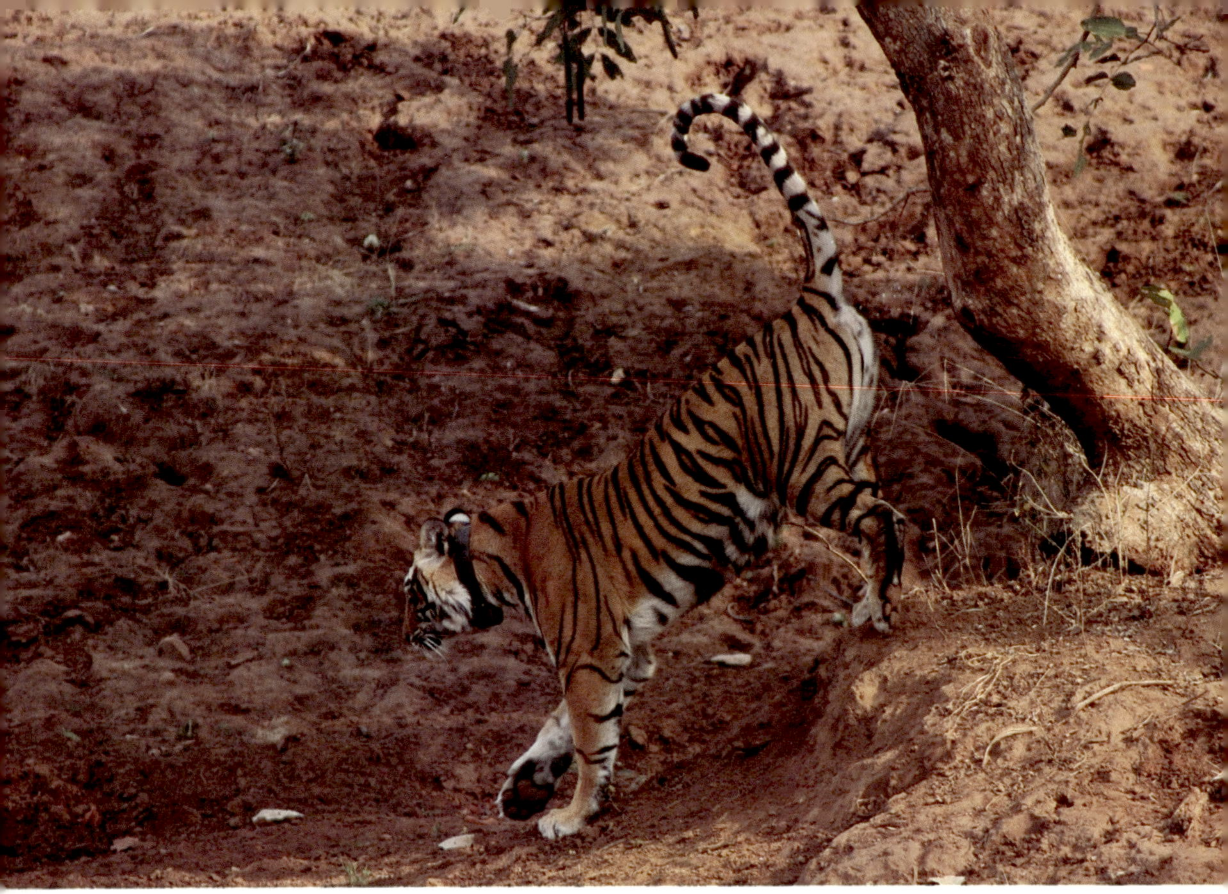

ABOVE:
Tigress Rani spraying urine to mark her presence

this water easily to Mala Johadka chowki using ordinary pipelines.

After Sariska had been bereft of its tiger population, the population of herbivores, especially sambar and blue bull, had increased considerably. Similarly, the cattle population inhabiting the Reserve in permanent camps had also increased. To support this increased animal population the management had to increase the carrying capacity of the Reserve. This can be possible only by habitat improvement by creating conditions favourable to better growth of desirable grasses and plants. Of course, an additional water point with stable water supply is an integral part of habitat improvement.

The Kalighati–Rajore plateau, with adjacent valleys as described above, with about 40 sq. km area was an ideal forest. This was an extremely rich area with high floral diversity. The entire plateau was full of palatable grasses as well. With the creation of three posts at vulnerable

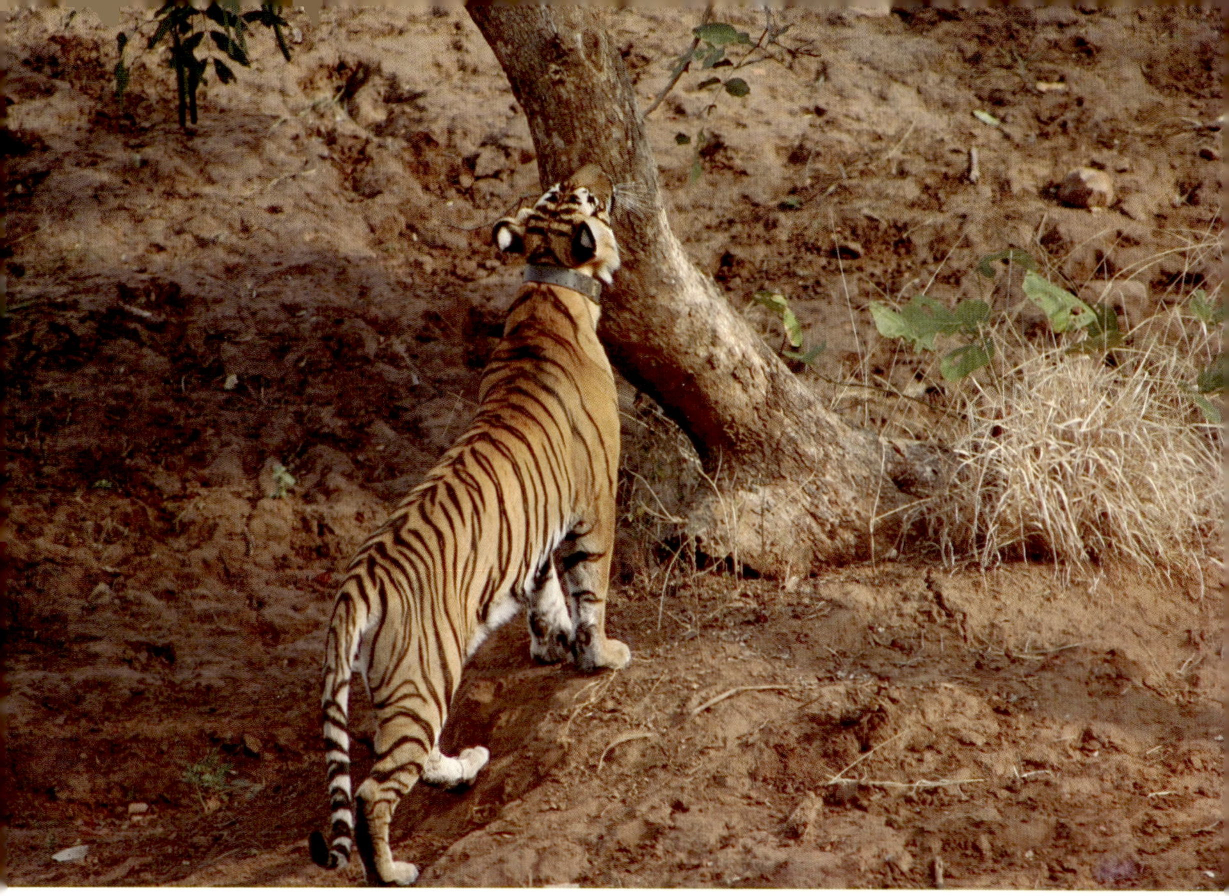

points, fair weather tracks with vantage points, and posting of protection staff in adequate number, regular patrolling had started which minimised human and cattle disturbance on this plateau. Now it only needed water points. I, therefore, drew up a plan to create several low-cost eco-friendly earthen water harvesting structures on the entire plateau. To begin with, three such structures were created in 2009–10 namely at Sunny Point, Phatyakhora, and Bana. Polythene sheets were spread on their beds to check water losses through seepage. The result was highly encouraging. The water hole of Bana was also connected to the pipeline carrying water from Kalighati. Thus it became perennial. A number of wild animals formed their niche around these water holes. Bana is an excellent meadow. Now with provision of perennial water hole, it began to attract a large number of wild animals. Very soon, a leopard family became resident and used the water hole regularly. The reintroduced

ABOVE: Tigress Rani smelling scent left by tiger Maharaja

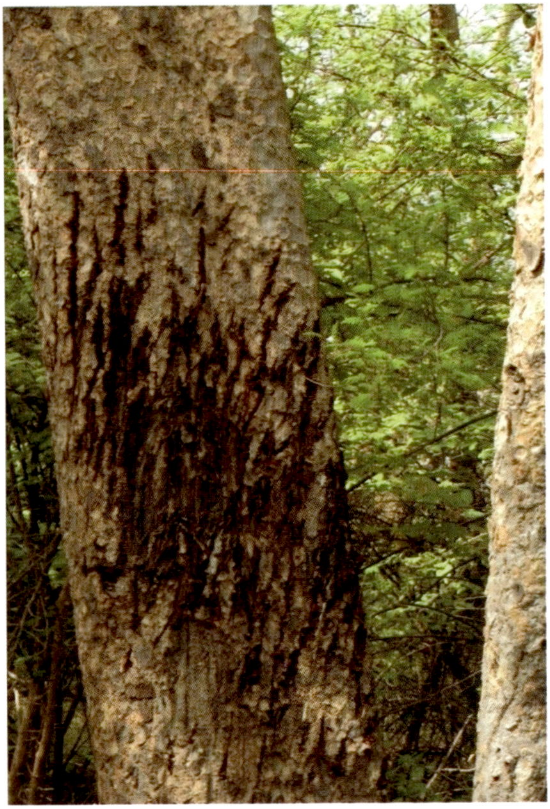

ABOVE: Nail marking by tigers in Bana forest

tigers also started visiting this water hole frequently.

I am convinced that several more such water holes should be developed on this plateau. Otherwise this drought-prone Reserve may witness heavy sambar casualty in dry years.

Kundli is another important valley very rich in vegetation but, again, without water. Animals are compelled to walk to Brahmnath and Kalighati water holes to drink water. These are located at a long distance from the valley. Also, they are located on the tarred road with heavy traffic round the year especially on Tuesdays and Saturdays when pilgrims are allowed free entry up to Pandupole temple. A permanent water hole in this valley, therefore, was highly desirable. With this objective, in March 2010 a 3-km-long pipeline was laid and a motor was used to lift water to the point where animal or human track to Kraska meets Kundli road. This also proved a boon for the wildlife of this area. Shy carnivorous animals with their nocturnal habits showed a special liking for this water hole. The frequency of tiger movement on Kundli road increased tremendously, especially during summer.

Similar to the Kalighati–Rajore plateau, earthen water harvesting structures were constructed at Boh chowki and Kalakadi valley also.

Construction of water holes in the remote areas is, however, a double-edged sword. On the one hand, it is an important tool to increase the carrying capacity of the area, while on the other, these attract poachers. This is a debatable issue. But I strongly believed in the development of the water holes in the interests of the wildlife. Undoubtedly, protection of wildlife from poachers is the basic responsibility of the management and no compromise should be made on this point. However, halting development of water sources in water deficit areas does not seem logical at all.

As part of strengthening the protection measures in the Reserve to counter repetition of the previous mishap of Sariska which wiped out the entire tiger population, many new patrolling tracks were created in the poaching-prone remote areas.

A 1.5-km-long track connecting Slopka–Pandupole fair weather road at Ghonsala Wali Johadi to the hill top overlooking vast forest area up to Siliberi, Baleta, Chimraj, etc., was constructed with two vantage points. One is highly picturesque and is gifted with a natural seat cut on a rock that provides an ideal surrounding for a memorable group photo.

BELOW: Dabli village in Sariska surrounded by hills

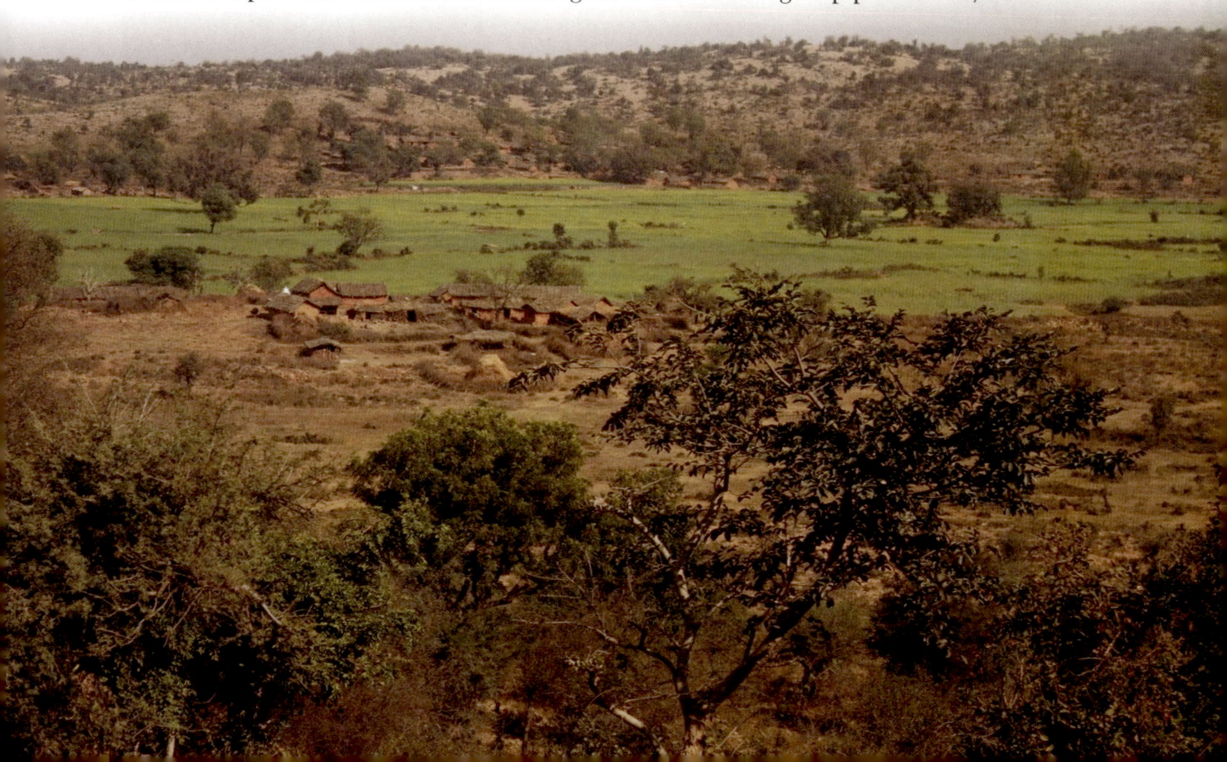

In December 2009 K.M. Chandrasekhar, the then Cabinet Secretary, during his visit to Sariska, had a family photo taken here with himself occupying this natural seat.

The famous Kraska plateau is situated on the eastern side of the Reserve. The two villages, Kraska and Lilunda, with huge cattle and human population, are situated here adjacent to each other. There is immense pressure on the forest which caused conflicts between the villagers and the management. Sukola and Dabli are the other two Gujjar dominated settlements on this plateau located on its eastern side. Beyond this plateau are thickly populated villages. Some of these are inhabited by Mev community, which is mostly non-vegetarian. People of this community were responsible for poaching of tigers and numerous other herbivores in the Reserve during 2002–04. The Kraska plateau, especially the Naldi area, had always been sensitive from this

BELOW: The deep Sariska forest (Tuda area)

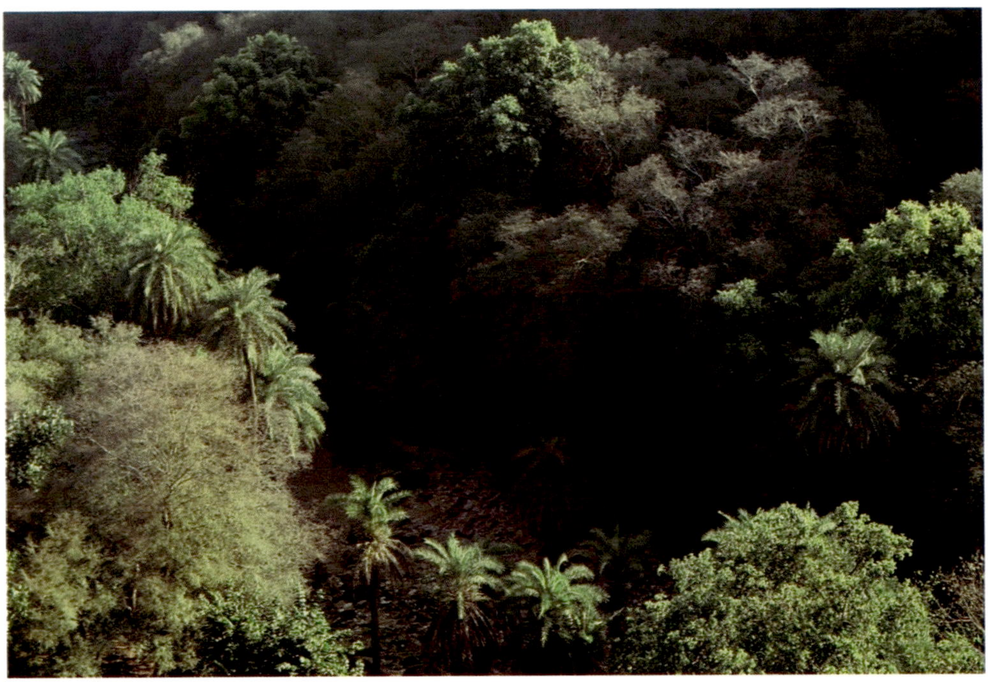

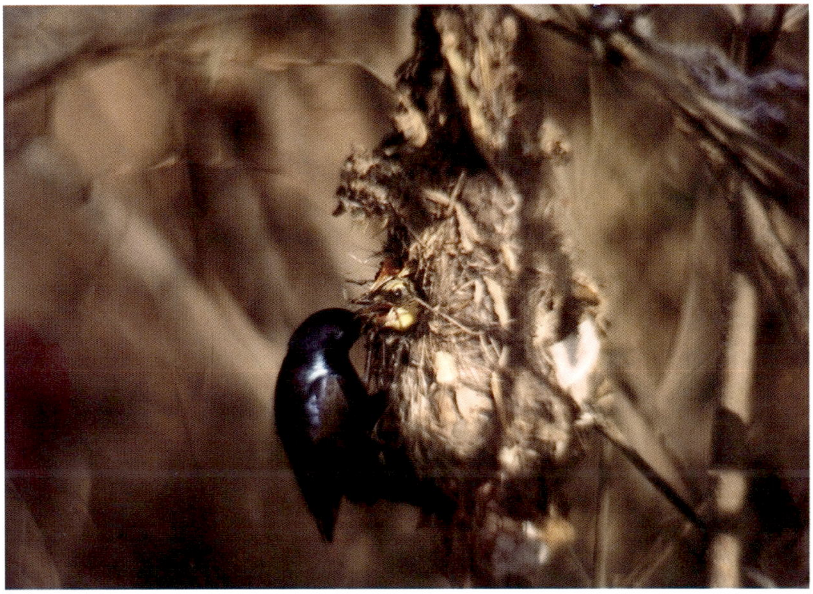

LEFT:
Purple sunbird feeding young ones

point of view. To strengthen protection here, a 7-km-long track was built on this difficult terrain with four vantage points between Kraska–Kund and Naldeshwar top. Strict vigil over a vast area has been possible from here with minimum staff.

Kalakadi valley, situated on the eastern side of the Reserve, is another poaching-prone area, as it is located closest to villages inhabited by the notorious *shikaris* (hunters) of Mev community. In fact, the entire area lying to the right of the Sariska–Pandupole road falling under the jurisdiction of the Malakheda police station had been threatened by these *shikaris*.

Like Kalakadi, the Siliberi–Rotkyala–Boh–Makrunda (Vulture Point) areas are equally poaching prone. Therefore, one patrolling track connecting Siliberi–Rotkyala valley to Kalakadi chowki and another connecting Rotkyala–Boh chowkies to Umri chowki via Makrunda were constructed in 2010 with many vantage points. Apart from protection, these vantage points, especially the Makrunda Point, give a wonderful overview of Pandupole valley.

I am sure that in future these tracks, if maintained properly, will prove important milestones in the protection strategy of the Reserve.

The construction of new water holes was the primary requirement of habitat improvement. Without substantial increase in the forage area, however, the carrying capacity of the Reserve could not be increased. A plan was drawn up to rid the important meadows of obnoxious weeds like *Adhatoda vasica*, *Cassia tora* and *Acrenthus* spp. etc. Dense growth of *Adhatoda vasica* was uprooted from Core I, particularly in Karna ka Bas, Jalebi Chowk, Tarunda, Buja, and Siliberi lest it germinates again through coppice. *Cassia tora* and *Acrenthus* spp. weeds were also removed from important grasslands between Brahmnath and Umri crossing.

The beautiful 7-km-long and 0.5–1.5 km wide Bhagani valley is blessed with natural perennial source of water. At Tuda, the spring never dries. In the lower part of the valley the water stays in small pools till early May. During the lean period of May–June, water from an underground well from an abandoned copper mine is pumped using a diesel engine to fill the water holes. An anicut was proposed to be constructed to harvest rain water during the monsoons in order to recharge the ground water system.

This beautiful valley too was infested with weeds such as *Adhatoda vasica* and *Cassia tora*. The presence of these weeds indicate excessive grazing. For several decades it remained the favourite grazing ground for cattle belonging to Gujjars who inhabited this valley till 2008.

A substantial area of this valley was cleared by removing these obnoxious weeds and was re-stocked with palatable grasses through seed sowing during the 2009 monsoons in the form of dung pellets. Now the grasslands are being developed through multiplication of grasses in the natural process.

Kankwadi is marked by the hills of Bhagani (Tuda) on the one hand

and Kalighati–Rajore plateau on the other. Bhagani valley had been made totally inviolate in 2008 by shifting Bhagani village out. Shifting of Kankwadi is in progress. After the shifting of Kankwadi village, an area of about 150 sq. km bound by Sariska–Ghanaka–Udaynath mud track on the one side and Sariska–Kalighati–Tehla road on the other, will become totally inviolate but for Haripura village which also is on the threshold of being shifted out sooner or later.

Similarly, by shifting settlements in Kraska–Sukola–Dabli plateau located left of Sariska–Kalighati–Tehla road, a much larger area can be made inviolate for wildlife. Consequently the traffic of pilgrims visiting the Pandupole temple will not be as damaging as it is now.

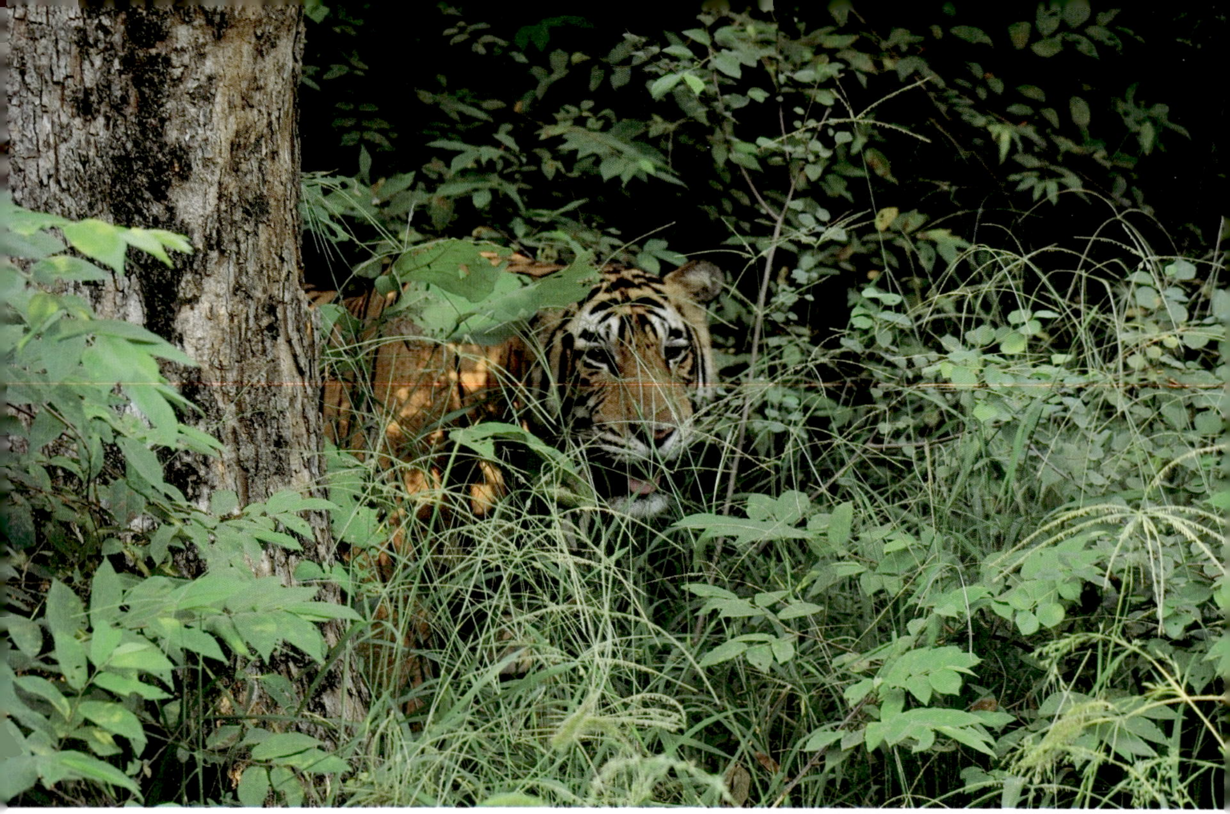

REINTRODUCTION OF TIGERS INTO SARISKA

As soon as the news of total tiger loss became public in 2005, the beautiful wildlife Reserve of Sariska suddenly lost its glory. Enquiry committees from state and central governments started camping in Sariska. The Central Bureau of Investigation (CBI), the prime investigation agency of India, also started questioning the staff and officers of the Reserve. It was a time when every employee of the Reserve was under suspicion. The media severely criticised the management. Some staff members were transferred to tough field postings in remote forests of Rajasthan. Other employees were also scared that they too would be transferred to destinations far away from their families. This panicky situation had totally demoralised the staff. The State Empowered Committee (SEC) and the central Tiger Task Force (TTF) had come out with several recommendations. The state and central governments were keen to see them implemented as soon as possible. Overall, it was a tough time for the Reserve management.

FACING PAGE: Sariska provides perfect habitat for tigers

BELOW: Getting acquainted with Sariska *(Photo by Dinesh Durrani)*

Villages and cattle camps located inside and on the periphery of the Reserve were quick to encash this situation. Cattle and goat grazing/browsing and wood poaching became rampant.

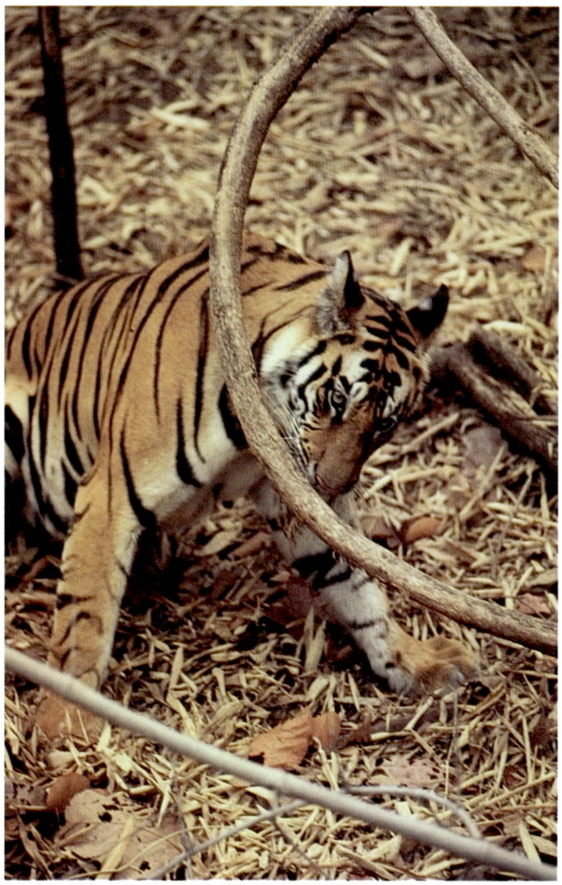

With the support of the local leaders, these mischievous elements started confronting the already demoralised staff. The survival of Sariska was at stake.

In the democratic setup in our country everything is weighed against its vote value. Alas, the poor wild creatures, who play the most important role in balancing nature, find no place in this political power game. As a result, barring a few, we find no saviours of wild treasure among politicians. They would go to any length to appease the vote bank. On receiving a signal from the local leader, the villagers may take no time in stripping the beautiful forest of its trees and grasses and extract the mineral wealth. Once a beautiful forest, it could soon become a wasteland.

WHY RE-INTRODUCE TIGERS INTO SARISKA?

Tiger is a magic animal. Loss of tiger brought havoc upon Sariska which put its very existence at stake. Can any sane person believe that one of the top politicians of the country then suggested in a public meeting in Sariska region that the land of the Reserve should be distributed to villagers for farming as Sariska, after losing its tigers, has no value! For saving Sariska from such politicians, it had to be restocked with tigers at the earliest.

It is a hard fact that Ranthambhore and Sariska have survived because of the presence of tiger, the prized animal. Presently, apart from the judiciary, very few advocates lend their voice in favour of wildlife and forests. Barring a few, conservation is not a priority for politicians because it has no vote value. Several greedy people look for an opportunity to use the mineral, wood, grass, and pasture resources

BELOW: The majestic tiger *(Photo by Dinesh Durrani)*

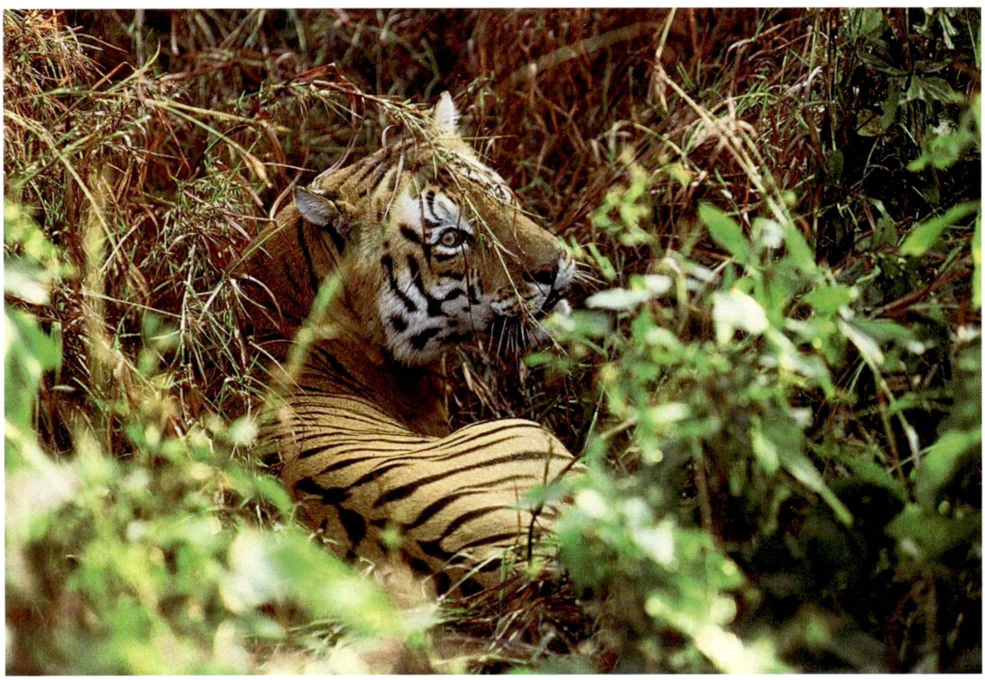

for personal benefit. A reserve without tigers does not also get any international support. Tiger brings in a lot of money for the tourism industry, which supports the preservation of tiger reserves. Ecologically also, such reserves are occupied by leopard which is the second largest carnivore. Once leopards establish themselves in the core areas, they are likely to kill cubs of tigers reintroduced in the future. No tiger population can be established unless the tiger cubs survive and grow to occupy independent territories.

TTF took serious note of this problem during its Sariska visit and mentioned in its report,

> After the news of disappearance of tigers, local politicians have convened meetings in the area demanding the Reserve be opened to grazing and agriculture. Bitterly resentful of park authorities, the leaders and villagers have threatened to take over the park, which they say have no reason to exist since the tigers are now gone. The Task Force therefore recommends that urgent steps need be taken to restore the park and to rehabilitate tigers in the Reserve.

The mesmerising charm of the tiger draws not only thousands of tourists but also powerful politicians and bureaucrats every year to the Reserve. This provides excellent opportunity to the Reserve management to gain political and bureaucratic support in protecting Sariska from greedy people. I am sure Sariska without the tiger would have deteriorated within a decade like several other important Reserves of Rajasthan, such as Van Vihar and Darrah.

The SEC emphasised on early action for reintroducing tiger into Sariska and observed,

> Usually introduction of large carnivore to an area from where they have been missing for a long time is not welcomed by local communities. Fortunately,

> this is not the case in Sariska and therefore, it is highly recommended; the sooner the re-introduction takes place, the easier it would be to bring the local communities into agreement with new conservation efforts.

The SEC also observed,

> Management of Park inter alia involves protecting a biological system, which is highly dynamic and functional. This process requires constant monitoring. With increasing anthropogenic and developmental pressures these highly sensitive ecosystems cannot be saved using the old *laissez-faire* approach, which prescribes *'Let nature take its own course'*. The current situation demands intensive monitoring of the system, restoration of habitat where it is necessary through appropriate management interventions. The bottom line is to keep the functionality of the ecosystem intact. Therefore, alert management systems responsive to the needs of wildlife populations are essential.

The SEC strongly endorsed the need for re-introducing tigers into Sariska, which forms the westernmost limit of tiger-occupied areas in India. Maintaining its population is imperative in the interest of forest and wildlife conservation. Subsequent to the report of this Committee, the Rajsthan government constituted a state steering committee under the chairmanship of V.P. Singh to implement the recommendations of SEC.

RECOVERY PLAN FOR TIGERS IN SARISKA

The disappearance of tigers from Sariska exemplifies the threat that exists to isolated tiger population in many parts of the country. Based on past trends and experience, it is sensible to assume that such losses and local extinctions in future will be more frequent and we will have

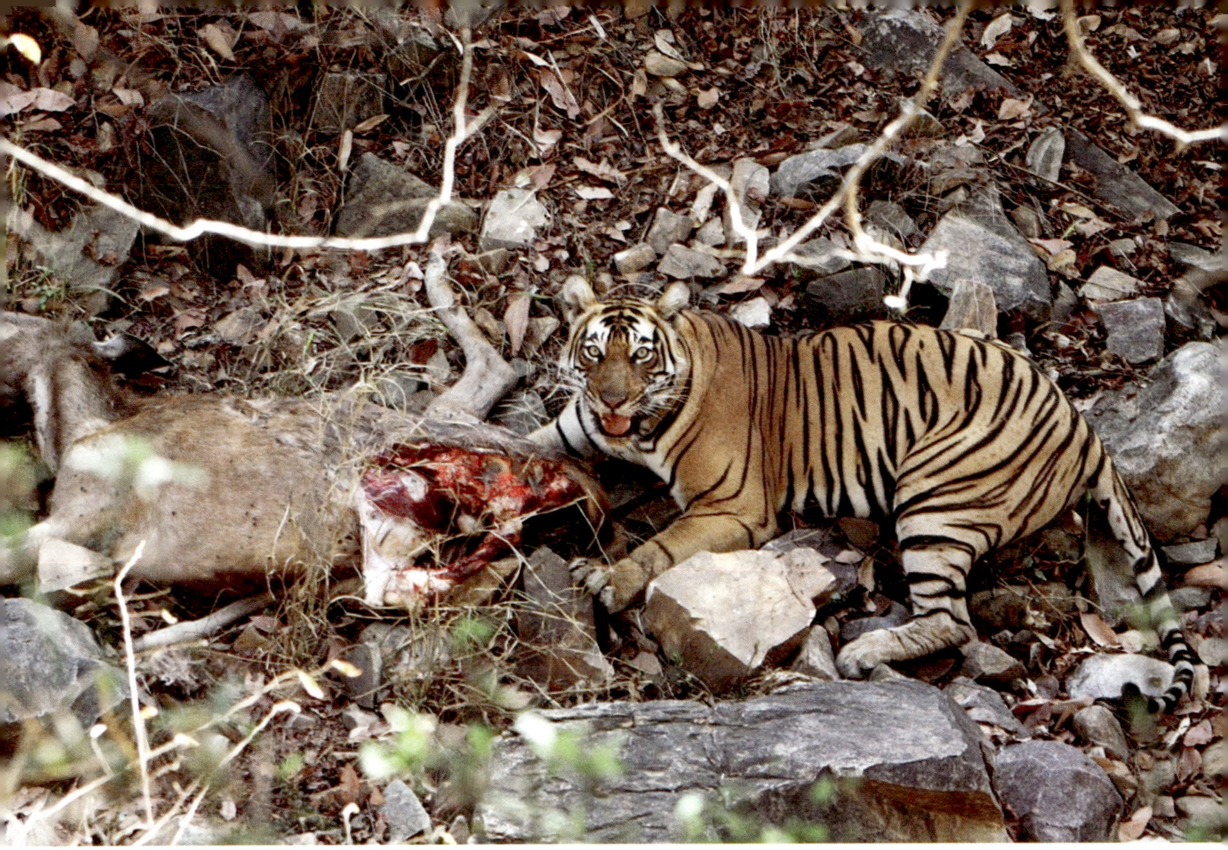

Above:
Rani looks happy in Sariska

to undertake immediate reintroduction and restoration programmes to save our natural heritage.

To re-establish tiger population in Sariska, it was important to remove the factors adversely affecting the habitat conditions and availability of prey to tigers. Reintroduction should establish self-sustaining population with high reproductive fitness in the wild environment.

Re-introduction of tigers into Sariska would restore the distribution limit of tigers in India which may otherwise influence the ecological structure of the semi-arid ecosystem.

The genetic stock of the tigers of Ranthambhore and Sariska could be assumed to be similar as both habitats are part semi-arid tracts in Aravalli hills. Therefore, to maintain the uniqueness of genetic stock of tigers in semi-arid tract, the best choice will be Ranthambhore tigers.

The tiger relocation from Ranthambhore Tiger Reserve to Sariska was based on the report entitled 'Assessment of Status of Tiger

(Panthera tigris) in Sariska Tiger Reserve' prepared by WII (2005) and subsequent 'Recovery Plan' developed by the Sariska Field Director. It was approved by National Tiger Conservation Authority in March 2008. Accordingly, WII developed a detailed protocol and plan of operation for immobilisation, radio-collaring, and translocation of tigers from Ranthambhore to Sariska.

The report had suggested that three tigresses and two tigers should be brought from Ranthambore to re-establish the tiger population in Sariska. It was also suggested that after establishing five tigers, two batches of two to three tigers each should be brought every three years to Sariska. The restocking is essential to maintain genetic and demographic viability of the tiger population. It was suggested that all selected candidates will be chemically immobilised. Tissue and blood samples will be collected to assess the level of heterozygosity and disease profile in these individuals. They will be fitted with radio collars having VHF and GPS transmitters. They will be transported to Sariska and released into a 100 ha. tigerproof enclosure in Nayapani area located in natural habitat with dense forest cover and a water hole. The tigers in the enclosure will be monitored for a period of two weeks and then released into the wild and their movements will be monitored continuously.

It was proposed to translocate one tigress between December 2007 and February 2008, followed by a male after a month.

In the second year two tigresses and in the third year one tiger would be brought to Sariska from Ranthambore for establishing initial population.

CONSTRUCTION OF ENCLOSURE AND THE LESSON LEARNED

According to the original plan, a 100 ha. enclosure was to be built at Nayapani, 5 km from Sariska headquarters. The size of the proposed

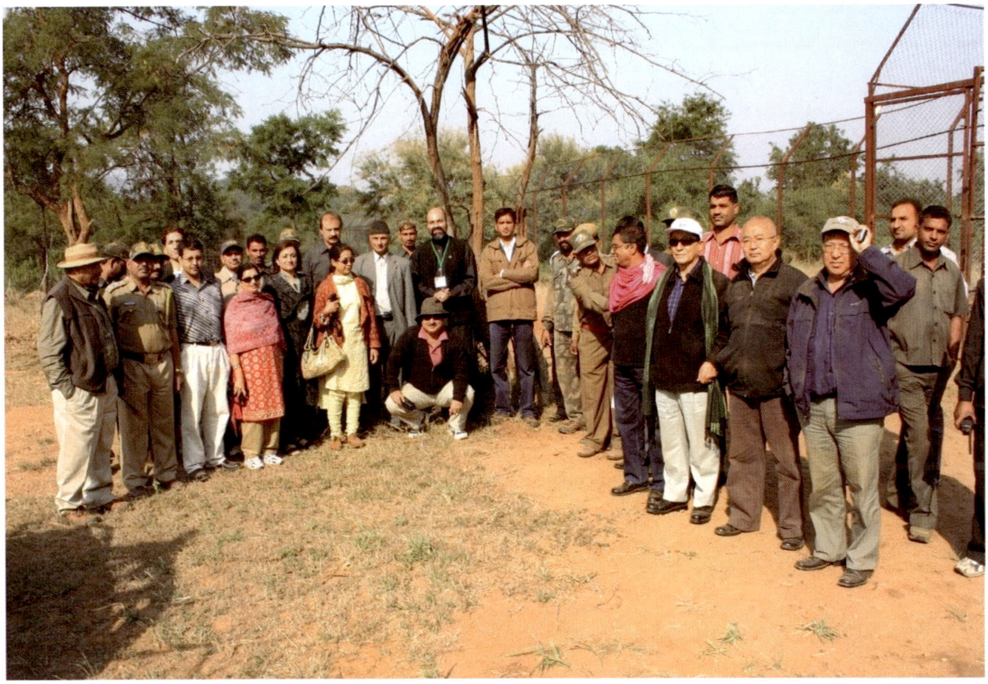

Above:
Forest ministers from SAARC countries visiting Sariska. Background shows the enclosures where reintroduced tigers were kept

enclosure was modified many times. Since this kind of experiment was being undertaken for the first time in the world, there was no prior experience to fall back on. Therefore, when the actual shifting took place it was felt that 100 ha. will be too big a size to monitor and will be too difficult to maintain involving huge expenditure. It was also felt that monitoring of the animal will also be very difficult in such a huge enclosure full of thick vegetation. It was, therefore, felt that a 50 ha. area would serve the purpose. Later, the size was again reduced to 20 ha., then to 10 ha. Finally, when required funds could not be made available, two enclosures of 1 ha. each were constructed side by side. This later proved to be the appropriate size. Keeping the translocated tiger in an enclosure for some time is part of the soft pad launching technique so that the animal remains safe against any kind of danger. For this purpose regular monitoring of the animal is necessary and it can be possible only in a small enclosure. Furthermore, large enclosures in such a reserve are contrary to the basic principle of providing free movement to wildlife inhabiting the area. Further, the area demarcated for the enclosure cannot be counted as part of the sanctuary or National Park. Therefore, it is always advisable to have the minimum required area for such enclosures. The Sariska model seems to be fine and may be adopted in other reserves if and when such a situation arises.

DELAY IN TRANSLOCATION OF TIGERS

Tigers are highly territorial animals. It is often said that the senses of a cat are so strong that it can travel hundreds of kilometers to reach its original home or territory.

A team from WII and Rajasthan Forest Department was deputed to conduct and facilitate the translocation operation.

Adult tigers of over two and a half years to four years of age

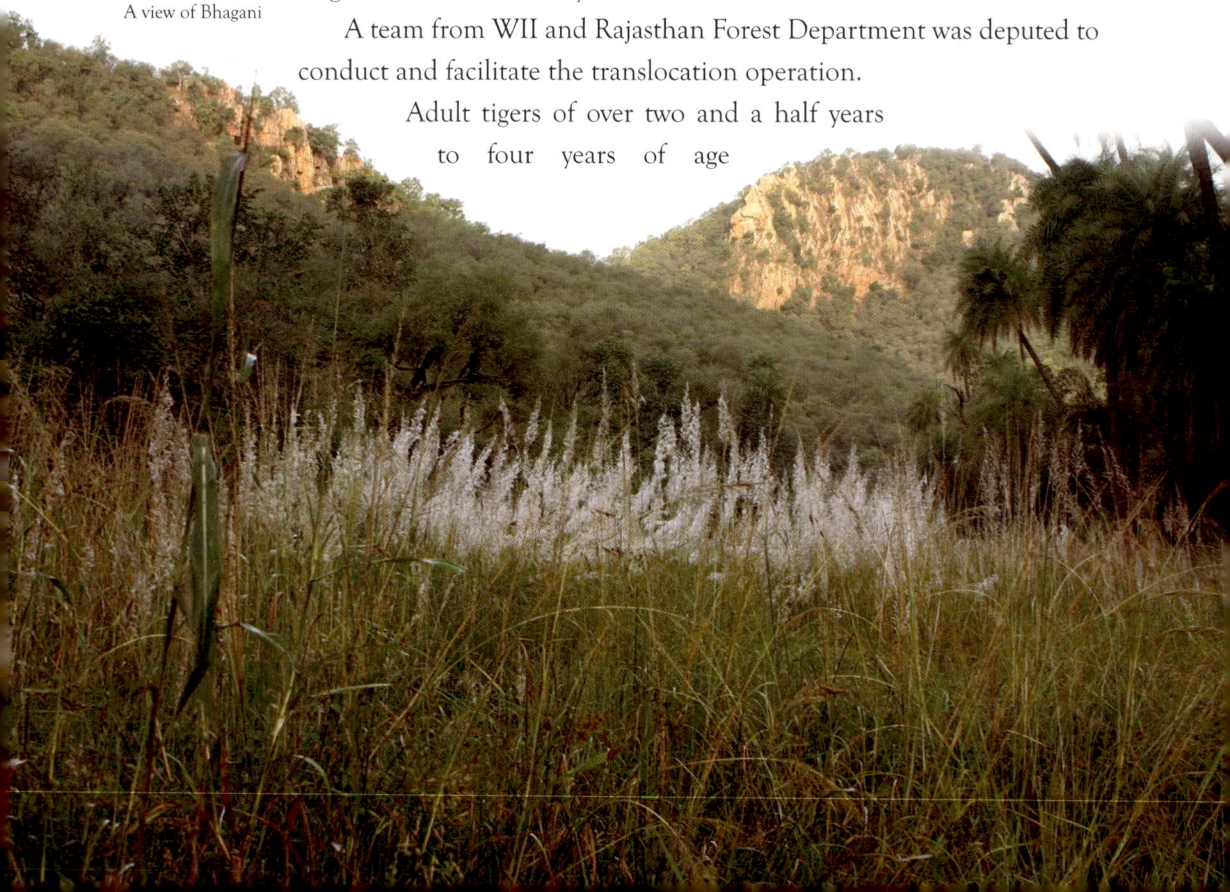

BELOW: A view of Bhagani

are considered suitable for translocation in view of medical fitness, as the body at that age has higher resistance to diseases and the physical strength to take on the stress of relocation. From the fertility point of view also such an age is good. The behaviour of tigers, when confronted with humans, is an important parameter for selection of candidates for translocation. Accordingly, young adults were selected depending on visual assessment and healthy body condition. These animals could not be translocated immediately due to opposition by the powerful anti-Sariska and pro-Ranthambhore hotel lobby. The State Steering Committee, chaired by V.P. Singh deserves all credit for relentless efforts and lobbying with the Central government. This obstruction delayed the original schedule by many months. Ultimately the final clearance for the tiger translocation was received on 25 June 2008.

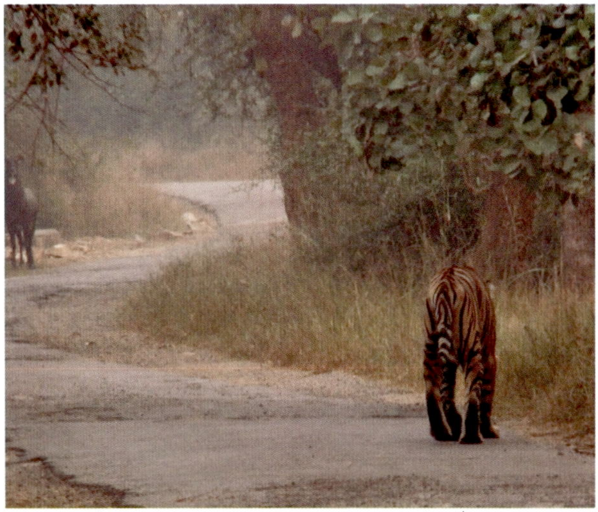

ABOVE: The blue bull is alert, but not scared because Maharaja is not hungry

The month of June in this part of the country is always very hot. This time is unsuitable to take up such sensitive operations. But the programme had already witnessed inordinate delay and the pro-Ranthambhore lobby was trying hard to scuttle this operation. The Committee, therefore, had no choice but to act immediately. There was miraculous interference that helped this pious programme by bringing in rains early that year. This took care of the feared heat waves.

In anticipation of the sanction, animal capturing and radio-collaring had started in June. In all, five adult tigers (three females and two males) were chemically immobilised and radio-collared in Ranthambhore

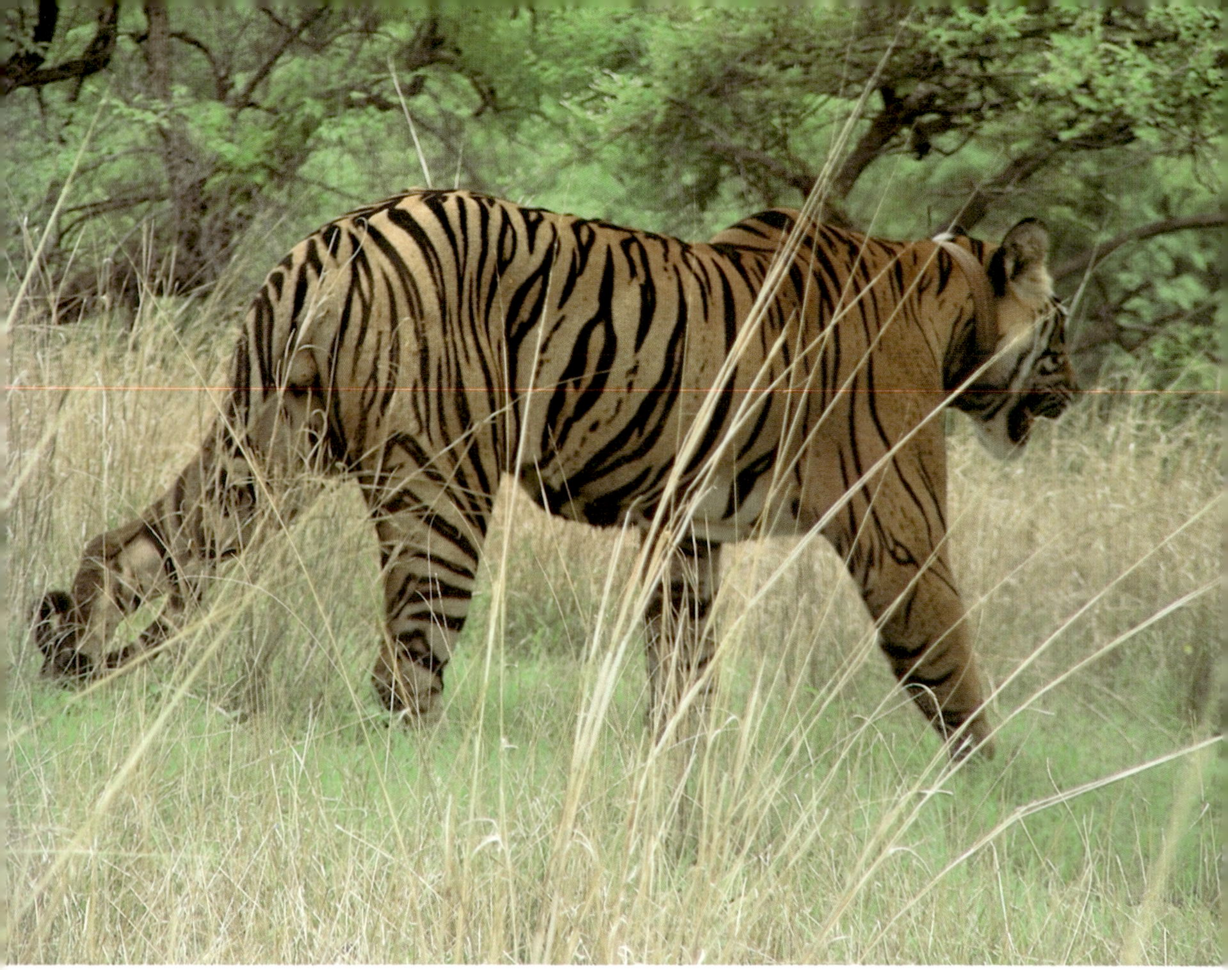

Above: Getting familiarised with Sariska

between 23 June and 4 July 2008. The drug used was a mixture of Xylazine and Ketamine. These animals had to be released in Ranthambhore itself for want of final sanction from the central government as well as due to non-availability of helicopter from the Indian Air Force.

TRANSLOCATION OF THE FIRST (MALE) TIGER (CP-1)

The first tiger was shifted on 28 June 2008 when the helicopter was made available. As per the original plan a tigress was to have been shifted first, which had been selected and radio-collared a few days ago. But on the day of shifting, she could not be located. A male tiger radio-collared earlier was located at Anatpura. There was no time left for further consideration as the entire field was ready. Therefore, it was instantly decided to translocate this 4-year-old young male. It was destined to enjoy the privilege of creating history and bringing back the glory of Sariska!

It was visualised that the immobilised animal may have to be kept under sedation for two to three hours considering the time required for radio-collaring (his earlier VHF collar had to be changed to one with two VHF and GPS transmitters through Argos satellite), caging, transportation up to helipad, air lifting to Sariska, and releasing in the enclosure. The drug (3.2 ml of HBM) was selected accordingly. A water container and sprayer were kept handy to counter the possible overheating of the animal's body due to sedation.

BELOW: Maharaja CP-1 in Sariska enclosure *(Photo by Shilpi Gupta)*

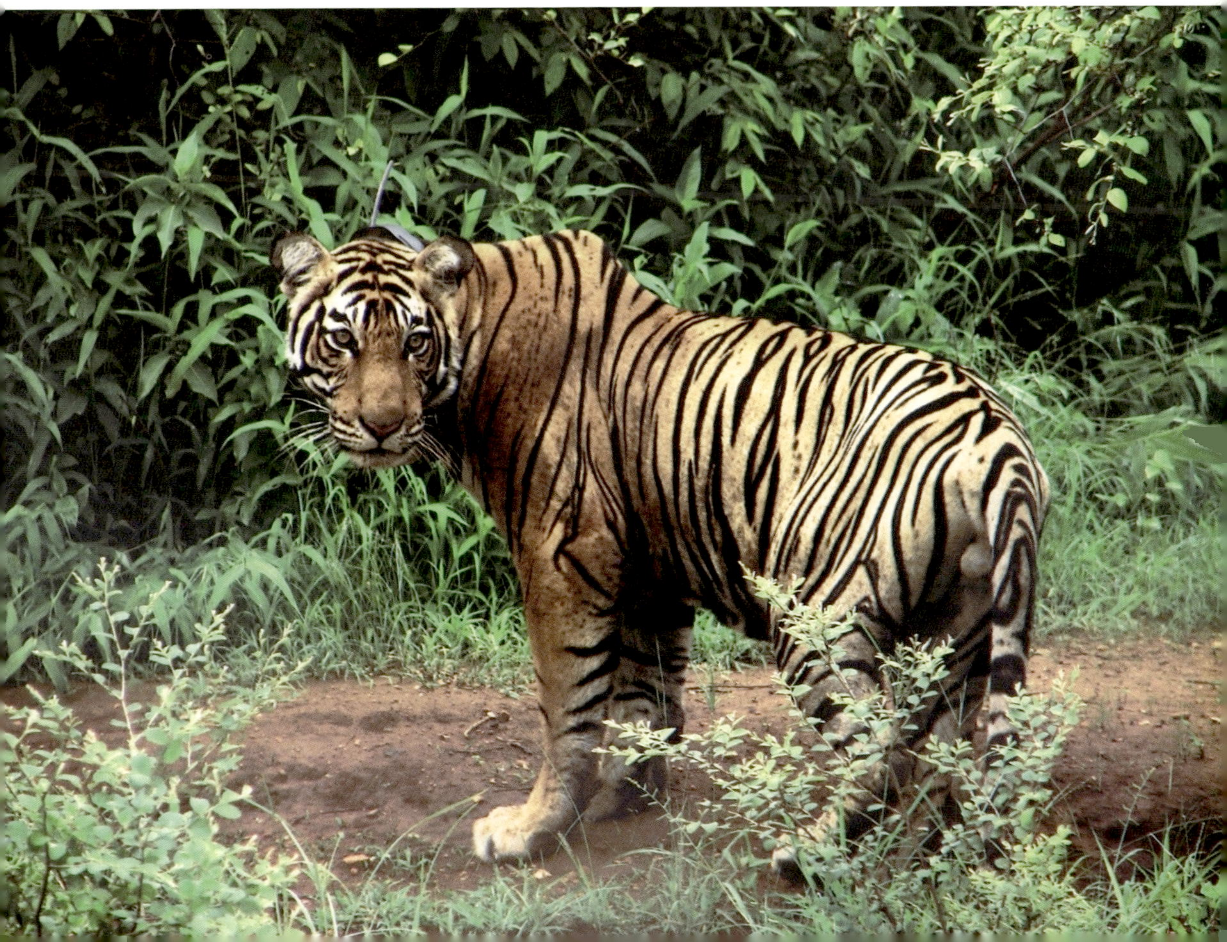

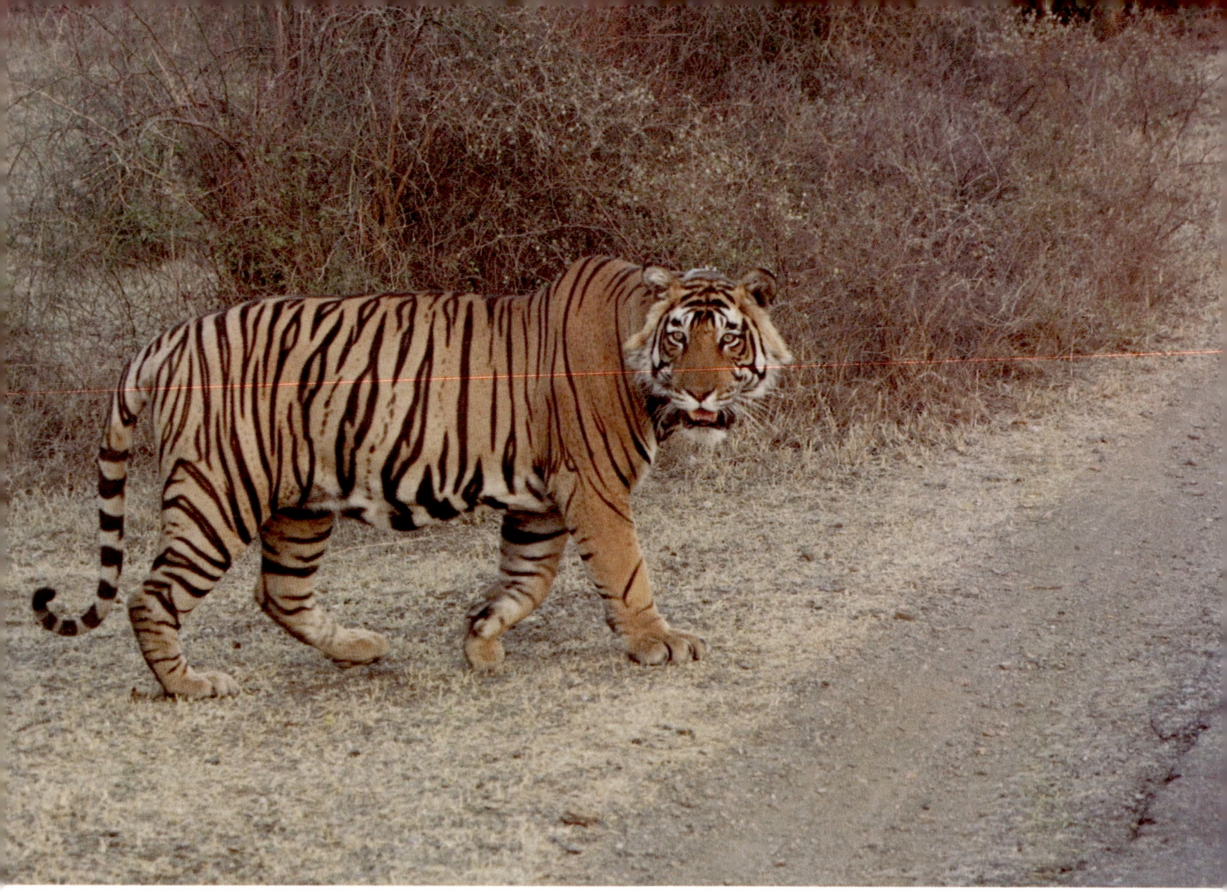

ABOVE: Maharaja on the prowl

A container with non-slip wooden planks at the bottom and angle iron frames on the sides and top was specially fabricated for transportation of the animals. Two small windows were provided on top and two sides for better monitoring of the animal during transportation and injection of medicines. The container was punctured with 25 mm holes all around for proper ventilation. The inside of the container was painted dark to keep the animal calm during transportation.

The sedation and other procedures including radio-collaring, etc. took about 40 minutes.

The loading and unloading of a cage weighing 250 kg, plus the weight of the sedated tiger was a huge task because of the wet soil and thick foliage. The first truck in which the cage was loaded at Ranthambhore got stuck in the wet soil and could not be dislodged.

The stand-by truck was, therefore, used to transport the cage to the helipad.

Ultimately the tiger was loaded on to the helicopter at about 11:10 a.m. It was partially revived at 11:30 a.m. The helicopter landed at Sariska at 12:27 p.m.

At Sariska Tiger Reserve all preparations were made to receive its first translocated tiger. The rain god, too, seemed to be enjoying at what was happening. The helipad prepared inside the Reserve, about 300 metres from the enclosure, was totally submerged in water. Helicopter landing in such circumstances seemed almost impossible. An alternative plan was, therefore, hatched and another landing site was identified, if the pilot decided against landing at the first one. These were anxious moments for everybody. If the second landing site was to be used, then it would mean an additional road journey through a broken tar road and another 2 km stretch through a waterlogged mud track. This was bound to put additional pressure on the tiger, which had now been under sedation for a considerably long time.

Sensing the anxiety of the team the pilot took a few low sorties over the original helipad and decided to land there. As soon as the helicopter touched the ground, it got stuck in the soft wet soil. But the landing was smooth and safe.

The cage was quickly transferred to the waiting truck and driven to the entrance of the enclosure. The tiger was soon revived and released into the enclosure. 28 June 2008 thus became a momentous day in the history of tiger conservation throughout the world. A light yellow cloth was hung along the fence of the enclosure to allow the animal to settle down without any stress or disorientation.

A monitoring team consisting of trained staff was set up to keep track of the animal in the enclosure. The team was stationed at a 20 metre high watch tower at a strategic location outside the enclosure equipped with VHF receiver, wireless handsets, and binoculars.

The tiger seemed restless from being caged and in a new location. It, however, adapted quickly to the new conditions. It made a kill on the first day itself.

Due to early monsoon, the foliage had grown very thick in the enclosure and keeping a visual track of the animal was not possible all the time. After eight days of monitoring, the tiger was released into the wild on 6 July 2008. Thereafter its movement was monitored round the clock and its GPS locations recorded. The forest department headquarters in Jaipur used Google Earth to plot the location of the animal every third day when the data on the locations was received directly through Internet from Argos satellite.

The tiger took to the new habitat almost immediately as was evident from the fact that it was making kills at regular intervals but it

BELOW: Radio collar of CP-1 being changed at Sariska

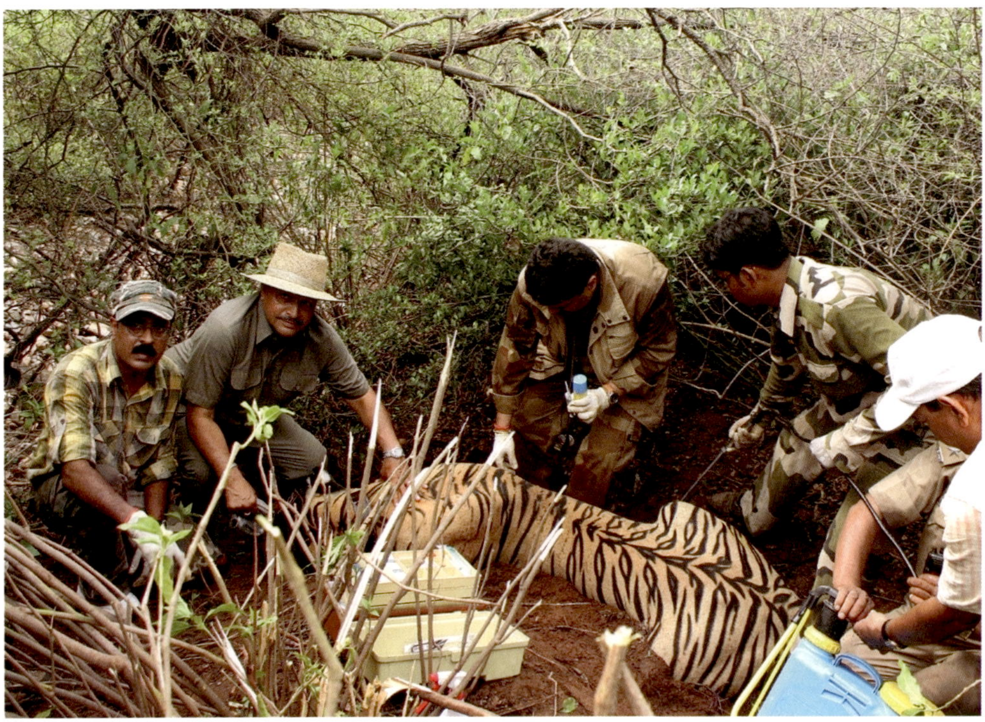

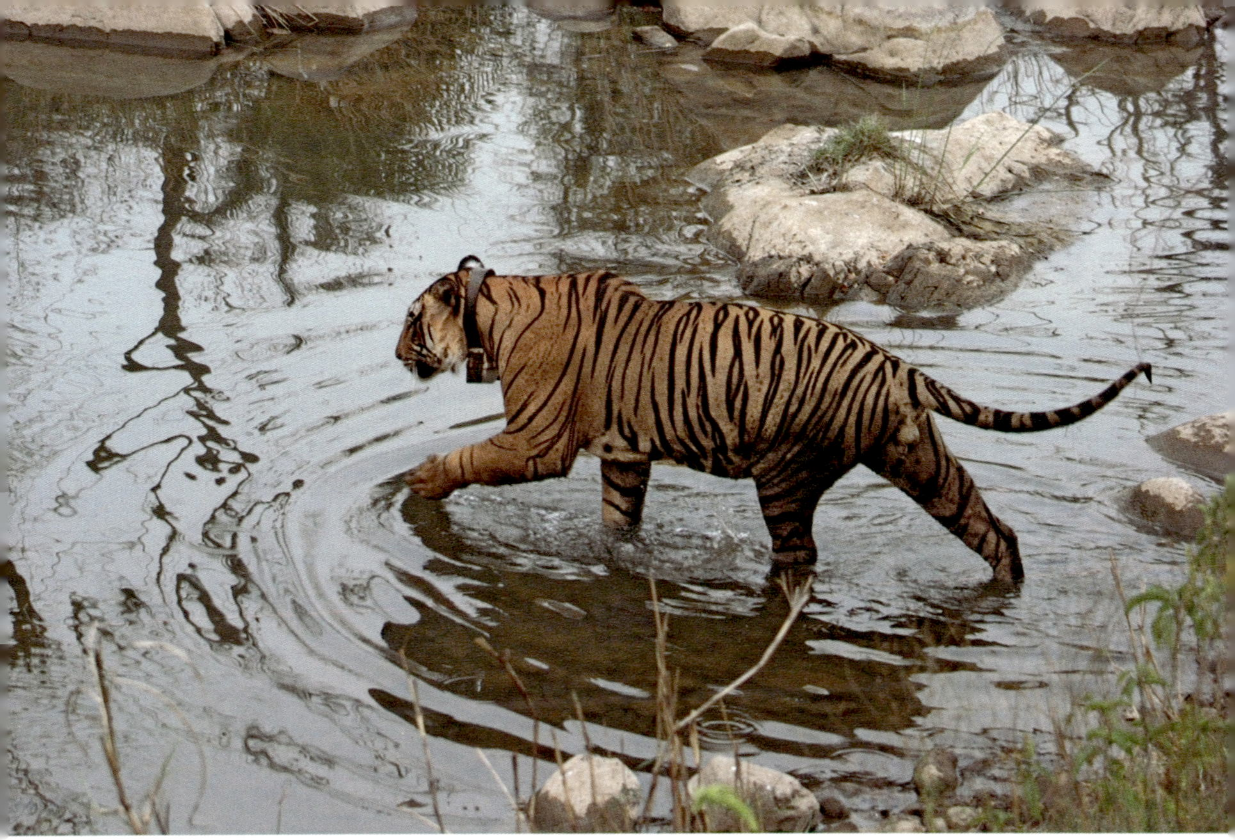

ABOVE:
Maharaja leaving Bhagani

moved towards the southern side of the Reserve, i.e. Tehla range, and reached Dabkan, a fringe area of the Reserve. The tiger could have strayed further towards human settlements had it not been for the alert monitoring team.

This team managed to steer the tiger back to the northern part of the Reserve. It continued its attempts to move beyond Dabkan, but could not because of the monitoring team. Ultimately, the animal took refuge in the Bhagani valley from where a village had recently been relocated. Bhagani had now become an ideal area with no disturbance and abundance of prey base like sambar, chital, nilgai, and wild boar. The area was blessed with a few perennial water holes as well. Bhagani valley thus played an important role in naturalising the tiger at Sariska. Since this was the only tiger in the entire Reserve, it started exploring larger areas and shortly expanded its territory up to Kalighati and Udainath.

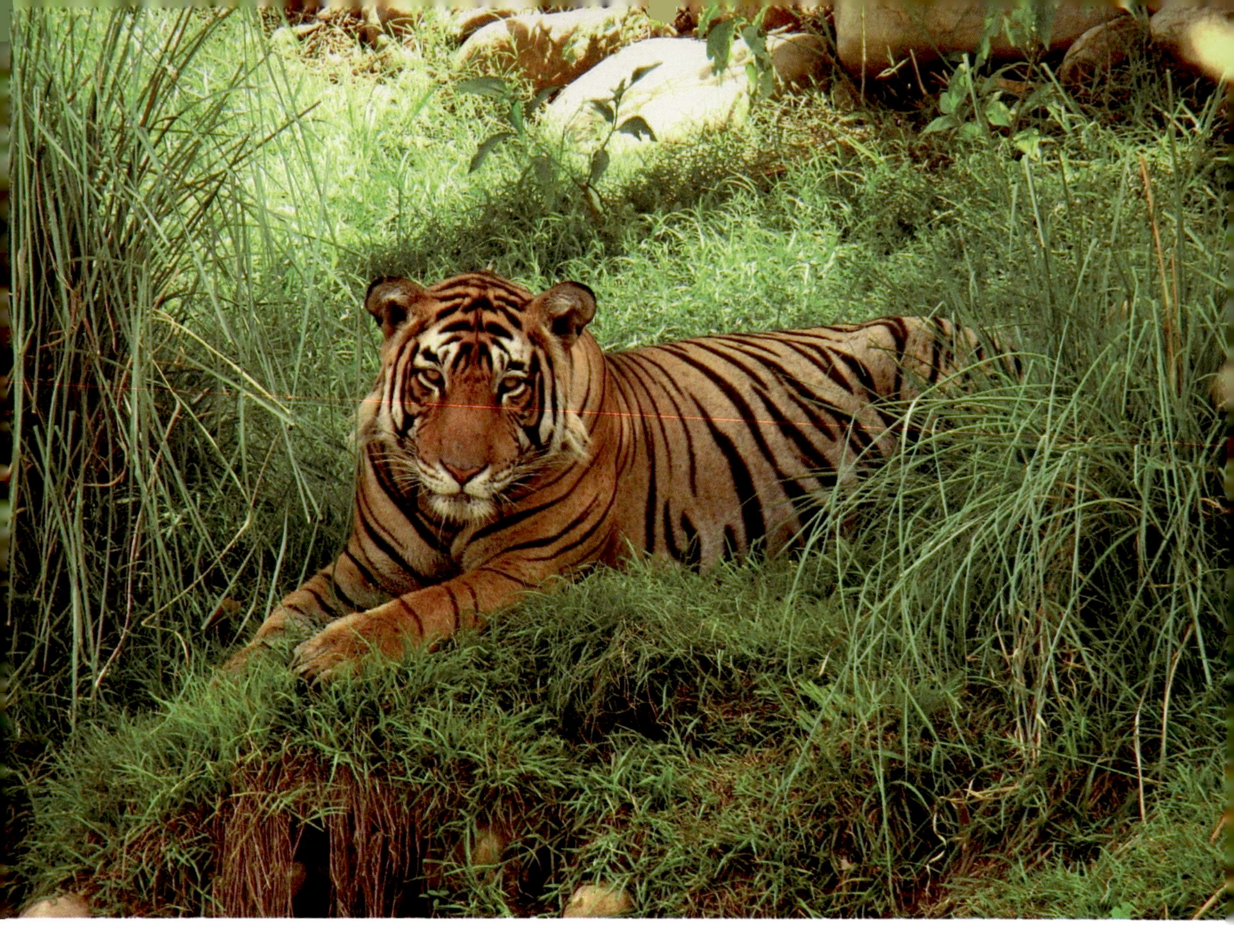

ABOVE: Maharaja in Bhensota Plateau

Once in Kalighati it made a kill of a chital. While feeding on it, a pack of wild pigs, which perhaps had never seen a tiger, made an attempt to snatch the kill from the tiger. Amazed at this foolhardy daredevilry of the pigs, the tiger charged at them and brought down the leader, while the others managed to escape.

To extend his territory, the tiger (coded CP-1), started exploring other areas such as Pandupole, Umri, Mahadev jungle, Slopka, Kundli road, Naya Pani, etc. Within a month it moved towards Bandipul area across state highway number 13. This was risky as the highway had heavy traffic all the time. Several animals have been killed on this road in the past including tigers and leopards. On a few occasions the anxious tiger ventured into the residential colony of the staff and officers of the Reserve

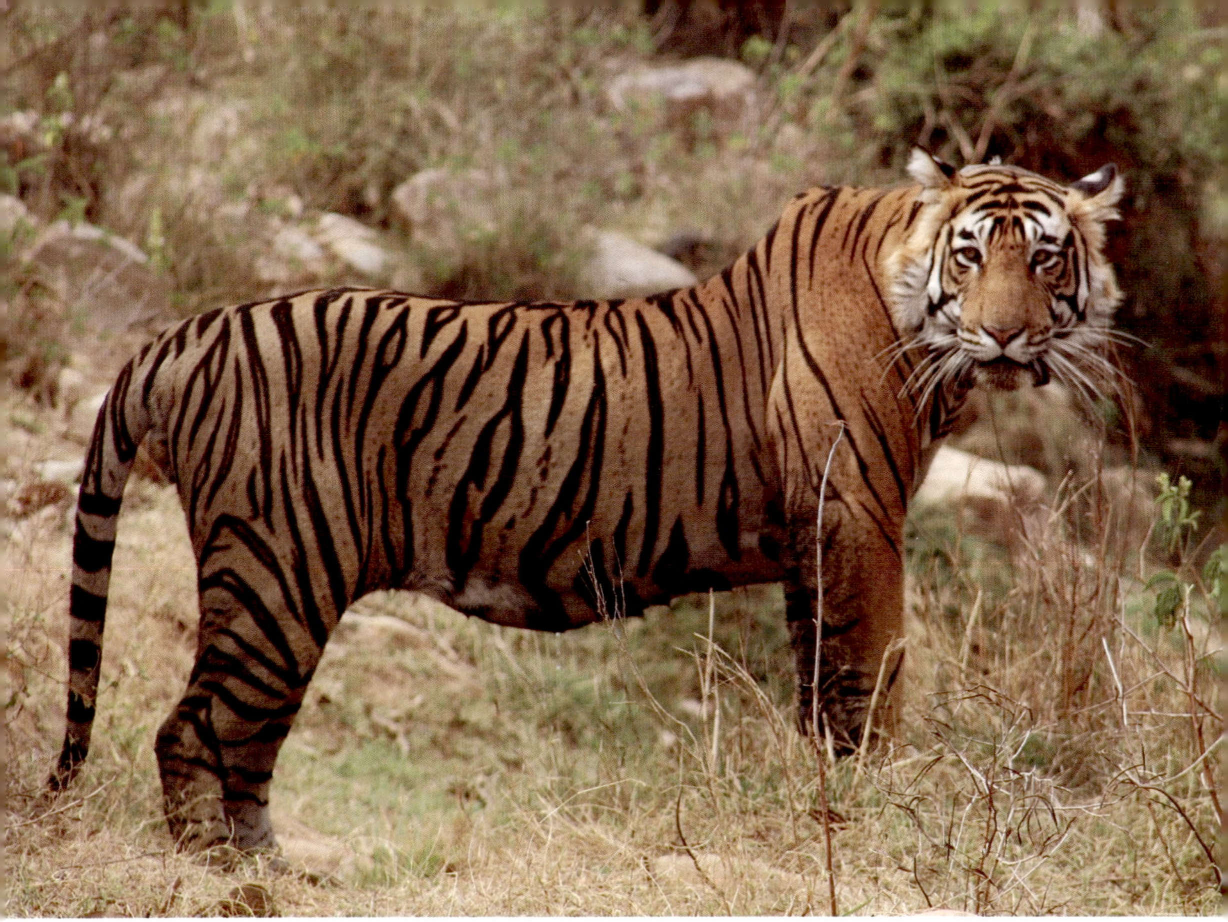

ABOVE: Maharaja, a majestic view

at Sariska headquarters. These visits were a matter of concern because of the possibility of an accident in the colony or in the adjoining Kundalka and Indok villages. The staff was put on high alert to steer the tiger towards the interior whenever it tried to come close to the highway. It was thus driven towards the core area. On the evening of 27 January 2009, close to Haripura village, almost on the main road between Sariska and Kalighati, it killed a buffalo calf but moved ahead without feeding on it.

At times during the night it would visit the waterhole behind my residence to drink water and often rub its body against the iron fence of my residence but did not venture into the compound. He was a bold and quite tourist-friendly animal. He kept wandering in the entire National Park area of the Reserve. He was a real king, so we decided to decorate him with the title 'Maharaja'.

TRANSLOCATION OF THE SECOND (FEMALE) TIGER (CP-2)

Encouraged by the success of the first tiger relocation, the State Steering Committee decided to shift a tigress. On 4 July 2008, a healthy tigress of about four and half years of age was tranquilised in Kachida valley of Ranthambhore, radio-collared, and airlifted following similar procedure and protocol as in the earlier translocation. Fortunately, it was a clear day and the entire operation was conducted with ease. At Sariska the cage was unloaded without any problem. Soon the tigress was released into the enclosure adjacent to the one where Maharaja had been kept. When the cage was opened, she jumped out without hesitation. However, once inside the enclosure, unlike Maharaja she remained hidden among the bushes and was hardly seen by the observers on the watchtower.

Since she was picked up at Ranthambore in the middle of a meal, everyone expected her to make a kill in the enclosure and have her full quota of food. When she did not, everybody was worried. Unlike Maharaja, she had been radio-collared for the first time and kept under sedation for a long time during the journey. Experts felt that this could be the reason for her abnormal behaviour. However, not willing to take any chances, it was decided not to hold her any longer in the enclosure. She was set free on 8 July, just two days after Maharaja was released into the wild forest.

Coming out of the enclosure she moved to Tarunda in the western part of the Reserve. Deciding not to stay there, she took a U-turn and headed towards Kraska hill which is inhabited by a large human population, mainly belonging to the cattle rearing Gujjar community.

Kraska is a huge plateau of over 30 sq. km where Kraska, Lilunda, Sukola, and Dabli villages are located. Due to over-grazing by livestock, the population of wild herbivore is very less here. After a while the tigress decided to move towards the hill slope on the north-east of the Reserve,

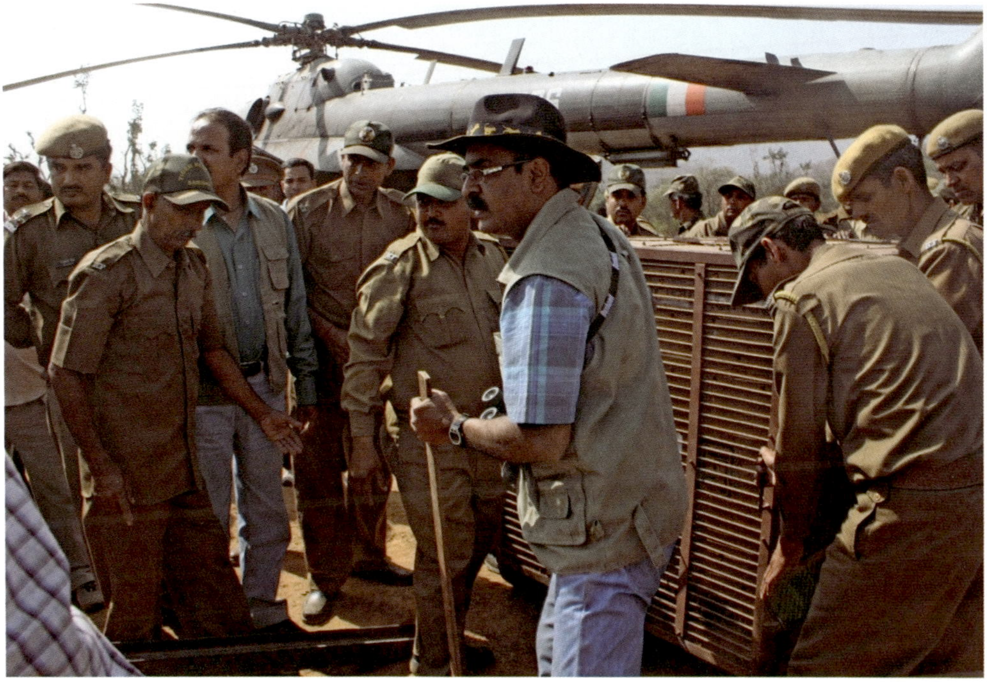

Above: The first tigress (Maharani) landing in Sariska from Ranthambhore *(Photo by Shilpi Gupta)*

spread between Lilunda and Naladeshwar. This area is extremely rugged and undulating with high gradients. The tigress, coded CP-2, was restless and was doing reconnaissance of the area as if trying to get back to the comfort of the plains and plateaus of her original home Ranthambhore. Heavy traffic on state highway number 13 discouraged her from coming down the hill.

A monitoring team of six personnel, which was following her constantly, might have added to her anxiety. But the surveillance could not be discontinued as she was not showing any sign of settling down. It was indeed a tough time for the monitoring teams as the male tiger was trying to break into the human habitations spread over the southern-western part of the Reserve almost every day and the female tiger was desperately patrolling Kraska–Dabli hill, overlooking the heavy vehicular traffic of the highway on the north-eastern side.

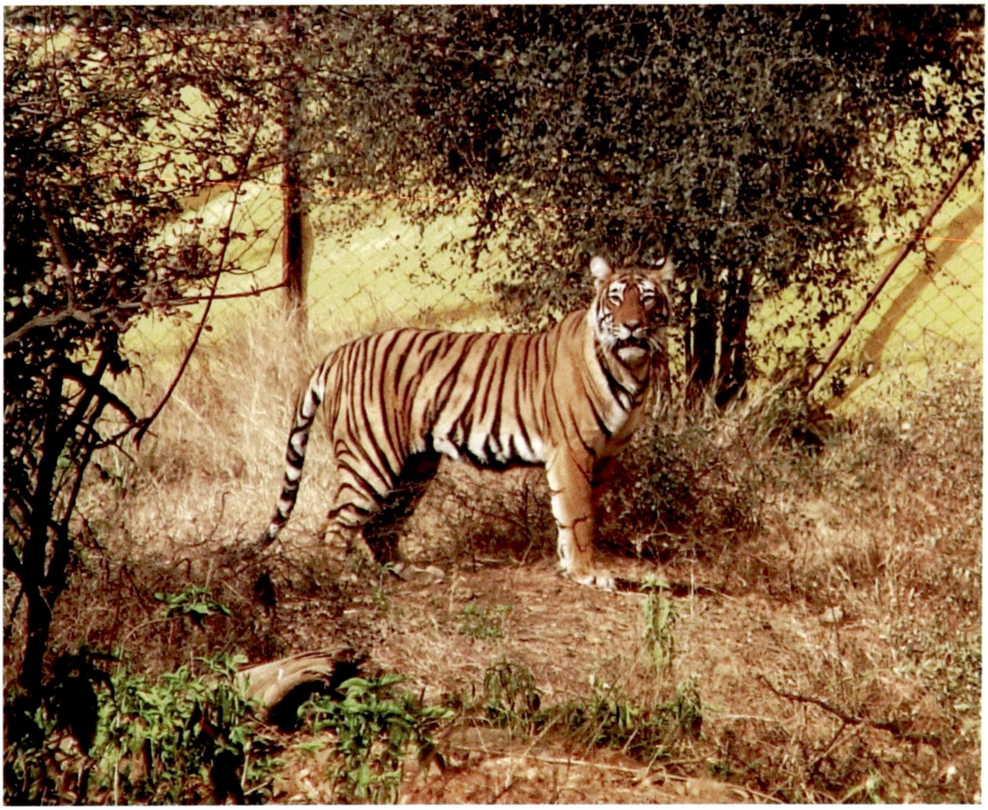

LEFT: Maharani in Sariska *(Photo by Shilpi Gupta)*

The monsoon had been very active that year and as a result the grasses and other ground growth was very thick, making the task of the monitoring team very difficult. This rigorous task was taking its toll on the staff of the monitoring teams.

To ensure alertness of the staff, monitoring duty was shifted from time to time.

On the evening of 29 July 2008 the monitoring party lost radio contact with the tigress. In spite of all attempts, contact could not be resumed. Additional staff from other ranges was summoned and an overnight search was mounted in the hills of Algual, Lilunda, Raika, and Sarunda without much success. That was a real panic situation. Even the satellite facility was not available. Satellite data from ARGOS could only be accessed every third day. In the meanwhile, the ground parties continued their search. Next evening, the satellite data revealed that the tigress was in Chandalia forest area under the Raika outpost.

Her presence in this area revealed that she managed to cross the state highway. Chandalia has been subjected to heavy grazing by cattle from Madho Garh and Raika villages. The area has very little prey base. If she moved further north, she would face even more difficult conditions. There is very little wild prey. Furthermore several hundred heads of cattle were present in Raika, Pani Dhal, and Loj-Nathusar villages. There

BELOW:
Maharani resting

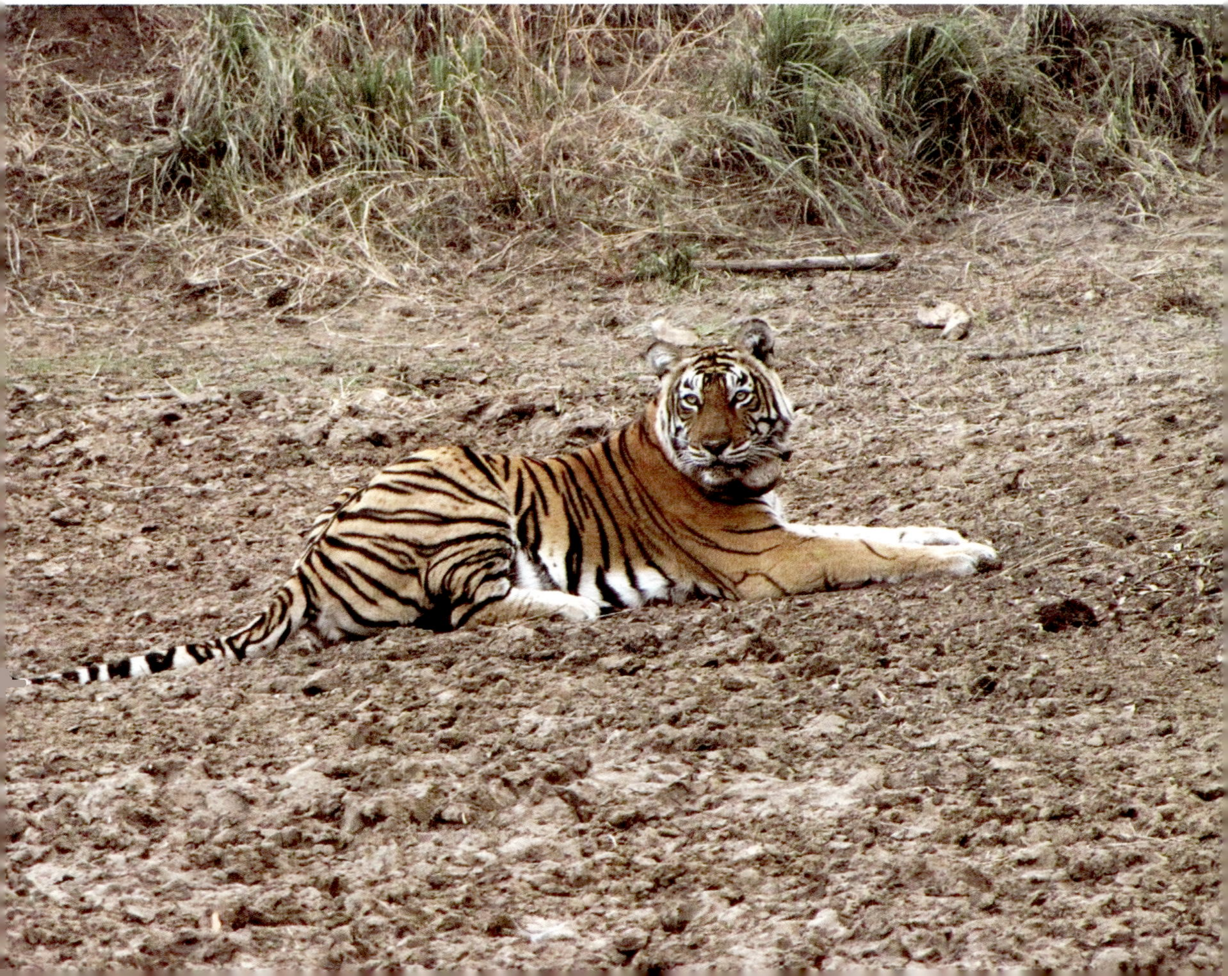

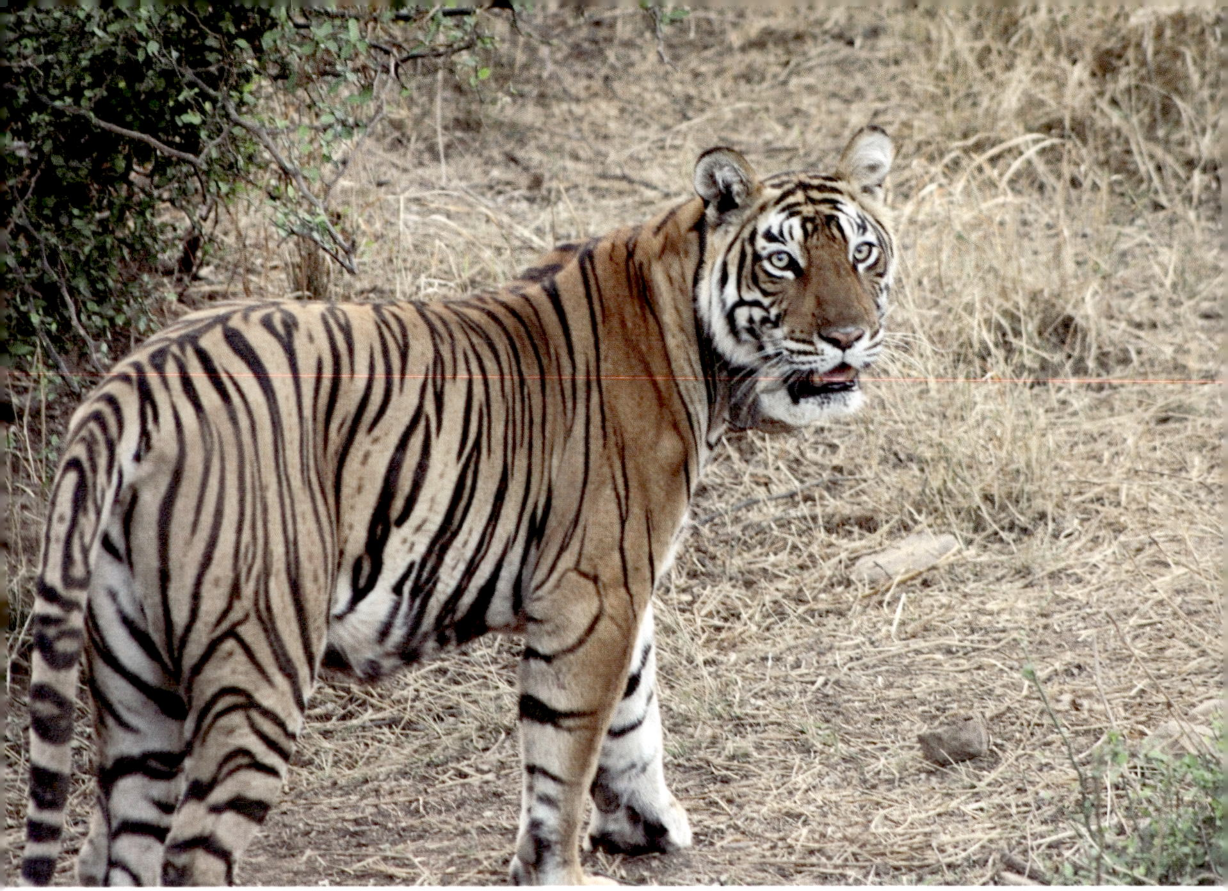

Above: Maharani on the prowl

was only one choice – the tigress had to be brought back to the safety of core area, once again crossing the highway.

With the reinforced search party, I rushed to the site and started the search with the help of the radio receiver. It was getting dark. Moreover, a light drizzle had also started making the operation even more difficult. Suddenly, after a loud call, a sambar jumped out of a thicket as if announcing the presence of the tigress. Though we could not see her, we figured that the tigress was very close to us.

Having located the tigress, a plan was drawn up. Using the available extra staff the area was cordoned off from three sides leaving only one opening towards the core area for the tigress to escape. The search party started with an old hunting style *haka*, that is beating the drums, tin cans, and using torches. The operation had hardly started when the skies opened up, forcing the operation to be called off abruptly.

In the morning, when the operation was about to start, the tigress was spotted on a sambar kill, perhaps a day old. She could well have been on the kill last evening when we were trying to steer her back to the core area. The logical explanation for her not moving out of the area overnight could be that she was hungry and did not want to give up her hard earned meal. I decided not to disturb her over her meal. I created a human barrier on the northern side, to discourage her from moving towards the degraded forests of Raika and Pani Dhal.

In the evening when the operation resumed, the tigress obliged and moved towards the highway but could not cross it due to a large number of pilgrims on the highway. Instead, she moved along the Rupareil river flowing parallel to the highway, and crossed the Kushal Garh–Talvriksh road. The following day she reached Lilunda after crossing the highway.

BELOW: Golden Oreole at Kalighati

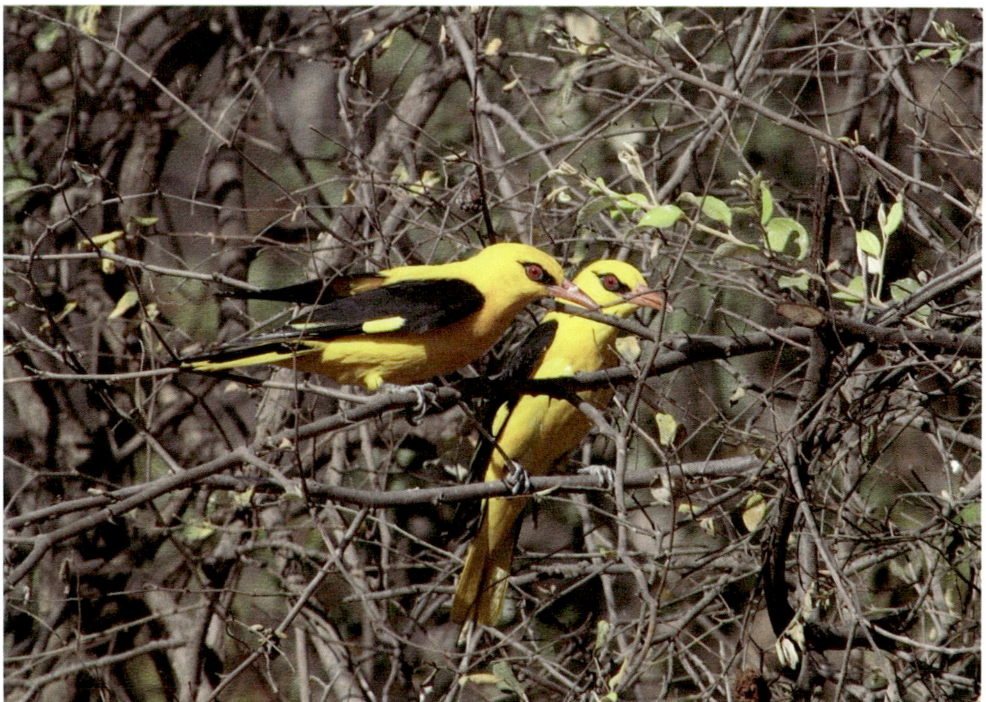

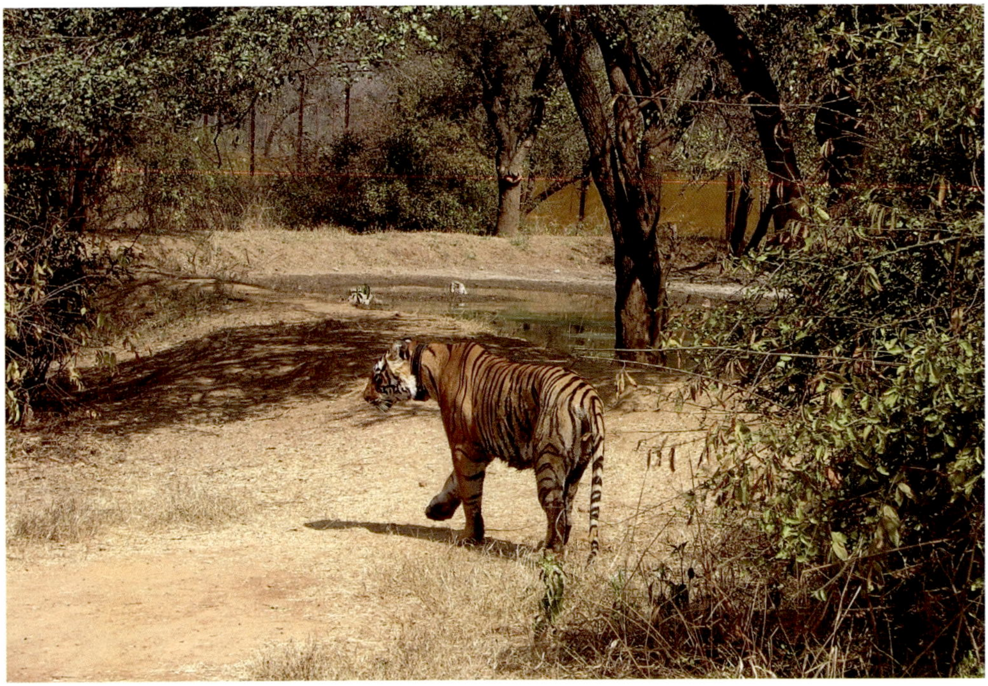

ABOVE: Rani soon after release in the enclosure at Sariska

Later on she came down the rough Kraska hill and moved to Ghanka forest. She had now started showing signs of settling down as she was regularly making kills and gradually developed confidence by increasing her range with every passing day.

In the first week of October 2008, she crossed over to Tarunda in the main Sariska valley and met the tiger Maharaja. She mated with him from 13 to 22 October 2008. The mating generated great excitement among the staff in the hope of seeing a litter soon. In the first week of November 2008 both the male and female tigers started sharing territories and were sometimes found hunting together. In order to reduce human presence near the animals, continuous monitoring was withdrawn from 7 November 2008. Later, both animals were monitored daily by their pug marks in respective beats, kill evidence and occasional VHF signals.

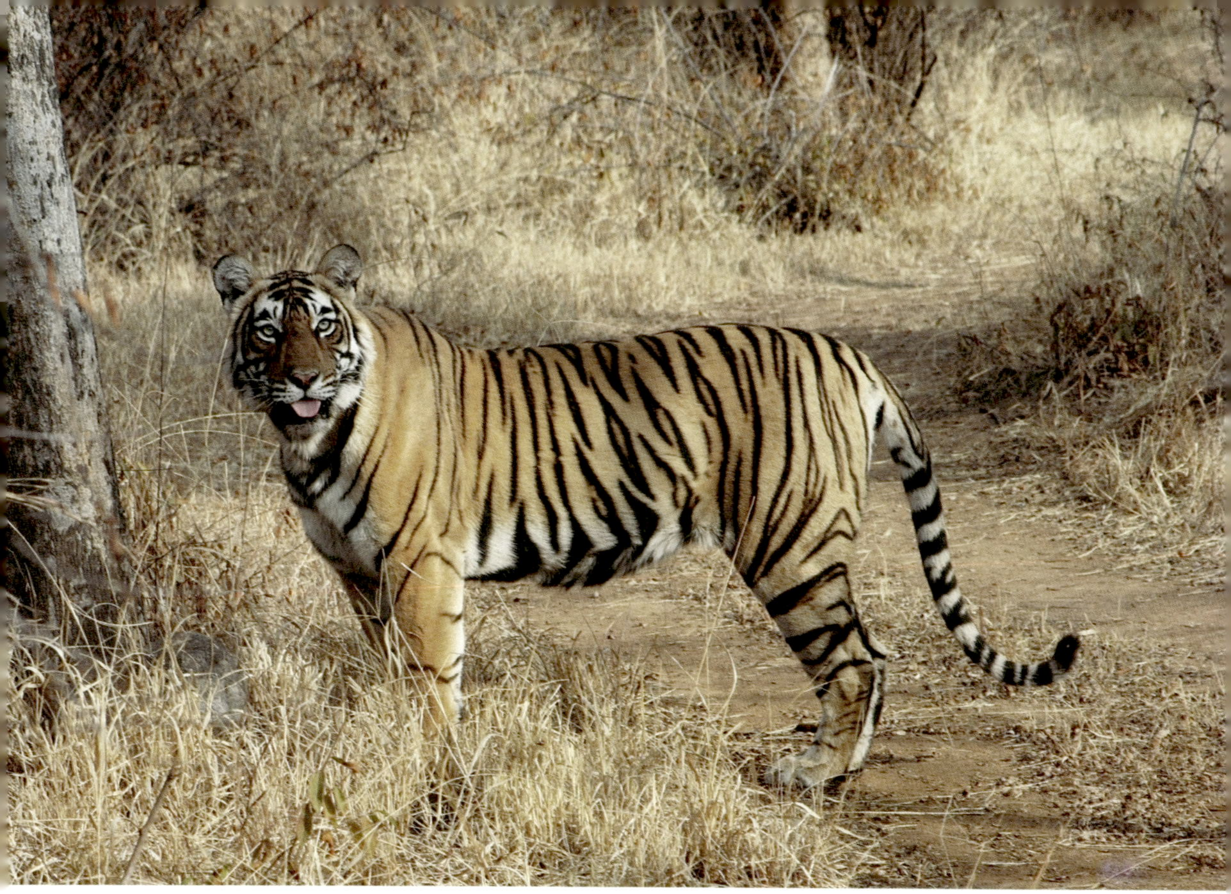

ABOVE:
Rani (CP-3), after her relocation to Sariska

TRANSLOCATION OF THE THIRD (FEMALE) TIGER (CP-3)

The third tiger to be translocated to Sariska was a young female about two and half years old from the Guda area of Ranthambhore. Guda is located on the periphery of the Reserve.

On 25 February 2009 she was chemically immobilised like the earlier tigers and fitted with VHF radio collar in the absence of a GPS enabled satellite collar. She was also airlifted to Sariska and was to be released in the same enclosure where the male tiger had been lodged. However, when the cage was opened, instead of jumping out, she preferred to stay in the cage. This strange behaviour perplexed us. Some felt that she was still under the effect of sedation. Water was sprayed over her body. Still she was reluctant to leave the cage. After nearly 20 minutes the tigress made her first move cautiously and came up to the opening of the cage. She peeped out, examined the surroundings, and with a lightening move, jumped out of the cage and disappeared into the bushes.

Apparently she was not very happy at being kept in quarantine though the smell of the male tiger still persisted in the enclosure. She did not make any kill and remained under thick undergrowth in the enclosure. This made us apprehensive about her well being. To get a better look at her, one of the researchers walked up to the fence of the enclosure and was immediately greeted with a full charge by the tigress in public view. She came crashing against the tiger proof chain link. This reassured the team as she did not show any signs of being sick or injured.

BELOW: Rani in the vacated Bhagani village

In consultation with scientists from WII, I decided to release the tigress into the wild on 27 February, two days after she reached Sariska.

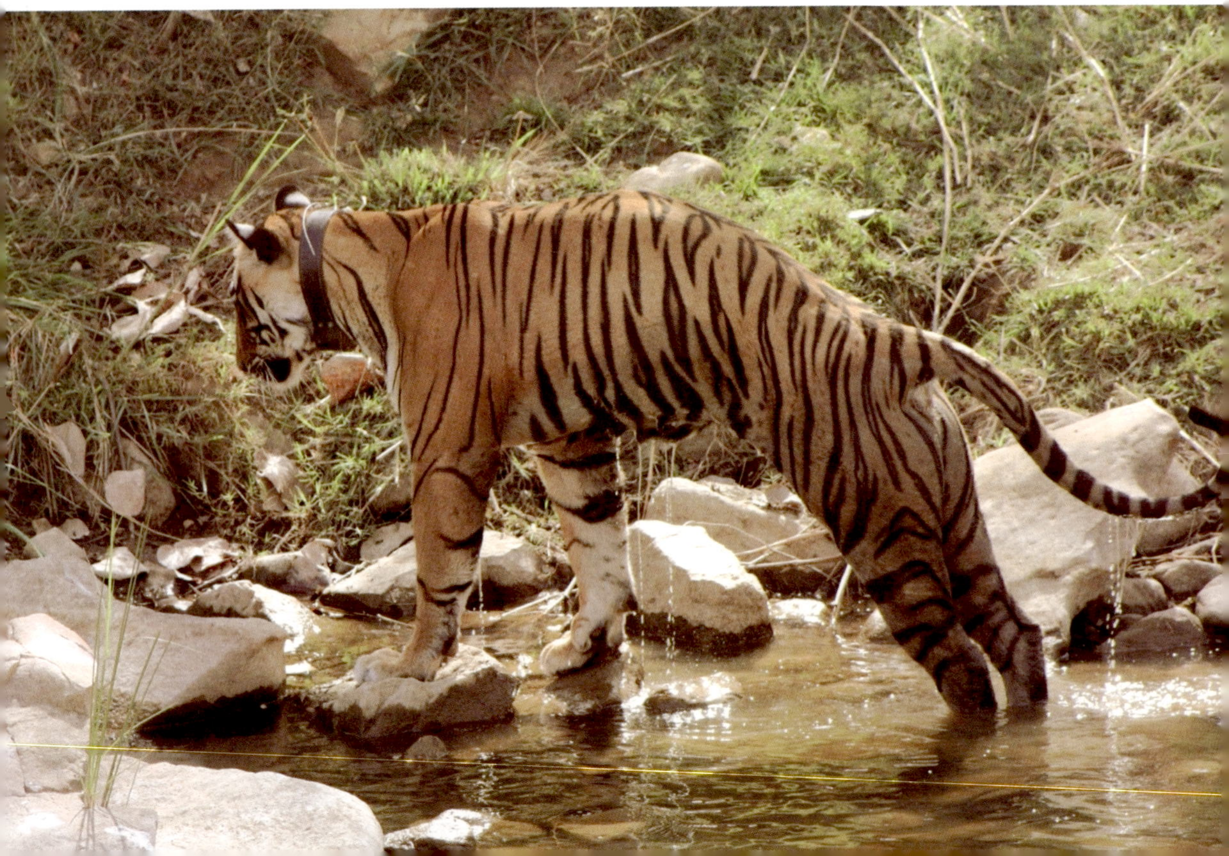

We, however, found that she had not moved at all from her position of the previous evening. She had not even come to the waterhole to drink water but was seen licking her paws. The situation warranted concern. Perhaps during the charge on the fence earlier she might have injured her claws. If this was the case then she could not be released as planned. In a hurried conference with the scientists, it was decided to wait and watch for some more time.

Meanwhile in order to see the reaction of the tigress, in the late evening it was decided to lift the blind (a lining of six feet high light yellow cloth) partially from the corner of the enclosure. As soon as the blind was lifted, the tigress charged, proving her total fitness. But looking at the earlier behaviour of the animal, Dr K. Sankar of WII wanted to keep the animal in the enclosure for a few more days for observation. Dr Parag Nigam, the veterinarian, was, however, of the opinion that the tigress should immediately be released; otherwise the agitated animal might injure itself seriously by charging at the fence with greater force. The CWLW Mr Mehrotra was briefed about the situation. After thorough consideration, he authorised me to take appropriate decision.

It was a difficult situation. The day-long behaviour of the animal suggested that she might be seriously injured, perhaps in the spinal cord. But her flawless jump after the partial removal of the blind suggested perfect fitness. I was in a fix. If the injured animal is released she will not survive. But if she is all right and is only unhappy at being in the enclosure, then her release will ease her tension. Weighing the pros and cons, I finally decided in favour of her immediate release. As soon as the gate of the enclosure was opened, she dashed out like a bullet. We checked the entire enclosure that night itself and again early the next morning. To our pleasant surprise not a drop of blood was found anywhere to indicate her injury. We were greatly relieved.

Leaving the enclosure, the tigress first stayed in a dry stream bed, close to the enclosure for some time. Then she made her way towards

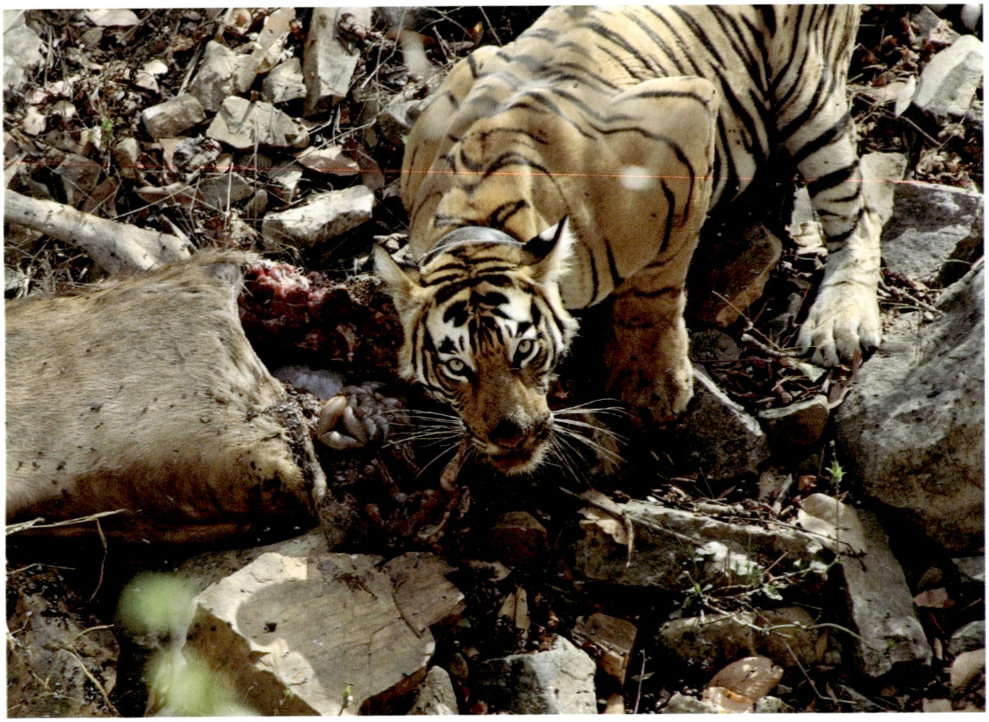

Above: Rani feasting on her prey

Tarunda and Bana plateau in the south-western part of the Reserve and then crossed Kankwadi to reach Garh–Rajore area. It looked like it was going to be a repetition of our old experience with Maharaja who had also ventured in this direction and reached Garh–Rajore village, located on the periphery of the core zone in the Reserve. Like Maharaja, she too made several attempts to get into human habitation. On one occasion, she made a sambar kill in Haripura Rundh (very close to Garh–Rajore). I told the patrol party not to disturb her till she is on the kill and wait until she is done with it. Afterwards, a drive was organised using drums and tin cans to steer her towards Bhagani–Kankwadi.

On another occasion she crossed Kalighati–Rajore hill plateau and entered the agricultural fields of Jodhawas and Kharrika villages, aggravating the problems of the patrol party. The constant beating of drums to steer her back irritated her. On the night of 16 March 2009, the agitated tigress even charged at the vehicle of the monitoring party. They had quickly to climb up a tree to save their lives.

On 19 March, the patrolling team managed to steer the animal to Bhagani during the day. Bhagani has a rich prey base. Water is available round the year, making it the ideal habitat for tigers. She stayed here for a few days but occasionally would go up to Rajore and Mala Johadka side. We hoped that she would stick to Bhagani for some time and then settle here permanently. This tigress, coded CP-3, however, loved to play truant. She had the habit of leaving the security of the core area and moving towards the edge of the Reserve near human settlements, giving us sleepless nights and frantic days. Every time CP-3 ventured out, we had to do 'haka' to steer her back to the core area.

We all wished for the male tiger to meet her soon so that she may naturalise here and make Bhagani her territory.

MATING AT BHAGANI ON 5 APRIL 2009

Revival of Sariska essentially means cubs from the reintroduced tigers to populate the forest up to its carrying capacity. The management was anxiously waiting for this to happen. In this context, there were reports about the presence of CP-1 and CP-3 at Bhagani. From the security point of view, a pair is more succeptible to poaching. So it was very important to visit the area frequently in order to strengthen the safety measures.

On 4 April 2009, I visited Bhagani. The staff posted here informed me about the presence of the tiger pair in Tuda area. I went to Tuda side and checked the entire stream but as the tigers were still in the thickets they could not be sighted. I stayed at the Bhagani check post during the night. Till late into the night, the staff told stories about their challenging experiences with CP-3 while following her day and night for almost a month. They were very enthusiastic about Maharaja mating with CP-3.

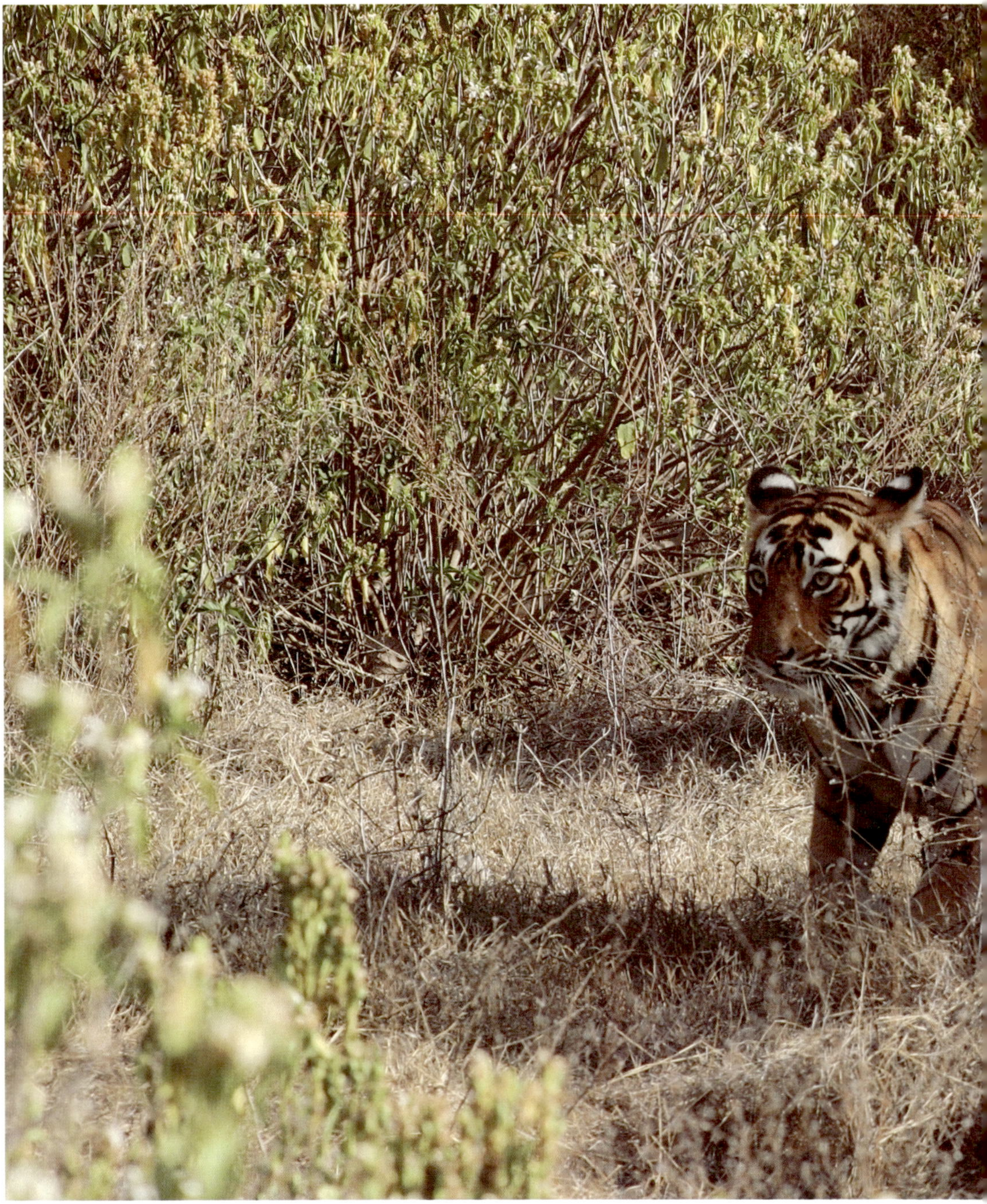

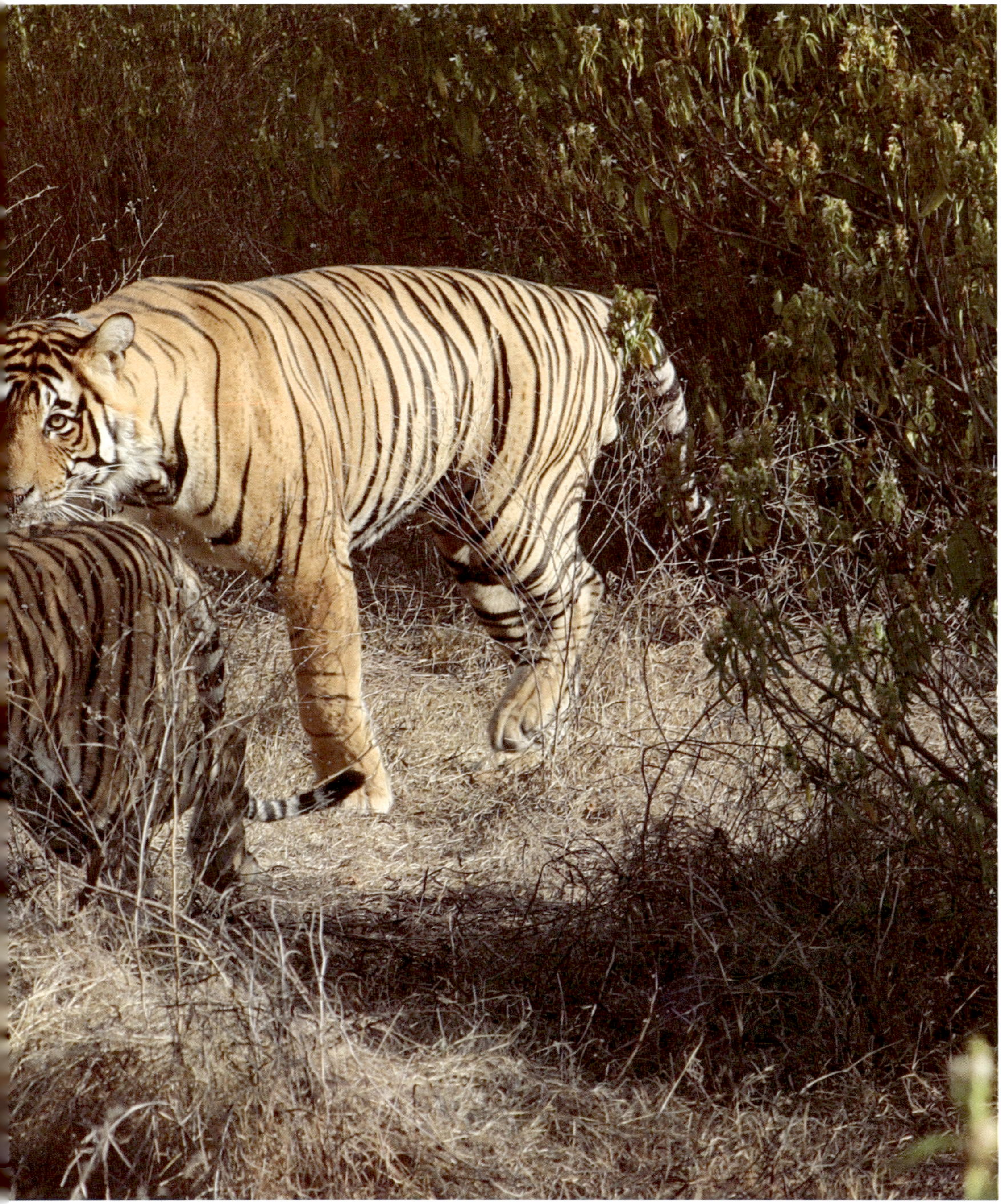

Next day I got up quite early in the morning. I wanted to see if I could spot the mating pair. The morning was clear and a cool breeze was blowing. I drove towards Tuda. Shortly I was rewarded with an alarm call of a chital from the valley ahead. I switched off the engine of the vehicle and waited for the commotion to follow that always happens when the lord of the jungle ventures out. Nothing happened. Everything was quiet; not a sound could be heard. After ten minutes of waiting I decided to move on.

After the shifting of villagers, Bhagani has now been secured by a boundary wall with an iron gate. Primarily rocky, with a few perennial stagnant pools of water, Bhagani is an ideal habitat for the tigers. Moreover, a large population of ungulates makes it a preferred hunting ground for the big cat.

On crossing the Bhagani nallah, I was received by a lone forest guard. The others had gone to patrol the area as there had been incessant tiger calls during the night confirming the presence of more than one tiger which could only mean one thing–the thing that we had all hoped would happen sooner than later–the single-most important factor–one that would ensure that the tiger was in Sariska to stay.

Praying to the Almighty, I went deeper into the forest. I drove for about a kilometre to find the Range Officer waiting under a Dhak tree. He informed me that some pug marks and tiger scats had been found but the tiger had not been sighted. I sat patiently in the vehicle, contemplating my next move, surrounded as I was by the dense under growth of shrubs with tiny white flowers. I did not want to disturb the tiger.

The sun had now climbed high and it was quite warm. The forest was quiet except for the faint flitting and twittering of purple sunbirds from these sweet smelling white flowers. The tiger had probably found a shaded spot and retired for the day.

Pages 166–167: Maharaja and Rani having a nice time together

Suddenly, the silence was broken by the loud metallic call of a sambar. After 30 seconds the call was repeated. It was picked up by a

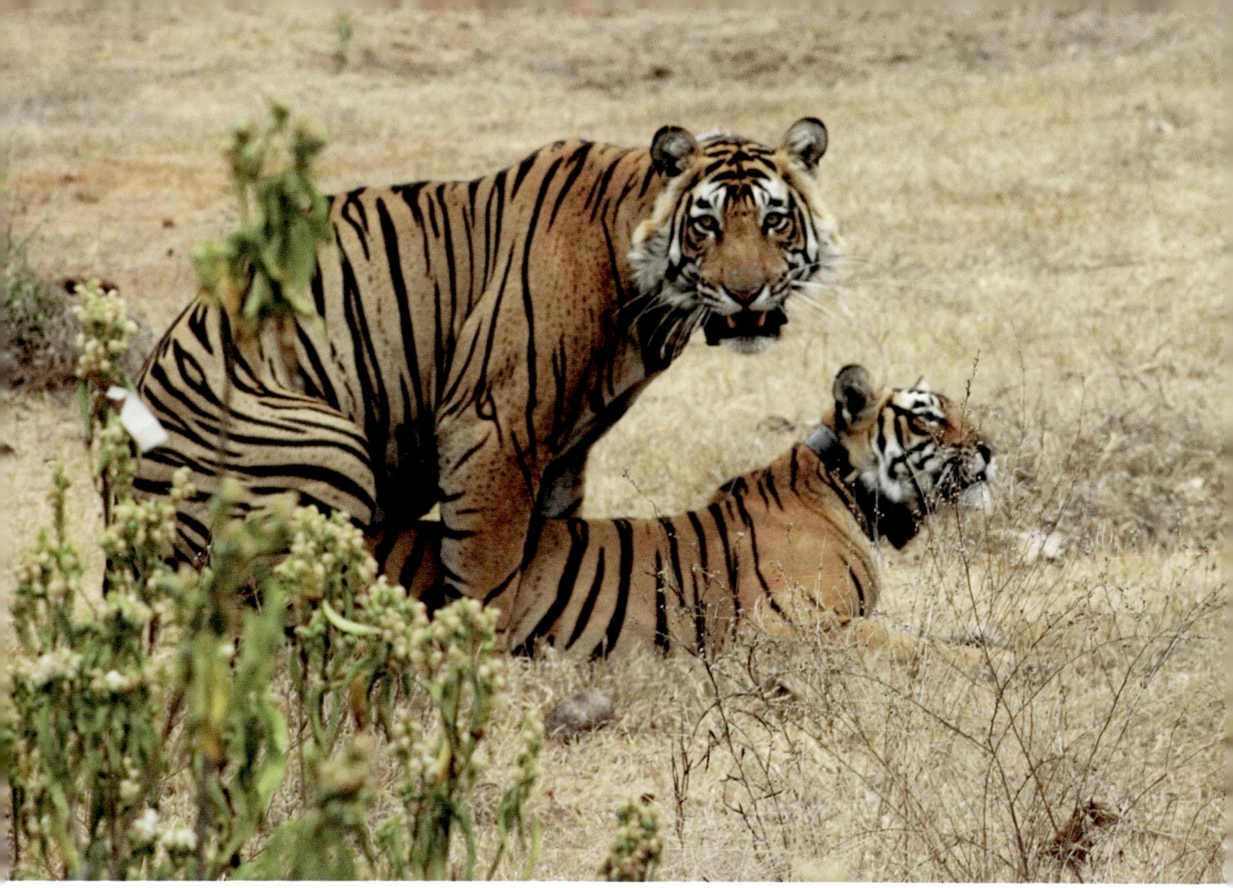

herd of chital feeding close by and the next moment the entire forest was resonating with animal alarm calls. Hanuman langurs sitting on tree tops started calling, followed by the piercing call of the peacock. The forest became action packed. Surely the tiger was on the prowl.

ABOVE: Maharaja and Rani mating at Bhagani

I received a message on the wireless set that the tiger had been seen at Tuda merely half a kilometre away from us. I drove in that direction cautiously, peering into the thick vegetation for a glimpse. The Range Officer pointed to my left and whispered '*Woh raha hokum*' (there he is, Sir). I scanned the region carefully and sure enough I saw tiger stripes. The bushes had beautifully camouflaged the majestic animal. He was sitting on his hind legs in the bushes and front legs and head out, looking straight at the approaching vehicle.

Oh, what a sight it was! In spite of having spent close to four decades in the forest and experiencing innumerable encounters with the tiger, I still cannot explain that feeling or thrill of the first glimpse. That one look is good enough to get you hooked for a lifetime.

Undoubtedly I was looking at the magnificent robust Maharaja, the first tiger to be brought to Sariska under the re-introduction programme. We switched off the engine of the vehicle and hesitantly looked at the tiger to see whether he was getting disturbed by our presence. He did not seem bothered by this intrusion into his siesta. I took out my camera and started clicking photographs. After about 10 to 15 minutes, there was a sambar alarm call a short distance away from us. Again it was picked up by chitals in the same direction. This alerted the tiger and he turned his head in the direction of the calls. Leaving the Range Officer to keep an eye on the tiger, I moved ahead in the direction of the calls.

We drove till the pool of water amidst loud calling but could not see the tigress. Then the Range Officer informed me that Maharaja had moved away into the thick undergrowth. We were wondering what to do next

BELOW: Finally tigers are back in Sariska

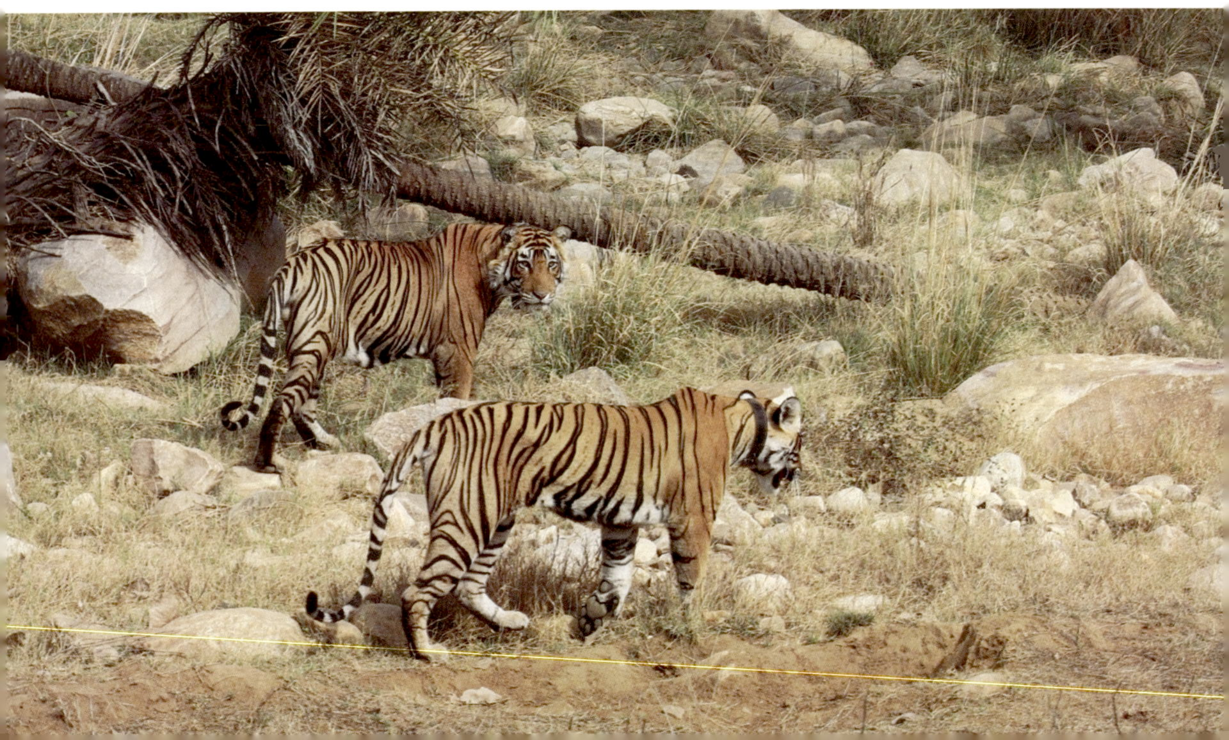

when we heard a very low growl, followed by an even lower 'ahawho'. Soon this turned into a regular low growling conversation between two tigers. We were thrilled to hear this vocalisation of the two tigers as it signified that they were already together. There was no point in our waiting out in the sun as there was little chance of getting a glimpse of the tigers hidden in thick cover. We drove back to the post for some rest. After an hour and a half, we drove back to the same spot accompanied by the Assistant Director and a researcher from WII, hoping to see the tigers. The weather had suddenly become cloudy and breezy and the sun had disappeared behind thick grey clouds. To our pleasant surprise, we found Maharaja relaxing out in the open under the shade of a small tree. We could not believe our eyes and luck, for, lying close to him, half hidden by the bushes, was a tigress! Her face was not visible. I asked my driver to move the Gypsy to the other side of the bush so that I could identify the tigress.

The noise of the engine startled the sleeping tigress who woke up and immediately got into a crouching position, looking at us and snarling for waking her up from a deep slumber. Then she stood up and walked towards the male tiger and stood facing him, with her back towards us. The tiger responded to her by gently nudging her on the neck as if trying to seduce or encourage her to mate with him. CP-3 moved a few metres into the bush and came out to the clearing on the far side. The tiger followed and moved behind her. The bushes in front of us partially blocked our vision. We moved back for a better view. The tigress had crouched submissively moving her tail slowly. Maharaja went around her sniffing closely and then it gently positioned himself on top of the tigress and started mating. The first mounting lasted some 10 to 12 seconds. After dismounting, the tiger surveyed the ground around him in a leisurely walk and then settled by her side.

In the next half hour, they mated twice more, again for short bursts of about 10 seconds each. The tigress looked a little exhausted now. Another attempt by the male tiger was not received well by her and she snapped at

> him. Thereafter, they both got up and went towards the water pool at the base of the hill.

What we witnessed that afternoon was history in the making. If all went well, Sariska could well be on the path to recovery with tigers roaming in the forest once more. We named this tigress Rani.

On the night of 6 April 2009 Maharaja moved back towards Kalighati leaving Rani in Richhunda area. The next morning I spotted and photographed him close to Bhramnath waterhole on a kill of a chital stag. It was quite evident that during the courtship it had not eaten anything. Another important point is that one week of togetherness with Maharaja had helped Rani to settle down and naturalise in the area of Bhagani. She was now freely making kills of sambars and chitals in and around this area.

It was interesting to monitor the courtship of Maharaja with Rani. After meeting Maharaja, Rani was now hardly moving out of Bhagani area. The tigress was fitted with a powerful dilope antenna. So monitoring her movements was easy. But there was some problem with Maharaja's transmitter because of which tracking him with the help of the antenna had become difficult. Therefore, we were depending mainly upon its pug mark trails. At that time the soil was already broken as a result of which the tigers were leaving behind clear pug marks. But as he was moving over a huge area, monitoring his movements had become very difficult. The entire field staff had been put on alert. I was thus getting information about his presence but not very timely.

On 10 April 2009, he started travelling from Udaynath, and crossing a series of hills, passed through Bhagani and reached Richhunda, about 6 km from Bhagani. His pug marks were seen in front of the Bhagani checkpost. He, however, did not meet the tigress who was very much present in that area. It is interesting to notice that after his first meeting with Rani, he did not venture very far from Bhagani. He had not gone

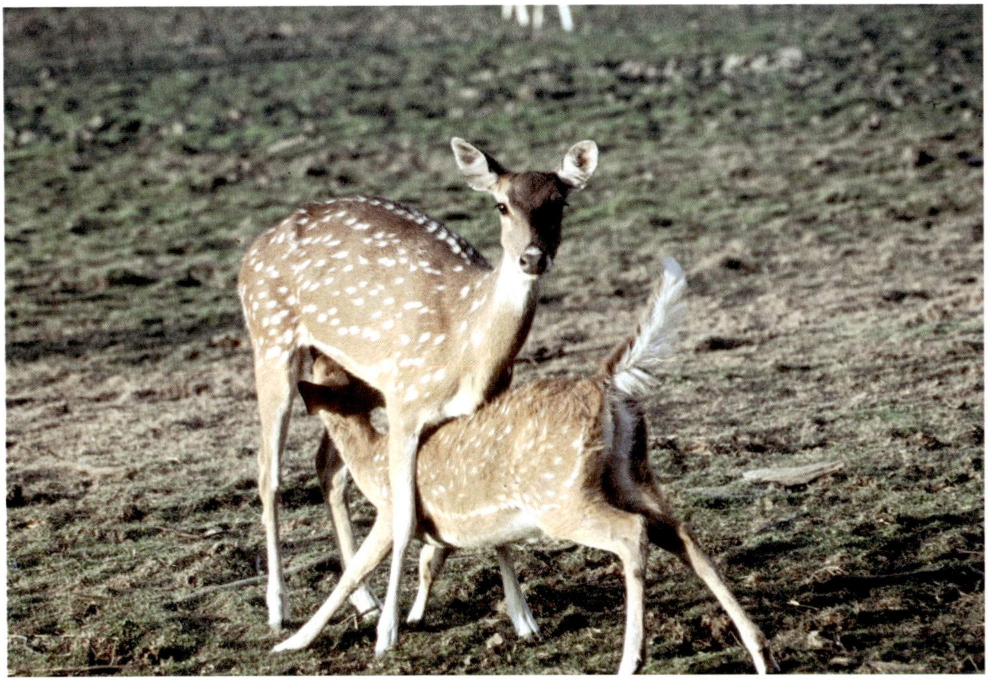

ABOVE: A spotted deer feeding its young one

beyond Bheru Ghati, 2 km from Kalighati. On 20–21 April 2009, he stayed in Tarunda and Karna ka Bas area in the company of the other tigress, who had since been christened Maharani. On 22 April, again he reached Bhagani and mated with Rani for the second time.

Since Maharaja reached Bhagani through hilly terrains, he did not leave any noticeable pug marks and silently joined Rani without anybody noticing it. On the morning of 24 April we got a clear signal from Rani's transmitter. She was about 2 km from the Bhagani post. We tracked the animal on foot. In the thickets of *Adhatoda vasica* (Adusta) one sambar carcass was found. It was almost fully consumed by Rani. She could not be seen due to the dense growth of Adusta shrubs. Maharaja too could not be sighted. But I had a gut feeling that the tiger was enjoying the company of the tigress in the thickets of shrubs, not very far from us!

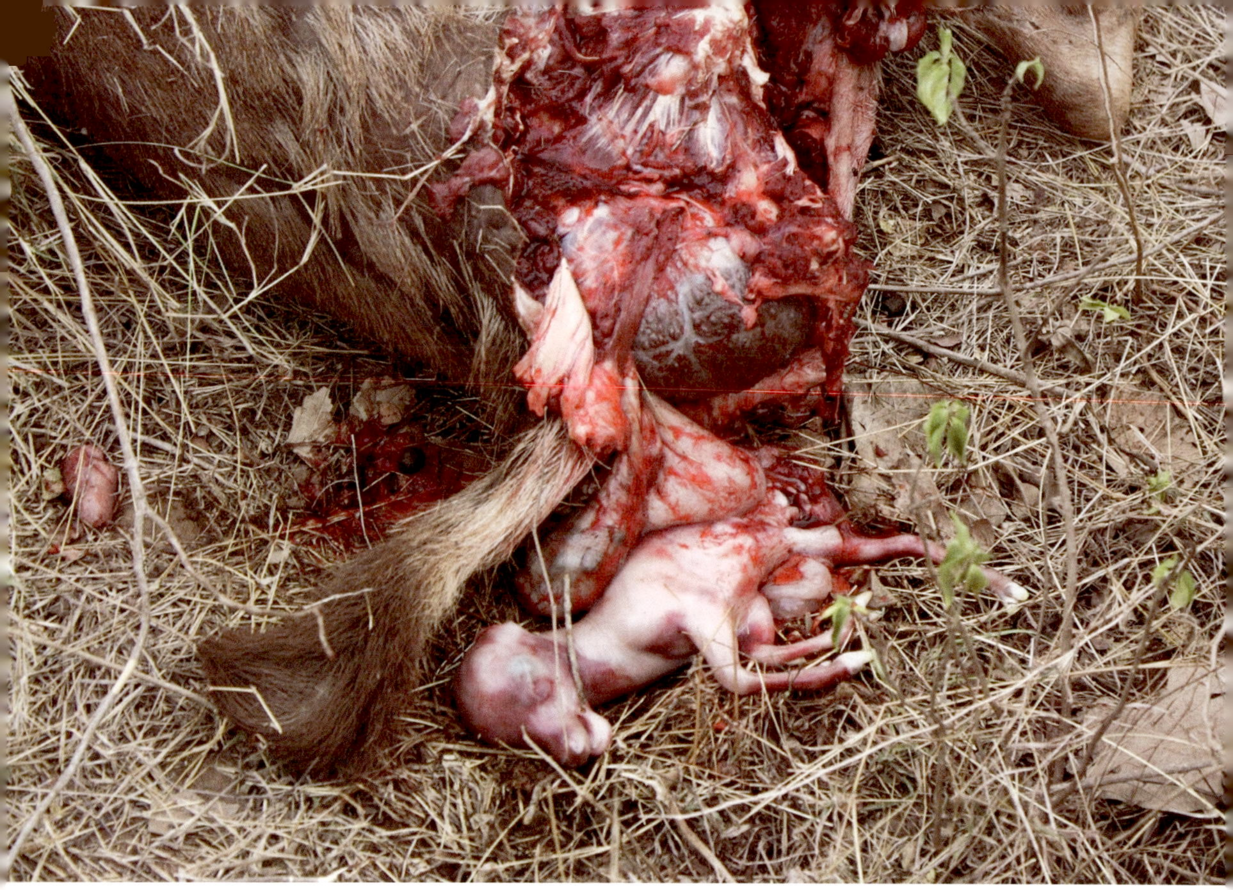

ABOVE: A foetus without a scratch left untouched by the tiger

Asking the staff to keep a vigil over the animals, I came back to the headquarters. Regular reports of mating were received from Bhagani. On the evening of 28 April, I again visited Bhagani. Prabhu Singh, the forest guard, told me that both the animals were at Dhaula Dah, an important water pool, about 1 km from the checkpost. We immediately rushed to the site. There was little water in the waterhole. The animals had moved from there towards another turn of the Bhagani nallah. While we were trying to locate them, suddenly there was an alarm call of a sambar. It was in panic. We cautiously approached. We found a fresh kill of a sambar doe. The tigress was on the kill and eating it leisurely. Maharaja was sitting about 7 m from her. They obliged me by giving excellent poses for shooting. Rani did not eat much and soon left the kill for Maharaja who also did not seem to be hungry. Leaving the kill behind, they moved towards Beri Wali Dah, another important water pool in the proximity. Rani went into the cool water of the pool and stayed there. Maharaja crossed the nallah and went up the hill on the other side of the nallah and disappeared.

> Later on, I came back to the kill. It was a young doe. A full grown foetus of the sambar was found near the kill. It must have come out of the mother's womb when the tiger had opened up its stomach. To my utmost surprise it was not touched by either of the tigers. Was it just by chance or had the tigers, too, showed respect to the unborn?

Another interesting observation about this pair was that Maharaja kept visiting Bhagani every now and then. Many times after making a kill, he left the area without feeding on it, as if he was providing food for his queen as sometimes humans do.

TRANSLOCATION OF THE FOURTH AND FIFTH TIGERS

Getting the fourth and fifth tigers to Sariska from Ranthambhore was virtually made impossible by the Ranthambhore lobby. It was due to the efforts of Mr Jairam Ramesh, the then Union Minister of State for Environment and Forests that the web was broken. On 20 July 2010 the fourth (male) tiger from Kundalka (core) of Ranthambhore was brought to Sariska. He was brought by road due to non-availability of a helicopter. A week later, on 28 July, the fifth (female) tiger was also brought from Gilai Sagar, fringe area of Ranthambhore. This completed the first phase of the reintroduction plan.

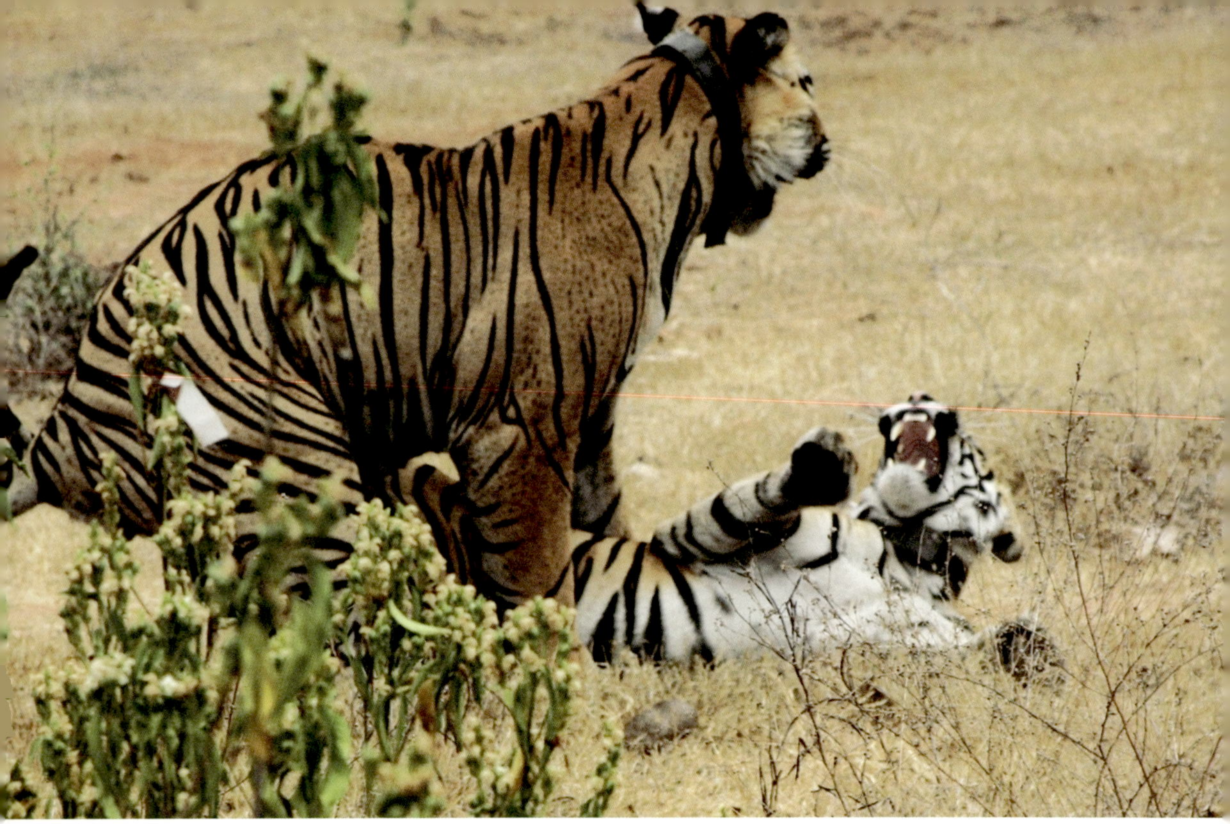

THE CONTROVERSIES

Reintroduction of Tiger into Sariska was routed in controversies from the very beginning. The proposal was vehemently opposed by a powerful lobby who did not want Sariska to recover lest it takes away a large share of the tiger tourism from Ranthambhore because of Sariska's ideal location vis-a-vis that of Ranthambhore. There were demonstrations by hoteliers, transporters, and guides on the streets of Sawai Madhopur. Their opposition is understandable because of their vested interests. But it was most unfortunate that some well known conservationists associated with Ranthambhore for a long time also supported this business lobby. Initially, they opposed the proposal on the premise that it is bound to fail as tigers are likely to die during the rigorous process of shifting. The first successful relocation proved them wrong.

Then they argued that the tigers would not accept the new location and die either out of hunger or will enter the villages and lift cattle or humans. Time proved them wrong on this aspect also. The translocation of Rani was opposed by them by proffering the argument that tigers with established territory should not be shifted; only those living on the periphery may be translocated. Is this theory backed by any studies? No. In fact, it does not stand on any footing except an effort to sabotage an ideal tiger rehabilitation programme for Sariska.

It is understandable that territories are formed by stronger tigers and tigresses of an area. Weaker animals are pushed out and are compelled

FACING PAGE: Maharaja and Rani mating

BELOW: Maharaja and Rani rest after mating

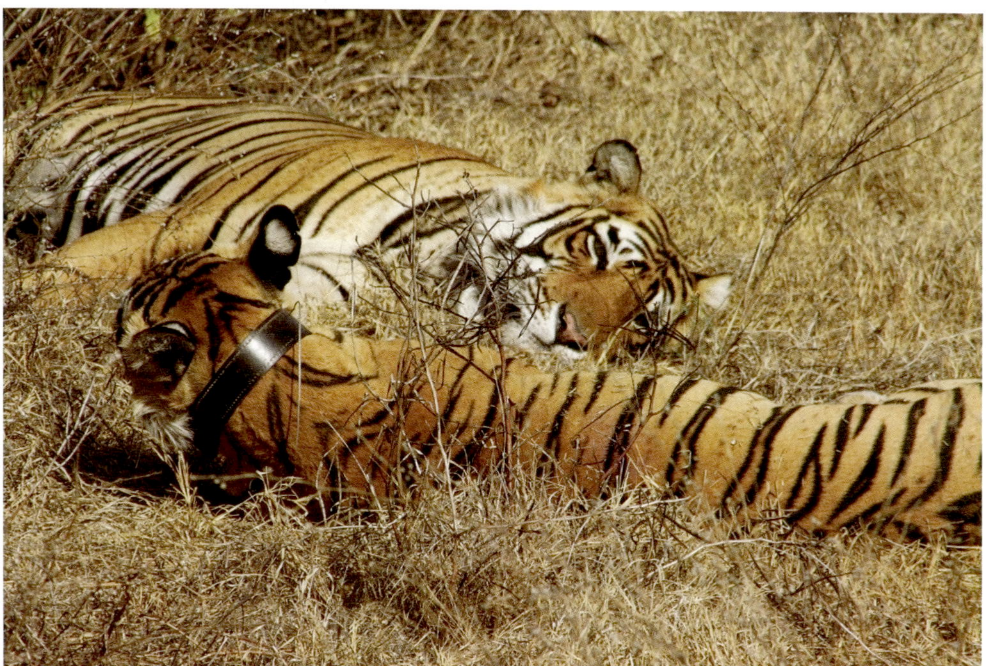

to take refuge on the periphery of a tiger land, which is often agriculture fields and adjacent villages. Since wild prey is scarce on the periphery, these tigers take to hunting livestock. If such tigers are picked up for translocation to Sariska, they are likely to be seriously injured or even killed by the tiger or tigress already established in the area. As a result, these new entrants, even if they survive, will be pushed to the periphery in Sariska as well, where the buffer is almost non-existent. These ousted animals, therefore, will have no choice but to resort to killing livestock in the surrounding villages or agricultural fields. It is bound to inflame the conflict between the Reserve and villagers within and on the periphery of the Reserve. These animals would thus become soft targets of not only poachers but also villagers. The entire project of restocking Sariska with tigers will then fall flat. It will obviously suit those opposed to the

BELOW: The water level goes down during summer

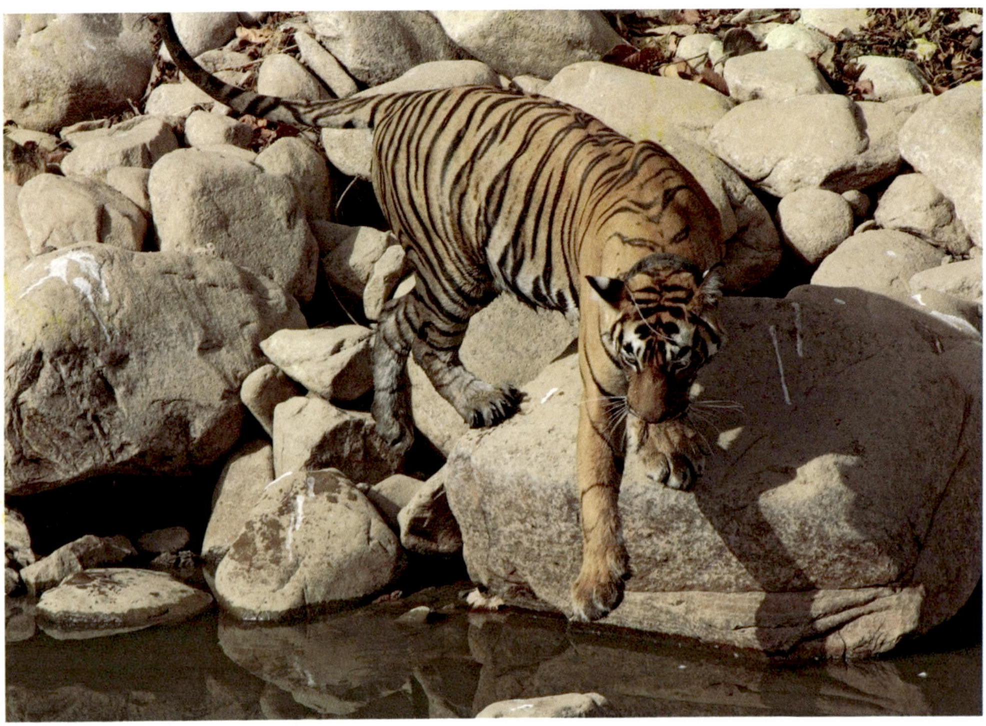

rejuvenation of Sariska. But will it be in the interest of the conservation of wildlife in general and tiger in particular?

I fail to understand the logic of advocating translocation of peripheral tigers. An unbiased scientific approach recommends the selection of strong tiger or tigress with well-established territories for such operations so that they can demand from the tigers translocated earlier enough room in the prime habitat to build their own territories. In Ranthambhore, the tigers pushed to the periphery will get an opportunity to occupy the space vacated by the stronger tigers. It will immensely help in reducing the tiger–villager conflicts around Ranthambhore also.

It is also worth mentioning that reintroduction of just three tigers enhanced tourism in Sariska by about 20 per cent in the first year itself. Tiger Den, the sick unit of Tourism Department of Rajasthan, had started making profits for the first time after 2004, when Sariska lost its tigers. This strengthens the suspicion that opposition to reintroduction of tigers in Sariska was a result of the cut throat business rivalry.

I would also like to mention that a Jaipur-based retired senior forest officer also opposed the tiger translocation to Sariska from Ranthambhore. He filed a writ petition in the Rajasthan High Court demanding an immediate halt to the translocation project. His plea was that the progenies of these relocated tigers will suffer from genetic problems as a result of inbreeding as tigers are genetically closely related. As a conservationist his

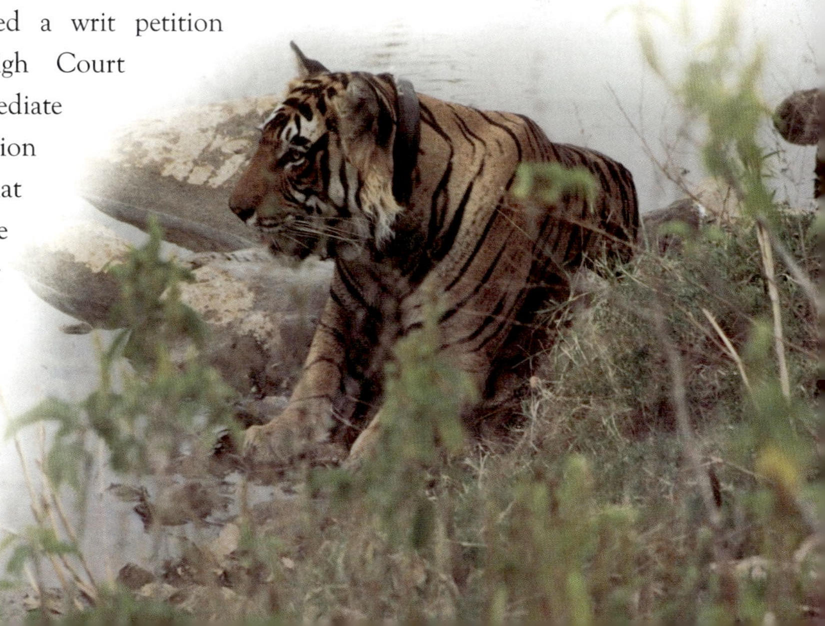

BELOW: Contemplating

concern about genetic diversity is appreciable. But should he talk of this when the very existence of Sariska depended upon its immediate restocking with tigers? He was well aware that if Sariska is not restocked immediately it was bound to fall into ruin just like many other important sanctuaries of Rajasthan and elsewhere in India.

Those genuinely concerned about the ill-effects of inbreeding should have waited till the completion of the re-introduction of five tigers into Sariska. Then quoting the example of this successful reintroduction they should have raised their voice advocating the interchange of tigers to and from not only Sariska and Ranthambhore, but from other tiger reserves in the country as well, as inbreeding is a severe problem in most of the tiger areas in India.

BELOW: About to start a meal

On the eve of the first anniversary of the tiger relocation, yet another controversy had been raked up. This alleges that all the three tigers (CP-

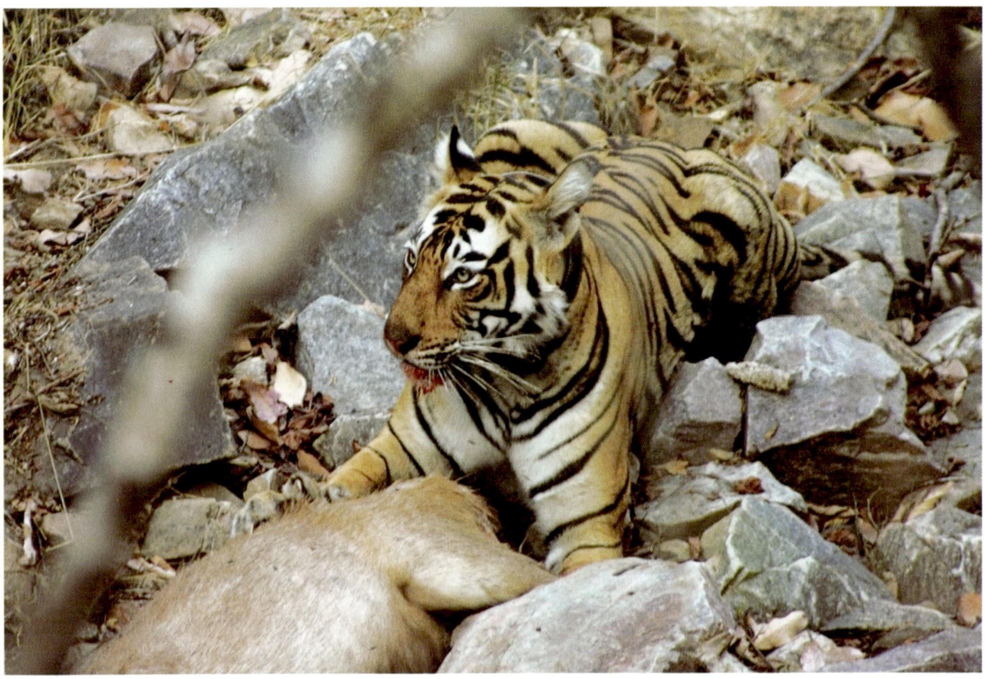

1, CP-2, and CP-3) relocated to Sariska are siblings from the same father, though the male is from a different mother.

The management of the Reserve and Wildlife Institute of India (WII) which actually performed this operation, as well as the Rajasthan government have denied this allegation. Looking at the attitude of the lobby, which has been trying desperately to scuttle this project, this new allegation also seems to be an arrow from the same quiver. If what they say is correct, then they should possess better knowledge about Ranthambhore tigers than the Reserve management or WII!

Ranthambhore was made a project tiger reserve in 1973. It reportedly had only 11 tigers then. The present large tiger population has been resulted from that small stock. Why did the experts not raise their voices against possible inbreeding then?

It is also surprising that this sibling controversy started only in June 2009, a year after the translocation. Did the experts take such a long time to complete their study or was this allegation used as the last resort because they failed to stop translocation of the third tiger in February 2009 in spite of their untiring efforts?

It is also striking that in the first week of November 2008 a team from WII reached Ranthambhore for undertaking the translocation of a tigress to Sariska. The anti-relocation lobby immediately became superactive and pressurised the member secretary of NTCA who ordered halting of this operation through letters to CWLW of Rajasthan and director of WII.

V.P. Singh, Member of Parliament and Chairman of the Steering Committee of Forestry and Wildlife Management, Rajasthan, took up this issue with the Prime Minister through his letter of 7 November 2008. The Prime Minister intervened and only then did it become possible to translocate Rani.

V.P. Singh's action provoked the Ranthambhore lobby to come out with the sibling theory. The propaganda of this theory brought them temporary success as the reintroduction plan was once again put on the back burner by the Central Government. It should also be considered that Ranthambhore is overflowing with a population of more than 50 tigers seemingly beyond its carrying capacity. There have been reports of fights between tigers. As a result, several of them have been pushed out of the Reserve. These tigers are in conflict with villagers on the periphery.

On 7 March 2010, two 17-month old tiger cubs from the litter of a Chiroli tigress were poisoned by villagers in Ranthambhore near Talwada village, on the banks of Banas river. A fortnight later, 50-year-old Badri Kumhar, a resident of village Edna, Shyampura, was killed along with his donkey by a tiger on the forest periphery. Again, on 3 July, 23-year-old Ghamandi Lal Saini was killed by a tiger near Ranthambhore Bagh Resort. Next month 22-year-old Hem Raj Gujjar was injured by a tiger. Two days later, in Bhuri Pahadi village a stray tiger seriously injured Daulat Singh Shaktawat, Range Officer of Ranthambhore. He was trying to steer this animal back to the Reserve after tranquilising it. Daulat Singh is one of the most experienced wildlife field officers in the country. He became a victim of the overflowing tiger population and lost his right eye apart from sustaining several other injuries.

Two tigers had crossed to Karauli area and a tigress to the ravines of Kota, travelling more than 150 km from Ranthambhore. After attacking Daulat Singh, this tiger, coded T-7, strayed towards Mathura and finally landed at Bharatpur after wandering more than 200 km. In October 2009 a tigress was poisoned by villagers while another made its way to Kalisind area. In all, eight tigers have strayed from Ranthambhore in a year out of which only one could be brought back. T-36 died in a territorial fight with T-42.

The stray tigers face the serious threat of being poached any day. The accidents, killings of villagers and their cattle by tigers, and killings of tigers by the agitated villagers in revenge are solely due to the over-population of tigers at Ranthambhore. Shifting of these tigers to an excellent habitat like Sariska is the best solution to this problem. But unfortunately, it is being opposed and that too, under the name of conservation and science!

It is a hard fact that in the last 30 years or so, due to genetic isolation, there has been potential inbreeding among the tigers in most reserves in India. In the absence of connecting corridors, long distance gene dispersal is no longer possible. Gene pools have shrunk in size as tiger reserves have become isolated from each other and are surrounded by large human settlements.

Tigers from similar reserves should definitely be exchanged liberally for bringing in new blood. Central Government and non-governmental organisations must take active interest in this. For Sariska also, it could be ideal to introduce some male and female tigers from central

BELOW: Rani drags the kill to safety

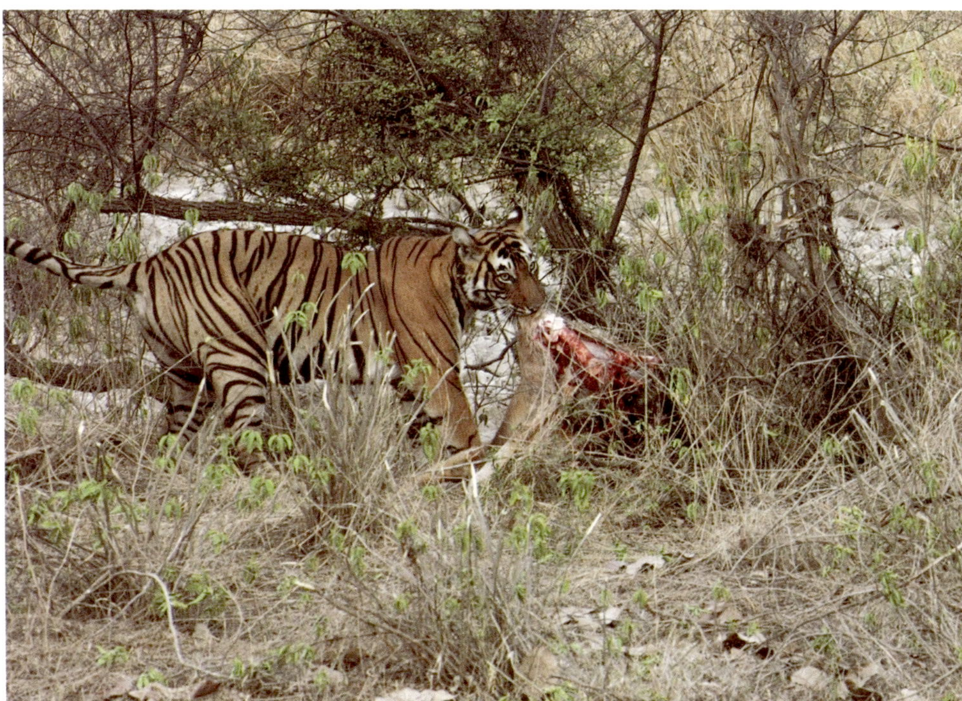

India's reserves like Kanha or Bandhav Garh. But under the present circumstances it does not seem possible. People with high connections and local business interests can influence government decisions. The present case of re-introduction of tigers into Sariska from Ranthambhore—both Reserves in Rajasthan—is a glaring example. When a state government has been stopped from introducing tigers from one reserve to another in the same state, how could one think of getting tigers from Reserves in other states?

According to Mr Jairam Ramesh, more tigers from Ranthambhore may be shifted to Sariska in order to ease out the pressure of over-population there, especially because the Madhya Pradesh government has refused to part with any tiger from its reserves. This further confirms that the hue and cry made by the Ranthambhore lobby did not bear any footing. Ultimately truth prevailed and Sariska got five tigers.

Government of India, through NTCA, must take the initiative to exchange tigers generously between various tiger reserves in order to give a shot of fresh blood to the endemic tiger populations trapped in most of the reserves in the country. This should be a priority in NTCA's agenda.

NON-BREEDING PROBLEM IN THE TRANSLOCATED TIGERS IN SARISKA

Amidst opposition of tiger translocation to Sariska, another cause of serious worry had surfaced. During 2008–10, three females and two males had been shifted to Sariska.

Another male tiger also joined this fleet in early 2011. Gestation period in tigresses is 90 to 105 days. Several breeding cycles have passed since these tigresses were brought to Sariska but so far none had bred. It is noteworthy that like Sariska, in Panna Tiger Reserve of Madhya Pradesh, after a total loss of tiger population, one male and four female tigers were brought in from Kanha, Bandhav Garh, and Pench Tiger

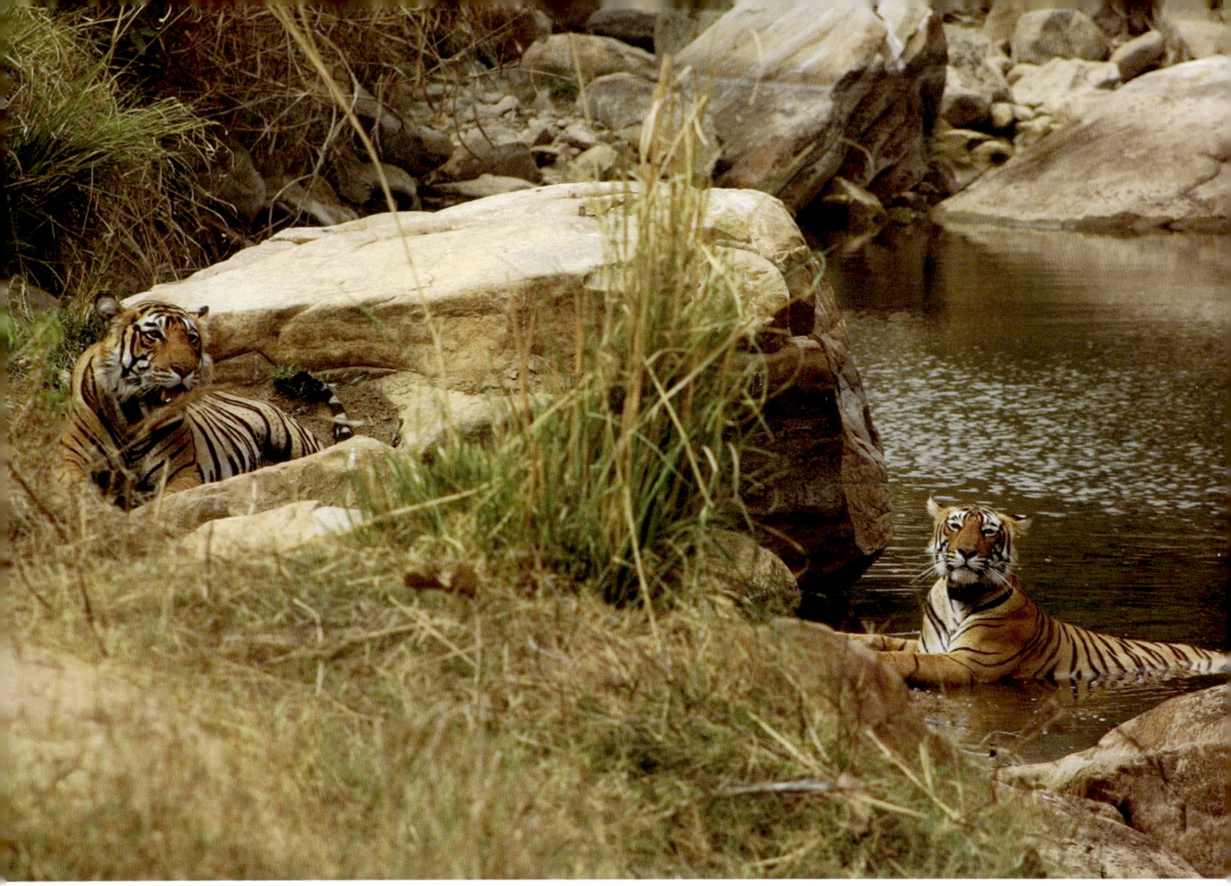

Reserves between 2009 and 2011. By January 2012, three females have littered 14 cubs there.

Sariska Tiger Foundation, a Thanagazi (Alwar) based NGO, organised two brain storming workshops in May 2011 and March 2012 at Jaipur and Alwar, respectively, to find out the cause for the non-breeding in Sariska.

Additional Chief Secretary (F&E), the entire team of forest officers, scientists, and experts including V.P. Singh (Member of Parliament and former chairman, SEC and Steering Committee), who were involved in the tiger translocation to Sariska, actively participated in the discussions. Chief Wildlife Warden, Madhya Pradesh, and Field Director, Panna, shared the Panna success story and their experiences. H.S. Panwar, India's top wildlife expert and member of the Government of India's Tiger Task Force, chaired the session.

ABOVE: Maharaja and Rani in their new home in Sariska

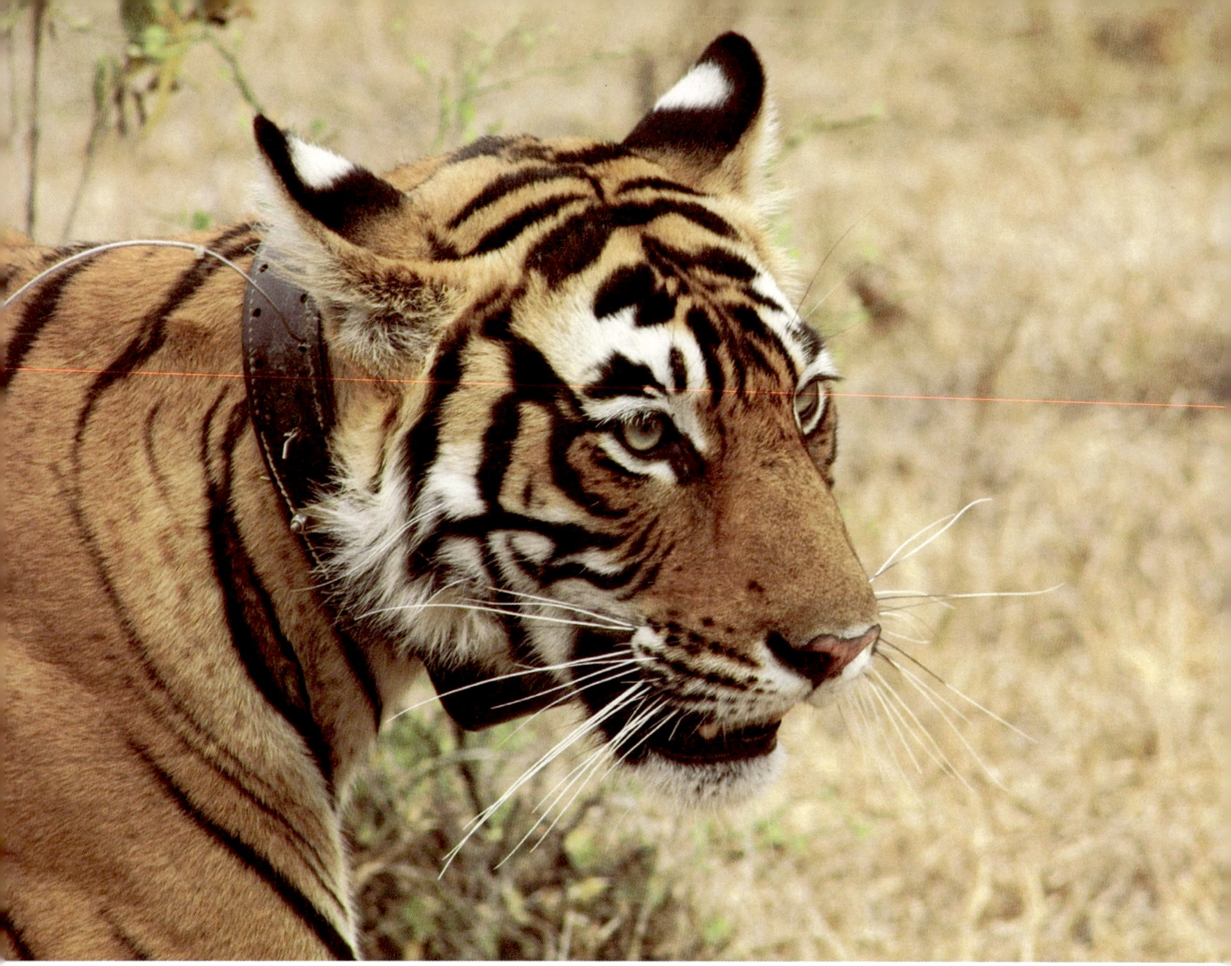

ABOVE: Rani with Dilope antenna (white wire) on the neck *(Photo by Shilpi Gupta)*

Different opinions were expressed by the participants. Dr K. Sankar (WII) said that according to the report of the scat analysis of Sariska tigers conducted at CCMB, Hyderabad, the two tigresses, Maharani and Rani, had conceived but pregnancy did not last long for reasons unknown. The reason was interpreted to be some stress on the tigresses. He held disturbance prevalent in Sariska in the form of human and cattle presence in core areas as well as heavy vehicular traffic, to be responsible for this. Many others supported his view. I had, however, a different view on this. The presence of villages, cattle camps with huge cattle population, and heavy traffic plying on state highways passing through core areas are all, doubtlessly, causing great disturbance which certainly needs to be curbed. But what we should not forget is that these disturbances had been persisting in Sariska since several decades when it used to be home to a sizable number of tiger population. Apart from this, Sariska is full of hills and valleys of which many are free from such disturbances where tigresses can fearlessly rear their cubs.

Some participants were of the view that the radio collars worn around the neck of the tigresses may be a source of stress and hormonal imbalance leading to infertility. Majority of the experts ruled out this idea citing the success story of Panna and elsewhere the world over. Though the Panna fact cannot be denied, I am unable to understand the reason behind keeping the tigers tied with belts around their necks. Surely tigers, too, need privacy for courtship and littering. This requirement takes them to interior forests which are generally inaccessible to humans. In such seclusion they freely mate, litter, and rear their cubs. The radio collar helps the management in chasing them in the name of monitoring even into those interior areas. One might choose to deny it but the fact is that the Reserve management cannot refuse permission to powerful politicians and bureaucrats who want to see the tigers hidden in such interior areas as well. Such disturbances can cause fear leading to stress in these tigresses as they are very cautious about the safety of the unborn. Such repeated disturbances may lead to abortion of the foetus.

Surprisingly, officers of the Reserve at every level, even those sitting at Jaipur and Delhi, insist that tigers should be kept belted in Sariska. Why? The animals are very well settled in their new home. There has not been even a single case of the tigers trying to run away. According to R.S. Shekhawat, Field Director, these tigers are happy in their new home. This means there is no fear of their running away. Then why keep them belted? The officers feel that to ensure the tigers' safety round the clock vigil on their movement is necessary and this cannot be done without the assistance of radio collars. I disagree with this protection strategy. This means that we shall have to radio collar the tigers and leopards all over the country because the threat to these animals from poachers and aggrieved villagers persists nationwide.

It is also worth mentioning that Sariska lost its first translocated tiger on 14 November 2010 at the hands of the villagers despite the 'round-the-clock' monitoring. This animal had a radio collar in working condition around its neck. This proves that belting tigers with radio collar, too, cannot necessarily ensure their protection. In fact there is no substitute for effective regular foot patrolling. This traditional protection strategy not only protects tigers but ensures protection of the entire wildlife inhabiting the Reserve along with the habitat. I am strongly convinced that radio collars must be removed from the animals as soon as they settle down in the new home.

According to Mr H.S. Panwar, founder director, Wildlife Institute of India (WII) and Dr H.S. Pabla, former Chief Wildlife Warden of Madhya Pradesh,

> Normally breeding population in the breeding area has an adult sex ratio heavily in favour of females viz. 1:3 or 1:4. Real dominant males ensure their territorial dominance and prevent

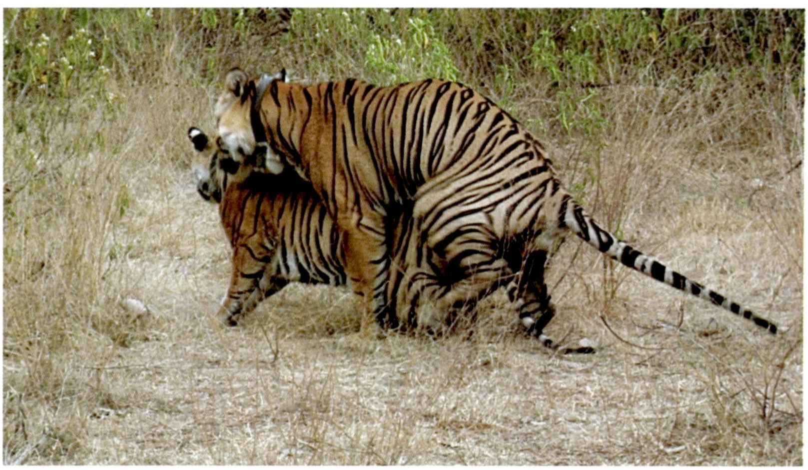

RIGHT: Another view of Maharaja and Rani mating

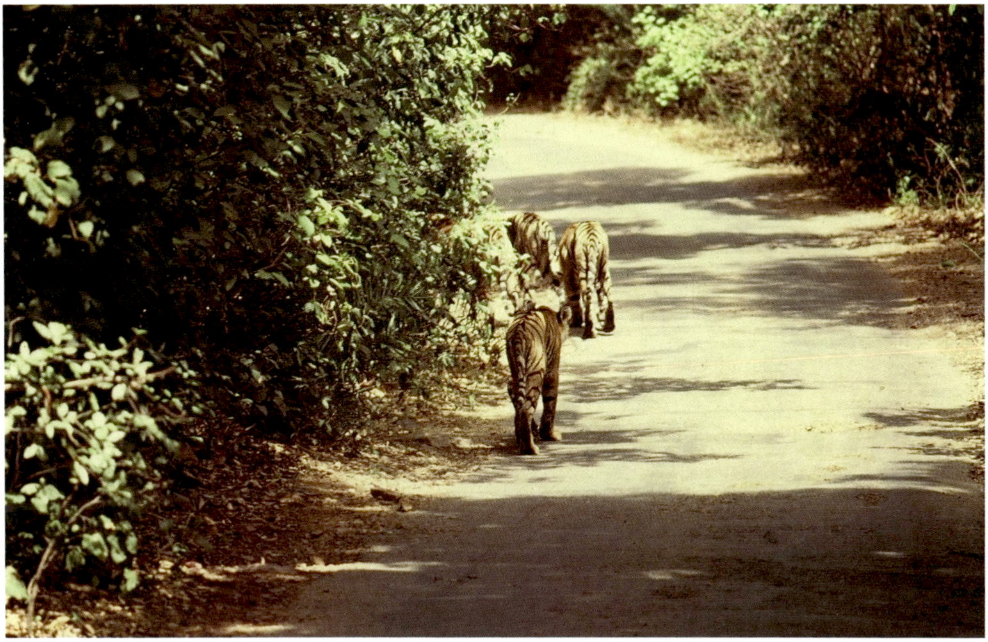

ABOVE:
A tigress and her cubs treading a dangerous path

> younger and past-prime males from frequenting the breeding area allowing females to breed and bring up their young with confidence. Perhaps the two-males-to-three-females combination is a stress cause that may be present among females, which results in stress during pregnancy causing miscarriage.

They suggested that under the present circumstances only one male should be kept in open free ranging condition in Sariska.

The introduction of one or two females of proven fertility in Sariska was also unanimously recommended in the workshop.

CUBS BORN IN SARISKA

Putting all questions and anxieties to rest, Maharani, the first tigress brought to Sariska on 4 July 2008 gave birth to a litter of two cubs. Of

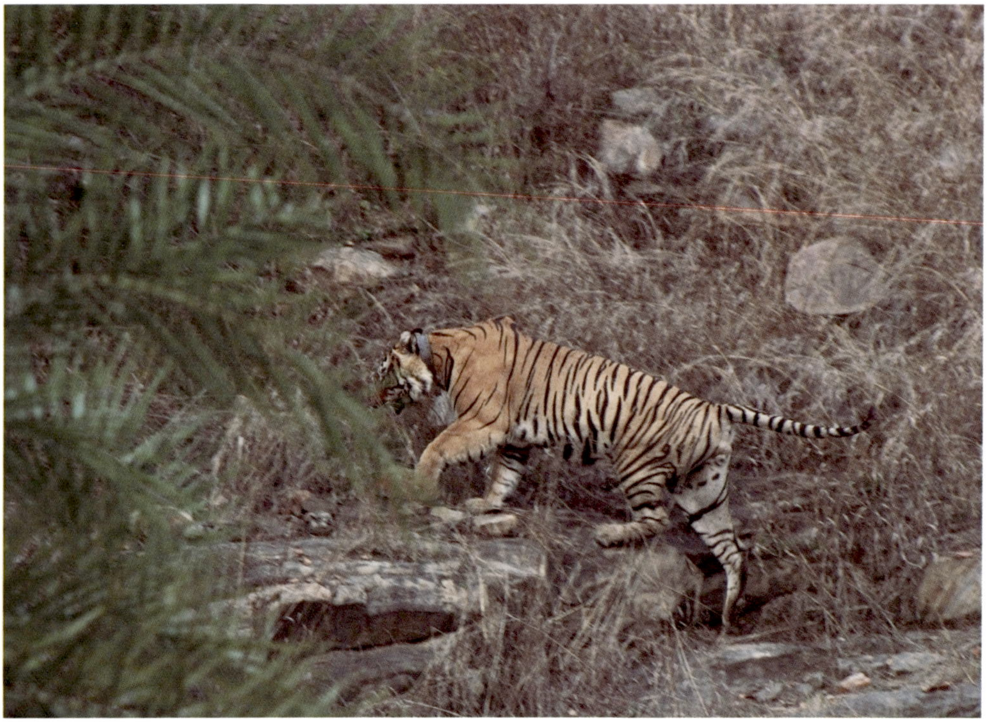

ABOVE: Tiger ST-6, father of the first cubs born of Maharani

course there had been rumours for some time but confirmation came only on 8 August 2012 when a trap camera placed close to Slopka anicut photographed this tigress with one cub in the evening hours. Evidence of the second cub came later in the form of pug marks in Pandupole area near a water point. Finally photographic evidence of both the cubs was collected by a trap camera on 30 September 2012.

It was a great moment as all tiger lovers, especially Sariska fans, were anxiously waiting for this good news for such a long time! But from a scientist's or a Reserve Manager's point of view, the inordinate delay in breeding still remained a question of debate. The experts who had been holding disturbance factor responsible for non-breeding may now give a second thought to their doctrine because nothing has changed in recent times in the habitat of Doraka where the tigress has delivered this litter.

I feel that the tigers brought from Ranthambhore are more sensitive to radio collars than those of Kanha and Bandhav Garh, reintroduced in Panna Tiger Reserve after the Sariska experiment. I reiterate that radio collars should be removed from reintroduced tigers as soon as they are settled in their new homes. This will help them naturalise and breed fast in the new habitat.

The birth of the cubs began a new chapter in the life of this Reserve. Sariska, however, is still passing through a tough time. Several important issues need to be addressed. This calls not only for a committed management but also for a strong will of the government.

Nature lovers are more than anxious to see this beautiful Reserve flourishing once again. I am sure one day Sariska will have its golden days back. The conservationists have to play their role with a positive frame of mind.

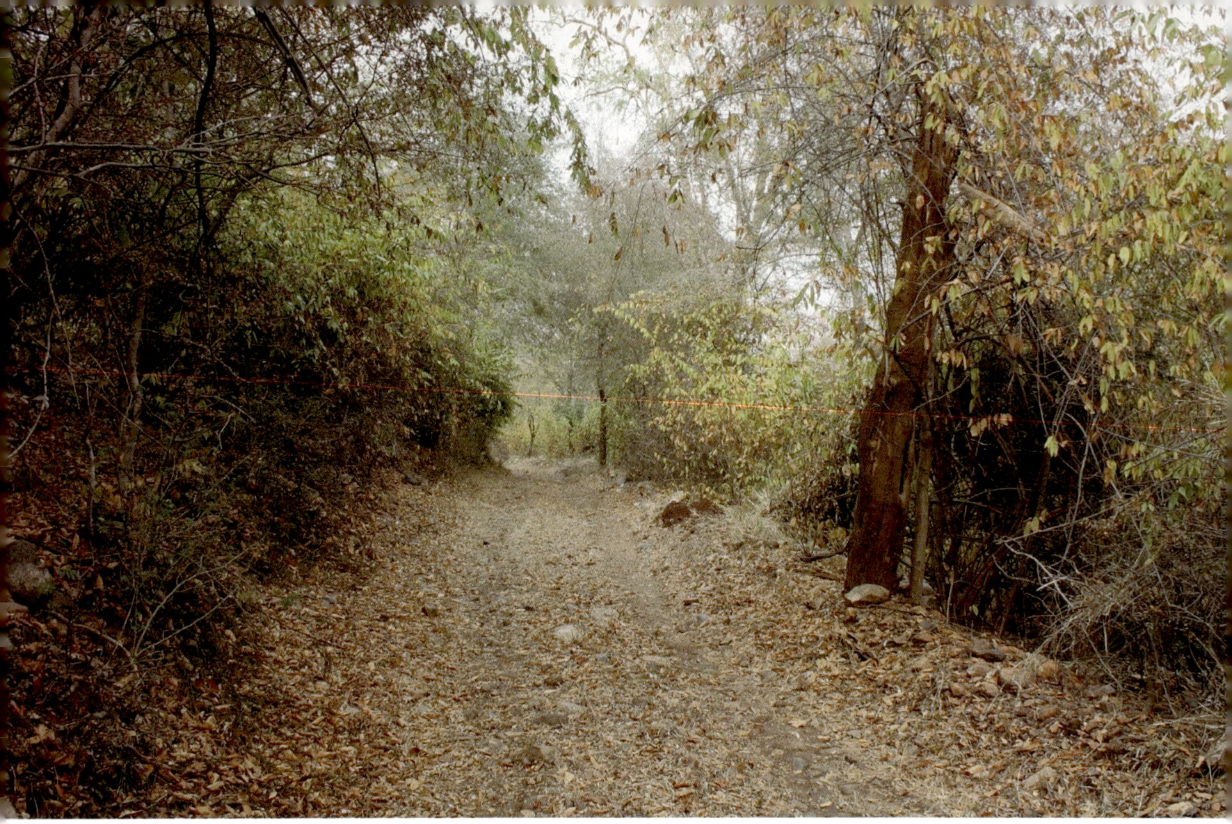

EPILOGUE

Sariska is a unique gift of nature to us. It has great potential of being developed into one of the best and most sought-after tiger reserves in India. After the scrupulous tiger poaching between 2002 and 2004 in which the entire tiger population of Sariska was decimated, a serious effort was initiated by the Rajasthan government to rebuild this Reserve. It set up a high-powered committee chaired by V.P. Singh.

Tigers were transported from Ranthambhore to Sariska. In areas where poaching was rampant, more protection posts were erected and patrolling tracks were built. Capable members of staff from other forest divisions of the state were transferred to Sariska. Efforts at habitat development were undertaken to support the huge herbivorous population which had grown multifold in the absence of tigers.

Forest resources cannot be saved without proactive and strong support from the government. Neighbouring villagers are partially or totally dependent on forests for their daily requirements of fuelwood, fodder, timber, and other produce in spite of the poor carrying capacity of the forest. This phenomenon is true of the entire country. The wildlife reserves possessing mobile wealth in the form of precious wildlife, such as tigers, are more susceptible to protection problems in such situations.

There are several villages with thousands of people in or near the Reserve who need to be shifted out of the area. Till 2008, only one village from the core area had been moved out of Sariska. The task of shifting 10 more villages from the core area and 17 from the remaining area of the Reserve, is enormous. The sudden withdrawal of government support has been a serious jolt to the rebuilding exercise of the Reserve. I joined this task in 2008 with great enthusiasm on the request of V.P. Singh. As I had only two years to retire, I was in a hurry to finish the task of ensuring foolproof protection to the wildlife of the Reserve and its development to support such a huge herbivore population.

I worked continuously and without rest. I succeeded in creating adequate enthusiasm in the field personnel to work hard in order to achieve this objective. I had, however, to be a bit tough with those who took their job casually. They approached the Rajasthan forest minister using their political connections. The minister got my transfer orders issued without even consulting the chief wildlife warden. It may be mentioned here that I had merely 4–5 months left for my retirement. A befitting reward for my sincere and hard work!

This incident gave me a shock. It also shocked some notable conservationists at the national level. They approached the chief minister who stayed the execution of the order. This allowed me to give finishing

FACING PAGE: A path through Sariska during autum

touches to the mission in hand. After my retirement in March 2010, however, the government did not bother to post a full time Deputy Conservator of Forests (DCF) at Sariska for a long time resulting in the deterioration of protection measures.

After about six months, a DCF was posted, who was initially reluctant to join. Moreover, soon after joining he proceeded on long leave. This further deteriorated the situation. As a result, Maharaja (CP-1) was killed by some miscreants of village Kaniawas located near Kankwadi inside the Reserve. Subsequently the DCF and ACF were suspended. Enquiries were conducted into the incident. No action, however, could be taken for want of political will. Meanwhile government appointed a new DCF who was also transferred within a few months. The next DCF also faced the same fate. The casual attitude of the government on this issue can be judged from the fact that Sariska had eight DCFs and four Field Directors in just three years!

Taking advantage of this fluid situation, villagers located inside and on the periphery of the Reserve started forced grazing in the prime areas of the Reserve. They also started pressurising the management for granting unrestricted entry throughout the day through all the gates of the Reserve, acquiring new proprietary rights over land located inside the sanctuary area, and repairing of roads passing through the core of the Reserve in contravention of the order of the Supreme Court. They also started challenging the boundary of the Reserve which was settled and, therefore, beyond dispute. These issues were raised as part of violent agitations with the support of local politicians.

The first agitation occurred during March–April 2012. The district collector, in subsequent discussions, gave them several assurances including resurveying the Reserve's boundary. Alleging of non-fulfilment of the promises, they started another agitation a month later, in May. The Reserve personnel were surrounded by several people and were not allowed to move. Tourists were stopped from entering the Reserve. There was utter chaos.

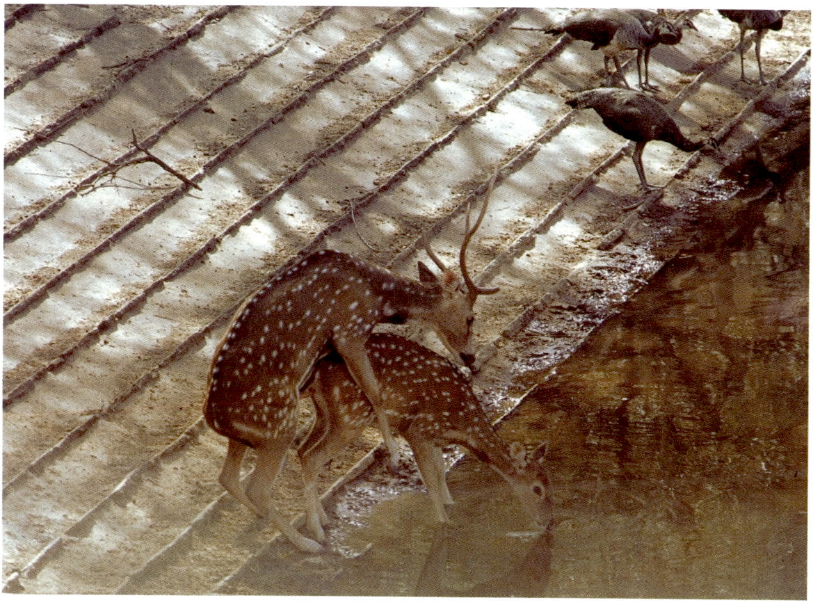

Left:
Spotted deer mating

The lives of the Reserve personnel were in danger as the unruly mob turned violent and started misbehaving and manhandling them. Following assurances and persuasion by the district administration and the Reserve management, they agreed to call off their agitation.

The district administration and the Reserve management took some conciliatory measures. These, however, did not satisfy the villagers and they started a dharna again in February 2013. This time the agitation continued for 53 days.

The government's passive approach in dealing with these agitations caused irreparable damage to the protection mechanism of the Reserve. There were several incidents where members of the patrolling staff were attacked by miscreants.

In July 2012 Ram Prasad, Nakedar of Sariska, and many other field personnel on patrol were attacked and even abducted by grazers. A police case was registered at Thana Gazi police station. No effective action was, however, taken by the police.

In February 2013, DCF Mahendra Sharma, Assistant Conservator, Range Officer, and other staff members were attacked with sticks and swords by grazers. They sustained serious injuries. Again a case was registered but once again the police failed to take any positive action. On the one hand, these incidents demoralised the already shaken staff and on the other, encouraged the miscreants to continue illegal activities such as grazing, wood poaching, and entering the Reserve with vehicles.

Amidst these disturbances there were some silver linings, too. Sariska made some positive developments as well. As a great consolation to Sariska lovers, two sub-adult tigresses were brought from Ranthambhore in January 2013. The then Rajasthan forest minister deserves full credit for this gift to Sariska.

In fact these tigresses had lost their mother at an early age. They were brought up under intensive care of the Ranthambhore Reserve management. Therefore, in Sariska they were allotted two separate but peripheral forests to avoid conflict with those tigers which had already established their territories. Being close to human settlements, the peripheral territories occupied by these sub-adults were not safe areas from the protection point of view. Another problem was their isolation from the tigers of the Reserve. An adventurous tiger, coded ST-6, brought from Bharatpur, met one of these tigresses, coded ST-9. Fortunately, no scuffle has so far been reported between the two. A few months later, the other tigress, ST-10, which confines itself to Loj–Nathusar area in the extreme northern forests of the Reserve, also has been visited by a tiger ST-4. They have also mated successfully. She has better chances of delivering cubs as this far flung area does not suffer from VIP visits. This will save her from undue stress unlike other tigresses of the Reserve.

The Reserve management has also succeeded partially in curtailing the number of vehicles reaching Pandupole temple located in the heart of the Reserve.

For some time after Maharaja was killed, the state and central governments showed some seriousness. The village relocation programme then gained momentum under the supervision of the new field director. Umri village was totally evacuated while Dabli, Rotkyala, and Kraska villages were evicted partially. Consequent to the transfer of this officer, the eviction process came to a standstill. After the gap of a year, in March 2014, the same officer was posted back to Sariska. This has generated some hope that the village relocation programme may gain momentum once again.

Sariska has not yet become self-sufficient as far as the tiger population is concerned. Since the first tiger relocation in 2008 there has been only one litter of two female cubs by Maharani, sometime in May 2012. After that, no good news has come from any of the tigresses in Sariska.

So far neither the Wildlife Institute of India (WII) nor any other expert organisation or individual has come forward with any logical

BELOW: Rani in vacated Bhagani village

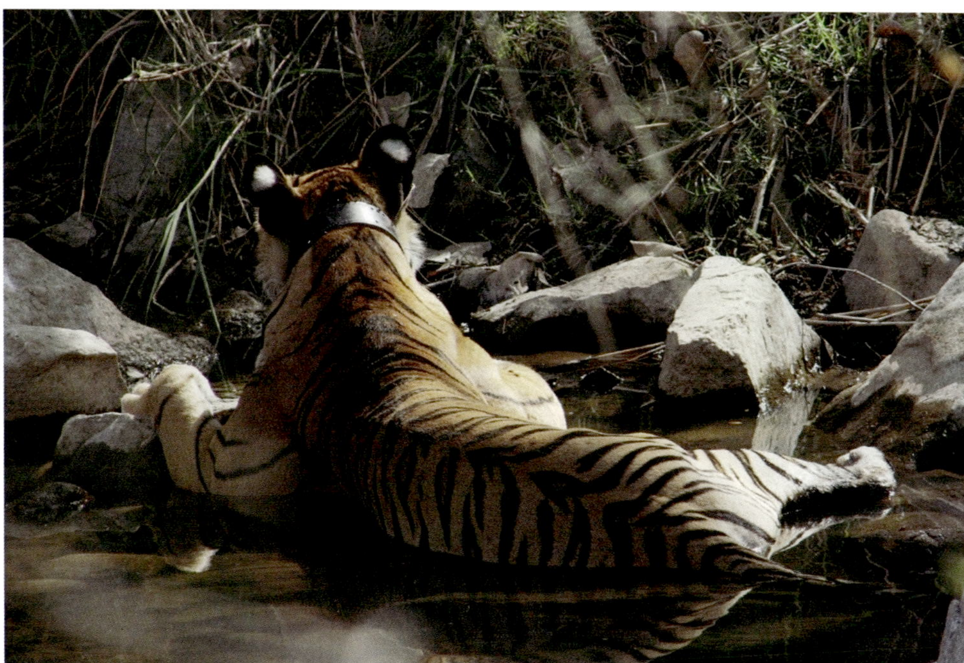

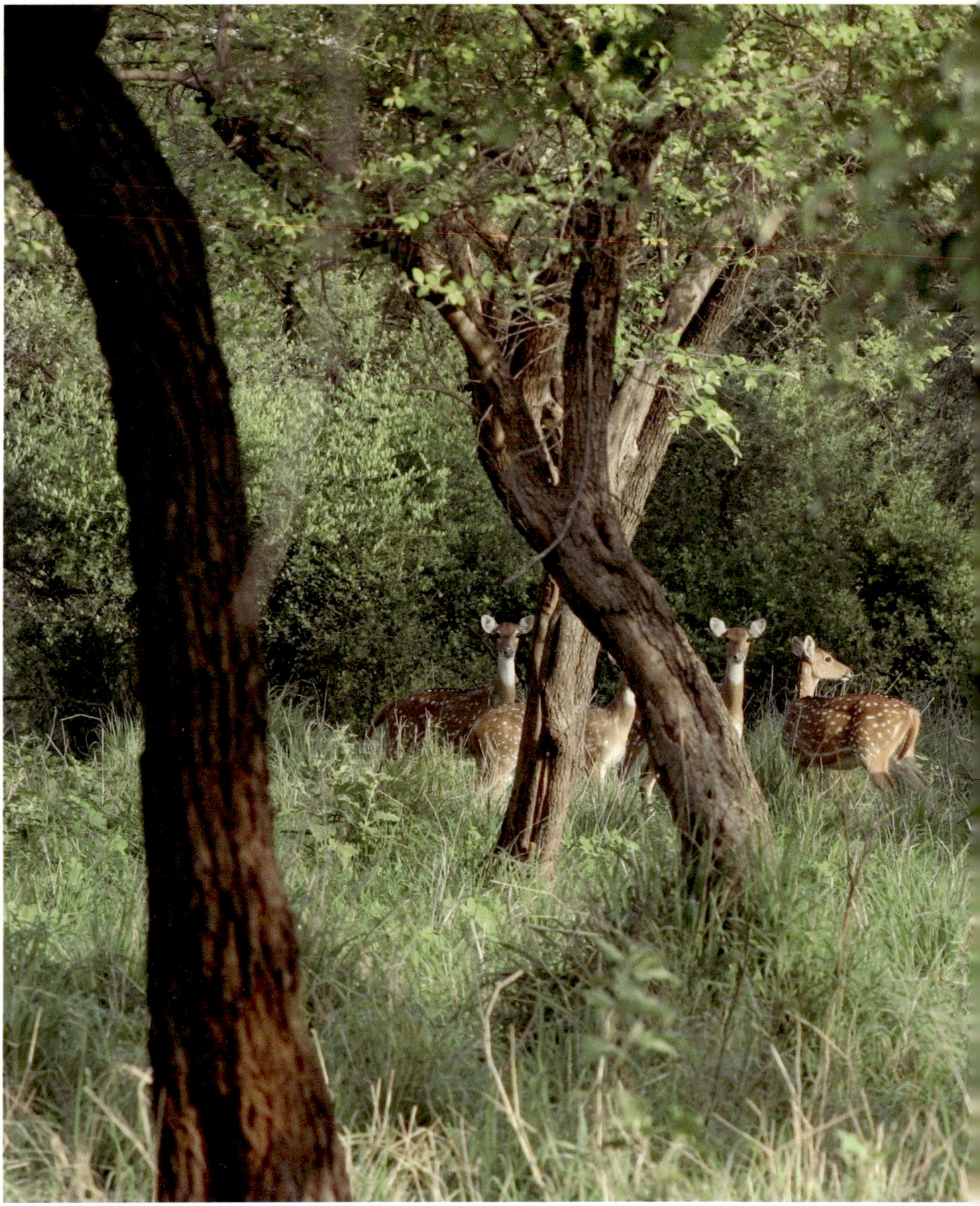

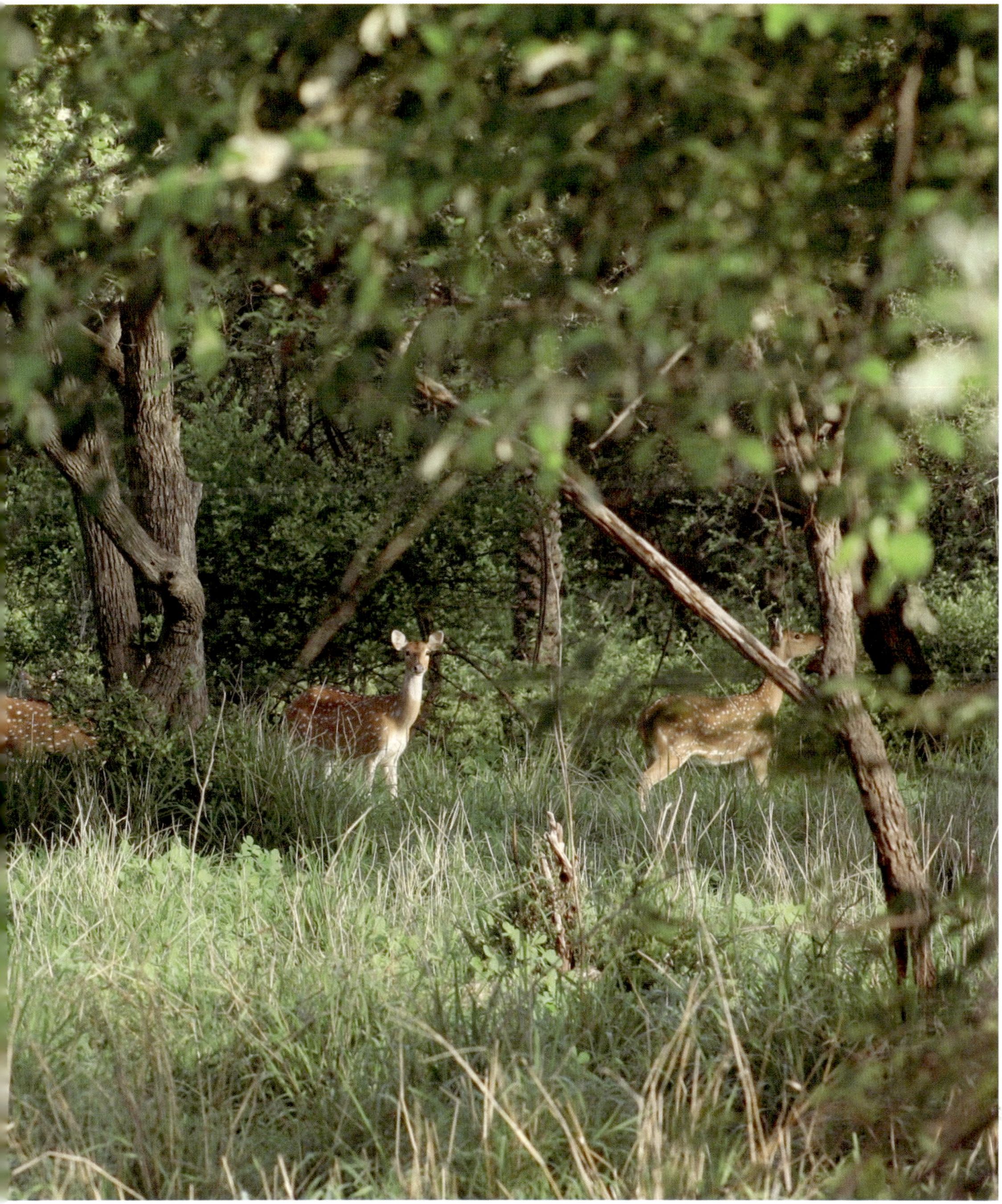

explanation for the non-breeding of tigers in Sariska. Sariska Tiger Foundation has been demanding the removal of radio collars of the tigers. Scientists, however, argue that radio collar has nothing to do with breeding. They also cite a few examples to support their theory. I feel that the Ranthambhore tiger population is somewhat extra sensitive to radio collars compared to other areas.

The radio collar, without doubt, helps us in regular monitoring of the tigers for their protection. But at the same time it also deprives the mating pairs and the conceived tigresses of privacy, thereby causing stress. This has resulted in repeated abortions as reported by Centre for Cellular and Molecular Biology, Hyderabad after examination of scat samples from Sariska.

PAGES 198–199: Bana Plateau in 2009
BELOW: A view from Mehrotra Point

It is also interesting to learn that in Ranthambhore, a few tigresses were radio-collared in 2007. None of them bred as long as the collars

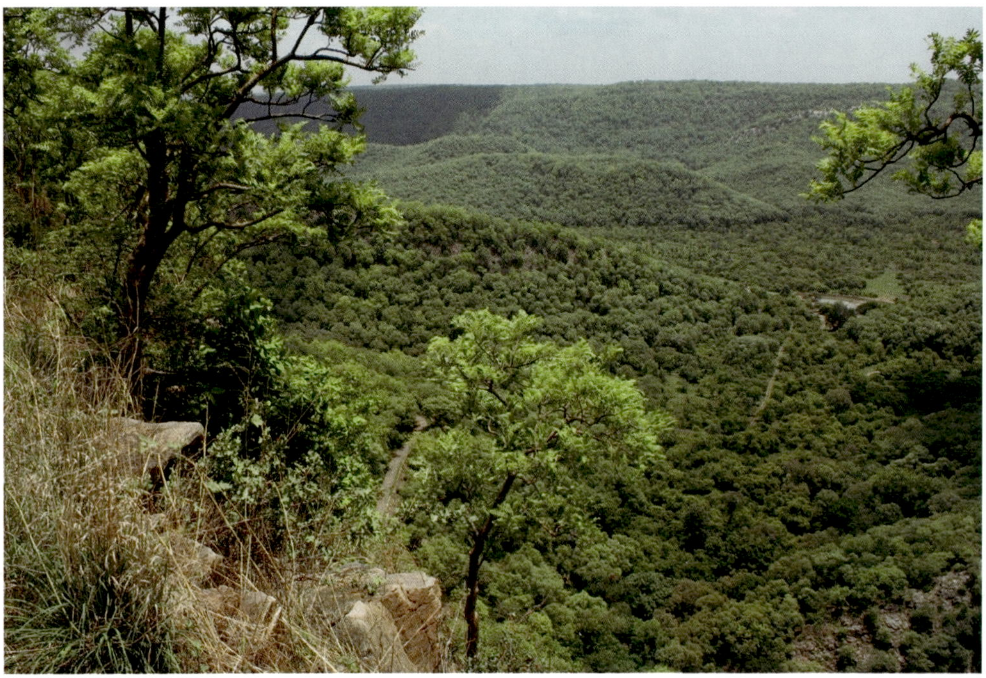

were on. They, however, bred successfully after the removal of the collars.

Tigress T-8 was collared in 2007. She did not breed in spite of her breeding age. The collar was removed in 2009 and she littered successfully around November 2010. Around March 2014 she gave birth to three cubs. Another five-year-old tigress T-17, collared in 2007, did not litter at all. Her collar was removed in November 2011 and she was seen with cubs in June 2012.

It may be incorrect to boast that we know everything about the behaviour of the tiger or, for that matter, any other wild animal. In fact we are always in the process of learning and should be receptive to new ideas. I strongly believe that removal of radio collars will help in the successful breeding among Sariska tigers.

While Sariska is facing the problem of non-breeding, Ranthambhore continues to overflow with tigers. In June 2014, Ranthambhore had 59 tigers including 24 adults and 15 sub-adults. The sub-adults above the age of two-and-a-half years are forced to stay close to their mothers for fear of the adult tigers all around them. This is ecologically very incorrect and unjustifiable.

This over-population, far beyond the carrying capacity of the Reserve, has compelled several weak tigers, especially sub-adults, to drift away from the safety of the Reserve. This has led to lifting of cattle and attack on humans, which in turn created conflicts between the Reserve management and the neighbouring villagers. It is significant that 17 tigers, including six cubs, drifted away from Ranthambhore Reserve between 2009 and 2013. Of this, eight were forced out between 2011 and 2013 alone. Many of these tigers have moved to places like Kota, Bundi, Dholpur, Bharatpur, and Kuno (in Madhya Pradesh) covering distances between 150 km and 200 km. Such movements are dangerous considering their own safety as well as that of humans and their cattle coming in contact with them.

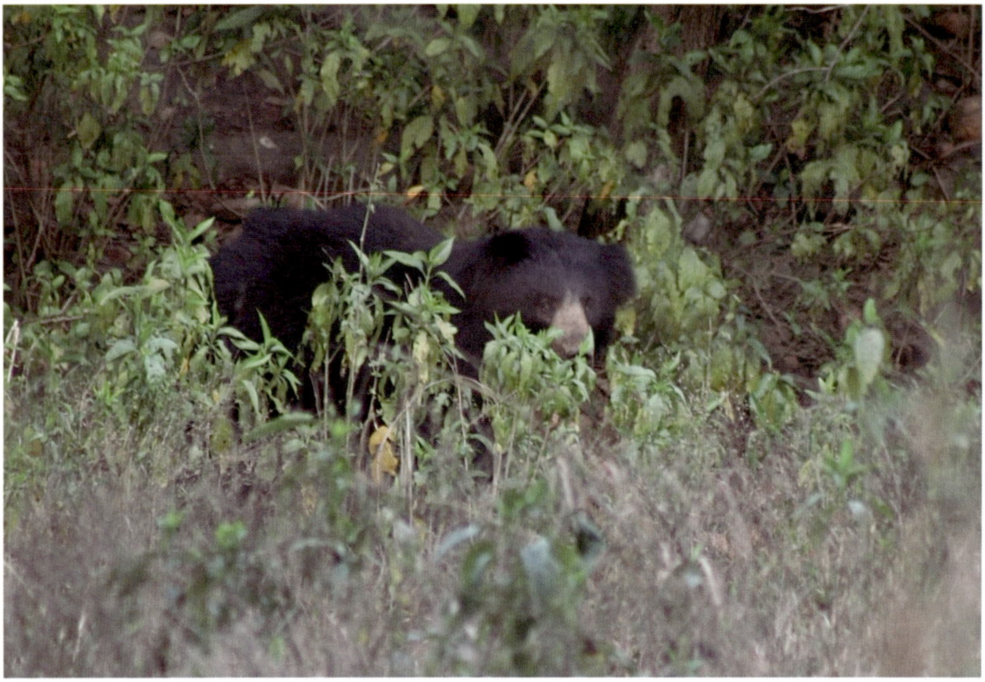

ABOVE: A naturalised wild bear in Sariska

In March 2010 two sub-adults were poisoned in Talwad village of Khandar. In December 2012 a tigress was poisoned by some villagers in Khandar range. In the last five years several cases of tiger–human conflicts have been reported.

A woman named Morpali Meena, resident of Baswo Khurd village, and the mother of a Nature Guide of the Reserve, was killed by a tiger in the adjacent forest area of the Reserve in February 2012. In March 2012 Asfaq Ahmed, a young man of 19 years, and a resident of Ansari Mohalla, was killed by a tiger in the fringe forest area of Mirza Ghati. In July 2012, a tiger attacked and seriously injured two people in Mei Kala village of Khandar range. The agitated villagers attacked the Sub-Divisional Magistrate and police officials with sticks and rods. They could be rescued only after the deployment of a huge police force. The Forest Minister assured that the boundary wall of the Reserve would be raised to stop the tigers from drifting into the village. This cannot be, however, called a logical and long-term solution. In October 2012, quite abnormally, a tiger attacked and killed Ghisu Singh, the head guard. He was supervising an ongoing development project in the Raj Bagh area of the Reserve.

Overpopulation of tigers can also cause the deadly disease called canine distemper (C.D.). Tigers in Russia and Indonesia were affected by this in the recent past. The disease spreads when shortage of space forces these cats to share space with humans and dogs. National Tiger Conservation Authority (NTCA) has issued an advisory in this regard in June 2013.

The simplest solution lies in regularly sending tigers from Ranthambhore to Sariska. But the tiger tourism lobby of Ranthambhore opposes this. It is a bit surprising that NTCA, too, is silent on this matter.

There has been another interesting development. A buffer zone of 332.23 sq. km area comprising 245.72 sq. km of forest land and 86.51 sq. km of revenue land around Sariska Tiger Reserve has been created by the state government through a notification on 9 July 2012. Though belated, it is certainly the right step in the interests of the Reserve and the people in the neighbourhood. If developed properly, it may provide pastures to villagers for their cattle without coming into conflict with the Reserve authorities, apart from providing protection cushion to the invaluable wildlife in the Reserve. This will also save the villagers and their cattle from carnivores venturing into fringe areas. Unfortunately, no step has been initiated so far to develop this buffer zone. I wish the government and the Reserve management would work on a time bound plan to develop this important zone in the interest of the Reserve and the people living around the tiger Reserve.

Richhunda is an important valley close to Kankwadi in Sariska. Richh means bear. This valley provides an ideal habitat for bear. Though no records can be found, it is said that about 60 years ago this

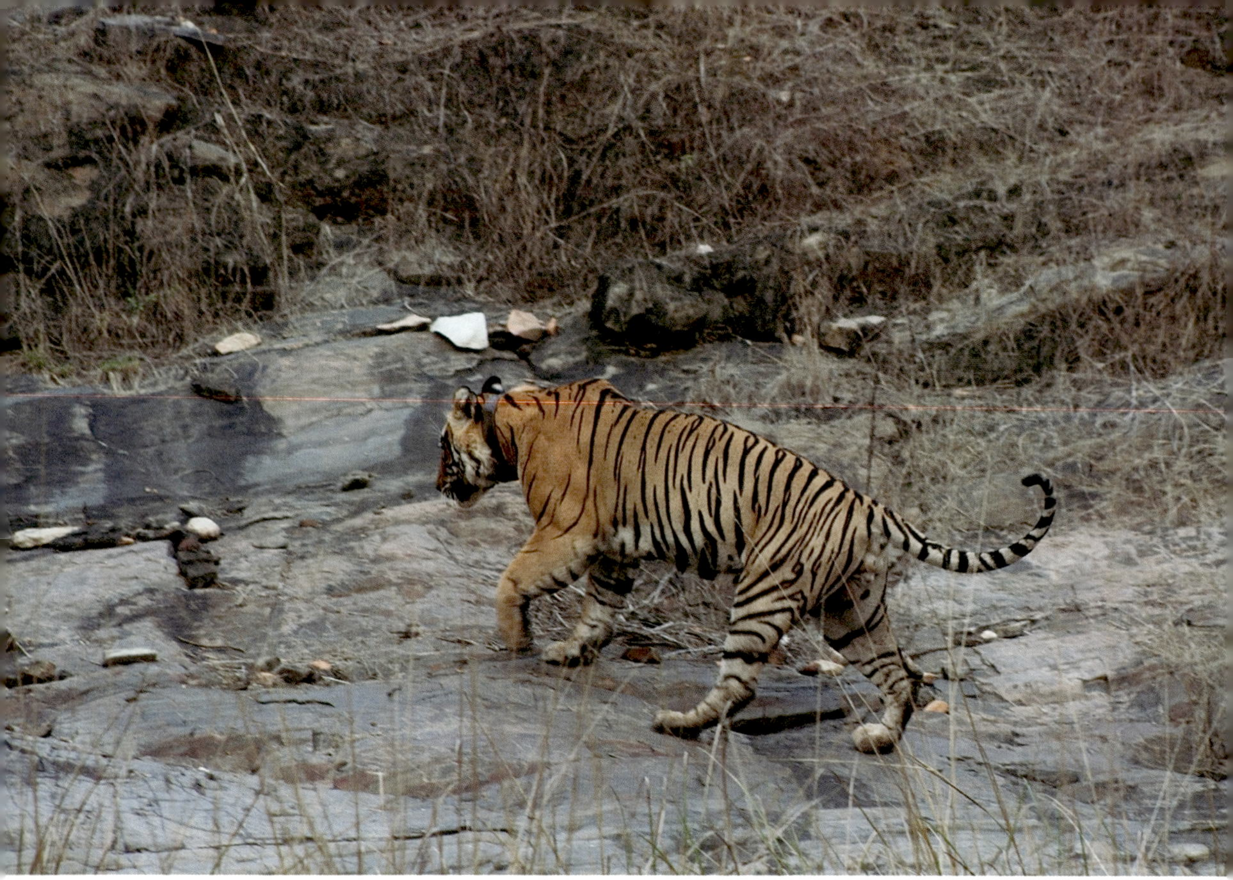

ABOVE: ST-6 in a vacated village

area had a sizable bear population. Bear is an aggressive animal and does not tolerate human interference. Unfortunately, no matter how aggressive they are, animals ultimately fall prey to crooked humans. After Independence, the Gujjar settlements in Sariska have grown in size. The bear population must have fallen prey to this development. Justice demands reintroduction of bears in Sariska at the earliest in the interest of the species as well as the Reserve. But lack of political will is the chief hindrance in fulfilling this ecological requirement.

In April 2013 a male bear was spotted by villagers in Raj Garh area, not very far from the south-eastern boundary of the Reserve. It was caught by the Reserve management and released in Richhunda area of Sariska. This animal has established itself well in this valley and adjacent Bhagani valley. But it needs special protection. It must be radio-collared and a dedicated team of personnel should be deployed to ensure its protection. It is also essential to introduce a female bear at the earliest to repopulate this Reserve with bear population, its lost glory.

I am optimistic that Sariska, the jewel of the Aravallis, will regain its lost glory very soon. Wildlife lovers and conservationists should persuade the government to focus on the development of this Reserve. Fortunately, in December 2013 Smt. Vasundhara Raje Scindia was sworn in as the state Chief Minister. It was under her leadership that the government had earlier constituted the steering committee under the chairmanship of V.P. Singh. This high-powered committee not only successfully reintroduced tigers into Sariska but also showed the strong will to rejuvenate this wonderful tiger land. But it could not complete its task due to change of government in the state. I wish and hope that the new government will soon resume this unfinished task and complete its mission of rejuvenating Sariska. I am confident that golden days will return to Sariska sooner rather than later.

REPRESENTATIVE LIST OF SARISKA'S FLORA AND FAUNA

HIGHER PLANTS

Typical habit of plant species is indicated along with some common local names, which can help in field identification.

Legends: T = Tree, S = Shrub, H = Herb, C = Climber

Scientific Name	Typical Habit	Common/ Local Name
Abrus precatorius	C	Chirmi/Murethi
Acacia catechu wild	T	Khair
Acacia leucophloea	T	Ronjh
Acacia nilotica (L.) Del.	T	Babul
Acacia seima Kurz	T	-
Acacia senegal wild	T	Gum Arabic, Kumta
Acanthospermum hispidum DC.	H	-
Achyranthes aspera L	H	Andhijhara
Acrocephalus capitatus Benth.	H	-
Actinopteris radita	H	-
Adhatoda vasica Nees	H	Bansa/Adus
Adiantum incisum	H	-
Adina cordifolia khook. F.	T	Haldu
Aegle marmelos Corr.	T	Bel
Aerva scandens Wall.	H	-
Albizia lebbek Benth.	T	Kala Siris
Allium spp.	H	-
Amaranthus spinosus	H	Jungli Chaulai
Anisameles ovata R. Br	H	-
Anogessus latifolia Wass.	T	Dhawa
Anogeissus pendula Edgw.	T	Dhok/Kardhai
Aplusa mutica L	H	-

Aristida funiculate Trin. and Rupr	H	Lapla
Asparagus racemosus Wild	C	Nharkata/Satavar
Azadirachta indica L.	T	Neem
Balanites aegyptica (L.) Del.	T	Hingu/Hingot
Barleria cristata L.	H	-
Barleria prionitis L.	H	-
Bauhinia racemosa Lam.	T	Jhinjeri
Bauhinia vereigata	T	Kachnar
Blainvillea rhombodies Cass.	H	-
Boerhavia repens L.	H	-
Bombax ceiba L.	T	Semul
Boswellia serrata Roxb.	T	Salai
Bothriochola ischaemum (L.) Keng.	H	-
Butea monsperma (Lamk.) Taub.	T	Dhak, Palash
Butea superba Roxb.	C	-
Calotropis procera	S	Akada
Capparis deciduas (Forsk) Edgw	S/T	Dela/Kair
Capparis sepiaria L.	S	Heens
Capparis zeylanica L.	S	-
Cardiospermum helicacabum L.	C	Balloon creeper
Carissa carandas L	S	Karanunda
Caseria tomentosa Roxb.	T	Chilla
Cassia fistula L.	H	Amaltas
Cassia occidentalis	S	Kasondi
Cassia tora	H	Panwar
Cayratia carnosa	C	Ramehana
Celosia argentea Wild	T	Malkangi
Celosia argentea L.	H	-
Cenehrus spp.	H	Anjan
Chloris barnata Sw.	H	-
Chloris dolichostachya Laga.	H	-
Chrysopogon montanus Trin.	H	-
Cleame viscosa L.	H	-
Clerodendrom phlomidis L.f.	C/S/T	-
Clerodendron multitlorum	S	Arni
Cocculus hirustus	C	Pilwani
Commelina hurzii CL	H	-
Commiphora wightii	H	Gugal
Corcchorous olitorious	H	Sanohari

Codia dichotoma	T	Lasauda
Cordial abligua Wild	T	Lasauda
Crataeve adansoli DC. Subsp. *Odora* Jacobs	T	-
Crotalaria medicaginea Lam.	H	-
Cascuta reflexa	C	Amarbel/Akashbel
Cymbopogon martinii (Roxb.) Wats.	H	Rosha
Cynodon dactylon	H	Dub
Cyperus compressus L.	H	Motha
Cyperus eleusinoides Kunth	H	-
Cyperus tagetiformis Roxb.	H	-
Dalbergia lanceolata L.	T	-
Dalbergia sissoo Roxb.	T	Sheesham
Dutura metel	S	Dhatura
Dendrocalamus strictus (Roxb.) Ness	H	Bans or Bamboo
Desmotachya bipinatta	H	Dab
Dicanthium annulatum stapf.	H	-
Dichristachys cinera W. & A.	T	Goya Kher
Dicliptera roxburghiana Ness	H	-
Diosphyros cordifolia	T	Bistendu
Diosphyros melanoxylon Roxb.	T	Tendu
Echinochloa colonum L.	H	-
Echinops echinatus	H	Untkatalo
Ehretia cararensis	T	Chamaror
Ehretia obtusifola Hochst.	T	Desi Papri
Elaeodendrom sp.	T	-
Eleusine indica Gaertn.	H	Jhania
Emblica officinalis (L.)	T	Amla
Eragrostic japonica (Trub.) Trin	H	-
Eragrostic tenella P. Beauv.	H	Underpooncha Chhota
Erianthemum purpurescens Ness	H	-
Erigeron sp.	H	-
Euphorbia granulata Forsk.	H	-
Euphorbia thymipholia L.	T	Dhundi
Euphorbia thymipholia	H	Dhundi
Ficus benghalensis L.	T	Bargad
Ficus palmata Forsk	T	Guler
Ficus racemosa L. Var. *Typica* Barrett.	T	-
Ficus jreligiosa L.	T	Peepul
Ficus infectoria	T	Pilkhan

Ficus rumphii	T	Parkhad
Ficus tomentosa Roxb.	T	-
Fimbristylis stolonifera C. B. CI.	H	-
Flacourtia india (Burn f.) Merr	S	Kandai
Flacourtia sepiaria Roxb.	S	-
Fluggea leucopyru Wild.	S	-
Garuga pinnata Roxb.	T	Kharpat
Grewia abutifolia Juss.	T	-
Grewia flavescens Juss.	T	-
Grewia hainesiana Hole	T	Phalsa
Grewia hirsuta Vahl (+ G. *Salvifolia* Heyne)	S	Kala Dhaman
Grewia populifolia Vahl	T	-
Grewia tilaefolia Vahl	T	Dhaman
Gymnosporia montana	T	-
Helicteres isora L.	C	Marorphali
Heteropogon contortus Roem. and Schult.	H	Kummeeria
Holarrhena antidysenterica Wall.	S/T	Kura
Helopteea integrifolia Planch.	T	Chirol/Churel
Ichnocarpus frutescens R. br	C/S	Dudhi
Imperata cylindrical (L.) P. Beauv	H	-
Indigofera cordifolia	H	Bekar
Indigofera crassiodes Roth. & DC.	H	Bekar
Indigofera spicata Forsk. (Jacq.)	H	-
Inga dulse	S	Jungle Jalebi
Ipomea aquatic	H	Nadi
Ipomoea fistulosa	S	Besharam
Ipomoea muricata Jacq.	C	Nishoth
Ipomoea pes-tigridis L	C	Besharam
Iseilema prostrates	H	Gandhel
Kigelia African (Lam.) Benth.	T	Sausage tree
Kirganelia reticulate	S	Makhi
Lannea cormandelica (Hout) Merr	T	Jhingan/Gurjan
Lantana camara L. var. *aculeate* (L.) Mold.	H	Lantana
Lawsonia inermis	S	Mehandi
Lemna paicicostata	H	Kai
Leucas mollissima Wall.	H	-
Limonia acidissima L.	T	Beli
Ludwigia octovalvis Jacq. Raven	H	-

Luffa acutangula	C	Kedwai Toria
Maeurua arenaria Hook. F. and Th.	C	-
Mallotus philippensis Muel-Arg.	T	Rohini
Mangifera India L.	T	Aam
Mitragyna parvifolia Korth	T	Kaim/Kalam
Momordiea diorea	C	Kakoda
Moringa oleifera Lamk.	T	Sainjna
Morus alba	T	Shehtoot
Mucunna prurita Hook.	C	Kaunch
Nelumbo nucifere Gaertn.	H	Kamal
Neptunia prostrate	H	Chhui Mui
Nyctanthes arbor-tristis L.	S	Harshringar
Nymphaea nocuhalli	H	Kumudini
Nymphaea stellata	H	Nili Kumudini
Nymphoides eristatum	H	Kumudini Nanhi
Nymphoides indicum	H	Chhoti Kumudini
Ocimum basilicum L.	H	Tulsi
Oryza spp.	H	Bagrru Dhan
Ougenia oegenesus	T	Sandan
Parkinsonia aculeate L.	T	-
Paspalum distichum L.	H	Aineha
Paspalum scrobiculatum	H	Kodra
Pennisetum orirntale Rich	H	-
Peristrophe bicalycalata (Retz.) Nees	H	-
Phoenix sylvestris L.	T	Khajur
Pipalia lappacea Juss.	H	-
Plumbago zeylanica L.	H	Chitrak
Prosopis cineraria (L) Druce	T	Sangar, Khejri, Jhand
Prosopis juliflora (sw) DC	T	Vilayti Kikar
Randia dumetorum Lam.	S	Maindal
Randia tetrasperma Benth. and Hook. f.	S	Bhedra
Rhus mysorensis Heyene	S	-
Rhynchosia himalensis Benth.	C	-
Rivea hypo-cratariformis Choisy	C	-
Saccharum munja	H	Munj
Sacharum spontaneum	S	Kans
Salvadora persica	S	Jal
Salvadora oleoides Dena	S	Pilu
Settaria verticullatta (L.) P. Beauv.	H	-

Spirodela polyrhiza	H	Kai
Solanum incanum L.	T	-
Solanum indicum L.	H	Makoy
Solanum nigrum	H	Makoy
Sorghum halapense (L.) Pers.	H	Barru
Sporobolum marginatus	H	Usari
Sterculia urens Roxb.	T	Keraya
Sterculia villosa Roxb.	T	Godgudala
Sterospermum sauveolens DC.	T	Padal
Syzygium cummini (L.) Skeels	T	Jamun
Tamarindus indica L.	T	Imli
Tamarisk aphylla	H	Farash
Tecomella undulata (Seem) Sm.	T	Roheda, Rugtrora
Tephoria hamiltonii	S	Dharmasa
Tephrosia purpurea Pers.	H	Dharmasa
Terminalia arjuna Bedd.	T	Arjuna
Terminalia belerica Roxb.	T	Bahera
Terminalia tomentosa	T	Sahaj/Sadar/Sain
Themeda quadrivalvis O. Ktrze.	H	-
Tinospora cordiforia	C	Sighi bel/Nimgiloy
Trema politoria Planch	S	Khakshi
Tribuls terrestic L.	H	Gokhru
Trichosanthes cucumerina L.	C	-
Tridax procumbens L.	H	-
Typha angustata	H	Patera
Vetiveria zizanioides	H	Khus
Vicia sp.	H	-
Vogelia indica Gibson	S	-
Wolfia arrhza	H	Kai
Woodfordia fruticosa (L.) Kurz.	S	V
Wrightia tinctoria R. Br	T	-
Wrightia tomentosa Roem. and Schultes	T	Dundhi
Xanthium strumarium L.	H	-
Zizyphus mauritiana Lamk.	T	Ber
Zizyphus nummularia R. and S.	S	Jharber

MAMMALS

Common Name	Scientific name
Caracal	*Caracal caracal*
Chausingha	*Tetracerus quadricornis*
Chinkara	*Gazelle bennettii*
Cheetal	*Axis axis*
Small Indian Civet	*Veverricula indica*
Fox	*Vulpes bengalensis*
Hare	*Lepus nigricollis*
Hyaena	*Hyaena hyaena*
Jackal	*Canis aureus*
Jungle Cat	*Felis chaus*
Langur	*Presbytis entellus*
Leopard	*Panthera pardus*
Common Mangoose	*Herpestes edwardsii*
Ruddy Mangoose	*Herpestes smithi*
Nilgai	*Bosephalus tragocamelus*
Palm Civet	*Paradoxurus hermaphrodites*
Pangolin	*Manis crassicaudata*
Porcupine	*Hystrix indica*
Rhesus Macaque	*Macac mulatto*
Ratel	*Mellivora capensis*
Rusty Spotted Cat	*Prionailurus rubiginosus*
Sambar	*Cervus unicolor*
Sloth Bear	*Melursus ursinus*
Five-striped Palm Squirrel	*Funambulus pennant*
Tiger	*Panthera tigris*
Wild Boar	*Sus scrofa*
Wild Dog	*Cuon alpines*
Wolf`	*Canis lupus*

BIRDS

Scientific Name	Common Name
Accipiter badius	Shikra
Accipiter gentiles	Goshawk
Accipter nisus nososimilis	Sparrow Hawk
Accipter virgatus	Besra Sparrow Hawk
Acridotheres ginginianus	Bank Myna
Acridothers tristi	Common Myna
Acrocephalus aedon	Thick-billed Warbler
Acrocephalus agricola	Paddy-field Warbler
Acrocephalus melanopogon	Moustached Sedge Warbler
Acrocephalus stentoreus	Indian Great Reed Warbler
Aegithina nigrolutea	Marshall's Iora
Agithina tiphia	Common Iora
Alauda gulgula	Eastern Skylark
Alcedo atthis	Common Kingfisher
Amauronis akol	Brown Crake
Amauronis phoenicurus	White-breasted Waterhen
Anas acuta	Pintail
Anas clypeata	Shoveller
Anas crecca	Common Teal
Anas falcate	Falcated Teal
Anas Penelope	Wigeon
Anas platyrynchos	Mallard
Anas poecilorhyncha	Spot-billed Duck
Anas querquedula	Garganey Teal
Anas strepera	Gadwall
Anastomus oscitans	Open-bill Stork
Anhinga rufa	Darter
Anmomanes deserti	Desert Finch Lark
Anmomanes phoenicurus	Rufous-tailed Finch Lark
Anser albifrons	White-fronted Goose
Anser anser	Grey-leg Goose
Anser indicus	Bar-headed Goose
Anthropoids wirgo	Demoiselle Crane

Scientific Name	Common Name
Anthus campestris	Tawny Pipit
Anthus hodgsoni	Indian Tree Pipit
Anthus novaeseelandiae	Paddy-field Pipit
Anthus novaeseelandiae richardi	Paddy-field Pipit
Anthus roseatus	Vinaceous-breasted Pipit
Anthus spinoletta	Water Pipit
Anthus trivialis	Tree Pipit
Apus affinis	House Swift
Apus melba	Alpine Swift
Aquila clanga	Greater Spotted Eagle
Aquila heliacal	Imperial Eagle
Aquila pomarian	Lesser Spotted Eagle
Aquila rapax nipalensis	Eastern Steppe Eagle
Aquila rapax vindhiana	Tawny Eagle
Ardea alba	Large Egret
Ardea cinerea	Grey Heron
Ardea purpurea	Purple Heron
Ardeola grayii	Pond Heron
Ardeola striatus	Little Green Heron
Arenaria interpres	Turnstone
Asio flammeus	Short-eared Owl
Athene brama	Spotted Owlet
Aythya baeri	Baer's Pochard
Aythya ferina	Common Pochard
Aythya fuligula	Tufted Duck
Aythya nyroca	White-eyed Pochard
Botaurus stellais	Bittern
Bubo bubo	Great Horned Owl
Bubo coromandus	Dusky Horned Owl
Bubo zeylonensis	Brown Fish Owl
Bubulcis ibis	Cattle Egret
Burhinus oedicnemus	Stone Curlew
Butastur tessa	White-eyed Buzzard Eagle

Buteo rufinus	Long-legged Buzzad	*Cercomela fusca*	Brown Rock Chat
Calandrella cinerea	Short-toed Lark	*Corvus macrorhynchos*	Jungle Crow
Calidris alpine	Dunlin	*Corvus splendens*	House Crow
Calidris canutus	Knot	*Coturnix chinensis*	Blue-breasted Quail
Calidris minuta	Little Stint	*Coturnix coromandelica*	Rain Quail
Calidris temminckii	Temminck's Stint	*Coturnix coturnix*	Common Quail
Calidris trestacea	Curlew Sandpiper	*Cuculus micropterus*	Indian Cuckoo
Caprimulgus affinis	Franklin's Nightjar	*Cuculus varius*	Common Hawk Cuckoo
Caprimulgus asiaticus	Common Indian Nightjar	*Culicicapa ceylonensis*	Grey-headed Flycatcher
Caprimulgus indicus	Indian Jungle Nightjar	*Cursoius coromandelicus*	Indian Courser
Caprimulgus mahrettensis	Syke's Nightjar	*Cypsiurus parvus*	Pam Swift
Carpodacus erythrinus	Common Rosefinch	*Dendrocitta vegabunda*	Indian Tree Pie
Centropus sinensis	Coucal	*Dendrocygna javanica*	Lesser Whistling Teal
Centropus toulou	Lesser Coucal	*Dicaeum erythrorhynchos*	Tickell's Flower-pecker
Ceryle rudis	Lesser Pied Kingfisher	*Dicaum agile*	Thick-billed Flower-pecker
Cettia cetti	Cetti's Warbler	*Dicrurus adsimilis*	Black Drongo
Charadrius alexandrines	Kentish Plover	*Dicrurus caeulessens*	White-bellied Drongo
Charadrius dubius	Little Ringed Plover	*Dicrurus leucophaeus*	Ashy Drongo
Charadrius hiaticula	Ringed Plover	*Dinopium benghalense*	Lesser Golden-back Woodpecker
Charadrius mongolus	Lesser Sand Plover		
Chillidonias niger	Black Tern	*Egretta garzetta*	Little Egret
Chlidonias hybrid	Whiskered Tern	*Egretta intermedia*	Smaller Egret
Chrysomma sinense	Yellowed Babbler	*Elanus caeruleus*	Black-winged Kite
Ciconia ciconia	White Stork	*Emberiza brunniceps*	Red-headed Bunting
Ciconia episcopus	White-necked Stork	*Emberiza buchanani*	Grey-necked Bunting
Ciconia nigra	Black Stork	*Emberiza fucata*	Grey-headed Bunting
Circaetus gallicus	Short-toed Eagle	*Emberiza melanocephala*	Black-headed Bunting
Circus macrourus	Pale Harrier	*Emberiza stewarti*	White-capped Bunting
Circus varius	Marsh Harrier	*Ephippiorhynchus asiaticus*	Black-necked Stork
Cisticola juncidis	Streaked Fantail Warbler	*Eremopterix grisea*	Ashy-crowned Finch Lark
Clamator jacobinus	Pied Crusted Cuckoo	*Erithacus alliope*	Ruby-throat
Columba eversmanni	Eastern Stock Pigeon	*Erithacus svecicus*	Blue-throat
columba livia	Blue Rock Pigeon	*Estrilda amandava*	Red Munia
Copsychus saularis	Magpie Robin	*Eudynamys scolopacea*	Koel
Coracias benghalenis	Indian Roller	*Falco biarmicus cherrug*	Lanner Egret
Coracias garralus	European Robin	*Falco biarmicus jugger*	Laggar Egret
Coracina melanopetra	Black-headed Cuckoo-Shrike	*Falco peregrinus japonensis*	Peregrine Falcon
Coracina novaehollandiae	Large Cuckoo-Shrike	*Falco severus*	Oriental Hobby

Scientific name	Common name
Falco tinnunculus	Kerstrel
Francolinus francolinus	Black Partridge
Francolinus pondicerianus	Grey Partridge
Fulica atra	Coot
Galerida cristata	Crested Lark
Gallicrex cineria	Watercock
Gallinago gallinag	Fantail Snipe
Gallinago minima	Jack Snipe
Gallinago stenura	Pintail Snipe
Gallinulla chloropus	Moorhen
Galloperdix lunulata	Painted Spurfowl
Galloperdix spadicea	Red Spurfowl
Gelochelidon nilotica	Gull-billed Tern
Glareola lacteal	Small Indian Pratincole
Glareola pranticola	Collard Pratincole
Grus antigone	Sarus Crane
Grus grus	Common Crane
Gyps bengalensis	White backed Vulture
Gyps fulvus	Griffon Vulture
Gyps indicus	Long-billed Vulture
Halcyon smyrnensis	White-breasted Kingfisher
Haliaeetus albicilla	White-tailed Eagle
Haliaetus leucoryphus	Palla's Fishing Eagle
Haliastur Indus	Bahmani Kite
Hieraaetus fasciatus	Bonelli's Eagle
Hieraaetus pennatus	Booted Hawk-Eagle
Himantopus himantopus	Black-winged Stilt
Hippolais caligata	Booted Warbler
Hirundo concolor	Dusky Crag Martin
Hirundo daurica	Red-rumped Swallow
Hirundo fluvicola	Indian Cliff Swallow
Hirundo nestica	Swallow
Hirundo smithii	Wire-tailed Swallow
Hydrophasianus chirurgur	Pheasant-tailed Jacana
Ixobrychus cinnamomeus	Chestnut Bittern
Ixobrychus flaviollis	Black Bittern
Ixobrychus minutes	Little Bittern
Jynx torquilla	Wryneck 353
Lanius cristatus	Brown Shrike
Lanius excubitor	Grey Shrike
Lanius schach	Rufous-backed Shrike
Lanius vittatus	Bay-backed Shrike
Larus argentatus	Herring Gull
Larus brunnicephalus	Brown-headed Gull
Larus ichthyaetus	Great Black-necked Gull
Larus ridibundus	Black-headed Gull
Leptoptilos dubius	Adjutant Stork
Leptoptilos javanicus	Lesser Adjutant Stork
Limicola falcinellus	Broad-billed Sandpiper
Linoasa linosa	Black-tailed Godwit
Locustella lanceolata	Streaked Grasshopper Warbler
Lonchura malabarica	White-throated Munia
Lonchura malacca	Black-headed Munia
Lonchura punctulata	Spotted Munia
Lonchura striata	White-backed Munia
Marmaronetta angustirostris	Marbled Teal
Megalaima haemacephala	Crimson-breasted Barbet
Melophus lathami	Creasted Bunting
Merops orientails	Green Eater
Merops philippinus	Blue-cheasted
Merops superciliosus	Blue-tailed Bee-Eater
Metopidus indicus	Bronze-winged Jacana
Milvus migrans givinda	Pariah Kite
Mirafra erythroptera	Red-winged Bush Lark
Mirafra javanica	Singing Bush Lark
Monticola solitaries	Blue Rock Thrush
Motacilla alba	White Wagtail
Motacilla cinerea	Grey Wagtail
Motacilla citreola	Yellow-headed Wagtail
Motacilla flava malanogrisea	Yellow Wagtail
Motacilla maderaspatensis	Leg Pied Wagtail
Muscicapa parva	Red-breasted Flycatcher
Muscicapa ruficauda	Rufous-tailed Flycatcher
Muscicapa superciliaris	White-browed Blue Flycatcher

Muscicapa tickelliae	Tickell's Flycatcher
Mycteria leucocephala	Painted Stork
Nectarinia asiatica	Purple Sunbird
Neophron pernopterus	Egyptian Vulture
Netta rufina	Red-crested Pochard
Nettapus coromandelianus	Cotton Teal
Nycticorax nycticorax	Night Heron
Onenthe deserti	Desert Wheatear
Oriolus oriolus	Golden Oriole
Oriolus xanthornus	Black-headed Oriole
Orthotomus sutorius	Tailor Bird
Otus bakkamoenaa	Collard Scops Owl
Otus scop	Scops Owl
Palagropsis capensis	Stork-billed Kingfisher
Pandion haliaetus	Osprey
Parus major	Grey Tit
Passer domesticus	House Sparrow
Passer hispaniolnesis	Spanish Sparrow
Passer montanus	Tree Sparrow
Pavo cristatus	Common Peafowl
Pelicanus onocrotalus	White Pelican
Pelicanus philippensis crispus	Dalmatian Pelican
Pelicanus philippensis philippensis	Spot-billed Pelican
Perdicula asiatica	Jungle Bush Quail
Pericrocotus erythrroyygius	White-bellied Minivet
Pericrocotus flammeus	Scarlet Minivet
Pericrotus cinnamomeus	Small Minivet
Pernis ptilorhyncus	Honey Buzzard
Petronia xanthyocollis	Yellow-throated Sparrow
Phalacrocoax carbo	Cormorant
Phalacrocoax fuscicollis	Indian Cormorant
Phalacrocoax niger	Little Cormorant
Phalaropus lobatus	Red-necked Phalarope
Philomachus pugnax	Ruff and Reeve
Phoenicopterus roseus	Greater Flamingo
Phoenicurus ochruros	Black Redstart
Phylloscopus affinis	Tickell's Leaf Warbler
Phylloscopus collybita	Brown Leaf Warbler
Phylloscopus fuscatus	Dusky Leaf Warbler
Phylloscopus griseolus	Olivaceous Leaf Warbler
Phylloscopus inornatus	Yellow-browed Leaf Warbler
Phylloscopus occipitails	Large-crowded Leaf Warbler
Phylloscopus subviridis	Brook's Leaf Warbler
Phylloscopus trochiloides	Greenish Leaf Warbler
Phylloscopus tytleri	Tytler's Leaf Warbler
Piciodes mahrattensis	Yellow-fronted Pied Woodpecker
Piciodes nanus	Pigmy Woodpecker
Pitta brachyuran	Indian Pitta
Platalea leucorodia	Spoonbill
Plegadis falicinellus	Glossy Ibis
Ploceus benghalensis	Black-throated Weaver
Ploceus manyar	Streked Weaver
Ploceus philippinus	Baya Weaver
Pluvialis domenica	Eastern Golden Plover
Pluvialis squatarola	Grey Plover
Podiceps cristatus	Great Crested Grebe
Porphyro porphyro	Purple Moorhen
Porzana fusca	Ruddy Crake
Porzana porzaza	Spotted Crake
Porzana pusilla	Baillon's Crake
Prinia buchanani	Rufous-fronted Wren Warbler
Prinia hodgsonii	Ashy Grey Wren Warbler
Prinia socialis stewarti	Ashy Grey Warbler
Prinia subflava	Plain Wren Warbler
Prinia sylvetica	Jungle Wren Warbler
Pseudibis papillosa	Black Ibis
Psittacula cyanocephala	Blossom-headed Parakeet
Psittacula eupataria	Alexandrine Parakeet
Psittacula krameri	Rose-ringed Parakeet
Pterocles exustus	Indian Sandgrouse
Pterocles indicus indicus	Painted Sandgrouse
Pterocles orientails	Imperial Sandgrouse
Pycnonotus cafer	Red-vented Bulbul

Pycnonotus jocosus	Red-whiskered Bulbul
Pycnonotus leucogenys leucotis	White-cheeked Bulbul
Rallus aquaticus	Water Rail
Recurviostra avosetta	Avocet
Rhipidura aureola	White-browed Fantail Flycatcher
Riparia paludicola	Plain Sand Martin
Riparia riparia	Collared Sand Martin
Rostratula benghalensis	Painted Snippe
Sakidiornis melanotos	Comb Duck
Salpornis spilonotus	Spotted Grey Creeper
Sarcogyps calvus	Black Vulture
Saxicola caprata	Pied Bush Chat
Saxicola ferrea	Dark Grey Bush Chat
Saxicola torquata	Collared Bush Chat
Saxicoloides fulicata	Indian Robin
Sitta castanea	Chestnut-bellied Nuthatch
Spilornis cheela	Crested Serpent Eagle
Sterna acuticauda	Black-bellied Tern
Sterna albifrons	Little Tern
Sterna aurantia	Indian River Tern
Streptopelia chinensis	Spotted Dove
Streptopelia decacto	Indian Ring Dove
Streptopelia oientails	Rufous Turtle Dove
Streptopelia senegalensis	Little Brown Dove
Streptopelia tranquebarica	Red Turtle Dove
Strix ocellata	Mottled Wood Owl
Sturnus contra	Pied Myna
Sturnus malabaricus	Grey-headed Myna
Sturnus pagodarum	Brahmini Myna
Sturnus roseus	Rosy Pastor
Sturnus vulgaris	Starling
Sulvia hortensis	Orphean Warbler
Sylvia communis	Whitethroat
Sylvia curruca	Lesser Whitethroat
Sylvia curruca althaea	Lesser Whitethroat
Sylvia nana	Desert Warbler
Taccocua lescenaultii	Sirkeer Cuckoo
Tachybaptus ruficollis	Little Grebe
Tadorna tadorna	Common Shelduck
Tephrodornis pondicerrianus	Common Woodshrike
Terpsiphone paradise	Paradise Flycatcher
Tockus birostris	Grey Hornbill
Treron phoenicoptera	Yellow-legged Green Pigeon
Treskiornis aethiopica	White Ibis
Tringa erythropus	Spotted Redshank
Tringa glareola	Wood Sandpiper
Tringa hypoleucos	Common Sandpiper
Tringa nebularia	Greenshank
Tringa ochropus	Green Sandpiper
Tringa terek	Terek Sandpiper
Tringa tetanus	Common Redshank
Tudoides malcolmi	Large Grey Babbler
Turdoides caudatas	Common Babbler
Turdoides staitus	Jungle Babbler
Turdus unicolor	Tickell's Thrush
Turnix suscitator	Common Bustard-Quail
Turnix sylvatica	Little Bustard-Quail
Tyto alba	Barn Owl
Upupa epops	Hoopoe
Venellus indicus	Red-wattled Lapwing
Venellus leucurus	White-tailed Lapwing
Vanellus malabaricus	Yellow-wattled Lapwing
Vanellus spinosus	Spur-winged Lapwing
Vanellus vanellus	Lapwing
Zoothera citrine	Orange-headed Thrush
Zosterops palpebrosa	White-eye

BIBLIOGRAPHY

- Champion, H.G. and S.K. Seth. A Revised Survey of the Forest Types of India. New Delhi: Government of India, 1968.
- Dang, Himraj. *Sariska National Park*. New Delhi: Indus Publishing Company, 2005.
- Government of India. Report of the Tiger Task Force. 2005.
- Government of Rajasthan. Report of the State Empowered Committee on Forests and Wildlife Management. August 2005.
- Government of Rajasthan. Mehrotra Committee Report on Tiger Disappearance from Sariska Tiger Reserve-3. 2005.
- Kumar, C.R. Ajit and K. Sankar. "Ichthyo-Fauna of Sariska Wild Life Sanctuary". *Journal of the Bombay Natural History Society* 90 (1993): 299–300.
- Panwar, H.S. "Protected Areas and People: The Indian Approach". Proceedings of the 25th Working Session of National Parks and Protected Areas, IUCN, May 1985.
- Parmar, P.J. "A Contribution to the Flora of Sariska Tiger Reserve, Rajasthan". *Botonical Survey of India* 27 (1985), 1–4: 29–40.
- Sankar, K., D. Mohan, and Pandey. "Birds of Sariska Tiger Reserve, Rajasthan, India". *Forktail* 8 (1993): 133–41.
- Singh, Guman. *Tales of Sariska* (unpublished).
- Wildlife Institute of India and Forest Department, Government of Rajasthan. "Recovery Plan for Tigers in Sariska Tiger Reserve", 2008.
- Wildlife Institute of India, Rajasthan Forest Department, and National Tiger Conservation Authority. "Reintroduction of Tigers, Sariska Tiger Reserve, Rajasthan". Annual Progress Report. July 2008–June 2009.

ACKNOWLEDGEMENTS

I owe a lot to the officers of Sariska Tiger Reserve who have not only served this Reserve with deep dedication but also have enriched my knowledge of the wild treasures of this Reserve. Daulat Singh, Uday Ram, Vidya Dhar (rangers); Ram Prasad and Jay Pal (Head Guards); Vipin Sharma (ex-Cattle Guard, presently in Panchayat Department); Heera (Cattle Guard); and Late Badri Payala (Driver) deserve special mention. Pushp Jain, Akhil Chandra, and Shakti Mohan immensely helped me in writing this book. I am highly indebted to Dr Anita Kothari for her literary inputs. My dear friend Vincent Van Ross, a noted journalist and wildlife enthusiast, deserve special thanks for his support in editing the manuscript.

I am highly thankful to Vikram Sisodia, my assistant at Sariska Tiger Foundation, and Anuj Gupta, computer designer, for their immense help in typing and designing the initial draft of this manuscript.

I am grateful to Dr H.S. Pabla, Dr V.B. Mathur, Dr K. Sankar, and Dr S.P. Goyal who shared their views and findings with me on various issues.

I salute my revered Guru Mr H.S. Panwar, Padma Bhushan awardee, for his invaluable contribution to the cause of wildlife conservation at national and international levels. He taught me the basics of wildlife management at the Wildlife Institute of India (WII). With all his knowledge on Indian wildlife, he is far too modest. I take this opportunity to pay my tributes to veteran wildlifers late Kailash Sankhala, Sanjay Debroy, and Fateh Singh Rathore whose contribution to the cause of wildlife conservation must be written in golden letters.

I thank Valmik Thapar, Ullas Karanth, Ms Belinda Wright, Bittoo Sehgal, and Brijendra Singh for their untiring support to tiger conservation in India. I hold Harsh Vardhan and K.L. Saini (ex-Field Director) in high esteem for their dedication to the cause of wildlife conservation. They have turned thousands of school children into conservationists and are still persisting with their crusade.

Former Prime Minister Indira Gandhi and minister Dr Karan Singh conceptualised and implemented Project Tiger. We salute them. Ms Vasundhara Raje, V.P. Singh, Maharaja Vishvendra Singh, and Bharat Singh in Rajasthan, all have passion for wildlife and its conservation. Conservationists place high hopes on them.

For Sariska's rebuilding, contributions of V.P. Singh, R.N. Mehrotra, and Raj Pal Singh deserve high appreciation.

Ravi Singh, Secretary General and CEO, WWF India arranged helicopters to airlift the first three tigers from Ranthambhore to Sariska. WWF also provided radio collars to monitor their movements round the clock, despite several procedural hurdles.

Last but not the least, my wife Renu, son Manish, daughter Bhawana, son-in-law Anshul, sister Pratibha, friend Dinesh Verma Durrani, and Kamal M. Morarka, noted industrialist, politician, and a wildlife enthusiast, deserve special thanks for their constant inspiration while preparing this manuscript.

INDEX